Social Services and the Ethnic Community

Alfreda P. Iglehart
The University of California, Los Angeles

Rosina M. Becerra
The University of California, Los Angeles

Allyn and Bacon
Boston • London • Toronto • Sydney • Tokyo • Singapore

Executive Editor: Karen Hanson
Vice-President, Publisher: Susan Badger
Managing Editor: Judy Fifer
Editorial Assistant: Sarah L. Dunbar
Executive Marketing Manager: Joyce Nilsen
Editorial-Production Service: TKM Productions
Production Coordinator: Eleanor Sabini
Cover Administrator: Suzanne Harbison
Composition Buyer: Linda Cox
Manufacturing Buyer: Megan Cochran

Library of Congress Cataloging-in-Publication Data

Iglehart, Alfreda P.
　　Social services and the ethnic community / Alfreda P. Iglehart,
　Rosina M. Becerra.
　　　p.　cm.
　　Includes bibliographical references and index.
　　ISBN 0-205-15712-2
　　1. Social work with minorities--United States--History.　2. Social
work with minorities--United States.　3. Social work with
immigrants--United States--History.　4. Social work with immigrants--
United States.　I. Becerra, Rosina M.　II. Title.
HV3176.I35 1994
362.84'00973--dc20　　　　　　　　　　　　　　　　　　　94-25718
　　　　　　　　　　　　　　　　　　　　　　　　　　　　　　　　CIP

This book is printed on recycled, acid-free paper.

Printed in the United States of America

10 9 8 7 6 5 4 3 2 1　99 98 97 96 95 94

Contents

8   Service Delivery to Diverse Populations: Interorganizational Pathways   241

9   Recurring Issues and the Next Steps   271

Preface

What is the focus of this book? This book is our attempt to pull together what is known about the history, evolution, and current state of social service delivery systems to ethnic communities in the United States. We base our analysis on a *theoretical framework of organizational and community behavior*. What have been the needs of these communities? Who has responded to these needs? What were those responses? And how much has changed today?

This book is for anyone who works with people or who does "social" work. In this line of work are social workers in the generic meaning—in the way that friendly visitors and settlement house workers were "social" workers even though "social work" did not exist at the time. This book is for anyone trying to make sense out of the contradictions that seem to occur whenever race, ethnicity, and service delivery merge.

We may be called *social workers, human services workers, caseworkers, case managers, practitioners, clinicians,* or some other title. We may be working in schools, hospitals, large public agencies, or small private agencies. Whatever the title, whatever the setting, all of us in the helping professions are part of a complex sociocultural, historical, and political context that defines who we are and what we do.

Social work as a profession becomes the anchor for some of what is to follow. This is because social work has been a dominant influence in defining how services are delivered and to whom they are delivered. It is because of this dominant influence that other helping professions have emerged to try new definitions and new approaches. Even in these cases, the power of the sociocultural, historical, and political context cannot be denied. The work we do and how we do it continue to derive from the society in which we live. Perhaps this book is not really about "social" work at all. Perhaps it is an example of how services and professions reflect the culture, values, and ideologies around them.

As we looked around us and saw communities becoming more diverse, we also saw these communities advocating for their own services in their own communities. They want their own agencies to serve their people. Is this necessary? Has this always been the case? How do existing service systems fit in with these ethnic service systems? Do these systems ever converge? These were some of the questions that motivated us to write this book. We wanted to know what led to the schism between ethnic communities and the rest of society that prompts these communities to want separate services for themselves. These questions could only be answered by reviewing the history of America—that part that speaks of the birth of a modern nation, the birth of social problems, the birth of social work, and the antisocial work movements. These questions could only be answered by looking at the evolution of service delivery in this country.

We found that, throughout history, ethnic minority communities were creating their own services and their own agencies. Social movements come and go, but the ethnic agency still persists. It may be similar to other agencies, but that similarity may be accidental because the ethnic agency, as a form and means of providing services to ethnic communities, predates most other agencies and movements. It seems to be a natural part of ethnic communities. We tried to understand this and to report, analyze, and interpret what the preponderance of literature indicated. To some extent, the literature spoke for itself. We are conduits for communicating what it had to say. We provide you with that literature for your review.

What do we hope to accomplish? Information and knowledge are forms of power. By passing this along to you, we hope you are empowered. There are signs of change as we helpers grapple with defining and implementing ethnic-sensitive practice. With this knowledge, you will know that some things reside with individual workers, some things reside in organizations, and some things reside in society at large. With this awareness, you will better understand why systems look the way they do and why workers define problems and intervene the way they do.

Our research communicated to us that what we are witnessing today is a continuation of a process that started decades ago. In addressing social problems, White America looked in the mirror and not out the window. In looking in the mirror, White Americans saw other White Americans who needed aid and support. Through this reflection, they could identify with the suffering of those who looked like them. Had White America looked out their windows, they would have seen others who needed help—others who did not look like them.

This history also told us that the same phenomenon was occurring in ethnic communities. African Americans were looking in the mirror. Mexican

Americans were looking in the mirror. As other groups came, they too looked in their mirrors. People were reaching out to help those who looked like them.

This history and its effects today are vital pieces to the puzzle of ethnic-sensitive practice and multicultural service delivery. The dualism inherent in the Welfare State is a product of the evolution of systems and not just of individuals. If there is to be cross-fertilization between or even convergence of these dual systems, then we need to learn how to inculcate in both of them an appreciation for the light in the window to complement the appreciation for the light in the mirror.

ACKNOWLEDGMENTS

In describing and analyzing the dynamics of ethnicity in service delivery systems, numerous examples from the field are used. We are indebted to those workers who shared their experiences and insights with us. Because of the sensitive nature of the examples provided, names and identifying information have been omitted from most of the illustrations. These workers embraced this opportunity to candidly and openly discuss the ethnic issue and for this we are grateful. The examples are theirs. The interpretations are ours. We assume full responsibility for the contents of this book.

We would like also to acknowledge Nelba Chavez, Jeanne Giovannoni, Jeanette Jennings, Harry Kitano, Del Martinez, Alex Norman, Dorothy Taylor, and Fernando Torres-Gil for the feedback and direction they provided in the development of this book. We wish to thank our reviewers: Joseph J. Mehr, Illinois Department of Mental Health and Developmental Disabilities; Felix G. Rivera, San Francisco State University; Bradford W. Sheafor, Colorado State University; and Cynthia Crosson Tower, Fitchburg State College, for their helpful input to this book.

Finally, we dedicate this book to all those who are grappling with the challenge of developing and providing ethnic-sensitive services.

Chapter 1

Introduction

Social service delivery systems appear to be at another crossroads. As the population of the United States becomes dramatically more diverse, numerous challenges and dilemmas arise about the most effective ways of providing services to ethnic minority groups. Although some cities are not currently facing these issues to any major extent, others are finding that the challenges thrust upon them are demanding immediate responses. Rapidly, however, the ethnic minority presence in the United States will move from concentrations in major urban areas to widespread presence in all areas of the country.

According to Census Bureau projections, by the year 2050, non-Hispanic Whites will drop from its present 75 percent of the nation's population to a low of 53 percent. This means that ethnic minority groups will make up almost half of the population. These Census Bureau projections further indicate that the minority population will be made up of 21 percent Hispanic, 15 percent African American, and 1 percent American Indian. Increased immigration and higher birthrates for ethnic minority groups mean that people of color are becoming more and more a felt and dominant presence in the United States.

At the turn of the century, Progressive Era thinkers and reformers were fearful that the massive influx of "new" immigrants—ethnic Whites from southern and eastern Europe—would seriously alter or even destroy the fiber and culture of native-born White society.[1] Widespread efforts to "Americanize" these new immigrants were launched with the intended effects of replacing immigrant language, traditions, and values with English and American values and culture.[2] The United States as the melting pot—an amalgam of people from diverse backgrounds with one language and one culture—was the belief that guided popular thinking of the day and continued to do so for numerous years.

1

As the new immigrants of today—Asians and Hispanics, for example—seek solace on the shores of this country and as other citizens of color continue to seek equitable treatment, the melting pot notion has given way to America, the mosaic society. In the intervening years from the new immigrants of the late 1880s and early 1900s to the new immigrants of the middle and late 1990s, social service providers and the rest of the nation have come to realize that language, culture, tradition, and skin color cannot be easily erased or ignored. People continue to cling to what is important to their individual and group identity. In addition, color blindness was more of a myth than a reality as particular ethnic groups were historically and continuously stigmatized by their color.

Demands and needs for social services will come from groups that are more likely to suffer from poverty, discrimination, and their attendant consequences—groups that have a disproportionate number of these ethnic minorities. Social service administrators and practitioners are urged to embrace the diversity surrounding these groups and implement culturally relevant and sensitive training for workers and programs for clients. As client populations change, the service delivery systems are now expected to successfully adapt to these changes.

In the era of the mosaic society, social service providers are charged with the task of responding to the needs of diverse groups in ways that recognize, respect, and tolerate group differences. In response to diverse client populations, the literature on clinical or treatment issues involved in ethnic-sensitive practice is proliferating.[3] These clinical issues include the manner in which ethnicity affects the worker-client relationship, cultural beliefs that influence both the worker and the client, and language and behavioral patterns that may determine treatment effectiveness.

The role of the worker-client relationship in the delivery of ethnic-sensitive services is, indeed, vitally important. The client experiences the agency through the worker as the worker interprets the policies of the agency and implements its services. In addition, because of the relationship established between the client and the worker during the treatment process, acceptance of and respect for the client's ethnicity and culture foster the rapport and trust needed for effective intervention.

In response to the growing diversity of society, social work is stressing the need for social workers to increase their sensitivity to the cultures and values of minorities.[4] Although treatment issues are crucial for effective individual, family, and small-group intervention, the worker-client relationship is but one aspect of service delivery to diverse populations. Furthermore, in some instances, the client's culture is treated as homogeneous and static while its social context and environment are overlooked.[5] Another aspect of service delivery requires recognition of the client's membership in other systems. Clients are members of groups, communities, and, frequently, other service delivery systems. They are not just individual cases but representatives of an array of networks. These systems are bounded by ethnicity, culture, and community. These client systems are shaped by the values and ideologies that define problems, help-seeking behaviors, and problem resolution. To ignore the other systems of which clients are a part is to ignore a significant element of their world. Effective ethnic-sensitive service delivery also includes the utilization and incorporation of the client's community and community services in the service delivery process. Many of these community services are offered through the ethnic minority agency—that is, an agency with ethnic minority staff who provide services to members of that ethnic minority group.

Still another aspect of service delivery involves recognition of the nuances of the service delivery system itself. Service delivery takes place in the context of a system that is also shaped by the culture, values, and ideologies of the groups and individuals planning and implementing those services. These systems determine the "appropriate" problems to address and the "appropriate" ways to address them.

The preponderance of literature on technologies for individual-level interventions and the pronounced paucity of comparable literature on interventions at other levels have been held as proof that helping professions, particularly social work, have a preoccupation with changing people and not systems.[6] Social work literature seems to implicitly accept existing social systems and explicitly omit critiques of social work and its nonclinical relations with minorities.[7] Consequently, the lack of data on the ethnic minority service agency can mirror a general disregard for the treatment *and* social value of these agencies.

Service delivery to ethnic minority communities illustrates the interface between service delivery systems and client systems. Consequently, the ethnic community is of central importance for the provision of multicultural social services. An examination of the ethnic community's responses to its own identified needs can provide a basis for understanding the ethnic community, its self-identified problems, and its problem interventions. The ethnic agency appears to capture an interface between a service delivery system and client system that blends service with community and ethnicity.

This book provides a social and historical overview of (1) social work's relationship to ethnic minority communities, (2) the organization of service delivery as it relates to ethnic minorities, and (3) the need for ethnic minority communities to develop their own social services. This overview becomes the foundation for the delineation of macropractice models that link mainstream social services with ethnic communities and ethnic agencies.

DATA SOURCES

The analysis and practice models presented in this book are derived from a compilation and synthesis of existing empirical and theoretical literature, case studies, and interviews with key informants. Historical records often provide indisputable documentation for the generalizations offered. Literature cited ranges from the historical *Charities and the Commons,* a turn-of-the-century journal, to more contemporary books and journals. Although these sources are varied, they all provide insight into social services and the ethnic minority community.

Literature that focuses on ethnic minority agencies—their history, forms, functions, and utilization—was reviewed in order to formulate the dimensions and tenets underlying ethnic agency practice. This literature included empirical discussions and a number of case descriptions and case studies. A systematic review of these cases and observations from key informants led to the identification of some "universals" governing ethnic agency practice. Contained within these pages is a comprehensive compilation of literature on the ethnic agency. From this compilation are drawn the core features of practice that integrate community and ethnicity in the service delivery process. The ethnic agency thus becomes a model for ethnic-sensitive practice that utilizes the social context of the client system. Practice models derived from ethnic agency practice are generated for implementation in conventional social services.

Literature on the history of formalized service delivery, organizational behavior, organizational change, and interorganizational relations was also surveyed to generate a sound foundation for the explication of models for linking mainstream social services with the ethnic agency. There is no one "right" way to bridge the gulf between these two service delivery systems, and the models presented take into consideration the range of factors that influence the interorganizational relationship.

Field examples are provided to illustrate the theoretical and analytical observations presented. These examples have been obtained from practitioners in the field through face-to-face contacts, telephone communication, and written communication. In some situations, small groups of practitioners discussed specific issues raised by the authors. These field examples are integrated throughout the chapters to provide depth and richness to the discussion.

HISTORICAL ANALYSIS

Mainstream social work and traditional social services have not historically shown themselves to be that flexible, adaptable, or malleable in service delivery structures and ideologies. The form and ideology governing social services have been evolving since the turn of the century. That evolution has only mildly flirted with deviating from its original underpinnings that were derived from the social, political, and economic context of the day. Indeed, social work and social welfare, then and now, are products of the environments from which they emerge. Conservative underpinnings were in the forefront of the formative years of the social work profession when the country was coping with the arrival of diverse, new immigrant populations. These conservative underpinnings were reflected in charity organizations and settlement houses that were derived from the White, Protestant, middle-class segment of U.S. society that sought to assist immigrants in adjusting to American life.[8]

The history of social work with ethnic minority groups cannot be denied, although much of it appears to have been rewritten to shroud or omit the extent of racism and exclusion operative in the charity organizations and even in the settlement-house movement—the reform arm of social work's birth.[9] Although some early services aided ethnic minorities, the general disregard for the needs, concerns, and rights of ethnic minority groups cannot be overlooked.[10] Actions on behalf of ethnic minorities were fragmented, sporadic, and sadly limited. Some ethnic minority groups were seen as unsuitable for assimilation. For example, a settlement house director declared, "You can Americanize the man from southeastern and southern Europe, but you can't Americanize a Mexican."[11]

There often appears, however, to be a glorification and a vaunted view of the social reform thrust of the early, turn-of-the-century settlement work, and this period is held as giving rise to the profession's commitment to social reform. Historical recollections, however, can often reflect more distortion and romanticism than realism. Although no deliberate deceit may have been intended, it has been fairly easy to equate the actions of the majority with those of a few reform-minded individuals. Today, service planners, administrators, and providers must recognize and confront the ambivalence that mainstream social services have historically held for ethnic minorities. Acceptance of a group's history as *the group* experienced it is a vital step toward reducing the gulf between mainstream social services and ethnic minority communities.

Years of distrust, apathy, neglect, and rebuff cannot, and should not, be minimized. The past must be confronted with all its undesirable baggage of differential treatment, benign neglect, and overt racism. Recognition of the past does not mean it should be condoned or condemned. It means that service delivery to today's diverse populations is predicated on history and responses to that history. This means that open doors and open arms will not result in the masses of color flocking to partake of the services offered. Knowledge of history should be skillfully used to inform the development of effective service delivery strategies for today's diverse populations.

The embryonic years of social work are an appropriate starting point for the development of models that unite mainstream social services with ethnic minority communities. An examination of the past can be useful in identifying pitfalls and patterns that should be avoided as well as highlighting those actions and trends that should be replicated. This historical overview is not just a synopsis of past events; rather, it is an analysis and interpretation of social work history that examines racial ideology, social control, and social reform as they relate to ethnic minority communities. In addition, manifestations of the self-help ethos in these communities are also explored.

DEFINITION OF TERMS

Ethnic group defines those who share a kinship system, a territory, belief systems, and biological characteristics. Thus, Mexican Americans, Cuban Americans, and Puerto Rican Americans may be members of the same race but belong to different ethnic groups. *Ethnicity* is more specific and recognizes distinct cultural and racial groups and is used here to refer collectively to both ethnic and racial groups. *Ethnic minority* defines those ethnic groups that have a subordinated or disadvantaged status in U.S. society. *Ethnic agency* refers to the ethnic minority agency,[12] which is an agency with ethnic minority staff who provide services to members of that ethnic minority group.

Ideology is defined as those beliefs that are held with great fervor, conviction, and tenacity that are accepted as fact or truth by some group.[13] It is mirrored in the prevailing political beliefs and is not typically alterable by science, logic, or rationality. The ideology of the group drives group action and defines social policy. These beliefs help the larger society in general and service providers in particular to define social problems and define solutions to these problems. Professions also have bodies of systematically related beliefs that guide practice.[14] Social work and social welfare embrace particular ideologies related to specific racial and ethnic groups.

Social control is defined as those practices and policies designed to encourage, persuade, and/or coerce individuals to conform to values and behaviors defined by the larger society. This larger society is comprised of political elites, economic elites, and special-interest groups. Social control, as conceptualized here, is not closely related to neo-Marxian theory that sees the functions of social welfare institutions and personnel as promoting and perpetuating a capitalistic system. Neo-Marxian theory does not adequately reflect the range of issues that define the ethnic minority experience in this country. In the United States, there seems to be a dominant or national culture of which capitalism is but a part and this culture reflects the imprint of a dominant ethnic group in the institutions, values, and character of the country. This imprint determines what is truly "American," who is truly "American," as well as social problems, social problem groups, and problem solutions.

The cultural imprint of U.S. society has historically made a distinction between racial minority groups and White ethnic groups. Although White ethnics have encountered deprivation and discrimination, they have not experienced the kind of exclusionary and dehumanizing treatment that deprived racial minorities of even the most basic rights and amenities for much of U.S. history.[15] The early years of what was to become social work practice dramatically emphasizes this point.

Social reform/social change is a concept whose definition often varies with the individuals using it. Conservative and liberal definitions abound that seem to represent opposite ends of a continuum. The concept can indicate major shifts and changes in the basic institutions of society or any change that is directed at levels other than the individual and groups of individuals. It is clear that when social reform is under discussion, the unit of analysis ceases to be the individual. The social reform nature of social work and social services will be examined as it relates to ethnic minorities, with particular attention to the way social change was defined and the actions resulting from these defintions.

Ethnic minority self-help describes those actions and activities undertaken by collectives and/or other groups that result in the creation and organization of a service delivery entity (a service, a program, or an agency) that provides direct services to some identified ethnic minority group or community. These efforts may encompass political activism but this activism is secondary to direct service provision for the amelioration or alleviation of particular social conditions. These efforts bring the service providers in direct, face-to-face contact with the service beneficiaries.

There seems to be a subtle irony in the use of the term *self-help*. The term connotes the ability of individuals to come together to develop their own solutions for the problem they identify; yet, the social and political environment surrounding the ethnic minority community poses constraints and conditions that often delimit community self-help goals and actions.

Welfare State refers to the institutionalization of policies and programs that support health, income maintenance, education, and welfare services. It reflects public (government) dominance in the policies, fiscal support, and implementation of a range of services that promote the general health and well-being of the citizens of the country. The private sector's influence is most noticeable in the implementation of social policy—through the operation of private institutions and programs.[16]

Mainstream, traditional, conventional social services are embodied in the practices of public and private, nonprofit, formal organizations established to address a particular problem or meet the needs of a particular group.

Many of these formal organizations implement the policies and programs mandated by the public through legislation, whereas others are sponsored by special-interest groups. In this analysis, there are service sponsors (public and private), service providers (social workers and other human services personnel), and service recipients (typically referred to as *clients*). Mainstream social services also emphasize formal organizations that tend to be complex and hierarchical. Ideally, human services organizations would seek to provide services to all who need them within a community, but, in reality, many minority groups are unserved, underserved, or inappropriately served by the established human services system.[17] Unfortunately, this type of service delivery has evolved over the decades. *Mainstream social services represent the social practices of the Welfare State.*

Mainstream social work refers to the particular professional practice involved in the organization and administration of the complex machinery supporting the policies and programs of the Welfare State. This practice is an outgrowth of the work of Charity Organization Societies and settlement houses of the Progressive Era (1895–1917). Clearly, professional social workers are but one piece of an intricate service delivery maze that includes numerous other human services personnel and professionals. The professional social work presence has, however, influenced the direction and tone of human services in this country. In fact, the development of the Welfare State and the development of social work have been interdependent. The emergence of the roots of the Welfare State in the New Deal of the Roosevelt administration contributed to a dramatic expansion of social work, as the number of social workers doubled during this period.[18] The Welfare State is dependent on a massive social practice labor force to carry out its policies. Social work is *the* social practice of the Welfare State, and professional social work represents the professionalization of this practice.

ORGANIZATION OF THE BOOK

Chapters 2 through 5 focus on the historical context of social work as it relates to services and responses to ethnic and racial minority groups. Because the history of ethnic and racial minorities in this country continues to influence social services and minority communities' reactions to these services, Chapters 2 and 3 provide a detailed overview of the social conditions surrounding specific groups during the Progressive Era, including White ethnics. The White ethnics are discussed to provide a backdrop against which to compare and contrast their experiences with those of the ethnic and racial minorities.

Urbanization, industrialization, immigration, and migration created densely populated slums and a new kind of poverty. Writings that cover the history of social work often include descriptions of these social conditions, but the plight of ethnic and racial minorities are generally relegated to a brief discussion or just a sentence or two. Those writings that do mention the social and discriminatory conditions of those groups often fail to discuss social work's specific responses to these conditions.

These chapters will present the unique histories of ethnic and racial minority groups to show that, although all groups suffered, all suffering was not the same. Furthermore, the histories of these groups are detailed so that students, practitioners, administrators, educators, policy makers, funding sources, and others interested in enhancing service delivery to diverse populations have a more in-depth knowledge of the histories of these groups. For those individuals who already possess this knowledge, these chapters serve as a stark reminder. These details are recounted for several reasons: to show that contemporary relations between social work and ethnic minorities are affected by the historical context of those relations; to emphasize that history can be dynamic with far-reaching consequences; to counter a tendency in social work to minimize its history with ethnic minority groups; and to stimulate thinking about how social work ought to relate to ethnic minority groups and communities.

Chapter 4 begins with an overview of the theoretical frameworks that are used throughout the rest of the book to analyze professional and community practices and processes. The political economy perspective and the systems perspective are examined for this purpose. With both perspectives, the ethnic community, the professional social work community, and organizations can be delineated along prescribed dimensions. These frameworks are also useful for formulating models for linking social services with ethnic communities and ethnic agencies. The chapter then moves on to present the profession's roots of direct practice emergent in the Progressive Era. The Charity Organization Societies and their legacies are discussed to document the patterns and responses that have become entrenched in the modern profession of social work. The manner in which early workers perceived racial and ethnic groups and responded to their needs created a foundation for the new profession that continues to be visible today.

Chapter 5 examines the way ethnicity and race affected the nascent profession's reform responses. The role of race and ethnicity in the settlement-house movement is presented because of the significance of the settlement houses in the development of indirect or macropractice. The chapter also includes discussions of professionalization and bureaucratization and how they affected the profession's reform impulse. Reform movements *within* the profession—the Rank-and-File Movement and the Human Services Movement—are also relevant for inclusion here.

In Chapter 6, the ethnic/racial minority community's efforts to address its own community problems are illuminated to depict the mission, ideology, and interventions embraced by this type of community. Each group developed its own approach to social service intervention and identified its own goals. Although some goals overlapped across communities, there were specific ways in which a particular group stamped the services with its unique culture and identity. As social work was evolving into a profession, the ethnic/minority communities were developing service delivery systems that, to a certain extent, paralleled the mainstream services.

Chapters 7 through 9 focus on the contemporary context of macroservice delivery to ethnic communities. Chapter 7 offers the parameters of ethnic agency practice as a way of understanding its strengths and weaknesses. This type of agency can serve as a model for service delivery to ethnic communities and has not received the attention and recognition that it deserves. The dimensions of ethnic agency practice as they relate to agency/ community interface, locality development, organizational climate/culture, organizational administration and leadership, and other aspects of macropractice are included. In addition, the issues and constraints of ethnic services are noted. The challenges that ethnic agency practice pose to mainstream social work are also analyzed.

The history of ethnic communities, the evolution of social work, the emergence of ethnic services, and the tenets of ethnic agency practice are used to generate models for contemporary service delivery to diverse communities. Chapter 7 also focuses on models that can be adopted by mainstream social services to more effectively serve hard-to-reach populations. These models address those areas in which mainstream agencies may seek to provide services themselves to specific communities.

Chapter 8 proposes models for partnership arrangements between mainstream social service organizations and ethnic agencies. These models target ways in which mainstream organizations may seek to utilize the ethnic agency as a conduit for service delivery.

The last chapter, Chapter 9, highlights the next steps in further developing ethnic-sensitive macropractice. Projections for the demographic shifts of the United States have implications for social services and the profession of social work. Particular issues need to be confronted if social work is to remain a viable profession in a multicultural country.

Historical analysis and organizational analysis are stepping stones to (1) the development of models for mainstream agency/ethnic community interface and (2) mainstream agency/ethnic agency interorganizational practice. Mainstream social services can incorporate dimensions of ethnic agency practice in their social service delivery processes that recognize and utilize the ethnic community. This agency/community interface varies in *form* and *content* and is influenced by a number of key factors.

Linking mainstream social services and ethnic agencies can be effectively accomplished through a thorough understanding of the history and functions of both types of service delivery systems. Organizational exchanges can promote ethnic-sensitive services and these exchanges also vary in *form* and *content* based on a number of key dimensions.

Social work emerged from the needs of a changing society that was becoming more diverse. The arrival of immigrants from southern and eastern Europe began to challenge the prevailing assumptions about Americanism while the country was grappling with the meaning of citizenship for African Americans. At the same time, Asians and Mexicans were legally ineligible for citizenship as the American Indians languished on the reservations as noncitizens and nonpersons. In this turbulent environment, forerunners of contemporary service providers addressed primarily the needs and issues surrounding the White ethnic immigrants.

As a result of the directions of these early workers, parallel service delivery systems emerged—one for mainstream social services and one for ethnic minority communities. These communities embraced a self-help ethos because not to do so meant, in many cases, limited or no relief from community problems. These ethnic minority services and programs were the forerunners of the ethnic agency and held significant meaning to the communities they served. At the same time, mainstream service providers often held patronizing and paternalistic attitudes toward these ethnic minority services. In general, ethnic agencies have been undervalued and unacknowledged by traditional social services and the social work profession.

Today, the future of social services and social work is again inexorably tied to ethnic groups, but in this case the ethnic groups are ethnic minorities of color. How well service providers are able to respond to the needs of these communities may determine the survival of the human services. To remain viable and relevant, service providers—professional social workers and other human services personnel—must demonstrate their efficacy in meeting the challenges of this decade and the next.

ENDNOTES

1. Roger Daniels, *The Politics of Prejudice* (Berkely: University of California Press, 1962), p. 66; Florette Henri, *Black Migration: Movement North 1900–1920* (Garden City, NY: Doubleday, 1975), p. 146; Richard Hofstadter, *Social Darwinism in American Thought*, Revised Edition (Boston: Beacon Press, 1955), pp. 170–200.

2. Ruth Crocker, *Social Work and Social Order: The Settlement Movement in Two Industrial Cities* (Chicago: University of Chicago Press, 1992); Allen Davis, *Spearheads for Reform, The Social Settlements and the Progressive Movement: 1890–1914* (New Brunswick, NJ: Rutgers University Press, 1984); Howard Karger, "Minneapolis Settlement Houses in the 'Not So Roaring 20's': Americanization, Morality, and the Revolt Against Popular Culture," *Journal of Sociology and Social Welfare* 14 (June

1987): 89–110; Alvin Kogut, "The Settlements and Ethnicity: 1890–1914," *Social Work 17* (May 1972): 22–31.

3. See, for example, David Burgest, Ed. *Social Work Practice with Minorities,* Second Edition (Metuchen, NJ: Scarecrow Press, 1989); Larry Davis and Joe Gelsomino, "An Assessment of Practitioner Cross-Racial Treatment Experiences," *Social Work 39* (January 1994): 116–123; Wynetta Devore and Elfriede Schlesinger, *Ethnic-Sensitive Social Work Practice,* Second Edition (Columbus, OH: Merrill, 1987); Donna Franklin, "Differential Clinical Assessments: The Influence of Class and Race," *Social Service Review 59* (March 1985): 44–61; John Longres, "Toward a Status Model of Ethnic Sensitive Practice," *Journal of Multicultural Practice 1,* number 1 (1991): 41–56; Jeanne Robinson, "Clinical Treatment of Black Families: Issues and Strategies," *Social Work 34* (July 1989): 323–329.

4. This is reflected in the content analysis of social literature on social work and minorities completed by Anthony McMahon and Paula Allen-Meares, "Is Social Work Racist? A Content Analysis of Recent Literature," *Social Work 37* (November 1992): 533–539.

5. William Banks, "Models of Culture and School Counselors: The Predicament of Black Youth," *Anthropology and Educational Quarterly 9* (Summer 1978): 137–147.

6. See, for example, Robert Vinter, "Analysis of Treatment Organizations," in *Human Service Organizations,* ed. Yeheskel Hasenfeld and Richard English (Ann Arbor: University of Michigan Press, 1978), pp. 33–50.

7. Miguel Montiel and Paul Wong, "A Theoretical Critique of the Minority Perspective," *Social Casework 64* (February 1983): 112–117.

8. Herman Levin, "Conservatism of Social Work," *Social Service Review 56* (December 1982): 613.

9. Numerous historical overviews of social work's history either omit or briefly review the way early service providers viewed and responded to ethnic minority groups. Examples of this oversight can be found in June Axinn and Herman Levin, *Social Welfare: A History of American Response to Need,* Second Edition (New York: Harper and Row, 1982); Mary Ann Jiminez, "Historical Evolution and Future Challenges of the Human Services Professions," *Families in Societies 72* (January 1990): 3–12; James Leiby, *A History of Social Welfare and Social Work in the United States* (New York: Columbia University Press, 1978).

10. Examples of this racism and exclusion are contained in Davis, *Spearheads for Reform,* pp. 94–96; W. E. B. DuBois, "Social Effects of Emancipation," *The Survey* (February 1, 1913): 572; Patricia Hogan and Sau-Fong Siu, "Minority Children and the Child Welfare System: An Historical Perspective," *Social Work 33* (November 1988): 493–498; June Brown, "Primary Prevention: A Concept Whose Time Has Come for Improving the Cultural-Relevance of Family and Children's Services in Ethnic-Minority Communities," in *Primary Prevention Approaches to Development of Mental Health Services for Ethnic Minorities,* ed. Samuel Miller, Gwenelle Styles, and Carl Scott (New York: Council on Social Work Education, 1982), p. 41; S. Wells Williams, "Chinese Immigration," *Journal of Social Science 9* (December 1879): 110–111; Paul Wong, Steven Applewhite, and J. Michael Daley, "From Despotism to Pluralism: The Evolution of Voluntary Organizations in Chinese Communities," *Ethnic Groups 8,* number 4 (1990): 217.

11. As quoted in Crocker, *Social Work and Social Order*, p. 182.

12. For further discussions of ethnicity and race, see Beth Hess, Elizabeth Markson, and Peter Stein, "Racial and Ethnic Minorities: An Overview," in *Race, Class, and Gender in the United States*, Second Edition, ed. Paula Rothenberg (New York: St. Martin's Press, 1992), pp. 145–155; Benjamin Ringer and Elinor Lawless, *Race-Ethnicity and Society* (New York: Routledge, 1989).

13. Lyman Sargent, *Contemporary Political Ideologies*, Seventh Edition (Chicago: Dorsey Press, 1987), p. 2.

14. Burton Gummer, "On Helping and Helplessness: The Structure of Discretion in the American Welfare System," *Social Service Review 53* (June 1979): 218.

15. Ringer and Lawless, *Race-Ethnicity and Society*, p. 27.

16. George Martin, Jr., *Social Policy in the Welfare State* (Englewood Cliffs, NJ: Prentice Hall, 1990), p. 1.

17. Wilbur Finch, Jr., "Alternative Service Organizations: The AIDS Community," in *AIDS—A Complete Guide to Psychosocial Intervention*, ed. Helen Land (Milwaukee: Family Service America, Inc., 1992), p. 79.

18. George Martin, Jr., *Social Policy in the Welfare State* (Englewood Cliffs, NJ: Prentice Hall, 1990), p. 27.

Chapter 2

White Ethnics, African Americans, and American Indians at the Turn of the Century: The Social Context of Early Practice

It is generally acknowledged that, up to the present time, minorities in general, and especially the Negro, have to a large extent been bypassed in the writing of American history. Social welfare history has, with some exceptions tended to reflect the mainstream in this regard.[1]

The historical emergence of social work was grounded in a period that was both complex and challenging. The historical and social context surrounding this emergence shaped the definition and direction of the budding profession. An analysis of today's social work interventions with diverse communities must be grounded in the history of these diverse groups in the United States. Thus, the Progressive Era becomes a significant starting point for this analysis.

Social work and human services publications do mention the Progressive Era, the social transition accompanying it, and, to some degree, the plight of ethnic minorities during this period. These topics often take up a few paragraphs or even a few pages that contain a broad, general, and rather simplistic overview without a serious analysis of the interplay between these social conditions affecting ethnic minorities and organized responses to them. The history of social work as it relates to particular groups cannot and should not be so easily dismissed, discounted, or denied.

General, brief historical summaries often erroneously convey a view that all groups suffered equally, horribly, and harmfully. Such a homogenized approach fails to distinguish the unique experiences of specific groups. These unique experiences were shaped by the way the larger society responded to each group—a larger society that included the nascent field of social work. For this reason, this chapter provides a more detailed description of the historical context in which social work emerged.

It is all too easy to believe that history has limited utility for contemporary practitioners and social delivery systems. Some people may even think that only contemporary issues are relevant for contemporary intervention—not the issues of the past. Yet, it is the specific history of each group that has contributed to the forms and functions of contemporary social work with that group. An understanding and acceptance of that history are paramount for explaining and overcoming the tensions that have long existed between ethnic minority communities and mainstream social work.

Thus, an understanding of social work's contemporary relationship with ethnic minority communities does not begin with the present. Rather, the profession's response to the needs of these communities has been developing over time and the visible results today represent an accumulation of that history. The social work/ethnic minority community interface is predicated on the evolution of the profession and the evolution of minority communities. Both sides had a specific agenda that led to the taking of divergent paths. It is the history of human services in general, and social work in particular, as it relates to ethnic minorities, that has shaped mainstream interventions in these communities. An understanding of social work's responses today is predicated on an understanding of responses during its formative years.

Modern social work has its roots in the Progressive Era (1895–1920), for it was during this period that increased immigration, massive migration, burgeoning industrialization, and unbridled urbanization dramatically changed the texture of U.S. society and created rampant social problems that begged for systematic, organized intervention. The acceptance of the idea that skilled professionals could assist individuals and families and that the attendant rise of the human services can be linked to social and intellectual movements in the Progressive Era set the stage for the emergence of social work, clinical psychology, and marriage and family therapy, among others.[2]

The actual years that define the Progressive Era appear to vary from author to author. For example, Cowan, Rose, and Rose described this period as 1900 to 1920,[3] whereas Jimenez used 1900 to 1917.[4] Davis targeted 1890 to 1914,[5] as did Kunitz.[6] Because of migration rates, immigration patterns, changing laws, and shifting economic trends, clarity in defining the Progressive Era years is vital for assessing this period. Although the addition or subtraction of a few years may seem insignificant, these variations determine the specific events chronicled and their immediate and long-range effects. Some events included or omitted are minor in nature; others, such as World War I, are paramount. The actual definition of the Progressive Era has implications for the analysis undertaken.

Here, the years 1895 to 1920 define the Progressive Era and those historical occurrences falling within this period are emphasized. These years are used because they capture the first signs of a change in the European immigration pattern, the peak of African-American migration to the North, World War I, and the period immediately following the war. World War I and its aftermath were particularly relevant in defining the minority experience in the United States. Where appropriate, historical antecedents and consequences of the Progressive Era are discussed as a means of capturing a more complete social context and not just snapshots.

PROGRESS OF THE PROGRESSIVE ERA

The Progressive Era was so named because of the economic, social, and political changes taking place during the time.[7] For example, this was the period that saw the railroad linking areas that had been separated by weeks of travel. In 1865, the United States had about 37,000 miles of railroad track, and by 1914, that figure had increased to 253,000.[8] Although the automobile was not a common family item, its presence was growing in U.S. communities. Evolving transportation technologies meant that manufactured goods and supplies could be carried to numerous parts of the country, thereby increasing their distribution. Furthermore, industries and factories developed with the utilization of cheap labor provided by migrants and immigrants. In 1914, there were 7 times as many industrial workers as there had been in 1859, production had increased by about 12 times, and 69 percent of the work force held nonagricultural employment.[9]

The Progressive Era is noted for the reform efforts undertaken by progressives and reformers on behalf of workers, children, and widows. Furthermore, this progressivism is generally associated with political liberalism directed toward ameliorating the problems and injustices accompanying the transition to an industrialized, urbanized society.[10] For example, in 1890, the National American Women's Suffrage Association was established; in 1899, Illinois and Colorado passed legislation that established juvenile courts; in 1904, the National Committee on Child Labor was organized; in 1909, the White House Conference on Care of Dependent Children was held; and from 1911 to 1920, numerous states enacted mothers' pension legislation and workmen's compensation.[11] Indeed, the first systematic welfare programs were enacted at the state level during this time, as reflected in the Illinois adoption of workmen's compensation in 1911, which was viewed as a progressive innovation.[12]

The paradox of the Progressive Era is rather striking because with this era came the dawning of a new American prosperity as well as a new American poverty. While thousands languished in the tenements of growing cities, thousands were also reaping the wealth of an industrializing country. At a time when poverty was taking on a new and even more abject meaning, numerous individuals were able to achieve success and wealth. During this era, the number of millionaires increased significantly and industries were monopolized by specific companies. The *World Almanac* named 4,000 millionaires in 1902, 47 percent of the nation's assets were held by 1 percent of the population during the early 1900s, Andrew Carnegie made $23 million in 1900, and steel, oil, and agricultural machinery production were dominated by U.S. Steel, Standard Oil, and International Harvester.[13]

The Progressive Era also gave rise to organized efforts to assist the less fortunate. The origins of U.S. social work were primarily in the Charity Organization Societies that emphasized control of pauperism by the regulation of charity through scientific principles ("scientific charity") and by the assimilation of the poor and immigrants who suffered the harsh slum conditions.[14] The settlement house movement—also a major part of social work history—provided for a focus on the environmental causes of poverty and on research into the factors leading to poverty.[15] These two roots of contemporary human services are well known among professional service providers and have received extensive coverage in social work and human services texts and journals. What is often lacking in these discussions, however, is the plight of racial minorities and the manner in which the charity organization societies and settlement houses responded to these groups.

This chapter and Chapter 3 provide a descriptive overview of the lives of White ethnics, African Americans, American Indians, Mexicans, Chinese, and Japanese in the United States during the Progressive Era. Chapters 4 and 5 detail the work of the Charity Organization Societies and settlement houses with these groups. The interaction between the needs of these population groups and initial social work responses to those needs is the foundation of today's mainstream practice with ethnic minority communities.

The significance of the past has been emphasized by Ringer and Lawless:

> Thus the historical past of an ethnic group is not something that is relegated to its archives to be viewed as a curious but interesting relic. Instead it functions to organize sentiments, needs, aspirations of the present. Consequently to understand fully the meaning of the past for an ethnic group, it must be seen as filtered through the prism of the present. As such the past and present are inextricably interwoven in the life of the ethnic group, and the interaction between the two does much to define the group's vision of its future.[16]

A review of the general conditions of this period, the unique history of specific ethnic minority groups, and early social work history can provide insight into bridging the gap that separates social work from ethnic minority communities. The conditions and early responses to them become a legacy for modern multicultural social work practice. The historical context of ethnic minority communities must be confronted for social work to gain the respect and acceptance of these communities.

THE SOCIAL CONDITIONS OF THE PROGRESSIVE ERA: URBANIZATION

The Progressive Era captures a snapshot of the urbanization of U.S. society along with significant population growth. In the decade preceding the advent of the Progressive Era—the 1880s—the U.S. population was 50.1 million, and 28.7 percent of this population resided in urban areas. At the beginning of the Progressive period, the population had grown to almost 63 million, and a little more than a third (35.1 percent) of the population was urban. By the end of this era—1920—the population had increased to over 105 million and slightly more than half (51.2 percent) was found in urban areas.[17]

Much of the population increase occurred in specific major cities as migrants from rural areas and immigrants from other countries were drawn to them by the magnet of jobs and economic prosperity.[18] In 1860, there were 8 cities with populations over 100,000, and by 1900, that number had grown to 33.[19] Baltimore, Brooklyn, Boston, Chicago, New York, Philadelphia, and St. Louis, for example, experienced unprecedented growth due to larger populations *and* changing city boundaries through annexation of adjacent areas that were already densely populated. For example, Chicago grew from 503,185 in 1880 to 1,099,850 in 1890—a rate of 118 percent; however, the city also grew in land mass from 35.66 square miles to 174.55 square miles—an almost 400 percent gain.[20] Consequently, immigration, migration, and annexation contributed to the urbanization of U.S. society and the growth of urban centers.

ETHNIC AND RACIAL GROUPS

White Ethnic Groups

European immigration was largely unregulated prior to World War I (1914–1918) but this changed after the war.[21] Between 1880 and World War I, strong antiforeign agitation erupted. This antiforeign sentiment was tied to the dramatic change in immigration patterns of the Progressive Era—from the immigration of the desirable, sturdy stock of "old" European immigrants from northwestern Europe to the immigration of the less desirable peasants and "pales" from eastern and southern Europe (the "new" immigrants).[22]

Numerous immigrant groups (Germans, Scotch-Irish, Swedes, Dutch, French, Spanish, Portuguese, Jews) contributed to the emergence of an American identity during the colonial period, although the Anglo-Saxon element was predominant in determining U.S. political, legal, and social development.[23] Many of these groups with cultures that did not vary greatly from the developing U.S. culture had been assimilated as they already espoused or adopted English and Protestantism. Catholic and Jewish populations were relatively small and nonthreatening to mainstream America. Belief in the Anglo-Saxon legacy shaped political thought in the 1880s and took form in *nativism*—the view that native-born Whites of old stock (Nordic and Aryan ancestry) were superior to all other groups. Darwinism and racist imperialism reflected an adherence to Anglo-Saxon supremacy in the literature and science of the late 1800s.[24]

During the 1880s and earlier, the majority of European immigrants hailed from Great Britain, Ireland, Scandinavia, and other countries of the northwest. Census figures indicate that, in 1870, the overwhelming majority (96 percent) of the foreign born in the United States had come from these countries, and 61 percent of those immigrating to the United States in that year were from northwestern Europe.[25] These immigrants were considered desirable because their appearance, culture, and values were held as more compatible with U.S. culture. Thus, these immigrants were considered easy candidates for assimilation. German immigrants, although from central Europe, provide an example of such a group. In an article on African Americans in St. Louis published in 1903, Brandt noted that there was no German problem, "though the Germans form a large part of our population, because they are already in line with American ideals before they came over, and quickly become assimilated."[26]

In 1880, only 5.4 of the European immigrants coming to the United States were from eastern and southern Europe and, in 1890, that figure was 21 percent. By 1900, 49 percent of the European immigrants were from the "undesirable" countries. Immigration reached its peak in 1914 as 1,058,391 European immigrants traveled to the United States. Of this number, only 12 percent came from northwestern Europe, while more than half (58 percent) came from eastern and southern Europe.[27] In the minds of native-born White Americans, the threat was very real and very immediate.

Discrimination
Nativism was widespread in the country and was fanned by the visible presence of the new immigrants—Italians, Poles, Russian Jews, and Greeks.

Native-born White Anglo-Saxon Americans believed themselves to be, through nativity and "stock," superior to others, while at the same time tolerating foreign-born people who were derivative of this stock.[28] Many of these new immigrants were Catholic or Jewish, while supporters of nativism embraced Protestantism. Progressives and other citizens feared that these new immigrants would outnumber the old immigrants from the sturdy-stock countries and threaten U.S. culture. These new immigrants also were of darker skin color and were thought to be stupid, dirty, loud, drunken, sexually uninhibited, violent, and dangerously radical by native-born Americans.[29] In 1903, Brandt also noted that the Russians, Hungarians, and Poles "require more assistance to be converted into desirable American citizens."[30] Nativism can be seen as not just an anti-immigration sentiment but as a racist one that did not discriminate against all foreigners but against those deemed inferior to White, Anglo-Saxon people.[31]

Many of the Catholic and Jewish immigrants sought to maintain their own religious practices and teachings by sending their children to religious-based schools, thereby resisting pressures to assimilate. These educational practices often clashed with progressive goals for a homogeneous society.[32] For example, the separatist policies of the Catholics that supported separate Catholic schools and institutions further kindled nativist, antiforeign sentiment.[33] This desire for Catholic and Jewish institutions was often interpreted as a rejection of U.S. values and further reinforced the view that these "new" immigrants were troublemakers.

Many of the immigrants faced harsh discrimination in employment and housing. From 1880 to 1915, about 2 million Jewish immigrants from eastern Europe came to the United States and were met with residential restrictive covenants that barred them from specific neighborhoods and employers who refused to hire them.[34] Much of this discrimination persisted beyond the Progressive Era as Jews were prohibited from holding particular offices and from entering most major universities.[35]

The wave of "new" immigrants was drawn to the United States for economic reasons as they left rural living behind them. Unfortunately, their agrarian skills could not be utilized in the large cities and they were forced to take whatever jobs and wages available. In 1900, 67 percent of the immigrants entered the country as laborers or without occupations.[36] They were forced to endure harsh slum conditions until they could better their plight through skill acquisition and assimilation.

Native-born American workers were bitterly opposed to Slavic, Italian, and other immigrants from eastern and southern Europe, and vocal proponents for immigration control advocated for the separation of the desirables from the undesirables.[37] Tensions between native-born Americans and the "new" immigrants influenced the U.S. labor movement as issues of class and ethnicity became entangled.[38]

Americanization

Thousands of the new immigrants were of slightly darker skin tones, were of peasant, country stock, espoused non-Christian and/or non-Protestant religions, and had cultural values and practices that were "foreign." Nevertheless, these so-called undesirables were still worthy of Americanization efforts. Although many "real" Americans were dubious because the task seemed so insurmountable, other reformers and progressives believed the problem to be resolvable. Indeed, many assumed that, over the years, the children and grandchildren of the new immigrants would blend in with the rest of America. This meant that the problems of Americanization were problems of the newly arrived, first generation of new immigrants.

President Theodore Roosevelt predicted that eventually *all* White immigrants, through Americanization, would become assimilated into U.S. society.[39] To Roosevelt, Americanization meant Anglo conformity in addition to assimilation. He firmly believed that immigrants should rid themselves of ethnic names, ethnic identities, ethnic customs, and ethnic loyalties in order to become fully Americanized.

Americanization became a popular doctrine of the Progressive Era and suggested that the problems of the newer immigrants were problems of a temporary nature. Public schools and businesses developed Americanization programs to hurry along assimilation.[40] In writing about immigrant education in the early 1900s, Seller noted, "Most old stock Americans, including educators, saw the southern and eastern European immigrants as morally, culturally, and intellectually inferior species which, if left un-Americanized, would destroy the American city.... Appropriate education for immigrants...was thought to be social and vocational rather than academic."[41] Eventually, Americanization was broadened to include nationalistic loyalty in addition to Anglo-Saxon conformity.

Health and Mortality

The new city dwellers and the cities themselves were ill equipped for the consequences of rapid demographic shifts. On one hand, the former rural life of migrants and immigrants was poor preparation for urban living with its dense population, poverty, poor working conditions, unemployment, and environmental conditions that fostered sickness and disease. Immigrants were also hampered by their lack of knowledge of U.S. culture and language. On the other hand, city services—such as sewer, water, street maintenance, and schools—often could not meet the needs of a swelling population. Housing needs also exceeded the availability of affordable, adequate housing. These factors contributed to the emergence of slums and tenement housing areas.

Conditions facing the poor of the urban centers were devastating.[42] Housing construction could not accommodate the thousands of people flooding the cities. Existing homes that had housed a single family were frequently partitioned so that several families could live in one room. The previous, more affluent owners deserted those areas destined to become slums. These families could afford more spacious housing in the country or in other, more desirable parts of the city. The housing crisis led to the hasty construction of unsafe housing. In addition, most apartments had no hot water, no baths, no indoor plumbing, no windows, no ventilation, no sewers, and no other sanitation facilities.

New York City provided one of the worst cases of overcrowding, as a little more than 42,000 tenements were homes for about 1.5 million people in 1900.[43] According to Ehrenreich, "The tenth ward on New York's Lower East Side, with a population density of more than 700 per acre, was one of the most densely populated places in the history of the earth."[44] Population density exacerbated the problems of fires and sewage disposal. Fires were a common occurrence because coal stoves were used for heat and, because the tenements were practically on top of each other, fires quickly spread. Cities were also grappling with ways of disposing of sewage generated by the massive population. Garbage pickup was often unreliable as piles and piles of trash covered city sidewalks.

Death and disease plagued the slums; infants were particularly susceptible. For example, in Massachusetts, the infant mortality rate was 163 per 1,000 live births from 1890 to 1894. In the same state, in 1895, the death rate for infants under 1 year of age was an incredible 216. Furthermore, cardiovascular-renal diseases, influenza and pneumonia, and tuberculosis were killing the urban population at alarming rates.[45] Tuberculosis was a particular health problem in the crowded, unsanitary slums. In the absence of proper sanitation and refrigeration, immigrants also battled food poisoning. Many of the immigrants feared hospitals because they associated them with death; as an alternative, folk medicine and midwives were frequently utilized. Some medications readily available on the streets and promoted as cure-alls often did more harm than good because of their toxic contents.

The general environment may have been more polluted and stressful than the ones left in the immigrants' countries of origin. The streets of the urban centers contained numerous seen and unseen hazards. For example, in New York, at the turn of the century, about 150,000 horses produced over 2 million pounds of horse manure, and about 60,000 gallons of horse urine fell on the streets while about 15,000 dead horses had to be removed annually.[46] The streets held other hazards in addition to unsanitary conditions. City crime rates were high as gangs roamed the streets, and public safety was further hampered by poor or minimal street lighting.

Working conditions posed another threat to the immigrants. About 35,000 Americans were killed and 536,000 injured each year during the Progressive Era. Railroad and steel plant jobs were particularly hazardous.[47]

It was often cheaper for employers to replace sick and injured workers than it was to improve the working conditions. Workers toiled long hours in unsafe conditions for wages that could not adequately support them. Factory safety standards and restrictions on work hours were either nonexistent or poorly enforced. Workers appeared to be at the mercy of their employers and were thankful for whatever employment they had. Unfortunately, in cases of injury or death, these employers were often absolved of any responsibility; thus, many families were left destitute. Rising insurance costs, dramatic increases in work-related injuries, and economic uncertainties eventually led many businessmen to support workmen's compensation programs.[48]

Factories themselves were fire hazards due to poorly constructed or nonexistent fire escapes, the presence of debris, blocked exits, and the absence of sprinklers. In 1911, a fire at New York's Triangle Waist Company killed 145 workers, most of whom were young female Italian and Jewish immigrants who were either burned to death, crushed, or impaled on a fence as they tried to escape.[49]

Children were especially vunerable as they succumbed to delinquency and/or lived on the streets as homeless street urchins. Those fortunate enough to secure employment found that employment could be more of a curse than a blessing. Because the use of child laborers was rampant at the turn of the century, the employment of children raised its own unique set of issues.[50] These workers toiled incredibly long hours for pennies in the canneries, factories, mines, mills, tobacco fields, and meat-packing plants where the work was often dangerous and poorly supervised. Others labored on the streets as vendors, messengers, and shoeshine boys. Children were often recruited from states with restrictive labor laws to those states with no such laws and worked as long as 12 to 14 hours a day for as little as 25 cents. In 1900, the number of child laborers in the South dramatically rose by three times over the previous decade and, nationally, over 1.5 million children were gainfully employed.

Racial Violence
Violence against the foreign born was particularly acute during the recessions of 1910 to 1911, 1914 to 1915, and the post–World War I years. In the latter years of the Progressive Era—the post–World War I years—bitter competition for jobs arose as the United States adjusted to its postwar economy. During this time, nativism and racism fueled mob attacks against the foreign born, many of whom were Italian. Much of American frustration surrounding the changing economy and job situation found form and expression in violence and discrimination against those deemed "undesirable."

The American Protective Association was formed in 1887 and was essentially anti-Catholic and extended membership to any foreign born who agreed to denounce Catholics. Other such associations were formed to protect U.S. society from encroachment by outsiders. Labor groups, including unions, engaged in violence against immigrants who appeared to be taking jobs away from "real" Americans. The Ku Klux Klan found new life in 1915 and was just about anti-everything and everyone except those who the Klan believed were all-American and all-pure. The Klan terrorized African Americans, Catholics, and Jews. Particular individuals—those perceived as troublemakers and/or group leaders—were often singled out for attacks that resulted in serious injuries or death.

Injustices of the Law Enforcement/Justice Systems

Numerous groups lobbied for anti-immigration legislation that would delimit immigration from the "undesirable" countries of Europe. In 1887, Congress passed a bill that would use a literacy test to restrict immigration—a test of the immigrant's ability to read and write English (or another language) before entering the United States. In addition, the head tax on immigrants was doubled and the discretion of immigration agents to admit or deport was increased. Such a bill was necessary, according to legislators and other supporters, to reduce undesirable immigration. Although the bill had numerous exemptions based on age, physical condition, and family status, it was vetoed by President Grover Cleveland. Some years and several presidents later, Congress was able to override a presidential veto in 1917 to enact the bill. World War I had rekindled the nativism flame and renewed agitation propelled the bill into law.

Neither race nor ethnicity was singled out as the thrust of the bill, but it was no secret that the wave of immigrants from eastern and southern Europe provided the impetus for the legislation. This was a subtle way of extending favoritism to one group without explicitly having to ban another. Since the poor, undesirable peasants among the new immigrants were limited in their literacy skills, the bill would curtail the flow of undesirables into the country.

Attitudes and legislation of the Progressive Era formed the basis of post-Progressive Era bills. Since the act of 1917 did not restrict immigration to the degree expected by its supporters, even more restrictive measures were passed later. For example, although the 1917 act implemented a process of screening applicants, the Quota Act of 1921 was passed to limit the *number* of immigrants entering the United States. A foreign country's quota was set as 3 percent of the number of its immigrant population in the United States in 1910. The Quota Act of 1924 went even further by setting the quota at 2 percent and using 1890 as the base year. This act favored the immigration of people from northern Europe because other immigrants were not a significant part of the U.S. population in 1890. Mexican immigrants were excluded from these restrictions because they were needed for labor in the Southwest farming industries and were not perceived as a national threat.

Interpreting the White Ethnic Experience

Over the years, the history of White ethnics has been written to extol the virtues of ambition, commitment, determination, and rising above insurmountable odds to achieve a legitimate place in the United States. Stories are written by and about the immigrants who came to America with nothing but the clothes on their backs and a burning desire to be an American.

In this era, the myth of the "melting pot" was born. The term was propelled into national consciousness by Israel Zangwill's play, *The Melting Pot*. In this play, a character utters, "There she lies, the great Melting Pot...Celt and Latin, Slav and Teuton, Greek and Syrian, black and yellow.... Yes, East and West, and North and South, the palm and the pine, the pole and the equator, the crescent and the cross.... Here they shall all unite to build the Republic of Man and the Kingdom of God."[51] The play opened in 1908 during the period of arrival of mass numbers of new immigrants, and the melting pot ideology offered optimism about the country's future. In addition, the playwright, an organizer of the International Jewish Territorial Organization, believed in America's ability to assimilate the disparate masses. The popularity of the melting pot perspective persisted long after the Progressive Era.

The history of the "undesirable" immigrants in the United States has been used to reinforce U.S. values such as: those able to excel without help—the independent, rugged individualists—represent the best of America; "making it" is of paramount importance; everything is possible; the desire for material gain is the basis of work motivation; and those who fail do so by their own hands.[52] With this perspective, the social, economic, and political conditions that surround people were reduced to mere obstacles that test the true worth and mettle of an individual. The new immigrants added another chapter to American history that perpetuated those beliefs tenaciously held in America.

RACIAL MINORITIES IN THE PROGRESSIVE ERA

In 1900, non-Whites made up about 12 percent of the U.S. population, and that figure varied only slightly during the Progressive Era.[53] Of the non-Whites in the population, African Americans totaled 11 percent, whereas American Indians, Japanese, and Chinese totaled slightly less than 1 percent. Mexicans were not counted separately in the statistics for this period. Thus, the 8.8 million African Americans in the United States at the turn of the century were the predominant racial minority. This means that the "non-White" statistics of this era appear to capture rather accurately the African-American population.

Non-Whites did not fare as well as Whites during the Progressive Era. The infant mortality rates for non-Whites was almost twice that for Whites, and non-White mothers were almost twice as likely to die during childbirth as White mothers. Furthermore, a White person born in 1900 could expect to live an average of 48 years, whereas a non-White could expect 33 years of life. Tuberculosis and influenza claimed a higher percentage of non-Whites than Whites. For example, in 1914, 260 non-Whites per 100,000 and 169 Whites per 100,000 died from these causes.[54] These figures are indicative of the type of social conditions surrounding the non-White population.

The belief that non-Whites represented a separate class of people is reflected in the social sciences of the day. Physiological and psychological studies were evoked to prove the innate inferiority of racial minorities. In 1916, one psychologist revealed that, according to test results, the low intelligence of Spanish-Indian, Mexican, and African-American children was confirmed and concluded that "their dullness seems to be racial." When using Army test results, another psychologist plotted ethnic and racial groups along an intelligence continuum that placed Nordics at the highest end, Alpines and Mediterraneans in the middle, and African Americans at the lowest end.[55]

Leading educators of the Progressive Era espoused views on the education of non-Whites that, today, would be called racist. For example, G. Stanley Hall, the educational reformer credited with bringing Freud and Jung to the United States, saw non-Whites as the *children* of the human race and advocated an educational approach that incorporated their culture and abilities. Decades ago, this position was considered one of reform; yet, it can be argued that it reinforced an inferior status for non-Whites.[56]

Although African Americans represented the dominant racial minority, it is important to look at them and other racial groups to determine their historical legacy in this country.

African Americans in the Progressive Era

With its reform and liberalism, the Progressive Era seems to have been anything but progressive for African Americans. During this era, African Americans were subjected to harsh, widespread discrimination; dire health and mortality rates; unbridled racial violence; injustices of the law enforcement/justice system; and biased analyses and interpretations of their conditions.

Discrimination
Prior to the peak northern migration of southern African Americans, African Americans were virtually invisible to the people of the northern and western states. During the early years of the Progressive Era, it was more cost efficient to U.S. businesses for African Americans to remain in the South as

cheap agrarian laborers. Those African Americans residing in the North were often less segregated than some of the "new" immigrant groups because their relatively small numbers in the population did not appear as a threat to other Americans.

Before the end of the Progressive Era, however, this situation changed drastically. The segregation of the South followed African Americans to the North. Even before the mass exodus of African Americans from the South, separation of the races was endemic to U.S. society. Indeed, in 1903, Brandt observed, "It is noticeable that there was a tendency to separation of the white population from blacks as early as there was a free Negro population of any consideration."[57]

When industrialization transformed farm work from labor dependency to machine dependency, when immigration restrictions curbed the flow of "new" immigrants, and when a major war drained the work force, African Americans ventured North in record numbers. In the early 1900s, changes in African-American migration patterns became apparent, and, by 1915, migration rates had risen significantly and peaked from 1916 to 1918. Figures for African-American migration indicate that less than 100,000 migrated in the 1870s and 1880s, approximately 200,000 migrated between 1890 and 1910, and from 1910 to 1920, between 300,000 to 1 million made the journey.[58] As many as 700,000 are estimated to have migrated during a peak period from 1916 to 1917.

From 1910 to 1920, the total African-American population of New York, Chicago, Philadelphia, and Detroit increased by about 750,000, and, after World War I, New York, Chicago, Baltimore, and Washington each had an African-American population over 100,000.[59] During this period, surveys of the reasons African Americans migrated found that poor wages, poor treatment by Whites, poor schools, problems with tenant farming, discrimination, and oppression were driving African Americans out of the South.[60] In 1917, DuBois noted that "the immediate cause was economic, and the movement began because of floods in middle Alabama and Mississippi and because the latest devastation of the boll weevil came in these districts."[61] DuBois also cited the cessation of European immigration and the violence against African Americans in the South as factors contributing to the migration.

Many African Americans assumed their own American nativity would foster acceptance by native-minded Whites. They found, however, that race took priority over nativity. Although they encountered similar prejudice as the immigrant groups, this prejudice was worsened because of race. In documenting African-American migration North, Goodwin observed, "Of all the major urban American immigrant communities of whatever ethnic or racial background, none faced the kind of systematic and restrictive measures upon its urban adaptation as did the American Black."[62]

African Americans appeared to represent a different class of people, and their growing presence in places where they had previously been rather invisible heightened racial problems. Even though they saw themselves as being as "American" as White Americans, they were confronted with a different reality. A group's self-identity is but one factor that defines its distinctiveness and status. The larger society also has its own set of definitions of the group and attempts to impose these definitions in its contact with that group.[63] To many Whites in the northern cities, African Americans were even more undesirable and "foreign" than were the "new" immigrants.

African Americans migrating North in search of economic security and freedom from oppression found the same conditions as experienced by the "new" immigrants—only more so. A 1905 issue of *Charities* described the housing problem facing African-American migrants: "Difficulty in obtaining a suitable place meets the Negro who comes to a large northern city. In many neighborhoods he cannot rent a house or apartment no matter how well able he may be to pay the price for it, and in those places in which he is permitted to live his accommodations are frequently worse than the same money would buy *for any other race*"[emphasis added].[64]

Sophonisba Breckinridge, an advocate of services for African Americans, provided a more detailed description in 1913 of the housing situation in Chicago: "While half of the people in the Bohemian, Polish, and Lithuanian districts were paying less than $8.50 for their four room apartments; the steelmill employees less than $9.50, and the Jews in the Ghetto less than $10.50, the Negro, in the midst of extreme dilapidation and crowded into territory adjoining the segregated vice district, pays from $12 to $12.50."[65] Breckinridge also observed that housing problems for African Americans were different from that of immigrants. While the *poor* Polish, Jewish, or Italian immigrant had to endure poor housing conditions, African Americans of *all* income levels suffered housing problems.

Many progressives in the North and the South saw education as the answer for African Americans. As with the newly arrived immigrants from southern and eastern Europe, manual training was at the heart of education proposed for African Americans. Although White philanthropists provided significant funding for education, many were only willing to support industrial education for African Americans.[66] In 1905, Gordon wrote, "The strain of commercial competition, as well as the added stress of race prejudice has had a tendency to limit the opportunities of the Negro boy or girl in securing necessary work…. It would seem then, that manual training in a school for Negro children is even more essential and helpful than it is in a school for whites."[67] Gordon went on to extol the benefits of bench work, forging, woodcarving, and mechanical drawing for African-American boys and the value of properly washing dishes, trimming lamps, making bread, and understanding the science of housekeeping for African-American girls. Although White southerners in general opposed African-American education, those who were somewhat sympathetic usually supported mechanical, industrial, and agricultural schools for this group.[68] Many Whites feared that too much of the wrong kind of education would make African Americans more difficult to control. African Americans themselves were more divided on the appropriate education for their people than were the Whites who actually controlled resources.

School attendance did not have the same meaning among African Americans as it did among Whites. In both the North and the South, since prejudice often prevented African Americans from working in the mills, factories, and other industries, they attended school instead.[69] Reformers who advocated compulsory education were ambivalent about the implications of such a bill for African Americans. Because school attendance was already high for many African Americans and compulsory education would put even more African Americans in the classroom, the potential threat of the "educated Negro" to White supremacy was widely debated.

As African Americans flooded the cities of the North, school segregation rose dramatically. Some schools were all African-American, and those that purported to be integrated assigned African-American students to the same classroom or sent them to branch schools. When African-American and White schools existed in the same cities, African Americans had the most deteriorated buildings and the fewest supplies.

Other reform efforts were retarded by fear that the reform would also have to be extended to African Americans.[70] For example, the age of consent in Georgia was 10 years old and remained there until 1918 (when it was raised to age 14) because legislators did not want to extend legal protection to African-American girls. Opponents of women's right to vote, particularly southerners, feared that extending the vote to women would lead to African-American women also voting. Thus, racism not only reduced the rights and privileges of African Americans but it also served to delimit the opportunities of Whites as well.

Pervasive racism against African Americans by persons outside this group affected the relations among members inside the group. For example, the "near-White" African Americans often saw themselves as different from the darker-skinned African Americans. Color became a status symbol that was associated with economic success. Because "whiteness" was more desirable than "darkness," African Americans adopted standards that favored the lighter-hued individuals of their race.[71] This may have carried over from slavery days, as mulattoes (as sons and daughters of slaveholders) and free African Americans had educational and economic advantages over the dark-skinned members of the race.[72] Furthermore, Whites may have extended preferential treatment to those African Americans who did not have the stereotypical "Negroid" features. The meaning of color in the African-American community and the etiology of those meanings have been widely debated over the years.

Health and Mortality

Living conditions contributed to the health and mortality of African Americans. Migrating African Americans experienced a significant decline in general health in the northern environment, particularly the areas of infectious diseases and maternal and child sicknesses.[73] These health and mortality patterns were present among African Americans in the North prior to the great migration period. In 1899, *The Charities Review* noted, "The negroes die twice as fast as the whites; but the whites have greater comforts and many advantages as regards skilled medical attention."[74] In 1897, *The Charities Review* attributed the high infant mortality rate among African Americans "to the fact that negro mothers are obliged, as a rule, to work out, thus leaving their homes and children, which is not only the cause of infant mortality, but also of neglected child life."[75]

While infectious diseases coupled with infant and maternal mortality decimated the African-American population, a study at the close of the Progressive Era revealed that African-American males were also more likely than Whites to be victims of homicides.[76] This fact underscores the violence that has historically stalked African-American communities, and "black-on-black" homicides have been a part of the history of numerous African-American communities. Violence of this nature in the African-American community has been linked to the concentration of alcohol and drugs (which are correlated with the incidence of violence) in these communities and the personal and social upheaval that accompanied African-American migration and urbanization.[77] The internalization of White attitudes that devalue African-American life has also been posited as an explanatory factor.

Racial Violence

Violence against African Americans also escalated during the Progressive Era. In the decade prior to the Progressive Era, more Whites than African Americans were lynched, and during this era, the actual number of lynchings decreased as the percentage of African-American victims rose. Mob action against this group increased, and lynchings as well as other acts of brutality became public spectacles. Of the 1,600 victims of mob action between 1890 and 1901, more than two-thirds were African Americans. A total of 3,000 known lynchings of African-American men and women stained American history from 1885 to 1915.[78]

Although this violence generally plagued the southern states, other parts of the country also witnessed lynchings and race riots as the numbers of African Americans in the North increased dramatically. Wherever large pockets of African Americans settled, they faced the same conditions as the earlier "new" immigrants *but their predicament was compounded by issues related solely to race.* According to Jansson:

> The situation was more favorable for African Americans in the North but only modestly so…. Residential areas occupied by African Americans were even more blighted than ones occupied by other immigrant groups, were more likely to be headquarters for organized crime and drug interests, and had virtually no health or other services. They experienced extraordinary discrimination in job markets since they were excluded from skilled trades and unions, often used as scabs to break unions, and were subject to race riots and mob violence when they competed with whites for jobs.[79]

Racial hostility and hatred directed toward African Americans were more pervasive and lethal than that directed toward any of the "new" immigrant groups. Mob violence erupted in East St. Louis in 1917 and in about 25 other cities, including Chicago and Washington, as mobs of Whites burned African-American ghettos and lynched, shot, and beat the inhabitants.[80] During the "Red Summer" of 1919, Chicago, Omaha, and other northern and southern cities were sites of brutal mob violence against African Americans that claimed numerous lives and left thousands homeless.[81]

The East St. Louis case is a vivid example of the magnitude and intensity of the racial mob violence that was inflicted against African Americans. The National Association for the Advancement of Colored People (NAACP) sent special investigators to collect data on the incident, and the results were published in the September 1917 issue of *The Crisis*.[82] According to this report, "On that day [July 2, 1917] a mob of white men, women, and children…drove 6,000 Negroes out of their homes; and deliberately burdered [sic], by shooting, burning and hanging between one and two hundred human beings who were black." Tension between Whites and African Americans had been unusually high for the past year in that city because African Americans from the South were used as strikebreakers when 4,500 White men in the packing plants decided to strike.

In a letter to delegates to the Central Trades and Labor Union, the East St. Louis union secretary wrote, "The immigration of the Southern Negro into our city for the past eight months has reached the point where drastic action must be taken if we intend to work and live peaceably in this community. Since the influx of undesirable negroes has started no less than ten thousand have come into this locality. These men are being used to the detriment of our white citizens."[83] The NAACP report, in response to this letter, noted, "It is not that foreigners—Czechs, Slovaks, Lithuanians—or whatever ethnic division is least indigenous to East St. Louis—it is not that *they* are ousting Americans of any color or hue, but the 'Southern Negro,' *the most American product there is,* [emphasis added] is being used to the detriment of our white citizens."[84] African Americans were faced with the stark realization that nativity did not override color and that they were considered the outsiders.

Injustices of the Law Enforcement/Justice Systems

Courts were not particularly sympathetic to African-American rights and status as citizens. It was during this period in 1896 that the Supreme Court handed down its *Plessy* v. *Ferguson* decision that made "separate but equal" treatment of African Americans the law of the land.[85] The Court had already upheld segregation in an 1890 decision that let stand a Mississippi statute that called for separate railroad cars for Whites and African Americans. The *Plessy* v. *Ferguson* decision dictated that the separate accommodations had to be of equal quality. This 1896 decision paved the way for widespread, court-sanctioned discrimination against African Americans.

In this historic decision, the Court declared that "legislation is powerless to eradicate racial instincts or to abolish distinctions based upon physical differences."[86] This ruling seemed to reaffirm the separation of the races as an innate or natural tendency that should not be challenged by law. Prejudicial attitudes thus became reified through laws that promulgated the inferior status of African Americans. Few people expected the "separate but equal" decision to be vigorously enforced. In fact, during the Progressive Era, other discriminatory laws were passed that limited African Americans' access to public education, housing, and jobs. (These laws were often referred to as Jim Crow laws, derived from a nineteenth-century song-and-dance act that stereotyped African Americans in an offensive way.) Because most of the African Americans (almost 90 percent) still lived in the southern states during most of the Progressive Era, Jim Crow laws and other discriminatory treatment occurred primarily in these southern states.

African Americans' belief in the power of the federal government to protect them from discrimination was further dampened by the actions of the nation's president. Many African Americans felt abandoned by President Theodore Roosevelt when he unfairly discharged "without honor" 167 African-American soldiers stationed near Brownsville, Texas, in 1906. An incident had taken place in which a White person was killed, and the soldiers refused to name those responsible. A military investigation yielded questionable evidence against the troops that may have been planted by Brownsville people as a way of having the troops removed.[87] Other White communities resented the presence of African-American troops, and conflict between troops and community often arose during this period. For example, in 1917, as a result of racial conflict between police and African-American soldiers in Waco, Texas, six African Americans were dishonorably discharged and sent to prison.[88] The Brownsville incident stands out because of the number of African Americans involved and because Roosevelt acted without the benefit of evidence.

African-American support for Roosevelt practically vanished after he refused to seat African-American delegates from the South at the 1912 political convention. This refusal may have been Roosevelt's attempt to regain southern White support that was lost after he invited Booker T. Washington, the noted African-American founder of Tuskegee Institute, to lunch at the White House. In the aftermath of White protest, Roosevelt later viewed the lunch as a mistake. These incidents led many African Americans to feel betrayed by a man who had once been regarded as an ally. These incidents were also indications of Roosevelt's belief that African Americans were inferior to Whites and needed aid to facilitate their assimilation into U.S. society.[89]

Actions by the federal government did little to raise African Americans' hopes for justice, fairness, and equal rights. The laws were against them and, as demonstrated in his arbitrary discharge of the Brownsville troops, so was the president of the United States. The evidence was overwhelming, mounting, and providing incontrovertible proof that "blacks were deserted by the federal government and must look after themselves."[90]

Because organized law-enforcement agencies were often perceived as agents for the social control of African Americans, these agencies also afforded little protection or security for countless members of this group. In almost every case of major racial conflict, the police refused to enforce the law and even led the mobs in attacking African Americans.[91] Consequently, poor or no law enforcement contributed much to the violence against African Americans.[92] A precarious relationship has historically existed between law-enforcement agencies and African-American communities. Because no arrests were made in 99 percent of the lynching cases occurring between 1882 and 1903, it appeared that law-enforcement authorities virtually refused to intervene in "lynch law."[93] This lack of action did nothing to change African-American attitudes about the police. The tensions between African Americans and law-enforcement agents are further captured in the 1921 study of homicides.[94] In this study, the majority of interracial homicides in the cities surveyed involved African-American males who were shot by *police* for "resisting arrest."

In looking at arrests in St. Louis from 1876 to 1901, Brandt noted that a large part of the police force was Irish, and this resulted in tolerance toward the offenses of foreign-born individuals as well as "an abnormal viligence over the Negroes."[95] In addition, the penal system has often been described as a replacement for the slavery system as a means of continued control of African Americans. For example, the state of New York legislated both the emancipation of slaves and the creation of the first state prison on the same day.[96]

Numerous African-American communities in both the North and the South were crime-ridden, drug-infested areas. African Americans were forced to live in districts that included these vices—vices that appear to have been tolerated by the police.[97] For example, New York's major African-American ghetto was home to saloons, gambling joints, prostitutes, pimps, and drug pushers. Also, African-American areas of Savannah, Georgia, were great sources of "crime and immorality."[98] In the North and the South, African-American crime rates exceeded that of Whites as African-American men, women, and children filled the jails and penitentiaries. In 1910, 11 times as many African Americans were incarcerated for grave homicide, 8 times as many for lesser homicide, 6 times as many for assault, and 3 to 4 times as many for prostitution, robbery, liquor law violations, burglary, rape, and larceny.[99] The debate raged then, as it does today, as to whether these excessive crime rates are the result of differential police activity or differential criminal involvement on the part of African Americans. Regardless of the cause, penal institutions were becoming increasingly institutions of color.

"Wayward" children and "fallen" women were particularly prevalent among the incarcerated population. Surrounded by crime, poverty, and minimal prospects, countless African-American children resorted to crime as a means of survival. In Georgia, for instance, children as young as 6 years of age were arrested and likely to be sentenced to the stockade or chain gang because of the absence of reformatories for African Americans.[100] Countless young African-American women who migrated to the North eventually relied on prostitution, as well as other illegal activities, as a way of earning money. In the absence of reformatories for African-American women, a significantly higher percentage was more likely to serve jail time than their White counterparts. Indianapolis, in the early 1900s, reflected this situation as White institutions refused to care for "fallen Negro girls."[101]

Interpreting the African-American Experience
Scholarly studies of African Americans during the Progressive Era offered valuable information about the conditions of African Americans but they often incorporated prevailing public attitudes about race and attempted to interpret the African-American experience. Brandt, in a study published in 1903 on "The Negroes of St. Louis," noted that African Americans were not generally found in parts of the city that had large foreign populations. Housing segregation was attributed to landlords not wanting African-American tenants because such tenants meant a depreciation of property value. Furthermore, African Americans were found to be excluded from all trades in St. Louis because of exclusionary attitudes of labor unions.

In explaining the high incidence of infectious diseases among African Americans, Brandt reported:

Negroes go insufficiently clothed in cold weather, are careless about wet clothing, are unwilling to call for medical attendance until the last moment, are ignorant of the laws of hygiene and sanitation, and live in surroundings that favor the spread of bacteriological diseases....These figures [for patients treated for smallpox], like those for consumption and pneumonia, point to constitutions weakened by bad sanitary conditions, poor food, and general carelessness.[102]

When reporting on the pauperism among African Americans in St. Louis, Brandt wrote:

The line between poverty and pauperism is farther down among the Negroes than among the whites, because of their lower standard of living....Fruit and vegetables, especially, are obtainable in season for almost nothing, and a "nickel's worth" of bananas or water-melon will content a Negro for a day. For this reason, although poverty is palpably as great and widespread among the Negroes here, it probably does *not mean so much suffering as one would at first view suppose* [emphasis added].[103]

Warner's 1894 poverty study offers another example of the permeation of social science research by prevailing racial attitudes.[104] He studied the causes of poverty in American cities and categorized 7,225 individual cases by ethnicity and nationality. The causes of poverty were grouped as (1) indicating misconduct (drink, immorality, shiftlessness and inefficiency, crime and dishonesty, and roving disposition); (2) indicating misfortune (lack of normal support as in the cases of an absent breadwinner, matters of employment as no work or insufficient work); and (3) matters of personal capacity as in cases of sickness or death of a family member, physical defects, insanity, and old age.

When reviewing findings, Warner observed:

Those who know the Colored people only casually, or by hearsay, may be surprised to find the misconduct causes running so low among them while sickness as a cause is of greater importance than in any other nationality. But to one who has worked in Baltimore or Washington it seems a natural result, and, indeed, a confirmation of the statistics. The Colored people are weak physically, become sick easily, and often die almost without visible resistance to disease.[105]

African Americans had the lowest percentage in the "Lack of work" category and the highest in the "Insufficient employment." Warner interpreted those two percentages as an indication of this group's "hand-to-mouth way of working at odd jobs rather than taking steady work."[106]

As these and other researchers offered subjective analysis of the social conditions of African Americans under the guise of objectivity, other writers sought to interpret the historical experiences of African Americans. Noted among these writers is Ulrich Phillips, a White scholar who helped to develop the history of slavery as a field of study.[107] Phillips held a rather sympathetic view of slavery and believed it to be a benevolent institution.

Even though racism and discrimination traveled with African Americans to the North, history often overlooks the treatment this group received in that part of the country. The South continues to stand out as the seat of anti-African-American sentiment while the North is left relatively untainted. The experiences of African Americans reveal that no place in the United States provided a haven from White hostility, racism, and discrimination.

The Progressive Era witnessed the continuation of discriminatory treatment of African Americans and ushered in a wave of unrelenting segregation, discrimination, and violence in the wake of record migration and the resulting urbanization.

American Indians in the Progressive Era

> Since the economic development of the United States could not have progressed without the displacement and neutralization of the Native population, the policies of extermination, isolation, and assimilation that have competed for ascendancy all required the definition of Natives as savage, inferior, and less than human, and their cultures as inferior and deservedly doomed to extinction.[108]

The history of the oppression of American-Indian tribes in the New World has been extensively documented and only those aspects relevant for understanding historical and contemporary dynamics between mainstream social work and American-Indian populations will be recounted.[109]

During the Progressive Era, reform aimed at the American-Indian tribes were, in fact, a continuation of efforts started decades earlier. Many groups, organizations, and individuals dedicated their time to American-Indian reform and set about to resolve the "Indian problem." This "problem" seemed to emerge when the tribes were dispossessed of their lands and America was struggling to determine what to do with the remaining American-Indian population.

The American Indians represented a unique conundrum. They were of significance because of the lands they held. As a group, unlike other populations of color, they were not needed for their cheap labor and they sought to maintain their separateness rather than strive for assimilation and integration into the U.S. society. The American Indians had rebelled against White encroachment of their lands, fought fiercely for their lands and their way of life, and blatantly rejected White domination. The eventual subordination of these tribes left hostility and antagonism rampant on both sides. With provisions in place for separating the tribes from their land, reformers could concentrate on "reforming" the American Indian.

Discrimination
According to Ahern, "The subordination of racial minorities by reform movements claiming principles antithetical to racism constitutes an important theme in the history of racism in the United States."[110] Reform efforts on behalf of American Indians at the turn of the century and earlier were predicated on assumptions, opinions, and beliefs that can now only be called racist. These reformers were typically White Protestants from middle- and upper-class society. Many were professionals or business people and, in their view, they were acting in the best interest of the American Indians to make them a part of America.

These "Friends of the Indian," as they were called, saw education as the proper vehicle through which American Indians could cast their lot with other Americans. Adequately prepared, American Indians could then succeed or fail by their own hand or by their own mettle. In 1819, Congress began allocating modest sums of money (about $10,000 annually) for the employment of "capable persons of good moral character, to instruct them [American Indians] in the mode of agriculture suited to their situation; and for teaching their children in reading, writing, and arithmetic."[111] The funds were distributed to various societies that already operated or were willing to develop schools on the reservation. Missionary societies were active in this area and used their own resources to help support the schools.

Without educational intervention, reformers saw the tribes as doomed to existence as paupers, dependent on public dole. Through education, children would move away from tribal communal values and learn the meaning of individualism. Indeed, according to Senator Henry Dawes, a leading political figure at the turn of the century, the "defect of the [tribal] system was apparent.... There is no selfishness, which is at the bottom of civilization."[112]

In the minds of the reformers, the day schools of the reservations were viewed as inadequate for raising American Indians to the standards of a Christian civilization. First, reading and writing alone were not enough to accomplish the goals desired by the reformers. Manual labor instruction was another element that became identified as the cornerstone of American-Indian education. Manual training would lead the tribes up the path to self-sufficiency and reduce dependency on government dole. In this regard, the requisite education would not only foster Americanism but also capitalism.

Second, and equally advocated, a move to locate the schools away from the reservations ensued. Many reformers believed that off-reservation boarding schools, in comparison to the day schools and the reservation boarding schools, provided the best setting for American-Indian education. The push for separate, off-reservation schools was based, in part, on earlier attempts at American-Indian reform. The reservations themselves had already been the target of reform efforts as reformers and missionaries tried to implement "civilizing" programs on them. A significant part of reforming focused on replacing American-Indian spiritual practices with Christianity. However, missionaries often moved beyond religious instruction and urged tribes to abandon their old ways for a life of farming—a life that meant permanent residence in one place rather than following the herds they hunted. Many missionaries and reformers were so committed to particular beliefs that they failed to learn about the customs and beliefs they were trying to erase.

Programs to Americanize the American Indians were often useless to people who suffered extreme poverty as they struggled with the passage of their old and independent way of life. This was particularly true for some of the plains tribes since the conversion from a hunting culture to agriculture was destined to take years. In the meantime, these tribes were dependent on government support for the necessities of life. In many instances, food and materials supplied were insufficient, inadequate, and often inappropriate. It is conceivable that the transitional process was taking much longer than government officials and reformers anticipated, and tribal needs may have surpassed specified allocations. Indeed, Prucha argued, "In such an unlooked-for circumstance, it was perhaps understandable that the rations supplied were insufficient and often poor in quality."[113] Hagan, however, attributed some of the problem to "blundering or outright fraud by White Christians" who profited from government contracts by supplying reservations with shoddy goods or no goods at all.[114]

The poverty conditions of the reservations did not encourage the tribes to enthusiastically embrace Christianity or the American way. Many tribal members were blatantly hostile to the reformers and missionaries while others were merely passively resistant. Lack of progress in Americanizing the reservations led reform and missionary groups to reject the reservations as the focus of their attention. As noted by Prucha, "The realization that the Indians were not changing as the reformers had so confidently believed they would led to an outright condemnation of the reservations as an unmitigated evil to be destroyed."[115] The reservations thus became the poisoned environment from which children needed to be rescued. In 1885, outspoken reformer Lyman Abbott told a reform-minded audience, "I declare my conviction then that the reservation system is hopelessly wrong; that it cannot be amended or modified; that it can only be uprooted."[116] These words captured the beliefs of numerous other reformers.

Surprisingly, poverty conditions of the reservations were held by some as necessary in order for American Indians to change their ways of life. Some argued that submission and destitution rendered the tribes more docile and obedient. Along the same line, others believed that the tribes needed to hit bottom before they would rise to a new and better life. Even in the midst of abject poverty on the reservations, American Indians continued to shun the guidance of missionaries and reformers.

Reformers and missionaries thus turned their zeal, attention, and force on the next generation of American Indians—the children. The tribal adults were already "lost" and could not be uprooted from "the blanket"—a reference to American-Indian ways. The resolution to the "Indian problem" was seen in helping tribal children to "shed the blanket" so they could become part of the American melting pot. Reformers believed that children literally had to be taken away from their families and their reservations in order to become "real" Americans. To facilitate American-Indian assimilation, the reformers would "kill the Indian and save the man."[117]

Separate, off-reservation schools for American Indians were proposed after American-Indian education had been tried at a school for another ethnic minority group. In 1878, American-Indian students were enrolled at Hampton Normal and Agricultural Institute, a manual training school for African Americans in Virginia. The school's administrator, General Samuel Chapman Armstrong, had been successful in securing the support of the American Missionary Association for the creation of the school in 1868. According to the memoirs of a Hampton teacher, a young White woman of "genteel New England upbringing," the American Indians formed a school within a school as the classes and dormitories "were entirely separate for the two dark races."[118]

Captain Richard Pratt, another military man and a vociferous advocate of American-Indian industrial education, had been instrumental in gaining the students access to Hampton. Pratt, however, grew displeased with the arrangement because of conditions at Hampton and because he feared that prejudices against the "colored" would be directed toward the American Indian as well.[119] Pratt obtained support for opening a separate school for American Indians and in 1879 opened the Carlisle Indian Industrial School in Carlisle, Pennsylvania—probably the most famous of the boarding schools. From its opening enrollment of 82, Carlisle eventually grew over the years to about 1,000 students. This school continued operating until it was closed in 1918.

While other boarding schools typically relied on private donations or churches for survival, Congress appropriated $67,500 to Carlisle in 1882 and the continued operation of the school became a certainty. With this and similar other appropriations, American-Indian boarding schools symbolized a new direction in national policy. In addition, the boarding school became the most prominent and popular way of Americanizing the American-Indian child and won substantial support from politicians, benefactors, missionaries, and other reformers.

The off-reservation boarding schools grew in importance to the reformers because such schools operationalized their belief that all vestiges of tribal life had to be stripped away before the new American could emerge. This meant that the children had to be separated from the reservation environment, tribal ways, and their old life. The boarding schools became the most dramatic, powerful way for American-Indian children to be "rescued" from the debilitating influences of the reservation. Children as young as age 6 were often enrolled at the schools that held hundreds, even thousands, of students in an institutional setting.

The boarding school period of American-Indian history had long-term, far-reaching consequences for the youths who attended them and for their families. Appearance was critical and children were immediately groomed and dressed in the manner of White American children. Even though hair had much symbolic value in their culture, boys received haircuts upon their arrival. Visually, with the exception of color, the children were transformed into "Americans" and this transformation symbolized the psychological transformation that was to follow. Each child was given an English name and was instructed to answer only to that name.

Although variations existed across the schools, some commonalities were evident. All schools emphasized industrial training, English, and Christianity. Boys were taught machinery skills and girls learned food preparation among other skills. Runaways were common and, when apprehended, were often harshly punished. Large numbers of students died at the schools, and cemeteries adjacent to the schools were filled with hundreds and hundreds of markers. Student attendance ceased to be voluntary as parents who refused to give up their children would not receive supplies or would suffer incarceration. Some children were kidnapped for the boarding schools.

While education was to be the great equalizer in U.S. society, opportunities were extremely limited and the boarding school experience did little to change public attitudes about the American Indian. Boarding school attendees continued to be outsiders to U.S. society and many also became outsiders among their own people. Hundreds returned to the reservation only to find that they could not communicate with their families because English had replaced the tribal language. Furthermore, the skills taught were often useless on the reservation.

The success of the off-reservation boarding schools has been long debated. Some graduates were able to secure mainstream jobs and "shed the blanket." Several became writers and eloquently described their thoughts about and reactions to the boarding education. Others saw the schools as a way of escaping the poverty conditions of the reservation. At the schools, children were regularly fed, adequately clothed, and life had a secure, predictable quality to it. Orphans could view the school as home and a place to belong. In general, however, this part of American-Indian history is not warmly or tenderly remembered by those who were the most affected by it.

While denouncing any differences between Whites and American Indians, the reformers, nevertheless, advocated educational policies that were both dramatic and devastating for the American-Indian people. *Separate* American-Indian schools were a major component of the educational saturation plan—schools that emphasized *industrial* training—yet, reformers saw nothing racist or discriminatory in their proposals.

Reform efforts were instrumental in obtaining federal support of American-Indian education. In 1870, the first federal appropriations were made, and by 1899, over $2.5 million was being spent annually on 148 boarding schools and 225 day schools that educated almost 20,000 children.[120] By 1913, 78 percent of all American-Indian children were in school—5,109 in mission schools, 26,028 in public schools, and 27,584 in the government's 216 day schools, 74 reservation boarding schools, and 37 off-reservation boarding schools.[121] The number of actual boarding schools decreased between 1870 and 1913, but the schools of 1913 boarded greater numbers of students than those of previous years.

Health and Mortality
Health and mortality are particularly important in this discussion of American Indians because during the turn of the century, these people had their *lowest* population census than at any other point—about 250,000. As with other groups, tuberculosis was a serious problem and morbidity and mortality rates among American Indians far exceeded those among Whites *and* African Americans.[122]

Injustices of the Law Enforcement/Justice Systems
The courts played a pivotal role in further reducing the amount of land held by American-Indian tribes. The Dawes Severalty Act of 1887 finally legalized what had been happening on a smaller scale. Prior to this act, numerous American Indians had either sold their land or had been defrauded of it. The Dawes Act stipulated that the president of the United States could allocate reservation land to American Indians with the title kept in trust for 25 years by the United States. Under the act, tribal land was divided into shares ranging from 40 to 160 acres. Family heads received the largest allotment and individuals received smaller parcels. After the allotments were made, any remaining "surplus" lands would be sold.

Under the Dawes Act, American Indians would become voting citizens if they lived away from their tribe and became farmers; however, since this stipulation went against tribal values, many American Indians would not concur and, consequently, lost their land.[123] Between 1887 and 1934, American Indians were separated from an estimated 86,000,000 of a total of 138,000,000 acres and most of the remaining land was desert or semidesert and worthless to the White population.[124]

The Dawes Act sought the redistribution of American-Indian lands and also sought to remove the tribe as the core of American-Indian power. Disbanding tribes and reservations would undermine the solidarity and cohesiveness of American Indians as a group and disperse tribal members throughout the territories. The separatism that promoted group identity and solidarity would be destroyed. This represents one example, albeit a legal one, of an attempt to force American Indians to assimilate into the American population.

Contracts and legal processes afforded little or no fairness for American Indians as treaties were routinely broken and congressional acts favored White Americans. Justice to Whites often meant injustices to the tribes. Violence against tribal groups was sanctioned and unpunished while similar acts by American Indians resulted in vigilante justice or indiscriminant punishment of American Indians—"guilty" or not. Consequently, American Indians had little protection under the law and no trust in the American legal system.

Interpreting the American-Indian Experience

Hagan referred to the coercive assimilation of American Indians as "acculturation under duress."[125] In order for the educational programs to be proposed and implemented, reformers and educators had to believe firmly that the "American way" was the best way for all people of the United States. These "reforms" were grounded in a philosophy that held American-Indian culture and people to be barbarian, savage, and in need of civilizing. The conversion to Christianity was a significant aspect of the Americanizing process.

With education, particularly off-reservation boarding schools, the American Indian was to acquire those tools necessary for American life. Education as a pathway to assimilation has been a cornerstone of an American belief system. With the proper skills, all people become equal in the race for success. Thus, the reformers believed themselves to be doing the tribes a favor by aggressively advocating for their education. Because the tribes were often closed to this way of thinking, reformers, missionaries, and government officials took on the role of acting in the "best interest" of this group.

As White Americans interpreted and wrote history to conform to their rationalizations, numerous aspects of the American-Indian experience were denied, ignored, or distorted. Only through prolonged interaction with Whites did the seemingly homogeneous group designation of "Indians" emerge.[126] Before these White–American-Indian interactions, American Indians were a diverse people, composed of many different Nations that had different languages and customs. Whites imposed a categorization that implied that all American Indians were similar, and from this similarity gross overgeneralizations could be made.

The early history of White domination of American Indians was not grounded as much in nativism or social Darwinism as was the subsequent domination of other groups. Rather, the colonists tenaciously believed they had a God-given right to take the land and its resources.[127] This idea of *manifest destiny*, a term coined in 1845, crystallized the belief that God wanted the continent developed as a utopian example for the world of the successful fusion of democracy, capitalism, and Christianity.[128] Colonists also believed they were encountering an inferior, uncivilized "Red Race" that had to be subordinated through whatever means were necessary—a race that would ultimately benefit from White presence and White influence.

Reformers defined American Indians as childlike, ignorant people who did not know what was best for them. They could thus justify their proposals for "raising" the tribes while at the same time denying the role White America played in creating the American Indian's disadvantaged status. Furthermore, implicit in the reform ideology that, through education, the American Indian would either "sink or swim" was an underlying belief that the individual would then be responsible for his or her own failure.[129] The manner in which these reformers interpreted American-Indian history and experiences, therefore, supported the coercive assimilation policies that were implemented.

This history underscores the tenacity with which reformers injected themselves and their beliefs into American-Indian life. In operating in the "best interest" of and by "knowing what was best for" the American-Indian tribes, reformers attacked tribal customs, values, and child-raising techniques. The removal of children from allegedly dysfunctional family and tribal environments was the most extreme case of racism and it heightened the antagonism between White America and American Indians. Education alone was insufficient in lowering the barriers that existed between the two groups, and the boarding schools often led to greater alienation rather than assimilation. Although children were greatly revered as the next generation in American-Indian culture, they also became a population that required protection from the good intentions of outsiders.

ENDNOTES

1. Alvin Kogut, "The Negro and the Charity Organization in the Progressive Era," *Social Service Review 44* (March 1970): 11.

2. Mary Ann Jimenez, "Historical Evolution and Future Challenges of the Human Services Professions," *Families in Society: The Journal of Contemporary Human Services 71,* number 1 (January): 3.

3. Ruth Schwartz Cowan, Mark Rose, and Marsha Rose, "Clean Homes and Large Utility Bills 1990–1940," *Marriage and Family Review 9* (Fall 1985): 53–66.

4. Jimenez, "Historical Evolution and Future Challenges of the Human Services Professions," p. 3.

5. Allen F. Davis, *Spearheads for Reform—The Social Settlements and the Progressive Movement 1890–1914* (New Brunswick, NJ: Rutgers University Press, 1984).

6. Stephen Kunitz, "Professionalism and Social Control in the Progressive Era: The Case of the Flexner Report," *Social Problems 22* (October 1974): 16–27.

7. June Axinn and Herman Levin, *Social Welfare–A History of the American Response to Need,* Second Edition (New York: Harper and Row, 1982), p. 127.

8. John Ehrenreich, *The Altruistic Imagination—A History of Social Work and Social Policy in the United States* (Ithaca, NY: Cornell University Press, 1985), p. 20.

9. Ehrenreich, *The Altruistic Imagination,* p. 20.

10. Ronald Berger, "The Social Construction of Juvenile Delinquency," in *The Sociology of Juvenile Delinquency,* ed. Ronald Berger (Chicago: Nelson-Hall, Publishers, 1991), p. 4.

11. Bruce Jansson, *The Reluctant Welfare State—A History of American Social Welfare Policies,* Second Edition (Pacific Grove, CA: Brooks/Cole, 1993), p. 111.

12. Joseph Castrovinci, "Prelude to Welfare Capitalism: The Role of Business in the Enactment of Workmen's Compensation Legislation in Illinois, 1905–12," *Social Service Review 50* (March 1976): 80–102.

13. Ehrenreich, *The Altruistic Imagination,* p. 23; Philip Foner, *History of the Labor Movement in the United States, Vol III: The Policies and Practices of the American Federation of Labor, 1900–1909* (New York: International Publishers, 1964), pp. 13–14.

14. As noted in numerous publications, including David Wagner, "Collective Mobility and Fragmentation: A Model of Social Work History," *Journal of Sociology and Social Welfare 13* (September 1986): 667; George Martin, Jr., *Social Policy in the Welfare State* (Englewood Cliffs, NJ: Prentice Hall, 1990), pp. 25–26.

15. As noted in numerous publications, including Louise Johnson and Charles Schwartz, *Social Welfare—A Response to Human Need,* Second Edition (Boston: Allyn and Bacon, 1991), p. 8.

16. Benjamin Ringer and Elinor Lawless, *Race-Ethnicity and Society* (New York: Routledge, 1989), p. 6.

17. U.S. Department of Commerce, Bureau of the Census, *Historical Statistics of the United States, Colonial Times to 1957* (Washington, DC: U.S. Government Printing Office, 1960), p. 9.

18. Edmund James, "The Growth of Great Cities in Area and Population," *The Annals of the American Academy of Political and Social Science 13* (January 1899): 1–30;

Johnson and Schwartz, *Social Welfare*, p. 37; U.S. Department of Commerce, Bureau of the Census, *Historical Statistics*.

19. Axinn and Levin, *Social Welfare*, p. 87.

20. James, "The Growth of Great Cities," pp. 18–19.

21. Carl Wittke, "Immigration Policy Prior to World War I," *The Annals of the American Academy of Political and Social Science 262* (March 1949): 5–14.

22. Milton Gordon, *Assimilation in American Life* (New York: Oxford University Press, 1964), pp. 87–88.

23. Wittke, "Immigration Policy Prior to World War I," p. 5.

24. Richard Hofstadter, *Social Darwinism in American Thought*, Revised Edition (Boston: Beacon Press, 1955), pp. 170–200.

25. U.S. Department of Commerce, Bureau of the Census, *Historical Statistics*, pp. 56–57.

26. Lillian Brandt, "The Negroes of St. Louis," *Publications of the American Statistical Association 8* (March 1903): 205.

27. U.S. Department of Commerce, Bureau of the Census, *Historical Statistics*, pp. 56–57.

28. Florette Henri, *Black Migration: Movement North, 1900–1920* (Garden City, NY: Anchor Press/Doubleday, 1975), p. 148.

29. Henri, *Black Migration*, p. 146; Ehrenreich, *The Altruistic Imagination*, p. 22.

30. Brandt, "The Negroes of St. Louis," p. 206.

31. Henri, *Black Migration*, p. 147.

32. Gerald Gems and Lucia Birnbaum, "Ethnic Education: A Clash of Cultures in Progressive Chicago," *Explorations in Ethnic Studies 14* (July 1991): 1–13.

33. Wittke, "Immigration Policy Prior to World War I," p. 10.

34. Harold Bradley, *The United States from 1865* (New York: Charles Scribner's Sons, 1973), p. 120; Henri, *Black Migration*, p. 148.

35. Ehrenreich, *The Altruistic Imagination*, p. 46.

36. U.S. Department of Commerce, Bureau of the Census, *Historical Statistics*, p. 60.

37. Wittke, "Immigration Policy Prior to World War I," pp. 10–11.

38. Ehrenreich, *The Altruistic Imagination*, p. 21.

39. Roosevelt's views of Americanization are recounted in Thomas Dyer, *Theodore Roosevelt and the Idea of Race* (Baton Rouge, LA: Louisiana State University Press, 1980), pp. 123–142.

40. Ehrenreich, *The Altruistic Imagination*, p. 31; Gerald Gems, "Ethnic Education: A Clash of Cultures in Progressive Chicago," *Explorations in Ethnic Studies 14* (July 1991): 1–13.

41. Maxine Seller, "The Education of the Immigrant Woman," *Journal of Urban History 4* (May 1978): 308.

42. Descriptions presented here of slum conditions during the Progressive Era are drawn from Otto Bettmann, *The Good Old Days—They Were Terrible* (New York: Random House, 1974); Ehrenreich, *The Altruistic Imagination*, pp. 20–22; Jansson, *The Reluctant Welfare State*, pp. 112–115.

43. Arthur Schlesinger, *The Rise of the City* (New York: Macmillan, 1951), pp. 110–111.

44. Ehrenreich, *The Altruistic Imagination*, p. 21.

45. U.S. Department of Commerce, Bureau of the Census, *Historical Statistics,* pp. 26, 30.

46. Bettmann, *The Good Old Days,* p. 3; Ehrenreich, *The Altruistic Imagination,* p. 21.

47. Bettmann, *The Good Old Days,* p. 70; Jansson, *The Reluctant Welfare State,* p. 114.

48. Castrovinci, "Prelude to Welfare Capitalism," pp. 80–102.

49. Foner, *History of the Labor Movement in the United States,* p. 21.

50. This discussion is based on the descriptions provided by Bettmann, *The Good Old Days,* pp. 77–79.

51. Clyde Kiser, "Culturalism Pluralism," *The Annals of the American Academy of Political and Social Science 262* (March 1949): 128.

52. A list of American values and myths, from which these were taken, is provided by Ralph Dolgoff and Donald Feldstein, *Understanding Social Welfare,* Second Edition (New York: Longman, 1984), pp. 5–6.

53. U.S. Department of Commerce, Bureau of the Census, *Historical Statistics,* p. 8.

54. Monroe Lerner and Odin Anderson, *Health Progress in the United States 1900–1960* (Chicago: The University of Chicago Press, 1963), pp. 114–120.

55. Both examples are based on Henri, *Black Migration,* pp. 326, 328.

56. David Muschinske, "The Nonwhite as Child: G. Stanley Hall on the Education of Nonwhite Peoples," *Journal of the History of the Behavioral Sciences 13* (October 1977): 328–336.

57. Lilian Brandt, "The Negroes of St. Louis," p. 220.

58. Henri, *Black Migration,* p. 51; Goodwin, *Black Migration in America from 1915 to 1960,* pp. 9–10.

59. David McBride, *From TB to AIDS—Epidemics among Urban Blacks since 1900* (Albany, NY: State University of New York Press, 1991), p. 35.

60. Goodwin, *Black Migration in America from 1915 to 1960* (Lewiston, NY: Edwin Mellen Press, 1990), pp. 11, 13–14; Henri, *Black Migration,* pp. 53–54.

61. W. E. B. DuBois, "The Migration of Negroes," *The Crisis 13–14* (June 1917): 63.

62. Goodwin, *Black Migration in America,* p. 15.

63. Ringer and Lawless, *Race-Ethnicity and Society,* p. 20.

64. "The Housing Problem and the Negro," *Charities 15* (October 7, 1905): 2.

65. Sophonisba Breckinridge, "The Color Line in the Housing Problem," *The Survey* (February 1913): 575.

66. William Pollard, *A Study of Black Self Help* (San Francisco: R & E Research Associates, 1978), pp. 93–99.

67. David Gordon, "Manual Training for Negro Children," *Charities 15* (October 7, 1905): 84.

68. Henri, *Black Migration,* p. 38.

69. John Dittmer, *Black Georgia in the Progressive Era, 1900–1920* (Urbana: University of Illinois Press, 1977), pp. 118–119; Henri, *Black Migration,* p. 242.

70. Detailed discussions of both examples given are contained in Dittmer, *Black Georgia,* pp. 116–120.

71. E. Franklin Frazier, *Black Bourgeoisee* (Glencoe, IL: Free Press, 1957).

72. Dittmer, *Black Georgia,* pp. 61–62.

73. McBride, *From TB to AIDS,* pp. 35-36.

74. "The Negro's Fitness," *The Charities Review 9* (September 1899): 323.

75. "The Negro," *The Charities Review 6* (June 1897), p. 379.

76. McBride, *From TB to AIDS,* pp. 41–42.

77. Henri, *Black Migration,* pp. 40–41; McBride, *From TB to AIDS,* p. 43.

78. Bradley, *The United States from 1865,* p. 146; Henri, *Black Migration,* pp. 43–44; James McPherson, Laurence Holland, James Banner, Jr., Nancy Weiss, and Michael Bell, *Blacks in America: Bibliographical Essays* (Garden City, NY: Anchor/Doubleday, 1971), pp. 140–141.

79. Jansson, *The Reluctant Welfare State,* p. 131.

80. Ehrenreich, *The Altruistic Imagination,* p. 46.

81. McBride, *From TB to AIDS,* p. 40.

82. *The Crisis 13–14* (September 1917): 219–238.

83. As quoted in *The Crisis 13–14* (September 1917): 221.

84. *The Crisis 13–14* (September 1917): 220.

85. Discussion of this decision is summarized from Harold Bradley, *The United States from 1865,* p. 146; and Henri, *Black Migration,* pp. 13–14.

86. As quoted in Henri, *Black Migration,* pp. 13–14.

87. Events surrounding the discharge are detailed in Henri, *Black Migration,* pp. 241–242.

88. "Riots," *The Crisis 13-14* (September 1917): 313.

89. Dyer, *Theodore Roosevelt and the Idea of Race,* pp. 89–122.

90. Henri, *Black Migration,* p. 52.

91. Henri, *Black Migration,* p. 261.

92. Dittmer, *Black Georgia in the Progressive Era,* pp. 137–138.

93. Bettmann, *The Good Old Days,* p. 106.

94. McBride, *From TB to AIDS,* pp. 41–43.

95. Brandt, "The Negroes of St. Louis," p. 252.

96. Scott Christianson, "Our Black Prisons," *Crime and Delinquency 27* (July 1981); 373.

97. Breckinridge, "The Color Line in the Housing Problem," p. 575.

98. Henri, *Black Migration,* p. 122; W. E. B. DuBois, *Some Notes of Negro Crime* (Atlanta: Atlanta University Press, 1904).

99. John Gillin, *Criminology and Penology* (New York: D. Appleton-Century, 1926), p. 60.

100. Pollard, *A Study of Black Self Help,* p. 93.

101. W. E. B. DuBois, *Efforts for Social Betterment among Negro Americans* (Atlanta: The Atlanta University Press, 1909), p. 125.

102. Brandt, "The Negroes of St. Louis," pp. 229, 230.

103. Brandt, "The Negroes of St. Lous," p. 251.

104. Amos Warner, "The Causes of Poverty Further Considered," *Publications of the American Statistical Association, New Series, 4* (September): 49–68.

105. Warner, "The Causes of Poverty Further Considered," p. 60.

106. Warner, "The Causes of Poverty Further Considered," p. 60.

107. John Smith, "DuBois and Phillips—Symbolic Antagonists of the Progressive Era," *Centennial Review 24* (Winter 1980): 88–102.

108. Luis Kemnitzer, "Native Americans," in *Racial Discrimination against Neither-White-Nor-Black American Minorities,* ed. Kananur Chandras (San Francisco: R & E Research Associates, 1978), p. 9.

109. This discussion is drawn from Wilbert Ahern, "Assimilationist Racism: The Case of the 'Friends of the Indian,'" *Journal of Ethnic Studies 4* (Summer 1976): 23–32; Stephen Cornell, "Land, Labour and Group Formation: Blacks and Indians in the United States," *Ethnic and Racial Studies 13* (July 1990): 368–388; Brian Dippie, *The Vanishing American—White Attitudes and U.S. Indian Policy* (Middletown, CT: Wesleyan University Press, 1982); Dolgoff and Feldstein, *Understanding Social Welfare,* pp. 72–73; Henry Fritz, *The Movement for Indian Assimilation, 1860–1890* (Philadelphia: University of Pennsylvania Press, 1963); William Hagan, *American Indians,* Revised Edition (Chicago: The University of Chicago Press, 1979); Jansson, *The Reluctant Welfare State,* pp. 87–88; Johnson and Schwartz, *Social Welfare,* pp. 96–97; Francis Prucha, Ed., *Americanizing the American Indian: Writings by the 'Friends of the Indian' 1880–1890* (Cambridge, MA: Harvard University Press, 1973); Francis Prucha, *American Indian Policy in Crisis: Christian Reformers and the Indians, 1865–1900* (Norman, OK: University of Oklahoma Press, 1976); Francis Prucha, *The Churches and the Indian Schools, 1888–1912* (Lincoln, NE: University of Nebraska Press, 1979); Russell Thornton, *American Indian Holocaust and Survival: A Population History Since 1492* (Norman, OK: University of Oklahoma Press, 1987).

110. Ahern, "Assimilationist Racism," p. 23.

111. As quoted in Prucha, *American Indian Policy in Crisis,* p. 206.

112. As quoted in Ahern, "Assimilationist Racism," p. 27.

113. Prucha, *American Indian Policy in Crisis,* p. 223.

114. Hagan, *American Indians,* pp. 126–127.

115. Prucha, *American Indian Policy in Crisis,* p. 224.

116. As quoted in Prucha, *Americanizing the American Indians,* p. 35.

117. The words of reformer Henry Pratt as quoted in Ahern, "Assimilationist Racism," p. 24.

118. Kay Graber, Ed., *Sister to the Sioux—The Memoirs of Elaine Goodale Eastman, 1885–91* (Lincoln: University of Nebraska Press, 1978), pp. xi, 19.

119. Prucha, *American Indian Policy in Crisis,* p. 273.

120. Hagan, *Native Americans,* p. 135.

121. Dippie, *The Vanishing American,* p. 186.

122. Thornton, *American Indian Holocaust and Survival,* p. 172.

123. Dolgoff and Feldstein, *Understanding Social Welfare,* p. 73.

124. Hagan, *American Indians,* p. 147.

125. Hagan, *American Indians,* p. 121.

126. Cornell, "Land, Labour and Group Formation," pp. 368–369.

127. Johnson and Schwartz, *Social Welfare,* pp. 96–97.

128. Jansson, *The Reluctant Welfare State,* p. 87.

129. Ahern, "Assimilationist Racism," p. 28.

Chapter 3

Mexicans, Chinese, and Japanese at the Turn of the Century

MEXICAN AMERICANS IN THE PROGRESSIVE ERA

At the beginning of the twentieth century, Mexican Americans in the United States were at a turning point in their history. In the middle to late 1880s, the vast amount of land they owned was coveted and eventually seized by White settlers through both legal and extra-legal means. As this seized land was mined, farmed, and developed, cheap labor was essential for production and profit. The indigenous people of Mexican descent in the Southwest and the immigrants from Mexico were significant to the nation because they filled this labor need. The quest for land and the need for labor determined the Progressive Era experiences and subsequent experiences of Mexican Americans and Mexican immigrants for years to come.

As more attention is directed toward issues surrounding the illegal immigration of Mexicans and Central Americans, the preimmigration history of Mexican Americans grows more obscure. The larger society may perceive anyone of Mexican heritage as being the first-, second-, or third-generation descent of a Mexican immigrant. Although this may be true for countless Mexican Americans, many others share a history in Texas and the Southwest that predates the establishment of White settlements. From the end of the Mexican War in 1848 to the beginning of unprecedented immigration from Mexico in 1910, the history of the Mexican people in the United States has been virtually unrecognized. This history, coupled with the treatment of Mexican immigrants, casts a shadow on mainstream social services to these groups today.

The history of Mexican Americans in the United States is tied closely to those events that occurred in Texas and the Southwest Territory.[1] White settlers moved into Texas in the early 1880s when it was still part of the state of Coahuila in the Republic of Mexico. Mexico welcomed these new settlers as long as they embraced Catholicism and pledged allegiance to Mexico. Once in Texas, however, the new settlers often forgot the oath and, in addition, continued to practice Protestantism. As a matter of fact, the settlers were able to circumvent numerous Mexican laws while challenging Mexico's power to enforce them. For example, Mexico's abolition of slavery in 1829 led many settlers to use lifelong indenture contracts signed by "former" slaves as a way of maintaining their slave population.

Hostility toward the Mexican government escalated and open rebellion ensued. The source of this hostility and antagonism can be traced to several issues. On one hand, the White settlers saw Mexican laws as interfering with their way of life, and their increasing numbers provided strength needed to openly rebel. On the other hand, it seems that the White settlers believed the Mexicans to be inferior in intelligence and refused to submit to a government that was also seen as inferior. At the time of the Texas War, the *5,000 or so Mexicans* inhabiting Texas did not join the White settlers in revolt against the Mexican government.

During the Texas revolution, the battles in San Antonio (at mission Alamo), Goliad, and San Jacinto were fought. Although Mexico was victorious in the first two, the revolution ended with the defeat of the Mexican army in 1836 at San Jacinto. With this defeat, the Mexican Texas died a violent death and the Republic of Texas was born. According to Acuña: "More important was the hatred generated by the war. The Mexican was pictured as cruel, treacherous, tyrannical, and as an enemy who could not be trusted. These stereotypes lingered long after the war and can still be detected in Anglo attitudes toward the Chicano. The Texas War left a legacy of hate and determined the status of the Mexicans left behind as that of a *conquered* people" [emphasis added].[2]

The Mexican-American War in the next decade recalled the hostilities between White Americans and Mexicans and land again emerged as the spark igniting conflict. During this period, belief in Manifest Destiny, social Darwinism, and nativism spurred White settlers into the Southwest Territory with a fervor that could not be stopped. The territory, however, was already inhabited by *75,000* Mexicans, many of whom were *mestizos*— descendants of the original Spanish conquistadors who created families with the American Indians of the area. In the aftermath of the Mexican-American War and the signing of the Treaty of Guadalupe Hidalgo in 1848, thousands of Mexicans became Mexican Americans—citizens of the United States—as Mexico gave up the Southwest Territory in exchange for $15 million. This Southwest Territory was later to become the states of

California, New Mexico, Utah, Nevada, and parts of Colorado, Arizona, and Wyoming.

People of Mexican ancestry residing in Texas and the Southwest suffered overt economic, political, and social subordination as White Americans began descending on the territory. This pattern was well established by the time revolution in Mexico drove thousands of Mexicans to the United States in the early 1900s. The Progressive Era captured the historical hostility held by many Whites toward Mexican Americans and this hostility was also directed to Mexican immigrants. These sentiments, coupled with differential treatment, have followed Mexican Americans throughout their history in the United States.

Discrimination

Mexicans in Texas and the Southwest Territory embraced a culture rich in Spanish, Mexican, and American-Indian customs, religions, and values. The Treaty of Guadalupe Hidalgo provided Mexicans "the enjoyment of all the rights of citizens of the United States according to the principles of the Constitution; and in the meantime shall be maintained and protected in the enjoyment of their liberty and property, and secured in the free exercise of their religion without restriction."[3] Unfortunately, this part of the treaty was not strictly enforced; as thousands of White settlers entered the territory, the rights of the indigenous inhabitants were trampled.

The Whites brought with them their own "American" values, customs, and laws. Implicit in this White presence was the belief that Whites were culturally superior to the Mexicans. Mexicans were not familiar with the "American" way of political and economic life and no means were provided to educate them in these areas. In addition, many of the Mexicans spoke only Spanish, were poor, and worked for the *ricos* (the rich) who often owned vast acreage. The Mexican population was generally scattered throughout the territory in villages and small towns.

The treaty was not powerful enough to overcome the racial attitudes so firmly entrenched in the minds of the White settlers and reinforced by the Texas Revolution. These Texas and Southwest settlers eventually deprived Mexican Americans of political power even in towns with a predominant Mexican-American presence. For example, in 1902, Texas adopted a poll tax that deterred Mexican Americans from voting.[4] In addition to losing political power, Mexican Americans were discriminated against in educational and economic opportunities. A master-slave caste system developed in which the Mexican Americans of Texas and the Southwest were relegated to the worst working and living conditions and became a cheap labor force for white farmers. As the territory grew in population, White establishments were known to post "No Mexicans Allowed," "No Mexicans Served," "Whites

Only," and other similar signs indicating that Mexican or Mexican-American clientele was not welcomed.

This anti-Mexican hostility had a tremendous effect on the Mexican-American population itself. This hostility was particularly fierce in the case of Mexican Americans who looked American Indian.[5] In Texas, *tejanos* (Mexican-American Texans) sought to distinguish themselves from Mexican immigrants, and eventually *Mexican* became a negative word to both Whites and tejanos.[6] The Mexican-American population was not a homogenous group but rather several groups as identified by their ancestry and physical appearance that ranged from the fairness of the Spanish to the darkness of the American Indian. These distinctions were captured in 1924 by McLean and Thomson, who wrote, "The *Mexicans* are those who were born south of the Rio Grande in the Republic of Mexico, and who have emigrated to the United States, usually within the last five or ten years. They are not American citizens, and usually do not wish to become so. In many cases *their skin is slightly darker than that of the Spanish Americans*" [emphasis added].[7] This gradation was often associated with class, as the designation *Spanish American* symbolized Spanish blood, aristocracy, and wealth, whereas *Mexican* reflected American Indian and peasant stock. Because of the tremendous amount of anti-Mexican sentiment, people frequently sought to dissociate themselves from this group. Thus, racism and discrimination permeated the Hispanic population and influenced the self-identification of group members.

Even though the descents of the Spanish were already in the Southwest before the arrival of the White settlers, the descendants of these Spanish pioneers were not exempt from Whites who exuded condescension, patronism, and superiority. For example, McLean and Thomson wrote further in 1924, "It must always be kept in mind, however, that they [Spanish Americans] look on themselves as *real* Americans, and cordially resent any accusation of lack of patriotism" [emphasis added].[8] These authors provided descriptions of both the Mexican and Spanish American that reveal just as much about the writers as about the subjects. The Spanish and Mexican are presented as childlike, docile people without much capacity for leadership in the mines nor appreciation enough for the value of education to send their children to school.

The hostility toward Mexican Americans was so strong that, in 1904, when 40 light-skinned orphans from New York were placed in the homes of Mexican Americans in the Arizona territory, the Whites in the area protested vehemently.[9] The protestors claimed that the parents fed the children strange foods and were too poor to care properly for them. The racism of the attack was mirrored in the Whites' description of the parents as "half-breeds." Vigilantes forcefully took the children from the Mexican Americans and gave them to White families. The Arizona Supreme Court supported the action of the Whites and referred to the vigilante groups as "committees." The New York orphanage that originally placed the children was legally powerless in retrieving the children from the White families.

The social conditions of Mexican Americans were exacerbated by the arrival of thousands of Mexican immigrants after 1900. Prior to 1910, Mexicans born in the United States made up 8 percent of the foreign born from the Americas and grew to about 25 percent in 1910.[10] From 1880 to 1910, the Mexican-born populations of Arizona, California, New Mexico, and Texas more than tripled. Jansson noted that many of these immigrants lived in remote areas and were subject to punitive labor policies of landowners who paid them little and brutally suppressed protest.[11]

At the turn of the century, Mexican immigrants and Mexican Americans made up 80 percent of the agricultural work force, 90 percent of the Western railroad workers, and 60 percent of the mine workers.[12] In addition, others traveled to the northern urban centers for work or became migrant farm laborers in other parts of the country. In a 1912 article on the experiences of Mexican immigrants in the United States, Bryan noted that in 1908 and 1909, about 86 percent of the Mexican immigrants working as railroad laborers earned less than $1.25 a day while the Greeks, Italians, and Japanese railroad workers earned more than this amount and some even earned more than $1.50 a day.[13] In addition to poor wages, the Mexican immigrant also suffered poor housing conditions that fostered diseases and criminal activities.

The Mexican immigrant was different from the Mexican American. Whereas the Mexican American was an American and saw America as his or her home, the immigrant had a much different view. According to Acuña: "Like the European, the Mexican came to the United States because of his hunger; but unlike the European, he did not intend to stay, nor did his masters intend him to remain. He came as a temporary worker...and was constantly shuttled throughout the Southwest and Midwest...and would return to Mexico when the work was finished."[14] This migratory pattern of the immigrant population and its supposedly temporary presence in the United States suggest that (1) assimilation was not the intended goal for this group in the eyes of the larger society, (2) many immigrant communities were transitory, (3) the Mexican immigrant developed a reputation for being a "floater," and (4) these immigrants were never to be real Americans. Many of these generalizations, however, were extended to Mexican Americans as well.

Racial Violence

Law enforcement agents provided no protection from the vigilantes who terrorized Mexicans in Texas and throughout the Southwest. For example, Mexican miners who were thrown out of the California mines were often attacked, shot, beaten, or even killed. In New Mexico and Arizona, violence against Mexicans was widespread and frequent.

The situation in Sonora, California, provides an example of how racial violence, coupled with legislation, robbed Mexicans of land and livelihood. Mexicans from Sonora, Mexico, settled the area and were successful in mining productive claims. They fought off White attempts to drive them from the land and the lucrative claims. Mexican miners became the victims of raids and killings as the Whites' quest for the land knew no boundaries. In 1850, the state legislature imposed a tax on all foreign miners (aimed primarily at the Mexicans). Using guns to implement the regulation, Whites forced about 2,000 Mexicans to leave Sonora. The tax was so high that other miners, Whites included, were forced out of the mines. The tax was eventually repealed a year later, but by that time, it was too late for the Mexicans.

In Texas, the Texas Rangers developed a reputation for shooting first and asking questions later in their dealings with Mexican Americans. A Mexican accused of a crime was often found guilty on the spot and punished on the spot. In retaliation for a crime thought to be committed by a Mexican, Rangers shot or beat numerous Mexicans and assumed that the guilty was somewhere among the bunch. To the Texas Ranger, a Mexican was a Mexican whether he or she lived north or south of the border.

Thus, the type of racial violence against African Americans in the South and later in the North was experienced by Mexicans in Texas and the Southwest, the overwhelming majority of whom were citizens of these areas. Many of the White settlers in Texas and the Southwest had migrated from southern states and merely transferred their racial animosity toward African Americans to Mexicans. In some places, Mexicans were referred to as "yeller niggers."[17] According to Moquin, the number of Mexican-American killings in the Southwest from 1850 to 1930 surpassed the number of African-American lynchings for the same period.[18] Many of these Mexicans were slaughtered for their land.

Injustices of the Law Enforcement/ Justice Systems

The Treaty of Guadalupe Hidalgo opened the door to one of the "greatest land grabs in American history" since the dispossession of the American Indian tribes.[15] Through Spanish and Mexican land grants, pueblos, missions, and individuals possessed thousands of acres of "good" land in the Southwest. Although the treaty protected the rights of these Mexican landholders, White settlers used the U.S. court system to challenge land ownership. Congress passed the Land Act of 1851 that was to help clear up "confusion" about land titles. This act, however, paved the way for Whites to legally challenge Mexican property rights. In some areas, up to 80 percent of the claims were ruled in favor of the challenger or plaintiff. Rather than being a system of justice, the courts became a means of stripping Mexicans of their property rights. Here, the foundation for lack of faith and trust in the U.S. judicial system was formed.

Not surprisingly, Mexican immigrants were overrepresented in the jails and prisons of Texas and the Southwest during the early 1900s. As their percentage of the population increased, their incarceration rate also increased. The proportion of the incarcerated among the Mexicans was greater than among other foreign-born groups or among the native born.[16] In Arizona and California, the chief offenses were gambling and drinking. As with African Americans, these incarceration rates for Mexicans raise the issues of law enforcement as a means of social control, the differential enforcement of laws, and the differential use of imprisonment as punishment.

Interpreting the Mexican-American Experience

The history of Texas and the Southwest is often painted with broad strokes of heroism, romanticism, and expansionism. Rationalizations are advanced to underscore the inevitability of outcomes. The Texas Revolution and the Mexican-American War are depicted as righteous, just consequences of attempts to oppress the frontier spirit that knew no containment. "Remember the Alamo!" is a battle cry for holding one's ground until the bitter end. The rugged frontier seemed to beckon the rugged individual whose dreams were as vast as the land. Whites are held as bringing civilization, productivity, vision, and the American way to undeveloped territories. The Texas Rangers are depicted as the keepers of justice who valiantly defended the Texas borders and protected settlers from dangerous, savage intruders. The Texas Rangers Museum in Waco, Texas, today offers visitors an overview of the glorious and well-honored history and tradition of the Rangers.

Acuña provided detailed descriptions of the romanticism that surrounds the Texas Rangers, the Texas revolt, and the Mexican-American War.[19] He cited noted historians who dismiss the brutality that accompanied the conquest of Texas and the Southwest as justifiable and unavoidable. Acuña's message echoes loudly from the pages: Mexican Americans have a far different view of these events and their consequences. This history, as recounted by Mexican Americans, is one of oppression, racism, discrimination, and colonization.

As institutions in U.S. society accepted mainstream interpretations of the past, the image of the Mexican American has greatly suffered. Over time, the distinctions between Spanish Americans, Mexican Americans, and Mexicans clouded and simply melted into one. Heritage and ancestry could not protect descendants of the first Spanish pioneers from being categorized as "alien" or "foreign" to U.S. society. As in the case of African Americans, nativity by birth and history could not shield Mexican Americans from the differential treatment accorded to "outsiders."

CHINESE IN THE PROGRESSIVE ERA

By the time the Progressive Era began, the "Chinese problem" had already been resolved in the United States by the Chinese Exclusion Act of 1882 that prohibited Chinese laborers from entering the United States and prohibited Chinese from becoming naturalized citizens.[20] Between 1855 and 1877, it was estimated that 191,118 Chinese had entered the United States. In 1860, one-tenth of the Californian population was Chinese, and, in 1870, the U.S. Chinese population was 63,199 according to census figures. The overwhelming majority of this 63,000 (99 percent) lived on the West Coast. Although immigrants of other countries were permitted unrestricted entry into the United States, Chinese were limited and, in some cases, those already in the country were driven out through a variety of means. Two years before the act, in 1880, Chinese constituted 105,465, or 2 percent of the 50,155,783 people in the United States. In 1882, the year the bill was enacted, 102,991 British and 250,630 German immigrants came to the United States in comparison to 39,579 Chinese. By the turn of the century, Chinese immigration was at a record low. Chinese in the United States had moved from being an invaluable labor supply to being the scourge of the earth. The rise and fall of this group in America traces the ebb and flow of public attitudes shaped by a changing social, political, and economic climate.

Although 2 percent of the population seems little cause for alarm, White workers viewed the Chinese as competitors who were willing to work any job for any wage. A country that had depended heavily on Chinese labor for the growth and maintenance of numerous industries was willing to denounce this group and deny any and all contributions it made to the economic development of the country. Consequently, during the Progressive Era, Chinese individuals had been reduced to nonpersons.

To grasp fully the status of Chinese individuals in the United States at the turn of the century, it is necessary to trace a series of events that climaxed in the Exclusion Act. In the mid-1880s, peasant uprisings, economic conditions, and political upheaval drove thousands of Chinese to flee China in search of new prosperity in other countries. The California Gold Rush acted to attract hundreds of Chinese, and the first arrivals were able to secure employment as cooks and servants. The Gold Rush period attracted some 35,000 Chinese, in comparison to the 2.5 million European immigrants entering during this same time. Many of the Chinese immigrants relied on resources, family assistance, or their own ingenuity to defray transportation expenses. With the later contract labor system, others entered into contractual agreements with U.S. companies that needed workers. These companies paid the travel cost incurred by workers and subtracted the amount from wages paid. Railroad companies used this system to meet the labor demands of the railroad construction. Some Chinese workers were recruited by large farming interests in the South with the expectation that these workers could fill some of the void left by the freed slaves. Many of the recruited Chinese eventually headed West when their contracts had been fulfilled.

When they came in modest numbers to the West before the 1850s, the Chinese were not perceived as any kind of threat. As a matter of fact, their style of dress, the pigtail, physical characteristics, and other indications of their cultural uniqueness made them a novelty in the Western towns. Many of the early arrivals worked in service areas such as restaurants and hotels that supported the growing population. Many were merchants and skilled craftsmen. When their numbers began to increase significantly in the 1850s, racism and discrimination became more blatant and more hostile. These were primarily Chinese peasants who were lured by the work in the mines. In the following decade, more Chinese immigrants were recruited for construction of the transcontinental railroad.

In the 1860s, Chinese workers were concentrated in the West in railroad and mining. The railroad industry had about 50 percent of the 30,000 Chinese work force and mining had a few thousand other workers. When the last spike was driven into the transcontinental railroad in 1869, about 25,000 railroad employers were out of work. By 1873, riches from the mines could no longer be extracted with an ax and a pan. More sophisticated mining procedures—those utilized by mining companies—were needed. The Chinese sought work wherever they could—in company mines, in factories, on farms, in domestic service. They often took jobs that were disdained by White workers and were working when thousands of Whites were not. The labor market thus became flooded and the depressions of the 1870s cast a negative, hostile shadow on the Chinese.

The Chinatowns that emerged were primarily male. For example, of the 100,686 Chinese in the United States in 1880, only 4,779 were females. About half of the males had left wives and families in China and anticipated going back to China. Some males returned to China to find a bride with the hopes of bringing her to America. Numerous immigrants planned to make the United States their new home and wanted to become Americans. About half of the immigrants were "sojourners" and the other half were "settlers." For all, the social activities were centered around the emergent Chinatowns as Chinatown shops and stores were established by the Chinese merchants to provide culturally based goods and services. A Chinese merchant class eventually evolved that catered exclusively to the Chinese community.

During the Progressive Era, the Chinese population in the United States decreased from 107,488 in 1890 to 61,639 in 1920. The exclusion acts (discussed later in this section) contributed to this decline. The development of Chinatowns and the migration of Chinese to other parts of the country were attempts to escape racism, discrimination, and brutality of the West. This search drove many of the Chinese to seek safety in the Southwest, the Midwest, the East, and the South.[21]

Some of San Antonio's Chinese population are descendants of the several hundred Chinese who were granted residence in the state by Congress because they assisted General Pershing in his 1916–1917 campaign against Pancho Villa. Hundreds of Chinese migrated to New York during the period of increased violence against them in the West. The Chinese population of Boston grew from 250 in 1890 to 1,000 in 1920. Small Chinatowns emerged in such cities as Chicago, Detroit, Minneapolis, New Orleans, and Augusta (Georgia). In some cases, they were brought in as cheap labor to work on specific projects and settled permanently in the area. In other cases, they migrated with the intent of establishing small businesses such as laundries, restaurants, and shops.

Discrimination

The Chinese were discriminated against from the time of their first arrival to the United States. The racism that was applied against African Americans, American Indians, and Mexicans was extended to the Chinese on the West Coast. In addition to being non-White and non-Christian, they were considered an inferior race that was clannish, deceitful, and guilty of lowering the wage standard for White workers. They were referred to as "coolies," a term that meant transient laborers but took on an even greater derogatory, dehumanizing meaning when applied to Chinese laborers.

There was also a strong sense among Whites that the Chinese could not be assimilated into U.S. society and that their loyalty would always be to China. In the eyes of the American people, the Chinese were contract laborers who were only passing through the country to steal employment and other resources from the more deserving White workers. Residential segregation led to the development of Chinatowns, which only reinforced public attitudes that saw the Chinese in a "we" versus "they" manner. Anti-Chinese sentiment grew so strong that societies were formed to attack the "Chinese problem" and lobby for anti-Chinese legislation.

Racial Violence

Chinese were the victims of racially motivated violence from the beginning of their history in the United States.[22] The first documented violence against Chinese people occurred in 1849 in Tuolumne County (California) when 60 Chinese workers were chased out of their camps by White miners. Similar violence erupted in other California mining camps. In San Francisco, one of the largest riots was sparked in 1866 when the wage demands of White workers were rejected and cheaper Chinese workers hired. By the 1870s, such violence against the Chinese was the result of organized attacks, many of which were organized by anti-Chinese societies. With the economic crisis of the 1870s, violence against the Chinese escalated as they were blamed for the depressed plight of White workers. In one 1871 riot, 21 Chinese were slain, 15 by lynching. Raging racism fueled by a stagnant economy made the Chinese perfect scapegoats for White frustration.

Chinese were attacked, injured, murdered, and/or driven from towns. Brutality against Chinese individuals took the form of shooting, lynching, burning, and stoning, and became integrated into the history of the West. In 1879, Williams noted, "No country, no government, I undertake to say, has ever permitted the indignities to be cast upon any race of people, that the government and municipality of San Francisco and California have permitted upon this class."[23] The violence was not limited to California. It followed the Chinese wherever and whenever their numbers began increasing. The Denver riot of 1880, for example, destroyed every Chinese business and home in the city.

Injustices of the Law Enforcement/Justice Systems

Perpetrators of brutality were seldom brought to justice. Law-enforcement agents many times looked on racial attacks without interceding. Chinese workers often retreated to the larger Chinatowns for protection. The police however, provided little assistance in preventing the riots but they were instrumental in quelling some of them. This was little consolation for those who suffered from these attacks. While law enforcement was lax in coming to the aid of the Chinese, the law itself was being used as another weapon against this group.

The laws and policies against Chinese were so powerful during this period that the expressions "not a Chinaman's chance" and "He doesn't stand a Chinaman's chance" were quite popular. Such expressions mirror that lack of rights and privileges held by the Chinese in America, particularly in California. The California Supreme Court ruled that "the term Indian included the Chinese or Mongolian race,"[24] thereby permitting the type of legal discrimination applied against American Indians to be extended to the Chinese. Chinese individuals, therefore, were barred from giving evidence against Whites in court. In writing of Chinese immigration in 1879, Williams asserted that this classification stigmatized the Chinese "by classing them with a race which has despised labor, has had no arts, schools, or trade, and in the midst of the Californians themselves were content to dig roots for a living."[25] This observation captures both the implications of the ruling for Chinese individuals and the extent of prejudice against American Indians.

A judge of the United States District Court of California further ruled that the Chinese could not become citizens because citizenship was extended only to aliens who were free Whites or of African nativity or African descent.

In California, numerous state and local anti-Chinese legislation was passed that taxed "foreigners," forced Chinese children to attend segregated schools, targeted Chinese businesses for "special" licenses, restricted Chinese fishing activities, denied Chinese admission to certain hospitals, and prohibited the hiring of Chinese workers for municipal jobs.[26] The anti-Chinese sentiment was running so strong that a Democratic Party anti-Chinese rally in 1876 had about 25,000 people in attendance.

It was the force of this sentiment that prompted Congress to pass the Chinese Exclusion Act of 1882. The act barred the entry of skilled and unskilled Chinese laborers into the United States for 10 years, denied Chinese naturalization, and prohibited Chinese laborers'spouses from entering the country. This act did not quell its supporters, and other restrictions were legislated. In 1884, the act was modified with more stringent restrictions, and the Scott Act of 1888 banned the return to the United States of any Chinese laborer. In essence, about 20,000 Chinese who had temporarily gone to China to see family and friends could never return to the United States. These people lost their businesses and whatever other possessions they had left behind in the United States.

During the Progressive Era, federal anti-Chinese acts continued to win support. In 1892, the Geary Act extended the Exclusion Act for another 10 years, and the Act of April 29, 1902, added yet another 10-year extension. Other acts restricted Chinese businesses, extended Chinese exclusion to the Philippines and the Hawaiian Islands, legislated funds for the use of a system to identify Chinese criminals seeking entry, and extended Chinese exclusion indefinitely. In 1913, one writer noted, "Every man in public life was under so binding a necessity to accept the popular belief in regard to the Chinese . . . that for one to seek the real truth of the matter was to end forthwith his political career."[27] Advocates for the Chinese people found themselves changing sides to avoid public attack. The exclusion act was not repealed until 1943.

According to Sung, "The Chinese were the only people specifically named in legislation to be excluded from the United States. It was an affront that still rankles in the hearts of many Chinese."[28] The racist nature of the exclusion acts and their legal perpetuation amplify the distinct history of this group in America—a history of how racism becomes converted into national policy.

Interpreting the Chinese Experience

The Chinese workers in early America went from a position of sought-after laborers to absolute rejection. Their contributions to the economic development of the West have often been rendered invisible. The type of racism and discrimination they endured required that their attackers deny or erase all positive attributes to categorize them in the vilest of terms. This shift in public attitude is captured in an 1877 California State Senate report:

> We admit that the Chinese were, in the earlier history of the State, when white labor was not attainable, very useful in the development of our peculiar industries....Now, to consider and weigh the benefits returned to us by the Chinese...they contribute nothing to the support of our institutions; *can never be relied upon as defenders of the State; they have no intention of becoming citizens;...and are a constant tax upon the public treasury* [emphasis added].[29]

These arguments subsequently were used against other immigrants of color, particularly undocumented Hispanics. In the case of the Chinese, the economic and political climates converged to identify a specific group of people as responsible for the ills befalling the West.

The power of opposition to the Chinese was strong enough to become a national policy agenda item. Once this happened, the history of the Chinese in the United States was rewritten. This was strikingly apparent during the 1969 centennial celebration of the transcontinental railroad when then Secretary of Transportation John Volpe omitted from his speech any reference to the 12,000 Chinese who helped build the railroad. He credited "Americans" with tunneling through mountains and chiseling through granite to lay miles and miles of tracks. Since the Chinese railroad workers were not American citizens, Volpe's speech rewrote history to exclude the contributions of these "foreigners." Much of U.S. history has denied or minimized the significance of this group's involvement in America's development and the lasting effects of national exclusionary policies.

JAPANESE IN THE PROGRESSIVE ERA

Japanese presence in the United States became significant, especially in California, in the late 1880s as laborers immigrated from Japan and Hawaii.[30] Prior to this time, the census figures reported only 148 Japanese in the United States in 1880. Japanese immigration peaked between 1901 and 1908 when about 127,000 entered the country. In the mid to late 1880s, Japanese workers had been recruited for the Hawaiian sugar plantations, and the factors leading to the transmigration from Hawaii to California are not entirely clear. The Chinese Exclusion Act of 1882 created, no doubt, a need for another supply of cheap labor. This first generation of Japanese (Issei) was able to find work in agriculture (planting and picking crops), mining, and domestic service. In comparison to the Chinese, the Japanese, in some cases did work for lower wages. For example, in the 1890s, Japanese workers generally earned 50 cents a day while the going rate for Chinese workers had been twice that amount.

The Japanese seemed committed to upward mobility, and low-paying jobs were only a temporary means to economic improvement. Over time, Japanese workers were able to organize strikes that often resulted in wages comparable to those of other groups. In addition, working for someone else was also a stepping stone to land ownership, and numerous Japanese were gradually able to purchase land. Further, in their own businesses, it was not uncommon for Japanese to employ other Japanese. This strong desire for economic mobility meant that, in general, many Japanese were not destined permanently to occupy menial and low-paying positions.

Those Japanese immigrating to the United States were primarily male. For example, of the 23,326 entering in 1900, only 985 were female, and males continued to dramatically outnumber females during the Progressive Era. These laborers lived in segregated areas, often dubbed "Little Tokyo" or "Little Osaka," and maintained their culture and language. Japanese merchants were able make a successful living providing goods and services specifically to the Japanese community. A strong sense of community existed in the Japanese ghettos, and workers cooperatively joined together to save money. In describing the Issei pioneers, Mass stated, "'Gaman,' which connotes emotional self-restraint and the maintenance of strength and endurance in the face of hardships, was a primary value in the character of the Issei. A strong sense of family honor and esteem, requiring that one conduct oneself in a manner that will avoid ostracism, was also highly important."[31]

The success of the Japanese was documented in the growth of businesses and property ownership. The number of Japanese domestic servants decreased and the number of gardeners—a position of status among the Japanese—grew. In 1909, 1,380 Japanese-owned businesses were counted; land ownership grew from 2,422 acres in 1904 to 16,449 in 1909. By 1919, Japanese farmers owned over 74,000 acres, leased another 383,287 acres, and shared crops in still another 59,000 acres. In 1920, the Japanese farm income reached $67 million.

Economic success was powerless, however, in protecting the Japanese from discrimination as their ambition and industriousness were met with growing anti-Japanese sentiments among California Whites.

Discrimination

According to Kitano, the Japanese were in "the wrong country, the wrong state" at "the wrong time."[32] As they rose to the level of economic competitors with Whites, much of the anti-Chinese sentiment was extended to include the Japanese. Fairchild summed up the similarity in public attitudes toward the two groups: "With respect to the Chinese and the Japanese, typical American opinion has followed a similar pattern: first, a cordial welcome to these 'quaint' and interesting foreigners who are willing to do unpleasant and menial work; then, as the numbers became sufficiently large to afford economic competition, violent and bitter opposition."[33]

Changes in public attitudes toward the Japanese coincided with the rise in Japanese worker strikes against White growers. Because there was not another readily available source of labor, growers felt cornered and thus yielded to the workers' demands for higher wages. This created an atmosphere of animosity in which employers held workers responsible for violating contracts.

By 1900, an anti-Japanese campaign was gaining momentum in California. This campaign may have been the perpetuation of anti-Asian attitudes that began earlier with the Chinese. In 1900, the mayor of San Francisco asserted: "The Japanese are starting the same tide of immigration which we thought we had checked twenty years ago....The Chinese and Japanese are not bona fide citizens. They are not the stuff of which American citizens can be made...they will not assimilate with us."[34] Much of the initial anti-Japanese activity originated with the farm labor leaders and spread to the rest of the population. The newspapers stirred public outcry with warnings of a takeover by the Mongolian race. The San Francisco *Chronicle* was fierce in its attack of the Japanese with such headlines as "Crime and Poverty Go Hand and Hand with Asiatic Labor," "The Japanese Invasion, the Problem of the Hour," and "Japanese a Menace to American Women."[35] The Japanese, as the Chinese before them, were described by such epithets as "filthy beyond belief," "an inferior race," and "aliens whose presence is inimical to health and public morals."[36]

Japan maintained an active interest in those Japanese who immigrated to the states. This interest was magnified by its response to the 1906 San Francisco earthquake. The largest contribution from another country came from Japan and totaled $246,000. Japan also maintained a watchful eye on the social and economic conditions of its former residents. While San Francisco did, indeed, need the money for rebuilding efforts, many Whites interpreted Japan's act of generosity as further indication that the bond between Japan and the Japanese in California was impenetrable. As with the Chinese, beliefs in the loyalty of the Japanese to Japan intensified. In the minds of many, the Japanese could never be loyal to the United States. Beliefs in the disloyalty of Japanese to America have haunted the Japanese throughout their history in this country.

Labor meetings were organized in San Francisco and other California cities to promote Japanese exclusion. Labor leaders were also instrumental in establishing anti-Japanese leagues; the Asiatic Exclusion League, formed in 1905, was prominent among them. Active participants in this league included labor leaders who themselves were European immigrants. These individuals firmly believed, as did thousands of other European immigrants, that assimilation could be achieved with the European nationalities but not with non-Whites. In their eyes, assimilation of Japanese and other non-Whites went hand-in-hand with a reduced standard of living, lower level of civilization, and a reduction of white superiority.

Boycotts were launched against Japanese businesses, and Whites were admonished to support White-owned and operated enterprises. The public was warned about the risks involved in eating food picked and prepared by unclean Japanese hands. Labor leaders and newspapers' unrelenting attacks on the Japanese heightened public fear of this group.

Japan's 1905 victory over Russia did little to ease White feelings about the Japanese. Prior to this demonstration of military force, the United States and Japan had cordial diplomatic relations. Japan's ascension to world power, however, altered public opinion about the country and led many to conclude that Japan's invasion of the states was possible, if not imminent. With the rise of "Japan and the Mongolian race," political and military leaders advocated strong military preparation to ward off attacks on Anglo-Saxon power. Social Darwinism moved from encompassing individual species to including nations as well.

The fear of invasion by Japanese immigrants and the fear of military invasion by Japan was captured by the popular phrase "yellow peril." The yellow peril underscored both a racial and racist ideology. The defined "menace" was a specific non-White racial group. In addition, adherence to the doctrine of White superiority and non-White inferiority gave the yellow peril its racist overtones. This menace became a battle cry and a rallying point for those who advocated the continued domination of White civilization in the United States.

Organized anti-Japanese activities and fears of the yellow peril persisted in the United States long after the days of the Progressive Era and erupted in full force with the World War II internment of Japanese Americans. This is but one example of how the Progressive Era formed the foundation of sentiments and beliefs that persisted over the subsequent years. The World War II internment camps represented the manifestations of the racism that was expressed and acted upon during the previous decades.

Racial Violence

Kitano observed, "It is perhaps surprising that in spite of the continuous verbal and printed attacks on the Japanese, there were never any equivalents to the Chinese massacres,…or to the many Negro lynchings in the South."[37] Japanese were assaulted and businesses were vandalized, especially during the labor-organized boycotts of their businesses. In these assaults, the Japanese victims typically did not sustain life-threatening injuries.

In cases of attacks on Japanese individuals, there were attempts by Whites to attribute the cause of the conflict to other than racial motives. For example, an attack on a Japanese businessman could be dismissed as simply caused by a labor dispute rather than by the victim's race. Furthermore, President Theodore Roosevelt authorized the use of troops, if necessary, to protect Japanese from mob attacks. This may have been done to protect the country's diplomatic relationship with Japan and not out of a belief in racial equality. Regardless of the motivation, this position may have tempered the use of violence against this group.

Injustices of the Law Enforcement/Justice Systems

Law-enforcement agents provided little or no protection to the Japanese or to their businesses. During the boycotts when assaults increased, the police failed to intervene and attackers routinely went unpunished. Complaints filed by Japanese individuals were also routinely dismissed. The law-enforcement arm of the criminal justice system simply refused to enforce the law against Whites who terrorized Japanese victims.

The most brutal battles fought by the Japanese were not fought in the street but "took place in the courts, and the most visible Japanese scars were from legal decisions."[38] The state of California was unrelenting in its quest for anti-Japanese ordinances. In 1906, the San Francisco Board of Education issued a resolution stipulating that all Japanese in public schools attend the Oriental school in Chinatown. Although President Roosevelt was able to have the order rescinded, discriminatory educational practices against children of Asian descent became as much a part of the West Coast as the Pacific Ocean. The discriminatory laws against the Chinese also applied to the Japanese who were also "Mongolian." Thus, the Japanese could not become American citizens and could not vote.

California's 1913 Alien Land Act stipulated that Japanese could lease agricultural land for up to three years and prohibited additional land purchases. Land already owned or leased by Japanese individuals could not be passed along to their children. This controversial act was passed despite the protestations of then President Woodrow Wilson who was concerned with Japan's reaction to the act.

Organized lobbying for restrictions on Japanese immigration led to a "gentleman's agreement" between the United States and Japan in 1908. Unlike the Chinese exclusion acts that explicitly prohibited Chinese immigration, the gentleman's agreement was negotiated, voluntary, and reflective of the United States' respect for Japan's status as a world power. This agreement seemed to be a compromise that was acceptable to both nations.

On one hand, the influx of Japanese immigrants could be curbed, and on the other hand, Japan itself would control the flow of Japanese to the states by restricting the number of passports given to laborers. The number of Japanese entering the United States was significantly reduced until 1914, when the number of wives entering the country caused the figures to increase sharply. American diplomats had not anticipated the number of wives coming to join Japanese men already in the United States. Many of the anti-Japanese leagues saw the unanticipated rise in Japanese immigration in spite of the agreement as another example of Japanese deception.

The Immigration Act of 1917 that instituted the literacy test also contained provisions for the curtailment of Asian immigration.[39] This act established the Asiatic Barred Zone that barred the entry of immigrants from southern and eastern Asia. The racially based immigration policies of the Progressive Era formed the basis of subsequent policies. The post–Progressive Era immigration bill of 1924 with its 2 percent quota based on 1890 census data also had restrictions directed specifically toward Japanese immigration. The bill placed *racial* restrictions on immigration by prohibiting the entry of persons who were ineligible for citizenship—a group that included Asians. In 1924, only White and "Negro" races continued as the only ones able to gain naturalization. Even if Japan had been permitted a quota, that quota would have been so minuscule as to be nonexistent. According to census figures, there were 2,039 Japanese in the United States,[40] and this base would have given Japan an immigration quota that was 2 percent of this figure—which amounted to only 40. This bill, in effect, wiped out Japanese immigration. Since the "Chinese problem" had been taken care of with the exclusion acts and since the Japanese were barred because they could not be naturalized, the "Asian problem" had finally been resolved. Immigration policy, as related to the Japanese, was not changed until 1952.

Interpreting the Japanese Experience

The Japanese immigrants in the United States at the turn of the century vigorously sought and achieved the American dream. They came to succeed and succeed they did. They rose from menial, low-paying jobs to affluence in agriculture and business. They epitomized the "rags to riches" story that was heralded as the American way. Something happened, however, on their way to grasping that gold ring of success. They apparently were too good, too effective, and too productive in living the American dream. They seemed better at the success game than the "real Americans," who often felt more deserving of the economic benefits of this country.

Those traits that had endeared Japanese workers to American employers (willingness to work at any job for any wage, ambition, determination) became weapons of attack. When the Japanese became staunch economic competitors to "American" businesses, they were recast as deceitful, greedy, and unethical. Restrictions, legal and other wise, had to be imposed to keep them in their place. A group with a commitment to upward mobility became feared as the "yellow peril" seemed destined to menace California and the world.

Over the years, this history of racism, discrimination, and legal restrictions against Japanese individuals at the turn of the century has faded in U.S. and social work history. Oppression seems less associated with Japanese Americans than with other people of color. In fact, the characteristics that helped the Issei achieve the American dream of economic success have been glorified and generalized, creating the stereotype of the "model minority." The myth of the model minority hides the history of oppression and has been used to counteract charges of racism. In an analysis of the model minority myth, Crystal asserted, "Asian Americans' apparently successful efforts at assimilation...have earned them the dubious moniker of the 'model minority.' According to this 'model minority' image, Asian Americans' cultural traits—diligence, frugality, and willingness to sacrifice—propel their upward mobility and win them public accolades."[41]

This rewriting of history and the emergence of this myth deny the differential treatment received by this group. Consequently, *oppression* and *discrimination* are words not typically used to describe the Japanese experience in America.

SOME CONCLUDING OBSERVATIONS

All ethnic and racial groups in the United States at the turn of the century suffered severe and extreme hardships. The White ethnics, with their darker skin tones and "deviant" religions, were in danger of polluting the melting pot with undesirable traits. African Americans represented a separate class of people altogether. After separating the American Indians from their tribal lands, the "Friends of the Indian" were deeply invested in rescuing children from the harmful effects of the reservation. Mexicans indigenous to the Southwest were driven from their land and were relegated, along with Mexican immigrants, to servile positions in a castelike system. The perception of Chinese as unwanted competitors for White workers and as unassimiliable culminated in national policy that banned Chinese from entering the country. Success with realizing the American dream caused the Japanese to be reviled as un-American, unassimiliable, and unwanted.

Suffering is suffering—regardless of which group is being victimized. It is not a matter of whether one group suffered more or less than another group. The key point is that all groups suffered *differently* and it is precisely this difference that should *not* be minimized, trivialized, or homogenized. Each group, then, has a history of contacts with White America, American institutions, and American policies. The United States, as a nation, responded differentially to each group and each group in turn was influenced by the history and form of America's response.

Although there is no doubt that thousands of White ethnics confronted nativism, discrimination, violence, oppression, deplorable living conditions, and life-threatening work environments at the turn of the century, racial minorities and ethnic minorities seemed to have fared even worse. White ethnics differed from these other minorities in a number of very clear, very distinct ways.

White Ethnics and People of Color

Although many old-stock Americans were hostile to the immigration of the "new" immigrants, national immigration policies did *not* explicitly target this group for immigration prohibitions. Immigration acts that affected these newer immigrants were acts based on *screening* procedures, not ethnic or racial membership. Through the literacy test, individuals rather than entire races of people were barred from entering the country. Chinese and Japanese immigrants were expressly singled out because of their race, and immigration acts specifically named Chinese immigrants and other immigrants not eligible for citizenship—a group that included Asians. This was, in effect, a *racial* barrier to immigration.[42]

White ethnics were seen as "undesirable" immigrants because of their cultures, religions, and peasant background. In addition, they were also people with darker skin tones. With all the storm of nativism and the drive to keep America pure and to keep America White, White ethnics failed to produce a national scare of the magnitude of the "yellow peril." There was no pervasive popular phrase or catchword that encompassed race as its focus as did the yellow peril. Although White ethnics significantly outnumbered Japanese immigrants, vehement racial protest was directed at the Japanese. With the rise of Japan's military position, the fear of Japanese invasion was captured in sentiment toward the country as well as its people in the United States. In his analysis of the anti-Japanese movement in the United States, Daniels indicated, "Most of the charges against the Japanese—their nonassimilation, their low standard of living, their high birth rate, their vile habits—were also made against European immigrants. But only against Orientals was it seriously charged that the peaceful immigrants were but a vanguard of an invading horde to come."[43]

White ethnics were shabbily treated and endured the worst of living conditions, yet they never experienced the loss of property that marks the American-Indian and indigenous Mexican history in this country. Through the force of physical violence and the judicial system, both groups were dispossessed of vast acres of land. These lands were needed to feed the insatiable appetite of Manifest Destiny, White superiority, and God's will.

White Americans had a tremendous sense of entitlement and nothing was permitted to block this great American quest.

White ethnics were not uniformly singled out for different treatment. Each city, each group, and each situation resulted in varying reactions from old-stock, "real" Americans. The treatment extended to the White ethnics was related to the economic climate, the type of work the groups sought, and the degree of perceived deviance of each group. This was not the case for African Americans who, *by law*, were mandated to receive separate treatment. Unlike White ethnics, African Americans were explicitly named and singled out in *national* policy for treatment that was at variance with the White population.

White ethnics and people of color were victims of racial attacks that claimed thousands of lives and injured even more. However, the magnitude and intensity of the violence levied against southern and eastern Europeans never matched that levied against American Indians, African Americans, Mexicans, and Chinese. In some cases, entire communities of color were literally wiped out by angry mobs of White men, women, *and* children.[44] These attacks, some of which can only be described as *massacres*, often involved the participation of White ethnics.

Some of the discrimination against White ethnics, Mexicans, Chinese, and Japanese can be attributed to the values, cultures, and religions of these groups. Even though American Indians were not immigrants, they still had cultures and religions that were "foreign" to Americans supporting nativism. Differences heightened antagonisms between groups and were used to rationalize harsh treatment. As a result, a "we" versus "they" posture emerged. Although White ethnics were outside mainstream America, in comparison to the racial/ethnic minority groups, they were much closer to the native stock "we" than were any of the other groups. In fact, many of the old-stock, native Americans favored any type of European immigration over immigration from China or Japan.

It is more difficult to argue that discrimination against African Americans was, in part, derived from cultural and religious differences or that their way of life was "foreign" to America. African Americans at the turn of the century were more native to the United States than many of the old-stock settlers who arrived in the country in the mid-1800s. African Americans were the products of U.S. society as they were transformed from Africans to Americans through years of coercive servitude. In the post–Emancipation years, African Americans were struggling to prove their Americanism and desired full integration into society. Nativity and cultural congruence, however, could not halt the discrimination and oppression heaped upon them. It seems that color alone was the paramount cause of their disfavored status.

At the turn of the century, White ethnics and people of color were "social problems" in America. Each group was in need of some type of intervention capable of producing desirable outcomes. The Progressive Era and its reformers did not provide equitable responses to these social problems.

Ethnicity, Race, and the Reformers

The Progressive Era is associated with reform, enlightenment, and liberalism. The middle class was beginning to turn its attention to the pressing social issues of the day. There were, however, limits to the progressivism of the period. Although progressives liked to think of themselves as free from prejudice, they simultaneously insisted that separate races could not mix.[45] The *Plessy* v. *Ferguson* decision echoed this view and the voluntary, and sometimes forced, segregation of other racial groups reinforced this position. In fact, the Chinese and Japanese were often described as "clannish" because they seemed to prefer communities composed of members of their own race. The segregation of African Americans was also linked to prevailing attitudes about the inferiority of this group.

The progressives further believed that Anglo-Saxons were responsible for the country's expansion and industrial growth. The continuing development of the country in the Anglo-Saxon way was predicated on the Americanization of the new immigrants. The White ethnics could gain coveted membership in the elite group through assimilation into the country's melting pot. Assimilation meant undergoing the process of Americanization that replaced ethnic values and culture with American ones. For the White ethnics, learning English and skills was the way out of the deplorable slums. With upward mobility, the "new" immigrants could become true Americans, with children and grandchildren who would be indistinguishable from descendants of the White pioneers.[46]

Americanization was set as a goal for all White immigrants—adults and children. The adults were an integral component of the process and were worthy of Americanization programs. This approach differed from the Americanization efforts undertaken by the "Friends of the Indian," who concentrated on the next generation—the children. The American-Indian adults were viewed as a lost cause that only interfered with the children's assimilation. The two interventions represent a stark and racist contrast. All members of the immigrant population could be Americanized, yet only American-Indian children were identified as the beneficiaries of this process.

Americanization, however, was not held as the goal for everyone. In fact, some groups were seen as unassimiliable and incapable of becoming part of the mainstream. In 1949, Kiser asserted, "In view of common social attitudes, it is not expected that a similar assimilation of the colored groups will occur in the foreseeable future."[47] Indeed, no amount of Americanization would make African Americans, Chinese, Japanese, and other groups of color indistinguishable from the descendants of White settlers. Even when it was introduced in the early 1900s, the melting pot perspective failed to embrace people of color.

One explanation for the assumption that people of color were unassimiliable lies in physical characteristics of these groups. Regardless of longevity in the United States, some groups will continue to look "foreign" and will continue to be linked with that group's country of origin. For example, in an 1992 undergraduate sociology class at a major midwestern university, a Japanese-American student offered emphatic support for the equalization of sex roles. A White student responded, "Would you feel that way if you were in your own country?" To which the Japanese American replied, "I *am* in my own country. I am a third-generation Japanese American." Ethnic/racial minorities are also expected to maintain some type of allegiance to that group's country of origin. Hence, Mexican Americans, Chinese Americans, Japanese Americans, and other Americans of color are perceived as being loyal to their "home" country. African Americans, however, are sometimes exempt from this stereotype.

These unassimiliable groups were also considered to be inferior to White groups. Regardless of status, all Whites were seen as superior to all people of color. In the words of a progressive spokesman, "Race...counts more than anything else in the world...an Italian of the commonest standing and qualities would be a more welcomed suitor [for the hand of an American's daughter] than the finest gentleman of Japan....The instinct of self-preservation of our race demands that its future members shall be members of our race."[48] Minority group status thus defined a castelike system in which people of color, especially African Americans, occupied the lowest positions. This is clearly reflected in Brandt's 1903 observation: "There are certain processes in the preparation of tobacco where the heat required is so great that white laborers cannot be used; in these departments the [tobacco companies] employ about 350 Negroes."[49]

By looking at race and ethnicity as elements dictating a caste system, Whites' responses to people of color during the Progressive Era can be more fully analyzed. With the exception of American Indians, people of color served as an invaluable source of cheap labor for menial jobs detested by Whites. African Americans, Mexicans, Chinese, and Japanese all filled the need for labor. As each group sought to rise above this lowly position, violent attacks, discrimination, and national policy served to contain their progress. African Americans were becoming too vocal and assertive in their drive for equality, and national policy acted as a ceiling for that drive. As Chinese and Japanese rose to the level of economic competition with Whites, various pieces of legislation halted their entry into the country and curbed their economic growth. Numerous Mexicans were robbed of their lands and forced to eke out a living in service to others. Vigilante, terrorist groups made sure that the Mexicans stayed "in their place."

Thus, the Progressive Era reformers were greatly influenced by race and color in their determinations of the appropriate place for various groups in society. Progressives defined which groups were assimilable and the Americanization process necessary for assimilation. They acted in "the best interest" of some groups (African Americans and Native Americans) and in blatant opposition to others (Chinese and Japanese). Nativism, as an ideology, gave people of color an inherently inferior status. They were *children* of the human race and, as children, they needed the direction and supervision of the superior race. Woodrow Wilson reflected this perspective about African Americans when he said, "[African Americans are] a host of dusky children untimely put out of school [by emancipation]."[50]

The Progressive Era was thus one stage in the country's continued movement toward its manifest destiny. Reform was not in the structures and institutions of society; rather, it was in the attitudes of the middle class and wealthy who began to take notice of the disenfranchised masses around them. Progressives felt that some of these masses should not be left to rot in the urban slums—that efforts should be made to raise immigrants to the level of Americans. To some extent, the Progressive Era was also a conservative period in that the activities of the progressives posed little threat to their economic or social positions.

Although the Progressive Era was a period of considerable change and reform in areas of social, legal, political and economic life, its history has been garnished with various myths.[51] Although middle-class progressives, reformers, and professionals were clothed in liberalism as they embraced the downtrodden, these groups also depended heavily on the financial and political support of big business, large corporations, and influential individuals. Orphanages, reformatories, welfare charities, Children's Aid Societies, and numerous similar groups conducted their activities and maintained their organizations with large donations from businesses and powerful people. As a matter of fact, most reforms enjoyed the support of big business. Although the Progressive Era stands for reform and liberalism in U.S. history, the role of big business in this era's emergence is often minimized. Progressivism was in part a businessmen's movement and big business played a central role in the Progressive coalition's support of welfare reforms.[52]

Big business served to guide many reform efforts and, in this role, may have also served to constrain efforts by defining appropriate and inappropriate areas for intervention. In order for business to be this influential, the reformers and the businessmen had to share similar ideologies and values. In this regard, the conservatism that comes with protecting vested interests and elite positions may have infiltrated Progressive Era movements, and reforms were to benefit those deemed deserving and appropriate. This progressivism and liberalism do not appear to have extended to non-White populations.

This is the era in which the roots of contemporary social work were planted. What were the positions of the Charity Organization Societies, friendly visitors, and settlement-house workers on the issues of race and ethnicity? How did they respond to the controversial issues surrounding particular groups of color? These and related issues are addressed in the next chapter.

ENDNOTES

1. This discussion is drawn from Rodolfo Acuña, *Occupied America—The Chicano's Struggle Toward Liberation* (San Francisco: Canfield, 1972); Frank Bean and Marta Tienda, *The Hispanic Population of the United States* (New York: Russell Sage, 1987); Arthur Campa, "Mexican Americans," in *Racial Discrimination Against Neither-White-Nor-Black American Minorities*, ed. Kanamur Chandras (San Francisco: R & E Research Associates, 1978), pp. 54–67; Bruce Jansson, *The Reluctant Welfare State—A History of American Social Welfare Policies*, Second Edition (Pacific Grove, CA: Brooks/Cole, 1993), pp. 131–132; Matt Meier and Feliciano Rivera, *The Chicanos—A History of Mexican Americans* (New York: Hill and Wang, 1972); Wayne Moquin, ed., with Charles Van Doren, *A Documentary History of the Mexican Americans* (New York: Praeger, 1971); David Weber, Ed., *Foreigners in their Native Land* (Albuquerque, NM: University of New Mexico Press, 1973).

2. Acuña, *Occupied America*, p. 19.

3. As quoted in Acuña, *Occupied America*, p. 29.

4. Weber, *Foreigners in their Native Land*, p. 147.

5. Meier and Rivera, *The Chicanos*, p. 82.

6. Meier and Rivera, *The Chicanos*, pp. 88–89.

7. Robert McLean and Charles Thomson, *Spanish and Mexican in Colorado* (New York: Board of National Missions of the Presbyterian Church in the U.S.A., 1924), pp. viii–ix.

8. McLean and Thomson, *Spanish and Mexican in Colorado*, p. 13.

9. This incident is detailed in Weber, *Foreigners in their Native Land*, p. 191.

10. Kingsley Davis and Clarence Senior, "Immigration from the Western Hemisphere," *Annals of the American Academy of Political and Social Science* 262 (March 1949): 76.

11. Jansson, *The Reluctant Welfare State*, p. 132.

12. Moquin, *A Documentary History of the Mexican Americans*, p. 253.

13. Samuel Bryan, "Mexican Immigrants in the United States," *The Survey 28* (September 12, 1912): 728.

14. Acuña, *Occupied America*, p. 131.

15. Moquin, *A Documentary History of the Mexican Americans*, p. 190.

16. Moquin, *A Documentary History of the Mexican Americans*, p. 259.

17. Weber, *Foreigners in their Native Land*, p. 152.

18. Moquin, *A Documentary History of the Mexican Americans*, pp. 190–191.

19. Acuña, *Occupied America*, pp. 10–31.

20. Discussion on this topic is drawn from Jack Chen, *The Chinese of America: From the Beginnings to the Present* (San Francisco: Harper and Row, 1980); Thomas

Chinn, "Chinese Americans," in *Racial Discrimination Against Neither-White-Nor-Black American Minorities*, ed. Kananur Chandras (San Francisco: R & E Research Associates, 1978), pp. 19–33; Jansson, *The Reluctant Welfare State*, p. 131; Louise Johnson and Charles Schwartz, *Social Welfare—A Response to Human Need*, Second Edition (Boston: Allyn and Bacon, 1991), pp. 100–103; Paula Rothenberg, Ed., *Race, Class, and Gender in the United States*, Second Edition (New York: St. Martin's Press, 1992); Betty Sung, *The Story of the Chinese in America* (New York: Collier Books, 1971); U.S. Department of Commerce, Bureau of the Census, *Historical Statistics of the United States, Colonial Times to 1957* (Washington, DC: U.S. Government Printing Office, 1960), p. 9; Carl Wittke, "Immigration Policy Prior to World War I," *The Annals of the American Academy of Political and Social Science 262* (March 1949): 5–14; S. Wells Williams, "Chinese Immigration," *Journal of Social Science 9* (December 1879): 90–123; Paul Wong, Steven Applewhite, and Michael Daley, "From Despotism to Pluralism: The Evolution of Voluntary Organizations in Chinese American Communities," *Ethnic Groups 8*, number 4, (1990): 215–233.

21. The Chinese presence in other parts of the United States is detailed by Jack Chen, *The Chinese of America*, pp. 248–269.

22. The history of violence against the Chinese is recounted by Chen, *The Chinese of America*, and Sung, *The Story of the Chinese in America*.

23. Williams, "Chinese Immigration," p. 108.

24. As quoted in Williams, "Chinese Immigration," pp. 110–111.

25. Williams, "Chinese Immigration," p. 111.

26 A list of anti-Chinese legislation is found in Chen, *The Chinese of America*, pp. 137–139.

27. As quoted in Sung, *The Story of the Chinese People*, p. 49.

28. Sung, *The Story of the Chinese in America*, p. 57.

29. As quoted in Chinn, "Chinese Americans," p. 29.

30. This section is drawn from Kananur Chandras, Ed., "Japanese Americans," in *Racial Discrimination Against Neither-White-Nor-Black American Minorities* (San Francisco: R & E Research Associates, 1978), pp. 34–53; Roger Daniels, *The Politics of Prejudice—The Anti-Japanese Movement in California and the Struggle for Japanese Exclusion* (Berkeley, CA: University of California Press, 1962); Richard Hofstadter, *Social Darwinism in American Thought*, Revised Editon (Boston: Beacon Press, 1955), pp. 189–191; Jansson, *The Reluctant Welfare State*, pp. 90–91; Johnson and Schwartz, *Social Welfare*, pp. 100–102; Harry Kitano, *Japanese Americans* (Englewood Cliffs, NJ: Prentice Hall, 1976).

31. Amy Mass, "Asians as Individuals: The Japanese Community," *Social Casework 57* (March 1976): 161.

32. Harry Kitano, *Japanese Americans*, p. 14.

33. Henry Fairchild, "Public Opinion on Immigration," *The Annals of the American Academy of Political and Social Science 262* (March 1949): 191–192.

34. As quoted in Daniels, *The Politics of Prejudice*, p. 21.

35. As quoted in Daniels, *The Politics of Prejudice*, p. 25.

36. David Crystal, "Asian Americans and the Myth of the Model Minority," *Social Casework 70* (September 1989), p. 406.

37. Kitano, *Japanese Americans*, p. 26.

38. Kitano, *Japanese Americans*, p. 26.

39. A detailed discussion of immigration policy can be found in Edward Hutchinson, "Immigration Policy Since World War I," *Annals of the American Academy of Political and Social Science 262* (March 1949): 15–21.

40. U.S. Department of Commerce, Bureau of the Census, *Historical Statistics,* p. 9.

41. Crystal, "Asian Americans and the Myth of the Model Minority," p. 405.

42. Edward Hutchinson, "Immigration Policy Since World War I," p. 18.

43. Daniels, *The Politics of Prejudice,* p. 68.

44. The 1917 East St. Louis, Illinois, riot that devastated the African-American community, for example, included attacks by White boys and girls. Details of this youthful participation are contained in *The Crisis 13–14* (September 1917): 219–238.

45. Daniels, *The Politics of Prejudice,* p. 49.

46. Clyde Kiser, "Cultural Pluralism," *The Annals of the American Academy of Political and Social Science 262* (March 1949): 128.

47. Kiser, "Cultural Pluralism," p. 128.

48. As quoted in Daniels, *The Politics of Prejudice,* p. 49.

49. Lilian Brandt, "The Negroes of St. Louis," *Publications of the Amercian Statistical Association 8* (March 1903): 238.

50. As quoted in Florette Henri, *Black Migration: Movement North, 1900–1920* (Garden City, NY: Anchor Press/Doubleday, 1975), p. 211.

51. Anthony Platt, "The Child-Saving Movement and the Origins of the Juvenile Justice System," in *The Sociology of Juvenile Delinquency,* ed. Ronald Berger (Chicago: Nelson-Hall, 1991), p. 10. Platt also provided a detailed discussion on the role of big business in the Progressive Era.

52. Anthony Platt, "The Child-Saving Movement and the Origins of the Juvenile Justice System," p. 13.

Chapter 4

Ethnicity, Race, and the Emergence of Direct Practice

According to Montiel and Wong, "A profound critique of the profession of social work and its relationship to minorities has not been made."[1] Such a critique, whether profound or not, would have to begin with the initial roots of the profession. The critique would then have to move forward with an analysis of significant milestones in the development of the profession that have had reverberating effects on the profession's relations with minority communities. Central to this historical analysis is the integration of a theoretical framework that illuminates specific events and their consequences. The application of such a framework moves the overview from the purely descriptive to the blending of theory, history, interpretation, and assessment. The incorporation of a conceptual foundation suggests that associations and predictive inferences can be drawn and advanced.

This chapter identifies the theoretical perspectives that underlie an analysis of social work's history and its relations with particular ethnic minority communities. A general overview of the profession's service delivery to those communities follows the theoretical discussion. The historical overview is not designed to be exhaustive, as detailed historical discussions have been presented by others. Rather, here the intent is to focus on those aspects of the profession's history that had major consequences for service delivery to ethnic minority groups and communities. Social work's current status in the eyes of those communities is, indeed, predicated on its unique history.

THEORETICAL PERSPECTIVES

The historical analysis and other analyses presented in subsequent chapters are derived from the political-economy and systems perspectives. Both are called on for interpreting the profession's responses to the needs of ethnic

79

minority communities. In addition, these frameworks are also used in analyzing the responses of these communities to their own needs.

Systems Perspective[2]

One of the unique advantages of the systems perspective is its applicability to numerous levels of social organization. The perspective can be used to discern the structure and behavior of groups, organizations, communities, professions, and other social entities. Bertalanffy, credited with originating the theory of general systems, wrote that "a system is defined as a complex of components in mutual interaction."[3] The systems perspective emphasizes the relationship between the system and its environment; interrelatedness of system components; steady state, equilibrium, or homeostasis; boundary maintenance; and system functions such as socialization, social control, communication, feedback, survival (adaptation and maintenance).

The environment is a significant aspect of the systems perspective. The importation of energy from the environment is necessary for system maintenance and survival. *Energy* here refers to those resources required for the system to act, affect change, and maintain itself. While the system is bounded, those boundaries are permeated by the dynamic exchange of energy between the system and the environment. Systems require inputs (people, raw materials, and/or other resources) from the environment and these inputs are transformed by throughputs (technology or the series of processes/activities applied to the inputs) into outputs (products) that are then released to the environment.

As organizational systems, many nineteenth-century public schools drew on an array of resources from the environment (such as pupils, personnel, financial support, and community legitimacy). Through the application of educational and Americanization technologies, the uneducated and "un-American" were transformed into educated Americans (the finished product) who were then returned to the environment with graduation. Geographically based systems such as communities at the turn of the century also imported energy from the environment (for example, new residents, financial support from outside employment, values, norms, social practices governing housing, and other services). These inputs were used to socialize members and maintain the community as a viable, dynamic social entity. A tangible example of community output was the individual who grew up in a particular community and left that community when he or she reached adulthood.

Systems can exist as tangible places such as organizations, communities, states, or nations. A formal organization has discernible boundaries, can be distinguished for the environment, has varying components or subsystems, has a structure, socializes new members, has internal communication patterns, applies sanctions to member behaviors, and seeks to maintain itself.

Systems perspective has been frequently used to analyze organizational processes and the organization-environment relationship. At the organizational level, systems characteristics appear more manageable for research and analysis. Organizational structure can be identified, formal communication channels can be investigated, and specific environmental factors can be explored.

The application of this perspective to communities and more complex levels of social organization has been more challenging because a community encompasses the individuals, families, other groups, organizations, and institutions within its boundaries. The United States also exists as a complex social system with the same systems characteristics as a formal organization, and would include communities and all their components, states, regions, and all the social institutions that make up the United States. At these levels, the complexity of disentangling systems characteristics seems overwhelming. Rather than being a guide for research, the systems perspective emerges as a guide for understanding the numerous dynamics that affect a system's actions and responses. Thus, the perspective provides a conceptual framework for organizing and assessing complex systems.

In addition to geographical or spatial areas and organizations, systems can also reflect networks of individuals who are bounded by kinship. This type of system is referred to as *nonplace communities*.[4] Kinship systems may be based on a blood, racial, or ethnic tie such as a family, an American-Indian reservation, or a barrio. The African-American community, the Hispanic community, or the Korean community may designate individuals who do not reside in the same geographical area but who are united by the domain of race or ethnicity. This blood, race, or ethnic nonplace system is bonded by values, ideologies, interdependence among members, a strong belief in mutuality of goals and expectations, and a commonality of history, tradition, and culture. Members of these kinship systems also have similar perceptions and definitions of social status within the group.

The early Japanese immigrants (discussed in the previous chapter) offer an excellent example of the dynamics of the kinship system. This immigrant community had a unity and cohesiveness that enabled them to pool resources for business ventures. This interdependence enabled numerous group members to become prosperous owners of businesses and land. They shared the values of ambitiousness, industriousness, and upward mobility. Particular occupations became equated with success and status because they provided a greater opportunity for the expression of individual effort, hard work, and ambition. Agriculture, small business, and gardening became symbols of self-employment, which was also valued. Furthermore, the Japanese immigrant community was dominated by single males who could respond to the seasonal nature of agricultural work. The cohesiveness of the group also led to the formation of work groups that could negotiate with employers for higher wages. The interdependence of group members, common values, and group cohesiveness has been held as significant in the economic success of early Japanese communities.

Another type of nonplace social system is one in which social network members share a like-mindedness, as is the case with religious groups or professions. According to Anderson and Carter:

> An established profession claims for itself and is recognized by society as responsible for a symbolic territory or domain. Almost by definition, when a group carves out for itself a societal function or some part of the society's stock of ideas, it becomes sanctioned as a profession.... The major commonality among the professions is that they are formally sanctioned by society to bring about change that is beneficial to the society and its components, as well as maintain the society.[5]

Members of a profession often share similar ideologies, values, and beliefs that define the profession's "culture." Members of the same profession typically identify with each other and have a common loyalty to that profession. In addition, the functions of socialization and social control of members occur within the boundaries of the profession. Members are further bonded by the specialized knowledge and set of practices that generally distinguish one profession from another and distinguish the professional from the nonprofessional. As systems, nonplace "communities of the mind" also strive to survive and maintain themselves and have all the other characteristics associated with systems.

A system can be both a part and a whole. That is, a system represents the parts that contribute to its wholeness while at the same time its wholeness represents a part or subsystem of some larger system to which it belongs. As a whole or complete system, the social entity strives to maintain its autonomy over the energy it receives, processes, and releases. Emphasis is on the internal dynamics of the system and its relationship with the environment. As a subsystem of a larger system, the social entity is perceived in terms of how it contributes to the larger system and responds to changes occurring in other subsystems.

A Mexican-American community may be concerned with the education its children receive in the public school system, employment opportunities for its members, the availability of affordable housing, the physical condition of neighborhoods, and the election of community representatives to public offices. If this community is in a city with other racial/ethnic minority communities, then the quality of services and equity of opportunities for the Mexican-American subsystem is relative to those of the other subsystems. Since the city as a system also seeks to maintain itself and achieve some type of steady state, a balance may be desirable among the subsystems so that resources (energy) are distributed throughout the system. If the Mexican-American community is not as organized, strong, or powerful as other ethnic minority communities or as the nonminority communities, the Mexican-American community may not amass as many resources as it may need. In addition, the ethnic/racial subsystems may end up competing with each other for positions, opportunities, and various other resources. The focus moves from the Mexican-American community as an autonomous system to the Mexican-American community as a subsystem connected to, affected by, and vying with other subsystems for vitally needed resources.

The larger environment also acts on a system and a system, in turn, acts on its environment. The American-Indian reservations (discussed in a previous chapter) provide a vivid example of these dynamics. The reservations were greatly affected by the policies, programs, and practices of the larger environment. The boarding school phenomenon removed children from their reservation systems and plunged them into a totally foreign situation. The larger environment also controlled the amount and type of resources that were sent to the reservations. Most of the reservations were poor because the means for self-sufficiency had been stripped away and replaced with meager supplies. The larger society literally controlled the destiny of the reservations.

Mexican communities (as systems) offer another example of how the environment can dramatically alter a system's homeostasis and shape the development of a new stability. Prior to the Mexican-American War, many Mexican communities of the Southwest were agrarian and populated by families historically tied to the land. As detailed in the previous chapter, after the signing of the Treaty of Guadalupe Hidalgo in 1848, thousands of White settlers invaded the territory and laid claim to the land. This massive displacement of Mexican farmers was, in systems terms, a critical disruption of the stability of these communities.

Because systems seek to control harmful environmental factors and adapt to external conditions, these Mexican communities survived by redefining their equilibrium. Land ownership, farming, and geographical stability were replaced with tenantry, other available employment (also defined by the environment), and geographical mobility. The subsequent influx of thousands of Mexican immigrants (another external factor) further reinforced the new stability emergent in Mexican-American communities at the turn of the century. This example also underscores the dynamic nature of systems equilibrium. For Mexican-American kinship systems, the resultant steady state was one in which frequent movement defined the homeostasis.

The larger society has, however, also been affected by the American-Indian and Mexican-American kinship systems in this country. Aspects of both cultures (language, clothing, art, food, traditions, values, beliefs) have found their way into mainstream society. As these groups developed and flexed their political muscle, their environments have been forced to change and adapt. For example, American-Indian tribes are reclaiming their lands, thereby blocking construction and other development plans forged by others. Tribes have challenged mainstream definitions of historical artifacts by demanding the return of American-Indian remains held by museums. Tribal groups argue that their ancestors should be properly buried and not displayed for public viewing.

The larger social system acted on and exerted influence over all the ethnic and racial groups discussed in Chapters 2 and 3. Legislation, discriminatory practices, racial/ethnic violence, and unprotecting law-enforcement agencies formed the parameters of the social system surrounding ethnic and racial communities and shaped the world views of community members. Ethnic and racial minority groups were more likely to perceive themselves as victims in a hostile world and cultivate a distrust of the larger society. In this respect, to some of these marginal groups, U.S. society had boundaries that were practically impenetrable. For White ethnic groups, those boundaries were more pliable and permeable to allow for a greater exchange of resources, including people.

Consequently, the systems perspective explicates systems functions, goals, adaptability, and boundary maintenance; the interdependence of subsystems; and energy exchanges (inputs and outputs) with the environment. The application of this approach to varying types and levels of social systems (from kinship systems to professions) adds to its significance for the topics covered in this analysis.

Because organizations are such an integral aspect of social work and service delivery, the political-economy perspective is also employed to further define and explain the dynamics occurring within organizational systems, between organizational systems, and between organizations and the larger environment.

Political-Economy Perspective[6]

According to Zald, "In its most generic sense, political economy is the study of the interplay of power, the goals of power-wielders, and productive exchange systems."[7] Power and economics guide the organization's development, goal direction, services, products, and definitions of effectiveness. The political economy of an organization defines its system of power (polity) and its system for acquiring and distributing resources (economy) and the interrelationship between the two. An organization's polity and economy also refer to dynamics inside and outside the organization. Thus, the organization is viewed as an arena in which various interest groups, external and internal, possessing resources needed by the organization, compete to optimize their values through it.[8]

An organization's internal polity defines its institutionalized patterns of decision making and its systematic processes for the exertion of influence in determining goals and defining ends to be met. This would encompass an array of structures, processes, and people within the organization. The power of individuals is derived from a hierarchical position or membership in the dominant elite faction that governs the organization formally or informally. This focus is on the manner in which goals and ends are determined and reified in the organization's political economy.

Workers have generally commanded a great deal of attention in discussions of internal organizational dynamics. Studies of employee morale and job satisfaction abound in the literature. In social work, numerous books and articles touch on the ways in which workers implement the organization's ideology. In the political-economy framework, staff attitudes and values are only important as they articulate with the organization's polity and economy.[9] Recruitment, socialization, and adherence of staff to the organization's political economy then become key organizational activities. For example, police officers of 100 years ago generally did not intervene in the attacks on ethnic/racial minorities. The political economy of law-enforcement agencies at that time had not defined the protection of those victim groups as their goals. Officers whose behaviors did not support the prevailing political economy of the organization were, no doubt, severely sanctioned.

Organizations have constitutions or normative structures that direct their political economy.[10] Within the organizational constitution, several tasks are accomplished: incentives for participation are illuminated; discretion and decision-making responsibilities within the hierarchy are specified; those parties to whom the organization is accountable are identified; and goals, clients, and technologies are articulated. Power plays between special-interest groups inside and outside the organization shape, create, and re-create the organization's constitution. This constitution represents the embodiment of those values optimized by special-interest groups (dominant elite) of that organization.

Within the political-economy framework, the internal economy is specifically defined as the organization's processes for motivating, organizing, and guiding organizational participants to meet the organization's goals.[11] The distribution of resources reflects the organization's constitution and value commitments. The achievement of specific goals (the optimalization of values) involves the commitment of staff time, incentives for staff participation, allocation of fiscal resources, delineation of technologies, specification of tasks, and a hierarchy that supports goal attainment.

Special-interest groups outside the organization help make up the organization's external polity. Government agencies, legislative bodies, licensing/accrediting bodies, sponsors/funders, other organizations that offer similar services, service beneficiaries, professional associations, and any other groups or individuals external to the organization with the power to influence the organization are examples of the external polity. These power brokers attempt to direct the organization in accordance with their own values that are derived from self-interests, moral imperatives, professional considerations, or some other mitigating belief system.[12] The Council on Social Work Education is part of the external polity of social work schools and programs because the council accredits such programs. In meeting accrediting standards, programs often have to modify their curriculum and/or structure. Thus, through the power of accreditation, the council influences what goes on in social work programs, departments, and schools.

The external polity also has the power to legitimize the organization and this legitimation acts as a magnet to attract clients, sponsors, and other resources on which the organization depends. Legitimation serves to reaffirm and sanction the organization's existence. In addition, legitimation reflects a correspondence between the external polity and the organization's constitution. When this correspondence is challenged, external power brokers may force the organization to modify its constitution, internal power brokers may attempt to fight these challenges, or the external and internal power wielders reach a compromise.

The organization's external economy includes such environmental factors as the available supply of services, service demands, personnel costs, prevailing technologies, and clients. These factors constrain the organization's choices and constitution. In the systems perspective, these factors were referred to as inputs needed by the system in order to maintain itself and survive. Shifts in the external economy can also affect the organization's constitution by redirecting the allocation of resources and shifting internal power relations. For example, the availability of funds for programs targeting client populations may lead to organizations developing new programs and recruiting new personnel, indicating that resources are being allocated differently. In addition, the new personnel with the requisite expertise for working with the new client population may form a dominant elite within the organization that reshapes the organization's constitution to optimize their values. In the 1960s, for example, funding priorities supported community organizing as a means of mobilizing low-income communities. Maximum feasible participation of community residents elevated those with expertise in grass-roots organizing. This represented a shift in power from casework to community organization. For a period of time, community organizers became the dominant elite of many human services agencies.

The political-economy perspective thus highlights the internal and external political (power) and economic systems that determine and influence what an organization is and what it does. The organization's relationship with its environment is specified in greater detail and particular factors of that environment are considered more significant than others. This perspective clarifies power as it relates to organizations and operationalizes the uses of that power.

The systems perspective and the political-economy perspective form the framework for examining the birth and development of social work as a profession. These perspectives are also incorporated in subsequent chapters.

THE BIRTH OF SOCIAL WORK

Most social work texts provide general descriptions of the origins of social work as a practice and as a profession. These descriptions include discussions of the Charity Organization Societies (COS) and the settlement houses. The COS and settlement houses represent the two distinct arms of social work that are referred to as direct practice and indirect practice; personal practice and social practice; retail and wholesale practice; social casework and social change/reform; or micro- and macropractice. These designations encompass the various systems in which the intervention occurs. The direct/clinical practice arm uses the individual, family, and/or other small groups as the treatment unit. Indirect/macropractice, on the other hand, targets social systems (organizations, communities, institutions, and other social entities) for change or reform.

Social work historians agree that the COS and the settlement houses were not as involved as they could or should have been in the concerns and problems of ethnic minorities. However, the determinants of this lack of involvement seldom receive in-depth discussion. In addition, the reform history of social work is often held as the premier example of the profession's investment in the plight of the less fortunate and the commitment to changing or reforming hostile, oppressive environments. There seems to be general adherence to the view captured by Ehrenreich: "The proto-social workers—charity workers, settlement-house workers, reformers, a group made up disproportionately of those of the middle class and who experienced more intimate contact with the poor, the immigrant, and the black, in daily life as well as in time of crisis—were perhaps *less susceptible to nativism and racism than were many others of their class*" [emphasis added].[13] Jansson also implied that "certain reformers *like many settlement workers* [were] *free from racism*" [emphasis added][14] This may be the history that social workers would like to believe existed at the turn of the century. This position elevates the early workers above the racism and ethnic animosities that preyed on the rest of society. This position also casts these workers as individuals able to accept people as people despite the prejudice and discrimination surrounding them.

Then, as now, every method of social work practice incorporates certain ideologies that serve to reflect either "dominant-subordinate" or "self-determining" social relationships among its participants.[15] These ideologies must be confronted directly and unflinchingly exposed if progress is to take place. Social work cannot be exempt from systematic scrutiny of its philosophies, practices, and popular myths.

Placing social work in the context of its political economy and viewing it as a subsystem of a larger social system can promote an understanding and appreciation of the dilemmas it faced during its emergence and evolution. An explication of the dynamics driving the early workers and organizations suggests that their goals and direction could have probably been predicted. In this regard, the question becomes: Could the long-term outcomes of the evolution of social work have been any different?

THE CHARITY ORGANIZATION SOCIETIES

The Charity Organization Societies (COS) predated the settlement house movement in the United States but both were inspired by similar activities in Great Britain. Prior to the importation of these interventions, almsgiving dominated U.S. responses to needy individuals and families. With substantial increases in the number of those requiring assistance came widespread concern that pauperism was threatening the moral fiber of America. There was also growing fear that coffers once swollen with philanthropic contributions would be completely drained by the demands placed on them. In response to the rising demand for alms and their decreasing supply, the Charity Organization Societies were established as a rational, scientific approach to serving needy populations.

The economic crisis of the 1870s brought with it unemployment, hordes of beggars and tramps, and huge relief bills.[16] The climate was ripe for the pursuit of alternatives to the fragmented, uncoordinated charity efforts that merely passed out money to those in need. A new approach was also supported by the prevailing belief that the existing responses perpetuated pauperism. The first American COS was organized in 1877 in Buffalo, New York, by Stephen Humphreys Gurteen, an Episcopal clergyman, and it seemed to be the answer to combating pauperism.

COS Inputs

From a systems perspective, the COS required numerous other inputs for its development and maintenance as an organizational response to a social problem. One major input was the ideology it adopted toward poverty and the poor. In *A Handbook of Charity Organization*, published in 1882, Gurteen detailed the philosophy and beliefs at the heart of the COS.[17] The COS captured the belief that people had a "natural tendency" to shirk duty and hard work for an easy and "unchurchly" life. This meant that, in the eyes of society, people were inappropriately seeking aid rather than supporting themselves. One of the dominant missions of the societies was to "investigate" the applications for assistance. Gurteen indicated, "No relief (except in the extreme cases of despair or imminent death) without previous and searching examination." In this manner, relief to the "accomplished cheat" could end while only "the deserving poor" would be helped. He cited the English rule of giving "no relief to able-bodied men, except in return for work done" and asserted, "This work-test is one of the most perfect touchstones for discriminating between the deserving and the undeserving that has ever been devised."

For Gurteen and other COS workers, charity had to be tempered with judgment in order to avoid fostering dependency among aid recipients. The COS axiom, according to Gurteen, was "Help the poor to help themselves." This was *not* to be accomplished by "small doles of money or by provisions supplied indiscriminately week by week." Rather, the COS sought to show the poor the way to independence, self-respect, and responsibility. In the minds of the organizers, COS could prohibit paupers from assuming that assistance was an entitlement and inhibit the long-term dependency of individuals on public dole.

Other ideological and value inputs bolstered the COS approach. According to Wagner:

> "Scientific Charity" originally favored the repression of pauperism by the regulation of charity by scientific principles as well as the socialization of the vast numbers of poor and immigrants who were crowding the urban areas. The ideology of "Scientific Charity" reflected the harshness of Social Darwinism and the Poor Law tradition as well as the benevolence of Christian revival and the *noblesse oblige* of service which had a long tradition.[18]

In the midst of poverty, numerous individuals were able to rise above their humble beginnings to achieve enormous success and wealth. In this era, the plight of the poor and the accomplishments of the *nouveau riche* were held as reflections of one's efforts, perseverance, motivation, and capacity to overcome seemingly insurmountable obstacles. The poor, in essence, were thought to be poor by their own hands and required a gentle nudge or a firm push in the right direction. It became the duty (Christian duty, for some) of those with abundance to reach down and help those in need. Indeed, views toward the poor were echoed in the writings of Robert Treat Paine, Jr., President of the Associated Charities of Boston: "Among the pauperized classes of a great city, the chief obstacles are two, usually found together: lack of all skill, and lack of all hope. They can do nothing well enough to get work, and they are sunk in despair. They will make no effort to help themselves, or if you succeed in inducing them to try, there is so little they can do!"[19]

Inherent in these ideological inputs about poverty were implications for perceptions of the larger society. For example, charity workers generally accepted the premise that America's abundance made it possible for all able-bodied persons to rid themselves of poverty through hard work.[20] In this light, poverty was a reflection of individual flaws that needed correction, rehabilitation, or socialization. Belief in the availability of work was so strong that after the 1890s depression, Mary Richmond asserted that "in ordinary times, there is still work somewhere for those who have the will and the skill to do it."[21] COS organizers failed to see that poverty could not be stymied with "benevolent stinginess" but was rooted in the structural societal transitions occurring on the economic and social level.[22]

Individuals also served as inputs for the development and maintenance of the COS. In numerous cities, three groups were involved in the COS movement: charity workers, who were usually paid agents and administrators; boards of directors, who oversaw the operations of the COS; and the volunteer friendly visitors.[23] In 1880, the President of the Associated Charities of Boston wrote, "The paid agents must become, if only after long study and patient practice and many failures, experts in the art of helping struggling families permanently upward, as well as experts making a diagnosis of the causes of need."[24] By 1910, the paid agents and administrators would be calling themselves "social workers."[25] The paid staff and the friendly visitors were the immediate predecessors of professional social workers, and the friendly visitors, in particular, were the forerunners of caseworkers.[26]

The paid agents were seen as peripheral to the core activity—friendly visiting—and were apparently employed to do the jobs that were frowned on by the well-heeled friendly visitors.[27] Administrative tasks were not deemed worthy of the time of the friendly visitors and, in essence, the paid agents were paid to be of service to the boards, COS committees, and the friendly visitors. Consequently, in the COS, each position carried its own responsibilities and a hierarchy was clearly in place. Agents often conducted investigations for well-to-do contributors and other interest groups; volunteer committees decided what approach to take with each case; and the friendly visitors used their personal influence to accomplish desired changes in the family.[28] Personal service and those who provided it ranked high in the hierarchy.

Boards were often composed of influential men from the business community and/or those of the upper class. Many board members donated money themselves or provided a liaison with other philanthropists and brought with them a desire to improve their tarnished image by demonstrating that wealth had social as well as personal significance.[29] Because the Charity Organization Societies were dependent on this group for funding and legitimation, the goals and technology were often defined by these board members.

Another major input to the COS consisted of the thousands of volunteers needed to conduct the friendly visiting. While the interest of dominant elite males dictated the course of action of the COS, women were primarily responsible for realizing the mission of the sanctioning boards.[30] The ideology of the larger society was embraced by the friendly visitors as they conducted their daily visiting with the poor. Indeed, the friendly visitors were from the privileged segment of society—the segment that sought to control the tide of pauperism. Through this cadre of female friendly visitors, the COS were able to act on the motto coined by the Boston Associated Charities, "Not Alms But a Friend."

The individuals and ideologies were staunchly middle and upper class. The Charity Organization Societies were a response to the fear that large numbers of poor people could become a dominant force in U.S. society and threaten the middle and upper classes. To a certain extent, the privileged classes banded together to create a mechanism for curbing the extinction of a society they cherished—a society with roots in small-town America and its small-town values. These groups were experiencing an America in a transition spurred by the urbanization, industrialization, and immigration detailed in the previous chapter. They were fearful that these changes would eventually lead to the demise of the America they loved and wanted to maintain. In a sense, the COS represented the middle and upper classes circling their wagon train against the onslaught of destructive forces. Although the COS promoted services to the lower classes, these organizations were a means of further solidifying the class boundaries that separated the haves from the have-nots. Through the COS, the poor could learn the ways and values necessary to raise themselves from their unfortunate plight. According to Lubove, "Charity organization represented, in large measure, an instrument of urban social control for the conservative middle class."[31] This view has also been expressed by other writers.[32]

Technologies of the COS

In 1880, Robert Treat Paine, Jr., President of the Associated Charities of Boston, detailed the goals of the friendly visitor: to make sure that children did not grow up paupers, to aid in finding work for all who are able to work, to train in skill all who are deficient, to make sure that health and home are as well as may be, and to inspire new hope and self-respect.[33] Through visiting the poor, the friendly visitor was expected to counsel family members and offer assistance in the context of friendship that was assumed to develop between the visitors and her charges. Through her presence, nurturance, concern, and example, the poor were to be moved to improve their lot. To some extent, assumptions about friendly visiting went beyond *noblesse oblige* because it captured the hope that interclass contact would benefit *all* classes and promote a sense of fellowship and community.[34]

While interclass contact had the potential of facilitating understanding between all parties, the role of the visitor in "showing" the poor the way to independence was the key element of friendly visiting. The Reverend D. O. Kellogg asserted in 1880 that pauperism was a "sign of moral weakness" and that the "victims of unsociable habits" needed "to see a world of pleasure and honor opened to them in the companionship of the refined and the pure-souled." He further noted, "Qualities of mind and heart are learned not only by imitation, but by contagion.... The educational power of association is of incalculable strength."[35] Also in 1880, Paine noted, "Volunteer visiting is the only hope of civilization against the gathering curse of pauperism in great cities."[36]

In the name of friendship, the friendly visitor would establish contact with a family. She sought to gain the trust of the family as she exerted her personal influence over the family. The visitor often approached the poor as one would approach a child in need of molding—a gentle push in this direction, a more forceful nudge in another direction. The poor were not seen as inherently bad or unsalvageable but as wayward children unable to know or act on what was best for them.[37] These attitudes reflect the paternalism that often dominated the personal service provided to the needy. The visitors, as they saw themselves, were simply being neighborly and trying to establish common bonds with a fellow neighbor. Although these may have been the images the visitors attempted to project, the visitors and "visitees" were definitely not equals and were separated by class and other boundaries. The likelihood of true friendships developing was minimized by these differences.

The use of personal service through friendly visiting was predicated on the assumption that the poor would be receptive to these visitors entering their homes. Indeed, the visitors were able to make hundreds, even thousands, of visits, and this could be used to attest to the value the poor placed in this service. It could also be argued that the visitors and visitees shared common goals and also had mutual interest. An alternative explanation for why the visitors were able to gain access to their cases can be found in the power-dependence relationship that existed between the two.[38] Because the friendly visitors had access to resources that were desired by the visitees, the friendly visitors were thus able to wield some influence over the families. In this case, a needy family would be unlikely to refuse the visitor entry to the home and even less likely to question or overtly resist her "guidance."

Although friendly visiting is championed as the mainstay of the COS and frequently cited as the core activity, it is not clear to what extent the COS actually utilized this personal service approach to attacking poverty. In research on the history of the charity society movement, Lewis provided some data on this subject.[39] It is difficult to determine a pattern from the available data, but numbers for specific societies in 1892 were reported. For example, Boston had 683 visitors, Brooklyn had 532, and Baltimore reported 195. These were the only societies that appeared to have a pool to accommodate a significant portion of their caseloads. New York had only 218 friendly visitors and served about 7,500 cases a year. Data further revealed that 53 societies reported having over 3,500 friendly visitors with 1,628 coming from the four societies just mentioned. Some 44 societies provided assistance to almost 75,000 cases. These figures, coupled with the fact that the visitors averaged a caseload from one to four families, led Lewis to conclude that "the service of a friendly visitor was available to a small minority of the societies' beneficiaries."[40]

It appears that the exercising of discretion was also a significant aspect of the COS technology. The societies had to make some determination about the distribution of their friendly visitors since every case could not be assigned a visitor. This means that specific case factors, specific friendly visitor factors, and/or specific organizational factors were instrumental in the decision-making process.

The Charity Organization Societies had three other primary aspects in addition to relying on friendly visitations: (1) the careful study of every case, (2) developing and maintaining central registration procedures, and (3) planning and coordination between charity agencies.[41] The thrust of the intervention was directed toward uncovering the circumstances surrounding a family's impoverished state and developing a response to the family. The technology was, in fact, derived from the manner in which the societies' organizers and their supporters defined poverty and individual responsibility. The focus on the individual in problem definition gave rise to the focus on the individual in the search for problem resolution.

The external polity and the external economy of the COS dictated that conservative approaches be pursued by the organizations. The organizations emerged from political boundaries that favored the middle and upper classes and defined the "appropriate" change strategies to develop. Within the organizations, the polity and economy favored techniques that focused on individual-level interventions. Case-by-case investigations could reveal the underlying causes for the family's plight and form the basis of directed assistance. The organizational constitution was framed by powerful volunteers who felt it was their duty to help the needy; the power held by the providers of financial support to the organization; and a reliance on investigation and friendly visiting.

Because the actual provision of monetary assistance was often secondary to scientific case investigations, the COS garnered a reputation for being miserly and stingy. An Irish poet, John Boyle O'Reilly, poked fun at the Boston organization by penning these sarcastic lines:

> The organized charity, scrimped and iced,
> In the name of a cautious, statistical Christ.[42]

This ditty also targets the role religion played in justifying the Charity Organization Societies' approach to financial assistance. Clearly, with the COS, personal service was seen as the major intervention rather than material help. The poor of the day may have not embraced this concept as enthusiastically as the COS organizers.

Case-by-case investigations was a means of curtailing the willy-nilly almsgiving that had dominated charity work in the previous years. This scientific approach to charity produced numerous detailed reports on the conditions of various groups in U.S. urban settings. For example, the Charity Organization Department of the Russell Sage Foundation, under the directorship of Mary Richmond, studied 985 widows known to nine COS in 1910.[43] This report captures both the emphasis on individual circumstances and the moralizing that so dogged COS efforts. Some 61 individual cases are presented to depict the most difficult cases. In noting the characteristics of these 61 widows as mothers, such categorizations as good, fair, immoral, untidy with poor children, untruthful and extravagant, very low standards, and intemperate are used.

According to this study, for the 799 cases for which the cause of the husband's death was recorded, 29 percent of the deaths were due to tuberculosis, and other health-related causes totaled about another 25 percent. This meant that over half of the wives became widows because of illness or disease. In addition, 9 percent had lost their husband through an industrial accident. Furthermore, over half of these industrial death widows collected no damages from the accident. As reported in the previous chapter, living conditions contributed to the incidence of illness among the poorer populations confined to the worst areas of the city. As also pointed out in Chapter 2, many workers toiled in unsafe jobs in hazardous settings. It is not surprising, then, that numerous families were thrust into destitution with the death of the breadwinner.

The COS did not tackle the larger structural problems surrounding the causes of widowhood. These organizations appeared to accept the environment as a given and to devote their efforts to helping families cope with and respond to their crisis. The COS helped families secure medical assistance, provided dietary instruction, and offered the services of volunteer visitors. Volunteers acted in a variety of ways. For example, they taught children housework; monitored the schooling of the children; secured special medical help; taught cooking, sewing, and record keeping; found work for some women; and met many emergencies.

COS responses were, thus, predictable. The external and internal polities and economies blinded these organizations to the larger picture that placed individual ills in a social context. Because those involved in the COS movement were beneficiaries of the fruits of society and were convinced that success was a combination of hard work and moral living, they saw hardships as tests of human nature. The fact that thousands of individuals were being harshly tested may have reinforced the view that poorer classes were defective and in need of moral guidance.

There was another means by which the COS sought to achieve their goals, and this vehicle is often overlooked in the COS history literature. The ideologies and individuals are not the only examples of the social control aspect of the COS. A more concrete and vivid example rests with the organizations' reliance on the police for controlling immoral, as well as illegal, behavior. For example, COS administrators often found poor communities with recreational activities consisting of penny arcades and small theaters to be a problem. Stage managers kept "a weather eye open for the social worker, with a policeman in tow, out to preserve the integrity of the American home."[44] Furthermore, the New York COS hired a detective in 1886 to investigate beggars and then had 200 loiterers arrested and jailed.[45] One Chicago district COS agent, Eugene Lies, advocated in 1905 for "close cooperation of police and charities"; the establishment of a "squad of state police" to apprehend and prosecute vagrants; and the "establishment of a mendicancy police corps in Chicago."[46] Although this position may have been extreme, its extremeness was not the reason for its lack of implementation. The massive politics involved in such a plan and the lack of interagency coordination can be blamed.

For numerous groups in society, police officers were not viewed as helpful or supportive. In some cases, as noted in Chapter 2, the police themselves were often involved in perpetrating acts of violence against specific groups. For the COS, however, the police became a significant part of the "treatment" process. Activities and individuals could be controlled with the swift action of a police officer and the societies were not hesitant in applying the force of the law.

Other organizations had special departments that enforced anti-vagrancy. For example, the New York COS maintained such a special department and reported on the 1885 activities of the special officer: "Our special officer, in addition to daily inspection of some of their [vagrants and beggars] various resorts, has caused the arrest, warned, and investigated upwards of 700 beggars, of whom 63½% were able-bodied men and women capable of earning an honest living…216 of these were arrested."[47] In some ways, the

COS exerted a heavy hand over those unfortunate enough to seek out an existence on the urban streets. These enforcement activities seemed to be aimed at the total removal of "immoral" people and "immoral" activities from city landscape. For many individuals, the law-enforcement aspects of the COS overshadowed the other COS interventions.

The COS and Immigrants

The COS devoted much effort in assisting immigrants in adapting to U.S. society. After all, it was the rapid growth of cities and the concomitant social ills (presented in Chapter 2) that triggered the search for more creative ways of responding to these societal transitions. The economic cycles of growth, recession, and depression added to the already long list of problems facing both the immigrant and native American populations. While the native-born groups faced primarily economic hardships, the foreign-born population faced this in addition to issues around adapting to their new home. According to Johnson and Schwartz, the COS did focus their concern on "this group of unadapted, newly urbanized people" in their hopes of helping them "establish a life-style congruent" with the "urban American societal system."[48] Ehrenreich went on to assert that charity agencies and social workers imposed their "ideas of proper living habits, family patterns, and behaviors" that defined "right living" in their work with immigrants.[49] In addition, immigrants were not conspicuous among the friendly visitors, paid agents, or directors, and this absence further attests to the middle-class Protestant American base of the COS.[50]

The COS thus became a vehicle for facilitating the Americanization of immigrant groups. Families were taught the art of housekeeping and the value of cleanliness. The social origins of the American emphasis on cleanliness can apparently be traced to the Progressive Era when immigrants were viewed as "dirty" and acculturation and assimilation required them to become "clean."[51] The COS became agents for transmitting the value of cleanliness. Many of the COS thus maintained the same position toward the new immigrants as did other Progressives (discussed in Chapter 2): They needed to be Americanized. With this goal in mind, numerous friendly visitors and paid agents set about the task of "encouraging" these newcomers to adopt American child-rearing practices, medical practices, diet, and clothing.[52]

The wave of "new" immigrants flooding the country at the turn of the century (described in Chapter 2), however, posed unique challenges for the COS. Indeed, the COS rose to meet these challenges but carried with them the same nativism that marked other Progressives. As noted in Chapter 2, these antiforeign sentiments were directed against those immigrants with darker coloring and starkly "foreign" cultures, languages, and practices. The *Thirteenth Annual Report* of the Associated Charities of Boston, published in 1882, captured the frustrations experienced by COS workers and volunteers: "Until the Italians became numerous, we had at least intelligent means of communication with most of the families we knew. . . [but the Italians] are truly foreign to us. We do not speak a common language; our standards have no meaning to them, and we may well doubt whether they have any applicability."[53]

In addition, in a review of the cases handled by the Minneapolis COS from 1900 to 1930, Stadum noted that culture and ethnicity were given slight attention and, in a third of the cases she studied, workers failed to indicate their nationality.[54] This slight attention may have been because the COS of this city did not include many of these "new" immigrants on their personal service caseloads. For example, the 1910 annual report of this organization stated that eastern Europeans did not understand America, nor did America understand them.[55]

These immigrants were not among those cases held in high regard by the friendly visitors. Although these families did receive services, it does not appear that services were offered with the same frequency and intensity as those offered to the more favored groups. This may be an area in which discretion was exercised to determine which cases would receive the attention of the friendly visitors.

The study of 985 widows known to COS in 1910 gives a glimpse into the caseloads of the COS.[56] In this report, 61 case summaries are presented with summary paragraphs that indicate the nationality of the widows. Of these 61, well over half were from the "desirable" immigrant countries of northern and central Europe. Only a quarter of the widows were from eastern and southern Europe. About another 16 percent were native-born Americans. Of those from the "undesirable" countries, 60 percent were Italians. These figures could mean that the friendly visitors and the paid agents were more comfortable working with those families who were more "American" and were further along on the assimilation continuum. It could also mean that those individuals with more "foreign" cultures were not socialized in the help-seeking process and did not have cultures that supported intervention by strangers. Whatever the reason, it does appear that personal and other services were available on a limited basis to the "new" immigrants.

Thus, the focus on the individual emerged in the COS work with the White ethnic groups. The key to the success of these groups, according to COS ideology, was adaptation, assimilation, and personal initiative. Many COS studied the extent of poverty within these various groups to ascertain those group characteristics that either encouraged or discouraged pauperism.[57] The Charity Organization Societies, therefore, were committed to assisting the "new" immigrants in eradicating those traits deemed undesirable so that Americanization could be facilitated.

The COS and Ethnic/Racial Minorities

Because the COS were products of the urban areas of the East and Midwest, the ethnic/racial minorities in those areas would appear to be the logical groups on which to focus. As noted in Chapters 2 and 3, American Indians were confined to reservations, the Mexicans were concentrated in the Southwest, and the Chinese and Japanese were primarily located in the West. African Americans were the only group with a significant population in those areas with COS, and this group dominates the discussion here.

It has been generally asserted that African Americans were rarely the beneficiaries of COS services.[58] Because the COS engaged in several types of activities, an overview of their activities and services to and on behalf of African Americans becomes necessary. One major COS activity, as previously indicated, was thorough investigations of social problems. African Americans were the focus of some of these studies.

The Charity Organization Societies were instrumental in publishing reports and investigations in their journals on the conditions of African Americans. Although studies of other ethnic minority groups were also reported, these studies were relatively infrequent.[59] The COS provided significantly more coverage of issues pertaining to African Americans. For example, the June 1897 issue of *The Charities Review* reported on the second Atlanta University conference on problems of the urban African American that was held the month before. The September 1899 issue of *The Charities Review* contained an article of "The Negro's Fitness" with statistics on African Americans in educational pursuits. In addition, the October 7, 1905, special issue of *Charities*, according to its introduction, was "devoted from cover to cover to the social interests of the Negroes in the northern cities."[60] This issue offered reports on such topics as the West Indian Migration to New York, the housing problems faced by this group, and a census on the African-American population of Baltimore.

Alvin Kogut, in an article entitled "The Negro and the Charity Organization Society in the Progressive Era," reviewed the discussions about "Negroes" in the journals of the COS and noted that interest in this group was probably at its highest from 1903 to 1906.[61] The review indicated that the COS did concern themselves to a certain extent with the issues surrounding the urban African-American population. The COS reports have been particularly useful in documenting the extent of discrimination in housing and employment facing this group. Indeed, much of the information used in Chapter 2 to compare the plight of the "new" immigrants with that of the migrating African Americans came from early COS publications.

Kogut, and others, have also concluded that African Americans "probably benefitted even less than other segments of the population from ongoing services of the COS and from COS support of such broader reform measures as housing code enforcement and labor legislation."[62] In writing of the African Americans of Philadelphia during the Progressive Era, DuBois likewise observed that, while African Americans receive "their just proportion" of the alms distributed, "protective, rescue and reformatory work is not applied to any great extent among them."[63] Consequently, the COS reports and investigations of the social conditions of Americans did not translate into hands-on services to African Americans.

According to Kogut's content analysis, some COS believed that discrimination prevented them from obtaining employment for African Americans; thus, this group created unique problems for the COS. Rather than try to combat the discrimination impeding employment of African Americans, numerous Charity Organization Societies concluded that their services were of little benefit to this group. This is further affirmed by the widow study conducted by the Russell Sage Foundation.[64] In the 61 case summaries, only 2 were "colored" widows. The lack of meaningful intervention between the COS and African Americans apparently fostered a particular reputation in this minority community. For example, one New York District COS experienced a substantial migration of African Americans but had few African Americans applying for relief.[65] Fueling the schism between the COS and African Americans was "the patronizing Lady Bountiful attitude of some of the social service groups" that irritated African Americans to the point that help from these social service groups was rejected.[66]

While the White friendly visitors may not have been visiting African-American families, several organizations were still active in training African Americans to be friendly visitors.[67] For example, the availability of African-American friendly visitors in the Baltimore area led to the establishment of separate boards in several districts. The Associated Charities of Washington had enough African-American volunteers to hold a class to train them for friendly visiting. Hence, some COS were active in helping African Americans to work with African Americans.

In general, COS participants were aware of the prejudice and discrimination faced by thousands of African Americans relocating to the North. Journals documented the extent of housing segregation and employment discrimination. The African-American community's inability to escape the slums and the vices that the slums attracted was known to the COS. In the midst of this knowledge, the COS apparently had little to offer this impoverished group.

The lack of COS hands-on personal service work with African Americans can be attributed to several factors. According to Axinn and Levin: "Such interest in the plight of blacks as might have developed from direct contact was stifled by the relatively few blacks in the caseloads of Charity Organization Societies. Again, the small number of blacks in the North was partially responsible. In Chicago in 1900, for example, blacks numbered 108,000 in a total of 1,698,000. They ranked tenth among the city's ethnic groups."[68] As the numbers of African Americans increased with the tide of migration, COS practices may have been so firmly entrenched that expansion to include the "new" migrants was beyond COS capabilities. There were apparently other factors driving the COS responses that may have been masked by the small percentage of African Americans in the urban centers of the North. As the numbers increased, these other factors were able to rise to the surface.

The COS participants were products of the society in which they lived and were not immune to the racial ideologies that permeated society. As noted in Chapter 2, Progressives and reformers believed some ethnic groups could be "Americanized" and assimilated into the mainstream of U.S. society. These Progressives also perceived some groups as poor candidates for Americanization. The COS organizers, who were also part of the Progressive fabric of America, held the same opinion. After studying the COS reports and periodicals, Kogut noted:

> Significantly missing from the discussion in the periodicals was talk of "assimilation," although assimilation played a prominent role in relation to immigrants and immigration…. The goal of assimilation was not, however, held out for the Negro..... This shift in goal…symbolized the profound difference in white America's perception of the white immigrant and the Negro migrant…. But perhaps the major reason for COS behavior in regard to Negroes lies in the *racism that permeated society*" [emphasis added].[69]

Thus, the COS were not active in fighting or even seriously advocating for the rights of African Americans.

The racial ideology of the COS is illuminated in specific articles of the COS periodicals. For example, the October 7, 1905, special issue of *Charities* endorsed the opinion of Booker T. Washington that "the masses of colored people are not yet fitted to survive and prosper in the great northern cities" and the position of anthropologist Franz Boas that the Negro "shows the traits of a healthy primitive people with a considerable degree of personal initiative, a talent for organization, an imaginative power, technical skill and thrift."[70] It is not surprising that Booker T. Washington was frequently cited in COS publications. No person better exemplified charity's goal of fostering individualism within an ethnic group than Washington.[71]

The COS aligned themselves with individuals, both African American and non-African American, who espoused their views of the status and inferiority of African Americans. These paternalistic, patronizing views were not thought to be racist by those who held them. These views were believed to be sympathetic and in the best interest of this racial group because they held an optimism that African Americans were in an early stage of group development and, with time, would make needed progress. It does appear, however, that, in the minds of the COS participants and other Progressives, no amount of progress would place this group on par with the native-born Whites or the White ethnics.

In this October 7, 1905, issue of *Charities,* an article on "West Indian Migration to New York" noted that among these migrants "it may be said that a very desirable class, including recently numbers of intelligent women, take to domestic work and are very much in favor with their employers."[72] Belief of the suitability of African Americans for domestic and manual work found among Progressives and reformers was also present among the COS members. The February 6, 1904, issue of *Co-operation,* the journal of the Chicago Bureau of Charities, echoed this view in an article on an industrial program for African Americans in Virginia: "In a single generation, these women [mothers of pupils in the program] had lost the practice of those domestic arts which made the cooks and seamstresses of the slavery period so celebrated."[73] The potential of this group for other kinds of pursuits was not recognized as COS defined the parameters of opportunities available to them.

Another explanation for the COS stance on African American lies in the fact that the COS movement was not a reform movement. Improvement in the status of people was the result of changing individuals, not in changing society. The host of ills facing African Americans could not have been effectively cured by friendly visiting. Indeed, the disenfranchisement of African Americans required some sweeping structural changes. The COS were not really invested in defining the problems of African Americans as structural problems and were not convinced the existing social system needed revamping. Consequently, the primary interest of the COS was not in African Americans and not in their deprivation or segregation as factors requiring broad social reform.[74]

Clearly, numerous problems confronted African Americans as they migrated to the North and fell victim to urbanization, industrialization, and immigration. No one denied that color was a liability that exacerbated the social evils erupting around most immigrant and migrant groups. The COS were swamped with applications from those they felt they could help and there was not much assistance available to the more difficult cases. It seems that whatever was to be done for African Americans, in the minds of the COS, had to be done by African Americans themselves. The COS and other reformers of the day supported and advocated individual responsibility while adding to it the concept of ethnic group responsibility.[75]

An adherence to the doctrine of ethnic group responsibility as emphatically applied to African Americans is identifiable in the COS writings of the period. COS journals routinely reported on the efforts of African Americans to reform, improve, and assist themselves. The October 1897 issue of *The*

Charities Review described and applauded the work of African Americans on behalf of their own people.[76] Named were a "colored philanthropist" in Chicago who established a home for the elderly and a man of youth, intelligence, and experience who was appointed as professor at Tuskegee Institute of Alabama. An industrial school in South Carolina "started by the colored people themselves" also received recognition.

The special issue of *Charities*, October 7, 1905, has several references to the efforts of African Americans to improve themselves and results of the Atlanta University study on Negro crime—a study that was directed by African Americans. Indeed, the section of the issue entitled "Opportunity and Responsibility" crystallizes the role of ethnic group responsibility: "In his [the African American's] deprivation of one or the other [opportunity and responsibility] lies the explanation of much of what we call the Negro's problem."[77] Examples are then provided to show how a lack of responsibility and accountability resulted in some of the social ills that befell African Americans.

The 1902–1903 annual report of the Indianapolis Benevolent Society observed that African Americans were becoming involved in philanthropic activities in their communities and stressed that "our citizens should give these movements all the encouragement and support possible."[78] The June 1897 issue of *The Charities Review* contained a report of the second Atlanta University conference on problems of African Americans in the cities, and this report conveys the COS doctrine of ethnic group responsibility. Although several resolutions were adopted at the conference, only one was actually quoted in the article—"that the negro must reform himself, and that he is not dependent upon charity or municipal regulations, but has the means in his own hands."[79] This resolution was synonymous with the sentiments of the COS and for that reason, was given prominence in *The Charities Review* article.

The COS did not entirely neglect or disregard the needs of African Americans. Investigations into the group's social conditions helped to expose the harsh realities surrounding the stigma of race in the United States. Doling out of alms to this community and the provision of personal services to a limited few should not go unrecognized. The contributions of the COS to this racial minority group is, however, significantly less than those provided to the White ethnic immigrants who also crowded the cities during this time. The Charity Organization Societies were products of their environments and were dependent on the public for funding, support, and legitimation. Those individuals inside the COS implemented the beliefs and ideologies that were extant in the larger society. In order to survive and maintain themselves, these organizations had to continue to embrace the groups and ideologies that gave them life.

The lack of COS emphasis on the needs of ethnic minority groups has often been minimized due to the prominent place of the settlement house movement in the quest for social reform. It is often assumed that whatever deficits incurred in the COS movement were more than made up for in the settlement houses. For this reason, a closer look at the settlement house movement is warranted.

ENDNOTES

1. Miguel Montiel and Paul Wong, "A Theoretical Critique of the Minority Perspective," *Social Casework 64* (February 1983): 112.

2. Discussion in this section is drawn from Ralph Anderson and Ira Carter, *Human Behavior in the Social Environment—A Systems Approach*, Fourth Edition (New York: Aldine De Gruyter, 1990); Ludwig von Bertalanffy, "General System Theory and Psychiatry," in *American Handbook of Psychiatry, Vol. I*, Second Edition, ed. Silvano Arieti (New York: Basic Books, 1974); Daniel Katz and Robert Kahn, *The Social Psychology of Organizations*, Second Edition (New York: John Wiley and Sons, 1978), pp. 23–33; David Nadler, "Managing Organizational Change: An Integrative Perspective," *The Journal of Applied Behavioral Science 17*, number 2 (1981): 192–194; F. Ellen Netting, Peter Kettner, and Steven McMurtry, *Social Work Macro Practice* (New York: Longman, 1993), pp. 139–140; Christopher Petr, "The Worker-Client Relationship: A General Systems Perspective," *Social Casework 69* (December 1988): 621–624; and Mary Zey-Ferrell, *Dimensions of Organizations: Environment, Context, Structure, Process, and Performance* (Santa Monica, CA: Goodyear, 1979), pp. 40–42.

3. Bertalanffy, "General System Theory," p. 1100.

4. Ralph Anderson and Irl Carter provide a detailed discussion of nonplace communities such as kinship and professional communities in *Human Behavior in the Social Environment*, pp. 69–96.

5. Anderson and Carter, *Human Behavior in the Social Environment*, p. 44.

6. The discussion presented here is drawn from J. Kenneth Benson, "Interorganizational Network as a Political Economy," *Administrative Science Quarterly 20* (June 1975): 229–249; Yeheskel Hasenfeld, *Human Service Organizations* (Englewood Cliffs, NJ: Prentice Hall, 1983), pp. 43–49; David Powell, "Managing Organizational Problems in Alternative Service Organizations," *Administration in Social Work 10* (Fall 1986): 59–61; Gary Wamsley and Mayer Zald, *The Political Economy of Public Organizations* (Lexington, MA: Lexington Books, 1973); and Mayer Zald, "Political Economy: A Framework for Comparative Analysis," in *Power in Organizations*, ed. Mayer Zald (Nashville: Vanderbilt University Press, 1970), pp. 221–261.

7. Zald, "Political Economy," p. 223.

8. Hasenfeld, *Human Service Organizations*, p. 44.

9. Zald, "Political Economy," p. 225.

10. Mayer Zald offers a detailed discussion of organizational constitutions in "Political Economy," pp. 225–229.

11. Powell, "Managing Organizational Problems," p. 59.

12. Powell, "Managing Organizational Problems," p. 59.

13. John Ehrenreich, *The Altruistic Imagination* (Ithaca, NY: Cornell University Press, 1985), p. 41.

14. Bruce Jansson, *The Reluctant Welfare State*, Second Edition (Pacific Grove, CA: Brooks/Cole, 1993), p. 130.

15. Michael Reisch and Stanley Wenocur, "The Future of Community Organization in Social Work: Social Activism and the Politics of Profession Building," *Social Service Review 60* (March 1986): 74.

16. Ralph Dolgoff and Donald Feldstein, *Understanding Social Welfare*, Second Edition (New York: Longman, 1984), p. 261; Roy Lubove, *The Professional Altruist* (New York: Atheneum, 1969), p. 2.

17. Stephen H. V. Gurteen, *A Handbook of Charity Organization* (Buffalo: The Author, 1882), pp. 27–35.

18. David Wagner, "Collective Mobility and Fragmentation: A Model of Social Work History," *Journal of Sociology and Social Welfare 13* (September 1986): 667.

19. Robert Treat Paine, Jr., "The Work of Volunteer Visitors of the Associated Charities Among the Poor," *Journal of Social Science 12* (December 1880): 112.

20. James Lane, "Jacob A. Riis and Scientific Philanthropy during the Progressive Era," *Social Service Review 47* (March 1973): 39.

21. As quoted in Verl Lewis, "The Development of the Charity Organization Movement in the United States 1875–1900: Its Principles and Methods" (D.S.W. diss., Western Reserve University, 1954), pp. 185–186.

22. Lubove, *The Professional Altruist*, p. 9.

23. Kenneth Kusmer, "The Functions of Organized Charity in the Progressive Era: Chicago as a Case Study," *Journal of American History 60* (December 1973): 659–660.

24. Robert Paine, Jr., "The Work of Volunteer Visitors of the Associated Charities Among the Poor," *Journal of Social Science 12* (December 1880): 105.

25. Kusmer, "The Functions of Organized Charity," p. 660.

26. Dolgoff and Feldstein, *Understanding Social Welfare*, p. 261; Louise Johnson and Charles Schwartz, *Social Welfare: A Response to Human Need*, Second Editon (Boston: Allyn and Bacon, 1991), pp. 8, 16. These roots of social work have also been noted in numerous other sources.

27. Wagner, "Collective Mobility and Fragmentation," p. 667.

28. Ralph Pumphrey and Muriel Pumphrey, "The Charity Organization Society," in *The Heritage of American Social Work*, ed. Ralph Pumphrey and Muriel Pumphrey (New York: Columbia University Press, 1961), p. 169.

29. Kusmer, "The Functions of Organized Charity," pp. 672, 674.

30. Beverly Stadum, "A Critique of Family Case Workers 1900–1930: Women Working with Women," *Journal of Sociology and Social Welfare 16* (September 1990): 74. See also C. A. Chambers, "Women in the Creation of the Profession of Social Work," *Social Service Review 60* (March 1986): 1–33.

31. Lubove, *The Professional Altruist*, p. 5.

32. See for example, Ehrenreich, *The Altruistic Imagination*; M. E. Gettleman, "Charity and Social Classes in the United States," I, II, *American Journal of Economics and Sociology 22* (April, July 1963): 313–329; 417–426; J. Leiby, "Charity Organization Reconsidered," *Social Service Review 58* (December 1984): 523–538.

33. Paine, Jr., "The Work of Volunteer Visitors," p. 114.

34. Kusmer, "The Functions of Organized Charity," p. 662.

35. D. O. Kellogg, "The Principle and Advantage of Association in Charities," *Journal of Social Science 12* (December 1880): 89.

36. Paine, Jr., "The Work of Volunteer Visitors," p. 113.

37. Lubove, *The Professional Altruist*, p. 14.

38. For a discussion of the power-dependence perspective, see Yeheskel Hasenfeld, "Power in Social Work Practice," *Social Service Review 61* (September 1987): 472–475.

39. Lewis, "The Development of the Charity Organization Movement," pp. 190–191.

40. Lewis, "The Development of the Charity Organization Movement," pp. 190–191.

41. Dolgoff and Feldstein, *Understanding Social Welfare*, p. 261; Ray Johns and David DeMarche, *Community Organization and Agency Responsibility* (New York: Association Press, 1951), p. 39.

42. Quoted in numerous sources, including James Leiby, *A History of Social Welfare and Social Work in the United States* (New York: Columbia University Press, 1978), p. 116.

43. Mary Richmond and Fred Hall, *A Study of Nine Hundred and Eighty-five Widows* (New York: Russell Sage Foundation, 1913).

44. Albert McLean, as quoted in Kusmer, "The Functions of Organized Charity," p. 663.

45. Lane, "Jacob A. Riis and Scientific Philanthropy," p. 35.

46. As quoted in Kusmer, "The Functions of Organized Charities," p. 669.

47. As quoted in Lewis, "The Development of the Charity Organization Movement," p. 170.

48. Johnson and Schwartz, *Social Welfare*, p. 38.

49. Ehrenreich, *The Altruistic Imagination*, p. 31.

50. Lubove, *The Professional Altruist*, p. 16.

51. Ruth Cowan, Mark Rose, and Marsha Rose, "Clean Homes and Large Utility Bills 1900–1940," *Marriage and Family Review 9* (Fall 1985): 53–66.

52. As noted in Jansson, *The Reluctant Welfare State*, p. 113.

53. As quoted in Lubove, *The Professional Altruist*, p. 17.

54. Stadum, "A Critique of Family Case Workers," p. 85.

55. As quoted in Stadum, "A Critique of Family Case Workers," p. 85.

56. Richmond and Hall, *A Study of Nine Hundred and Eighty-Five Widows*, pp. 50–78.

57. Steven Diner, "Chicago Social Workers and Blacks in the Progressive Era," *Social Service Review 44* (December 1970): 394.

58. This conclusion can be found in, for example, Andrew Billingsley and Jeanne Giovannoni, *Children of the Storm* (New York: Harcourt Brace Jovanovich, 1972), p. 38; Patricia Hogan and Sau-Fong Siu, "Minority Children and the Child Welfare System: An Historical Perspective," *Social Work 33* (November 1988): 494.

59. An example is the report on "Mexican Immigrants in the United States," that was published in *The Survey 28* (September 7, 1912): 726–730.

60. The Negro in the Cities of the North," *Charities 15* (October 7, 1905): 1.

61. Alvin Kogut, "The Negro and the Charity Organization in the Progressive Era," *Social Service Review 44* (March 1970): 14–19.

62. Kogut, "The Negro and the Charity Organization," pp. 19–20.

63. W. E. B. DuBois, *The Philadelphia Negro: A Social Study* (New York: Schocken Books, 1967), pp. 357–358.

64. Richmond and Hall, *A Study of Nine Hundred and Eighty-five Widows*, pp. 50–78.

65. Kogut, "The Negro and the Charity Organization Society," p. 13.

66. Florette Henri, *Black Migration: Movement North 1900-1920* (Garden City, NY: Anchor Press/Doubleday, 1975), p. 126.

67. Kogut, "The Negro and the Charity Organization," pp. 13–14.

68. June Axinn and Herman Levin, *Social Welfare—A History of the American Response to Need*, Second Edition (New York: Harper & Row, 1982), p. 151.

69. Kogut, "The Negro and the Charity Organization Society," p. 20.

70. "The Negro of the Cities of the North," p. 1.

71. Steven Diner, "Chicago Social Workers and Blacks in the Progressive Era," *Social Service Review* 44 (December 1970): 394.

72. "West Indian Migration to New York," *Charities* 15 (October 5, 1905): 2.

73. As quoted in Diner, "Chicago Social Workers and Blacks in the Progressive Era," p. 395.

74. Axinn and Levin, *Social Welfare*, p. 151.

75. Andrew Billingsley and Jeanne Giovannoni, *Children of the Storm* (New York: Harcourt Brace Jovanovich, 1972), p. 23.

76. "The Negro," *The Charities Review* 7 (October 1897): 718.

77. "Opportunity and Responsibility," *Charities* 15 (October 7, 1905): 1.

78. As quoted in Kogut, "The Negro and the Charity Organization Society," p. 13.

79. "The Negro," *The Charities* 6 (June 1897): 379.

Chapter 5

Ethnicity, Race, Reform, and the Evolution of Social Work

The settlement house movement has the distinction of being the precursor to social work's interest in and commitment to social reform. Community organization, advocacy, and other methods facilitate interventions with numerous types of social systems. Social workers have boasted about the settlement houses, often to counteract attacks on what some have perceived as an indifferent stance on social reform. There is, however, a hidden side to the settlement houses—a side that is too infrequently mentioned. For the most part, the settlement house movement is little more than a penumbra, with the social reform elements receiving all the attention while the core settlement house technologies remain hidden from view.

This penumbra has prevented the profession from critically analyzing its reform role as it related historically to ethnic/racial minority groups. The egregious treatment of these groups at the hands of the larger social systems in which they were situated seemed to warrant aggressive economic, political, and social interventions. For this reason, the reform nature of the forming profession was a potentially more powerful ally for the ethnic and racial minorities in this country. Consequently, an examination is warranted of the historical role of social work's social reform in mitigating the conditions of minorities. This analysis also contains an examination of the effects of professionalization and bureaucratization on the social reform thrust of social work.

THE SETTLEMENT HOUSE MOVEMENT

Settlement houses, like Charity Organization Societies (COS), were English imports.[1] In England, the houses provided opportunities for university men to dwell in the poorer sections of town to provide services and to contemplate the best approaches to society's social problems. As developed in that country, the settlement house "was simply a residence for university men in a city slum."[2] The first settlement house in the United States was the Neighborhood Guild, renamed University Settlement, established in New York in 1886. The mission of the first settlement house was to provide a place for the educated to live or settle among the poor immigrants to generate the sense of neighborliness that would develop good citizens.[3] Many of the first settlement houses in the United States were affiliated with educational institutions and religious groups. The idea soon caught on as settlement houses proliferated in cities across the country. According to the *Handbook of Settlements* (1911), there were 74 settlements in 1897, 103 in 1900, 204 in 1905, and 413 listed in this 1911 handbook.[4]

The University Settlement provides a vivid example of the goals and activities of a large settlement house located in a major urban city. It was located on the Lower East Side of New York City in a slum neighborhood.[5] As outlined in its constitution, this settlement sought to "bring men and women of education into closer relations with the laboring classes in this city, for their mutual benefit. The society shall establish and maintain in the tenement house districts places of residence for college men and others desirous of aiding in the work, with rooms where the people of the neighborhood may meet for social and educational purposes."[6] The charter of Hull House, another well-known settlement established in 1889 by Jane Addams and Ellen Starr, described its mission: "To provide a center for the higher civic and social life; to institute and maintain educational and philanthropic enterprises, and to investigate and improve the conditions in the industrial districts of Chicago."[7]

According to the *Handbook of Settlements*, residents of the University Settlement conducted sociological investigations of the neighborhood, advocated for improved housing, worked for improved sanitation conditions, secured play areas and equipment for neighborhood children, served as school trustees, aided in the organization of unions, protested against corrupt politicians, opened their doors for a branch of a loan society to help ease economic hardship accompanying depressions, educated neighborhood residents about local politics, helped in the passage of a juvenile court law, and testified before state and national committees. The activities of Hull House and numerous other settlement houses were similar in nature to those of the University Settlement.

The settlement house represents the reform history of social work because of the energy that was directed toward improving the conditions of the slum neighborhoods. Efforts were undertaken to promote legislation for improving the social climate of the neighborhoods in which they existed. Settlement house workers lived in the blighted areas and learned from personal experience the extent and consequences of poverty. These workers attempted to mobilize neighborhood residents to organize, advocate, and press for needed changes. Locally based actions often grew into social action as settlement organizers recognized the power of the environment in the lives of individuals and fought to change that environment. The environment and its array of deleterious social conditions were the targets of change. Social casework started in the COS, whereas the settlement house movement gave rise to social group work, community organization, and social action.[8]

In the midst of its focus on social reform, Charity Organization Societies and the settlement houses were still similar in several areas.[9] Both organizations were devoted to teaching the poor the middle-class way of life and attached a morality to poverty. For both, the road to self-sufficiency was paved with hard work, commitment, and not yielding to the vices of life. In addition, Protestantism was a driving force in both the COS and the settlement house. Furthermore, the settlement house worker was, to a certain degree, similar to the friendly visitor. The friendly visitor of the settlement house, however, worked from the inside out, rather than from the outside in, and did not just visit but moved in for a rather sustained period of time.

Like their COS counterparts, the settlement house workers also felt obligated to help those who were less fortunate and "to give something back" in exchange for the privileges they enjoyed. They wanted to use their education and class position to make a significant difference in the world in which they lived. Because the manner in which they made their contribution was so dramatic (changing their lives as well as place of residence), these organizers were also fulfilling a personal need to participate actively and meaningfully in the world around them—a world that included poverty, destitution, and countless examples of harsh human suffering.

Inputs for the Settlement House Movement

The ideology of the settlement house movement reflected in varying degrees *noblesse oblige*, social gospel, socialism, social reform, and a belief in cooperation between social classes.[10] Settlers believed in the capacity of people, regardless of their social status, for personal, economic, spiritual, and social growth. Settlement house residents extended their beliefs to encompass the duty of society in assisting its citizens in maximizing their growth in these areas. Although the targeting of pauperism by the COS reduced the social problem to the individual level, the targeting of *poverty* by the settlement house organizers expanded the social problem to a more global, societal level. The settlement house philosophy also placed the "settlement" in the midst of the slums, to live among the poor, to share their lives and culture with the poor, to become a part of the neighborhood, and to experience life's hardships firsthand.[11]

Although it is difficult to summarize the settlement outlook (the word *settlement* was eventually used freely and loosely[12]), the writings of those closely affiliated with the movement provide some insight into the ideologies driving the movement. Jane Addams of Hull House (Chicago) saw the settlements as attempting "to add the social function to democracy." According to Graham Taylor of the Chicago Commons, "It [the settlement] seeks to unify and help all other organizations and people in the neighborhood that make righteousness and brotherhood....[The settlement] aspires to be a center of the best social life and interests of the people." The second annual report of New York's East Side House reads, "All men of every class have something to give and something to get. Let the disposition to do good through others' agency be supplanted as far as possible by the desire to know and to do it first hand." Vida Scudder of the Philadelphia College Settlement echoed the significance of personal experience in the slum neighborhood by asserting that, through such an experience, "one has at least placed one's life at the point of greatest need in the modern world, between those alienated classes which cry out for a mediator."[13]

Jane Addams summarized three major motives she felt drew settlers together: (1) a desire to push society from political democracy to social democracy by translating democracy into social terms, (2) a desire to "share the race life" of the masses and aid in racial progress, and (3) the desire to "express the spirit of Christ" by stimulating a Christian movement toward humanitarianism.[14] The settlement houses offered reformers an opportunity to practice their beliefs in a way that put them in direct contact with the impoverished classes. Unlike the friendly visitors who visited and then went home to their comfortable surroundings, the settlers changed their lives by moving into the slum neighborhoods, putting on their work gloves, and working alongside the poor. According to Wagner: "The settlements were the Peace Corps or Vista of a generation of young people (primarily women) in the 1890–1914 period who sought to escape home and join a vibrant, altruistic movement which also linked economic, political, social and philosophical concerns."[15]

Settling in the slums and ghettos of the city was a tremendous challenge for the settlement house residents. They faced all the unsavory conditions of the slums that were detailed in Chapter 2. These educated, genteel men and women of comfortable means were willing to forego or temporarily put aside their lifestyle in order to touch a foreign, unseemly world teeming with every social ill imaginable.

The settlement house movement also achieved uniqueness by focusing attention on the socialization of the "normal, adequately functioning family."[16] With adequate resources and sufficient opportunity, the poor were envisioned as rising from the grips of destitution to take their rightful, respected place in society. The social ills confronting impoverished communities were attributed less to the moral weaknesses of the individual and more to the social and economic climate surrounding the individual. Thus, neighborhoods and communities were the target of intervention and the individual became the vehicle for affecting change at these levels. The settlers believed in the power of cooperation between settlement residents and community residents in the quest to vitalize slum neighborhoods.

Even though the settlers sought a "oneness" with the slum residents, settlers were often aware of the schism that existed between them and those living around them. The settlers rarely actually suffered or experienced the poverty and destitution that afflicted families in the neighborhoods. Some settlers even believed that their presence in the neighborhoods was a sham and that the settlement was "nothing but a high flown 'ambassador' among these suffering swarms."[17] Although the mission of the movement was to reduce the social distance between the classes, some traces of that distance were difficult to erase. In addition, within the settlement house itself, settlers often maintained their own separate, insulated world, which further suggests that, for many settlement houses, integration into the communities was somewhat superficial.

Socialization for life often meant socialization for American life or Americanization of the immigrant communities. In fact, the Americanization movement was spearheaded by the settlement houses and spanned the period from the 1890s to the 1920s.[18] Settlers believed that immigrants needed to learn about U.S. culture and values in order to benefit from the riches offered in America. The settlement houses incorporated an adherence to the melting pot view of society that was discussed in Chapter 2.

Examples of the significance of Americanization to the settlement house movement can be found throughout the 1911 *Handbook of Settlements*.[19] For example, a description of the neighborhood surrounding the Northwestern University Settlement of Chicago noted, "All about us the problem of the Americanization of foreign peoples is being slowly worked out, and 'Americans in process' is the order of the day."[20] The goals of Friendship House, in Washington, DC, were aimed "to promote temperance, thrift and self-control" and to "awaken an interest in civic improvement and establish the foundations of honest and progressive citizenship"[21] Zion House, in New York, was founded in 1893 to provide a place "where the elements of good citizenship can be inculcated and fostered."[22] In Erie, Pennsylvania, the Neighborhood House sought "to raise the standard of living and make better citizens of the foreigners in the neighborhood."[23]

In addition to ideology, another significant input for the settlement house movement was the pool of settlers that resided in the houses. The American settlement house movement drew on two sources for settlers—the clergy (as did the British movement) and the college woman (who was not part of the British movement)—and relied heavily on women, as college women made up 70 percent of the settlement residents.[24] As were the friendly visitors of the COS, the settlers were generally middle-class women.

The charter of the College Settlements Association, an association that was organized in 1890, specifically addressed the role of women in the settlement house movement: "The association would unite all college women... in the trend of a great modern movement; would touch them with a common ideal. Young students... should be quickened in their years of vague aspiration and purely speculative energy by possessing a share in a broad practical work."[25] The settlements provided these women a chance for personal fulfillment, self-realization, and accomplishment beyond home, family, and the traditional role of teacher.[26] Many college-educated women felt stifled by prevailing norms that prohibited their participation in politics and gainful employment. Through the settlements, these women could satisfy their desire to do, be, or accomplish while at the same time helping the neighborhoods achieve their potential.

Jane Addams, daughter of one of the richest men in northern Illinois,[27] wrote of the betrayal of educated women by a society that constrained the choices available to them. Addams saw settlement house work as the salvation for these women, including herself, because through "social mothering" and "civic housekeeping" the traditional role of nurturer was preserved.[28] The friendly visitors may have been responding to a similar need. Thus, women were creating a place for themselves through their helping activities.

While creating a place for themselves in administering to others, women were also defining for themselves a role steeped in service and practically void of substantial financial remuneration. Because many of the settlers either relied on the benevolence of others or had family funds, the volunteer nature often came to be assumed. The reward for the work, consequently, lay not with financial compensation but with the meaning of the mission for the workers. For many, especially daughters of ministers, settlement work was an extension of the missionary movement as the settlers tried to uplift the poor.[29] Even today, the "calling" to a mission is still part of social work as the worker's motivation, moral incentive, and rich awareness of the greater ends to be served continue to be prominent.[30] Thus, the work itself becomes its own reward.

Another significant input to the settlement house movement was the external economy and external polity. Settlement houses required legitimation and financial backing in order to be maintained and to expand. For many of the political Progressives of the day, the settlement houses were "politically correct" in their focus and activities, and received support from philanthropists and corporate donors.

As was noted in Chapter 2, few reforms were enacted without the tacit approval, if not the guidance, of large corporate interests.[31] Within the dominant elite class of society, the Progressives were able to join forces with settlement house residents to push for reforms that were perceived as liberal. Many of the corporate leaders sought to polish their rather tarnished images by supporting worthy causes and groups. Numerous welfare reforms of the Progressive Era were the result of the businessmen's movement teaming with the settlement house movement.

This teamwork would suggest that major reforms during the Progressive Era provided some relief for the masses while at the same time offering something to the big business sector. The child labor, or child-saving, movement is an excellent example. Historical accounts of the fight for child labor legislation indicate that the abolition of child labor was, to some degree, a means of driving out marginal tenement operators and other marginal businesses. Such legislation was generously supported by those business interests that did not depend on cheap, child labor. Children could be protected from exploitation, and big business could be stabilized, consolidated, and run more efficiently. At the same time, compulsory education was gaining more support, and child labor legislation fit neatly with compulsory education legislation. Furthermore, this child-saving movement was aligned with the traditional interest of women and was an appropriate area in which women could exercise social mothering.[32] In their quest for legislation to protect children, the settlement house leaders had the support of powerful, wealthy business leaders. This external economy and external polity were necessary for many of the reforms to be achieved.

The external polity and external economy also supported the settlement house Americanization efforts. Americanized workers were more productive and efficient workers. The settlement programs complemented the numerous programs provided by large companies. For example, the Ford Motor Company had mandatory English classes for the foreign born, and the first lesson commenced with a reading entitled "I Am a Good American."[33]

On the other hand, these inputs acted as constraints to the reform activities of the settlement houses. Settlers had to be careful not to alienate wealthy supporters by taking up unpopular causes.[34] Settlement houses depended on large donations to operate their programs and this dependency often defined the parameters of their reform targets.

The philosophy, the populace (service providers and service beneficiaries), external polity, and pecuniary base converged to form a service movement that has been heralded as the reform roots of modern social work.

Technologies of the Settlement House Movement

The settlement houses achieved goals through a number of means: local action; gathering and promulgating facts; preparing legislation; mobilizing forces for the passage of legislation; securing employment for community members; teaching English, occupational skills, domestic skills, and hygiene; teaching the poor the middle-class values that contributed to success; and stressing the value of self-help.[35]

The settlers, as did the COS participants, emphasized the importance of gathering facts and documenting the existence of problems. Jane Addams, Florence Kelley, and Julia Lathrop pioneered the social survey at Hull House and University of Chicago Settlement.[36] *The Hull House Maps and Papers* (1895) was the first systematic and detailed attempt to describe immigrant communities in an American city.[37] Harry Kraus, in *The Settlement House Movement in New York City, 1886–1914*, presented a detailed overview of the surveys and investigations that were completed by settlement house leaders.[38] The settlers saw the need to document social problems and compile data on housing, health, and employment. With this documentation, the settlers could then develop strategies for addressing and attacking the causes of social problems. More so than the COS, the settlers forged links with sociology and, therefore, colleges and universities. The basis for these linkages was reinforced by the college affiliation of the settlers and the settlement house appeal to the college-educated woman.

In terms of specific practices, the settlement houses offered space for union organizers to meet, provided a range of classes, organized clubs that facilitated community interaction, offered night classes, developed organizations that advocated for and protected the rights of immigrants, provided information and referred community residents to appropriate agencies for services, organized community residents to clean and improve their surroundings, invited community residents to house-sponsored recreational activities, and organized community residents to press local governments for such things as playgrounds, stricter enforcement of housing codes, and better city services. Settlers contributed to the push for child labor laws, women's labor laws, institutional care of the disabled and mentally retarded, child welfare services, and juvenile courts.[39]

Not all settlement houses, however, engaged in all these listed activities. Some houses were concerned only with the provision of club activities, whereas others were actively involved in advocacy and legislation. The most notable and large houses—Hull House, Chicago Commons, University Settlement, for example—are frequently cited as the prototypical settlement houses; however, they probably fall at the reform end of a continuum that ranges from extremely conservative to extremely liberal (reform oriented). The number of settlement houses peaked at 500 in 1915[40] and only a fraction of that number had ever participated in social reform work. The overwhelming majority had, however, developed clubs, classes, and recreation for their communities.

Children and young girls received a great deal of settlement house attention. Settlements generally provided day nurseries and kindergartens that freed mothers to work. Noel House (Washington, DC) settlers believed, as did most other settlers, that "the young people" were "in special danger."[41] With the exploitation of child workers and the seemingly inhumane treatment of juvenile offenders, passage of child labor laws and the creation of special services for youthful lawbreakers rose to the forefront of legislative activity. Settlers lobbied elected officials, sat on key boards and committees, ran for public office, and solicited the support of powerful individuals and groups. The perceived vunerability of the young female worker facilitated launching efforts to protect this segment of their population. For example, the University of Chicago Settlement wanted "to secure a boarding house for immigrant girls in order to mitigate the evils attendant on the 'boarder' habit of immigrants."[42] Consequently, these vulnerable groups enjoyed the benefits of the "social mothering" provided by settlers seeking to find a niche for their skills.

The deplorable housing and sanitary conditions of the densely populated urban settings (as detailed in Chapter 2) naturally led the settlers to focus on these areas. Creating a healthy, pleasant environment became the goals for numerous houses. Groups were organized to clean the streets themselves and/or to lobby for better services. Because children had no play areas except for the trash and manure-littered streets, playgrounds were also a priority. The settlement sometimes devoted some of its space to recreation activities for children. Cleaner streets and play areas were the products of the "civic housekeeping" of numerous settlement workers.

The settlement houses also evoked the strong arm of the law and law enforcement to assist in cleaning up neighborhoods. For example, the Settlement School in Frankfort, Kentucky, was able to have saloons closed, and the Irene Kaufman Settlement in Pittsburgh was instrumental in closing "obnoxious dance halls."[43] The work of the Thomas H. Swope Settlement in Kansas City, Missouri, vividly illuminates this side of the movement: "After two years' agitation in regard to the motion picture show and mutoscope halls, valuable and necessary legislation was secured. [This settlement] cooperated with its neighbors in an effort to drive out prostitution and to exercise a certain moral supervision over the district."[44] Just as the COS worked to improve the recreation activities of the communities, the settlement houses also attempted to rid neighborhoods of "undesirable" entertainment and recreation. To this end, the police assisted in driving out immoral elements by enforcing specific ordinances.

The primary settlement house technology used consistently across all houses was that of interaction with and between community residents. The contact the settlers had with each other and with their neighbors stimulated them to act on behalf of their neighborhoods. The energy flowing from these interactions inspired people to envision change in themselves and their surroundings and then work to achieve those changes. The core technology was the *process* of human dynamics derived from the interactions occurring in the houses. The importance of interaction was reflected in the goal of Hull House: "to make social intercourse express the growing sense of the economic unity of society."[45]

Settlement Houses and Immigrants

The settlement house movement is almost synonymous with immigration and Americanization as the houses emerged to meet the needs of the immigrants.[46] Since the settlement houses were residentially based, they experienced the transition of neighborhoods as the so-called new immigrants supplanted the old. The new immigrants were not shunned by the settlement houses; instead, they were embraced as groups that required more rigorous and extensive Americanization. The Chicago Commons noted the challenge that the new immigrants brought with them: "In the place of every German, Scandinavian and Irish family removing, immigrant families still stranger to our American life and conditions arrive. Like the surf upon the sand, each new wave of immigration from southern Italy, Sicily, Poland, Armenia and Greece, breaks over us here, where twenty-four or more nationalities meet and try to live and work together."[47]

The University of Chicago Settlement also reported that the old Irish, Scotch, and English neighbors were supplanted by the Bohemian, Pole, Slovak, Lithuanian, Croatian, and Slovenian.[48] The same phenomenon was occurring throughout other parts of the United States as the settlement houses responded by opening their doors to their new neighbors. From Baltimore to Boston, Chicago to Cleveland, St. Paul to St. Louis, the new immigrants were changing the fabric of the neighborhoods as well as U.S. society.

While the doors were swinging open for the new immigrants, the welcome they received varied from enthusiastic to disdainful. Alvin Kogut provided an examination of the attitudes of key settlement house directors and concluded that these directors were guided by veiled racism or the spirit of egalitarianism.[49] Jane Addams of Hull House espoused cultural pluralism, recognized the special needs of the new immigrants, and valued their distinctive cultural heritage. Robert Woods of Boston's South End House, however, had a markedly different view of the new immigrants. He saw these immigrants as barriers to achieving national unity and advocated for immigration restrictions by joining the Immigration Restriction League. These examples highlight the diversity in opinions held by the settlement directors and their residents.

These attitudes toward immigrants are captured in the settlement house descriptions contained in the 1911 *Handbook of Settlements*. The La Grange house, one of the few settlements in the south (Augusta, Georgia), boasted of being in a neighborhood with a population "of pure American stock."[50] The Wrightsville House of Philadelphia was situated in an Hungarian neighborhood and the Hungarians were "almost over-thrifty, lacking the power to find the best of life, doing little else than earn, eat and sleep."[51] Furthermore, settlement house workers, in general, lacked wide variation in their position on legislation to restrict immigration. For example, according to Davis: "Most settlement workers also accepted the passage in February 1917 of the first immigration bill requiring a literacy test. There had always been disagreement over immigration restriction, but in 1917 not even the Immigrant Protective League launched an effective protest against the bill."[52]

The new immigrants were often seen as possessing values and customs that were not supportive of the American way of life. The answer for them, in the eyes of the settlers, was through the Americanization process. In fact, the push for Americanization was directed solely toward immigrants. They were seen as redeemable, and the English, sewing, cooking, housekeeping, mechanical drawing, and manual training classes were offered as the tools for success in America. Thus, the settlers agreed with many of the Progressives of the day: With proper training and guidance, the new immigrants could be transformed into true Americans. According to Jansson: "Although commonly identified with 'social reform' by some historians, some settlement house staff could be quite condescending to immigrants, such as by seeking to convert them to the eating and living styles of Americans. Or they could be preoccupied with socialization and recreation services with scant attention to social reform."[53] Indeed, the early settlement house movement was encircled by the "benign form of paternalism" that prevailed during the Progressive Era.[54]

For the new immigrants, residence in the blighted neighborhood was but a stepping stone. With economic success, a family could relocate to better sections of town. In this regard, immigrant status could be held as a legitimate reason for living in a poor community. For "real" Americans, continued existence in a community of destitution was often taken as personal failure or weakness. The native-born Americans did not have the excuse of immigrant status to protect them. Attitudes toward the "real" Americans living in poverty areas are also found in the *Handbook of Settlements*. For example, the Union Bethel Settlement of Cincinnati described its neighborhood in these terms: "Much of our constituency is composed of the defective and dependent class. The people are largely Americans and Irish-Americans."[55] For the Southwark House in Philadelphia, the "Americans" in the neighborhood are described as "the dregs of a once prosperous community."[56] The Nashville Wesley House was faced with many who were "of the unfortunate, shiftless, or immoral class."[57]

The settlement house movement, therefore, cannot be neatly summarized as reflective of a particular point of view or a particular vision. The views and visions were as diverse as the individuals moving into settlement work. In the telling of social work history, a few major settlement houses are singled out to exemplify settlement house work. The history that involved anti-immigration sentiment, belief in the individual as the cause of his or her plight in life, the role of Americanization in settlement house work, and the social control aspects of this work is frequently minimized or ignored.

Settlement Houses and Racial/Ethnic Minorities

All racial and ethnic groups suffered—but not in the same manner nor to the same extent. The social suffering of the minorities was exacerbated by their minority status. Whatever was happening to the White ethnics was happening to an extreme with the minority groups. What were the settlement houses doing for the African Americans who migrated to the North in search of economic security? For the Mexicans who were displaced from their land? For the American Indians confined to the reservation? For the Chinese being driven out of the country? For the Japanese who were punished for being too successful in realizing the American dream?

Because African Americans greatly outnumbered the other groups and moved into those cities in which the settlement houses flourished, the work of the settlement houses with this group is of particular interest. Generally, the settlement houses responded in one of five ways to the influx of African-American migrants in those communities that had once been primarily composed of immigrants: (1) provided services to the new migrants, (2) established African-American branches, (3) refused to provide services to this group, (4) closed their doors rather than serve this new clientele, or (5) relocated to areas that did not include African Americans.

Those settlements that welcomed African Americans were relatively few in number and, in addition, there were few settlement houses to serve predominantly African-American sections of town.[58] By the 1920s, when African-American migration had already peaked, numerous cities were adjusting to the dramatic increase in their African-American population and the settlement houses were experiencing the effects of these demographic shifts. The settlement house movement was a residentially based movement and, as such, could not ignore the changing complexion of the neighborhoods. The Abraham Lincoln Center of Chicago responded by offering integrated services that included African Americans, and this response has been attributed to the center's "ultra-liberal" leaning.[59] Initially, the Abraham Lincoln Center, founded in 1905, was situated in a neighborhood with people who were "largely American; many of them German, Irish and Jewish extraction."[60] The center controlled membership so that 50 percent African-American membership could be maintained, provided interracial activities, and later sponsored a series of lectures by Melville Herskovitz, author of *The Myth of the Negro Past*.[61] Neighborhood House also approached a turning point in its history as African-Americans replaced the immigrant population.[62] In 1925, the settlement staff decided to remain in its present location and begin providing services to these newest arrivals. By 1929, the settlement had hired its first African-American social worker but it was not until the 1940s, when its membership was two-thirds African American, did an African American join the house's board of trustees.

Examples of typical settlement house responses to African Americans are numerous: The board of the Eli Bates House in Chicago voted to close the house rather than admit African Americans; Kingsley House in Philadelphia excluded African Americans entirely; one New York settlement substantially increased its membership fee to discourage African Americans from joining; the director and board of Christamore settlement in Indianapolis decided to move the settlement rather than integrate it; the Friendship House of the Washington, DC, excluded African Americans; the Marcy Center of Chicago followed the Jewish families out of the neighborhood rather than provide services to the incoming African Americans; the Central Presbyterian Chapel and Settlement House in Kansas City (Missouri) accepted "all but Negroes" in its classes; and the Neighborhood House of Ft. Worth noted that in its neighborhood the "people are Americans, foreigners, and many Negroes, the latter not touched by the work."[63]

Judith Trolander provided a rather enlightening overview of the racial segregation practiced at Chicago's Hull House.[64] By the 1930s, the second largest African-American community was situated in the Hull House neighborhood; yet, African Americans were not represented in the programs and services of the house. Even though the *Hull House Yearbook* listed a "black mothers' club," a club organized in 1927 by Jane Addams, African-American club members were not invited to participate in house programs, were not on any of the house's mailing lists, and were not receiving any benefits from the program. Trolander described the practices of Hull House as de facto segregation.

Some houses opened separate facilities for African Americans. For example, the Women's Federation of Elmira, New York, operated a small settlement "in the Negro quarter of Elmira"; the Henry Street Settlement in New York City established the Still Branch for Colored People; the College Settlement in Philadelphia opened the Starr Center to serve African Americans; Boston's South End House established the Robert Gould Shaw House for Africans; and the Wendell Phillips Settlement in Chicago was started with the help of Hull House residents.[65] According to Allen Davis in *Spearheads for Reform*, these separate houses for African Americans were based on specific beliefs of the settlers: "Many of the settlement house workers decided that special segregated facilities would best serve the interest of Negroes. This attitude was based partly on the idea that each neighborhood should have its own social center and partly on the fear that the presence of Negroes would drive others away."[66]

Those houses that served African-American communities were generally not controlled by those communities. Most had White boards of trustees or White-dominated boards that directed the operations and guided the future of the house. For example, the Presbyterian Colored Missions of Louisville, Kentucky, was maintained by White Presbyterians and specialized in religious services and industrial classes, while the White Episcopalians supported settlement work in an African-American section of New York and enrolled over 400 African-American girls in cooking and sewing classes.[67] This point is significant because it mirrors the tendency of individuals outside the group to identify the group's problems and identify solutions to those problems.

Booker T. Washington received the support of many settlers because they agreed with his perspective that African Americans were not yet ready for equality and that the road to equality was paved with manual training. Such a position continued to place responsibility for overcoming discrimination at the feet of the discriminated. Indeed, African-American settlement houses were not always designed to speak for the African American; rather, the separate houses often served to perpetuate racial segregation.[68]

The Eighth Ward Settlement House of Philadelphia is a stark example of the way White settlers perceived and approached an African-American community. It was established in 1895 by private citizens for settlement work among African Americans. This population is thus described: "In sharing its life with the colored people, our settlement has its unique problem, for it deals not with a race that is intellectually hungry, but with a race at the sensation stage of its evolution, and the treatment demanded is different.... The very material we have to deal with prevents us from being either attractive or successful.... And the peace we have not, we wish for others."[69] The Eighth Ward Settlement House concentrated on cleaning and improving the streets. It provided sanitation work, kindergarten, public baths, saving funds, basket weaving, hammock making, a women's club, and a dancing class.

Most of the settlements providing services to African-American communities focused on morality, temperance, religious instruction, neatness in domestic life, industrial uplift, singing classes, social meetings, drawing classes, instruction in thrift, and lectures.[70] One of the reports of Chicago's Frederick Douglass Center (founded by White settler Celia Parker Woolley) acknowledged, "Our treatment of the colored people in this country constitutes the greatest charge that can be made against our patriotism, our religion, our humanity"; however, the center' activities consisted primarily of "a women's club, sewing-class, children's singing-class, study-class, an orchestra, quartette and religious services Sunday afternoon."[71] Overall,

White-controlled settlements that served African Americans, "instead of promoting racial reform, displayed a cautious reformism that bowed to racism and oppression."[72]

Fear of alienating White members was only one reason for settlement houses to discourage African-American participation in White programs. Funding was often difficult to secure for programs that focused on African Americans. In writing of social settlement work among African Americans, Sarah Collins Fernandis observed in 1905: "The limitations of our activities may be easily measured by the fact that a year's expenditure, including three salaried workers, was six hundred dollars! That larger scope may be given to all our activities through generous financial assistance is our hope; that this line of work has its peculiar value as a corrective for delinquent conditions in districts where Negroes, ignorant and poor, form a segregated mass, is our firm belief."[73]

In 1908, Fernandis was continuing to seek funds for African-American settlement work. She wrote, "Social settlement work for the colored people in needy centers should be helped in the struggle for financial foothold."[74] Trolander also noted that African-American settlements, particularly branch houses, were poorly financed operations.[75] Established charitable organizations differentiated between White and African-American clients and little money was allocated for relief work with African Americans.[76] Although contributions were sufficient enough for the widespread settlement work with immigrants, the dearth of donations for work with the African-American population reflected the attitudes of the external polity and external economy of the settlement houses. Even with the advent of the coordinated fund-raising activities of Community Chests, African-American services still suffered from inadequate funding[77] and agencies were seldom rebuffed for their discriminatory practices.

African Americans represented a kind of anomaly to the settlement houses. Many were more "American" than the native-born population who may have had "foreign" stock in their family backgrounds. Consequently, African Americans did not need the "Americanization" treatment to which the immigrants were exposed. They already were Americans and were already grounded in U.S. values, beliefs, and culture. These Americans did not require proselytizing to direct their faith and souls to Protestantism, for they had already converted years before to American religion. Thus, it seems that the mission and technologies of the settlement houses would have to be modified for these groups to deemphasize Americanization and emphasize social reform.

Another factor in the settlers' response to African Americans can be found in the attitudes of the settlers. Numerous settlers shared the attitudes of the larger society toward African Americans. For example, Graham Taylor of Chicago Commons saw African Americans as a problem—a "de-

praved" people who society was obligated to uplift and treat humanely.[78]
Even Jane Addams seemed to hold that African Americans were in the early
stages of their development. At the 13th Annual Conference for the Study of
the Negro at Atlanta University in 1908, Addams remarked during her talk:

> The thing I feel most strongly as the difficulty among the Italians,
> among the Greeks and among the Russians (for these are the ones
> whom I constantly see), is the contrast they find between the life
> they have led at home and the life they are obliged to live in
> Chicago....The advantages are that you are ready *to make your*
> *adaptation;*...the disadvantages are that *you lack some of the restraints*
> *of the traditions which the people I mentioned bring with them.* [emphasis
> added].[79]

The voices of the settlement house movement did not convey a uniform
attitude about African Americans. Some believed in racial integration while
others endorsed racial segregation. Because the movement did not reach out
to embrace the African-American communities, those voices that echoed
racist, separatist beliefs may have been the loudest.

The verdict on the settlement house movement is that African Americans find the settlement houses guilty of overlooking the needs of African-
American communities. W. E. B. Dubois observed that social settlements
excluded African Americans and "even where they are not actually discriminated against, they are not made to feel welcome."[80] Fannie Williams
observed in 1905, "Only recently has it occurred to the social workers that
those who speak a foreign tongue and belong to the 'submerged tenth' are
not the only ones in need of guidance, protection and encouragement."[81]
While this may have occurred to social workers, few were involved in
extending that guidance, protection, or encouragement. In a 1936 analysis of
settlement work with African Americans, Lindenberg and Zittel raised a
critical question and then offered an answer:

> "What is the Settlement, the sponsor of the underprivileged and the
> champion of the immigrant, doing for the Negro who has settled on
> his doorstep?" ...We find three factors which are altering...the com-
> position of the settlement neighborhoods.... They are, namely, the
> decline of immigration, the shifting of the successful foreign born
> immigrant and his children out of the slum areas...and the influx of
> the Negro.... Let's face the issue! What are the settlements doing for
> the Negro in their neighborhoods? *In most instances absolutely noth-*
> *ing.* [emphasis added][82]

Consequently, the settlement house movement expended most of its ener-
gies on the immigrant groups.[83]

The doctrine of ethnic group responsibility may have been another factor influencing the practices of the White settlers. Perhaps the settlers felt as the friendly visitors—the responsibility for meeting the needs of African Americans rested with African Americans. It may have been expected that African Americans, when they reached that point in their evolution, would organize their own services for the benefit of their own people. This belief survived the Progressive Era and was reflective in the emerging social institutions of society. For example, John Murchison of the Department of Interior wrote in 1935, "It is difficult, however, to convince the Negro that he, himself, must accomplish his own deliverance and economic security."[84]

The establishment of the National Urban League seems indicative of this doctrine of ethnic group responsibility. It was organized in 1911, governed by a board composed primarily of conservative Whites and African Americans such as Booker T. Washington, operated primarily by African Americans, and had "Not Alms, but Opportunity" as its self-help slogan.[85] Settlement house worker Mary Simkhovitch was a member of its 39-person board.[86] Although the league was considered an African-American organization, its goals and visions were set largely by Whites who acted in accordance with their views of what African Americans should be doing for themselves. Hence, the White-controlled external polity and external economy of these organizations dictated the technologies used by these organizations. These polities supported the doctrine of ethnic group responsibility.

Although the movement did not distinguish itself as the champion of the African American, several individuals were able to distinguish themselves because of their work with and commitment to this group. Notable among these reformers are Jane Addams, Edith Abbott, Sophonisba Breckenridge, Lillian Wald, Mary White Ovington, Florence Kelley, Frances Kellor, and Celia Parker Woolley. Several of these individuals worked with African-American community leaders to develop settlement houses for African Americans. For example, Lillian Wald was instrumental in the establishment of Stillman House in 1906 and Celia Parker Woolley established the Frederick Douglas Center in the African-American section of Chicago. Mary White Ovington worked to improve housing in African-American communities. Edith Abbott and Sophonisba Breckenridge advocated for services to African-American children.[87]

One of the major contributions of settlement house reformers was the organization of the National Association for the Advancement of Colored People (NAACP). The organization was founded and funded by Whites, many of whom were associated with settlement houses and opposed racial discrimination. All of the original officers of the association were White, with the exception of W. E. B. DuBois.[88] Those who started the association feared that it would be perceived as too radical, so they enlisted the help of a journalist "to counteract the impression that the Association was made up of crackpots and radicals."[89] In its creation days, the NAACP may have been "radical," but the group envisioned carving a path to racial freedom through the established structures of society rather than through attacking or challenging the validity of these structures. Foster described the early days of the NAACP in this manner: "In the beginning, the wealthy Northern white philanthropists who were interesting themselves in the Negro people, looked askance at the N.A.A.C.P....Later on, however, the organization, by its increasingly conservative course, was able to win the support of these people."[90] The NAACP organizers set the tone for an advocacy organization that sought reform by working within and through the existing legal and political system. These founders were also keeping within the trend of "outsiders" defining the problems and defining the appropriate solutions.

The external polity was strong enough to silence even the strongest reform voice. For example, when Roosevelt refused to seat an African-American delegation from southern states during the 1912 presidential convention of the Progressive party, Jane Addams debated leaving; however, she decided to remain.[91] Addams may have realized the futility of her protest but, by remaining at a convention of a supposedly reformist party that squelched the rights of African Americans to participate, she exemplified the fact that reform efforts did have their limits.

As far as African Americans were concerned, the settlement house movement cannot be generally characterized as a reform movement. The discriminatory practices that existed outside the settlement house found their way inside the settlement house. In addition, the creation of separate facilities to serve African-American populations was a perpetuation of the prevailing belief that the races should be segregated. As with other services, segregation meant less—less service, less attention, less advocacy—for this group. The reform arm of the nascent social work profession was handcuffed by the pervasive racism that dominated the external polity and external economy, as well as by the racism that permeated the internal polity and internal economy of the settlement houses.

African Americans were victims of the same and even greater discrimination, racism, and violence that followed the immigrants. The immigrants received assistance from religious groups, political groups, and social workers; however, no comparable group felt an equal compassion for or commitment to African Americans.[92]

Settlement Houses and Other Ethnic/Racial Minorities

If the settlement houses did little for African Americans, they did even less for other minority groups. The few settlements that developed in areas populated by other minorities provided segregated services or no services. The College Settlement in Los Angeles stands out as an exception because its participants included Mexicans. Settlement workers wanted to establish contact with the Mexicans newly arriving from Mexico, but the 1904–1905 report of the settlement asserted, "A race seeks its own."[93] This belief may have been the reason that house activities were often segregated by the ethnicity of the participants. Workers in this settlement house were active in lobbying for juvenile court services and served on numerous boards and commissions. The extent to which Mexicans were the beneficiaries of these activities is not clear because the neighborhood was changing from Mexican to Italians and Slovenians. As Mexicans left the Southwest and moved to other parts of the country, they continued to encounter racism and were generally excluded from participation in settlement houses.[94] In fact, the *Handbook of Settlements* makes little mention of the Mexicans as a service group.

As neighborhoods experienced changes in ethnic composition, exclusionary policies were, in some cases, reversed. The board of Neighborhood House, in Gary, Indiana, decided on November 17, 1925, to admit Mexicans to the agency.[95] In its work with Mexican families, the settlement house appeared to focus on bringing the religious teachings to this group. To reach this population, the house had sermons and preachings delivered in Spanish. There is little indication, however, that the economic and political issues facing Mexicans were addressed.

In general, those few settlements that mention the Mexican population seemed more concerned about saving souls than facilitating social reform. The Wesley House of Houston, Marston Hall of Thurber, Texas, and the Spanish Settlement of Brooklyn illuminate this emphasis.[96] Wesley House was located in a neighborhood that included native-born Americans, Germans, Armenians, Syrians, and Mexicans. Activities included night school for foreigners, kindergarten, nursing services, sewing school, and religious services in Spanish. Thurber, Texas, was a mining town with a population of 800 to 1,000—about three-fourths were foreign born and largely Italians and Mexicans. Thurber provided religious services for foreigners, temperance society meetings, night school, kindergarten, housekeeping classes, and an array of clubs. The Spanish Settlement of Brooklyn taught English to Spanish adults and had classes in Christian Doctrine, sewing, singing, and dancing. Advocacy and reform work on behalf of the Mexican population was not mentioned. To an extent, the limited settlement work with Mexicans was an extension and continuation of the missionary work with this group that predated the settlement house movement.

Other groups received practically no settlement house attention. For example, only one Chinese settlement is listed among the settlements in the *Handbook of Settlements*.[97] True Sunshine Mission of San Francisco was established to provide work among the Chinese and was located in a Chinese quarter of San Francisco, across the street from the Chinese school. The mission maintained a playground, provided classes in English for adults, taught classes in sewing and kitchen gardening for children, had a dispensary, and conducted religious services. These activities focused on Americanization, not social reform; the anti-Chinese sentiment that dominated much of the West may have muffled any attempts at reform. In addition, the settlers of True Sunshine Mission may not have recognized or accepted a need for any other types of activities.

Although not listed in the *Handbook of Settlements*, the Cameron House in San Francisco helped "Chinese women enslaved by the tongs in their brothels."[98] This work had begun in the 1870s with the Presbyterian Mission of Chinatown and was eventually led in 1895 by a Scotswoman named Donaldina Cameron. She was able to enlist the aid of the police in her efforts. This may be the only organized work on behalf of Chinese women during the Progressive Era.

Although located in the Chinatown and Bowery of New York, the Chinatown Rescue Settlement and Recreation Room was organized "for neighborhood work among erring" American, English, German, French, Hebrew, Italian, and Bohemian girls who "live with the Chinese and American men in Chinatown."[99] Substance abuse, disease, and prostitution associated with dance halls and saloons prompted settlers to intervene to rescue girls from this environment. Not surprisingly, the work of a settlement in Chinatown targeted the White ethnics in this community.

Settlement work never reached the Japanese communities. This may have been due to this group's economic success and the anti-Asian feeling that prevailed on the West Coast. It is doubtful that university or religious groups would commit their resources to assist a population that was perceived as taking property and business away from the "real Americans who deserved them."

American Indians were a special case; their confinement to reservations rendered the settlement house movement irrelevant. The reformers who advocated and implemented the boarding school model (discussed in Chapter 2) were drawn from the same pool as were the friendly visitors from Charity Organization Societies and settlement house workers. In addition, many educated middle-class women ventured to the reservation to teach and provide Americanization activities. These young women were called *missionaries* rather than social workers.

The reform of the settlement house movement excluded racial and ethnic minorities as the beneficiaries of that reform. The child labor reforms, the juvenile court reforms, and the creation of reformatories for children failed to incorporate minorities. According to June Brown: "The literature of the era reveals a notable scarcity of the concern for the plight of Black children trapped in the neoslavery of sharecropping; for American Indian children subjected to many forms of...'acculturation under duress'; or for Hispanic and sometimes Asian children working in the fields of California and the Southwest."[100] Consequently, from its very inception, social work was alienating ethnic minorities through practices that implied that the needs of these groups were not paramount.

Many of the issues confronting the ethnic minority groups were civil rights issues—issues that dealt with discriminatory policies and practices and racist perspectives. In general, social work, in its infancy and in its adulthood, has not been a civil rights movement. With a little stretch of the imagination, social work could be loosely perceived as a subtle civil rights movement for educated women who wanted to escape the confines of home and hearth. For these women, social work became a liberating force in their lives. Unfortunately, this liberation did not extend to other oppressed groups.

THE EVOLUTION OF A PROFESSION

The COS and the settlement house movement evolved into the profession of social work. It is not the purpose of the discussion here to delve into the details of that evolution; rather, the intent is to analyze significant components of that evolution that had specific implications for service delivery to minority communities.

The Quest for Professionalization

As an emerging occupation, social workers moved to transform social work from a volunteer, lay activity to one that derived professional status from the recognized and respected expertise of its members. This means that the paid social agent eventually replaced the volunteer friendly visitor as the dominant presence in the budding profession. Numerous factors shaped the direction of the new profession's development and this development widened the schism between social work and ethnic/racial minority communities.

Leaders in the field were alarmed by Abraham Flexner's pronouncement during his speech at the 1915 National Conference of Charities and Corrections that social work was not a profession because it lacked a specific skill as used with a specific function.[101] Social work leaders embarked on a mission to prove Flexner wrong, and to do this, they would carve out their own particular niche of expertise. These individuals desired the professional designation enjoyed by other professions and the acceptance of the significance of the work they did. It may have seemed to some social workers that, in the absence of professional status, social work would be destined to remain an adjunct service rather than one that was indispensable and fully integrated into society. No doubt, professional status also carried a special degree of significance to the educated women who wanted to elevate their "social mothering" and "civic housekeeping" to a higher plane.

Professionalization became, in itself, a cause.[102] Volumes of time, energy, and other resources were invested in the establishment of social work as a full-fledged profession. This meant that numerous social workers were invested in advocacy on behalf of themselves. Professional associations, training, and degreed educational programs became the goal as social workers attempted to define and redefine their work in terms compatible with the norms of professionalism. In essence, these pioneers believed that "the promise of American life" could be achieved if people placed their trust in the skills of those "exceptional" individuals who were expert in the control of social problems.[103] By pursuing professionalization, social work was following in the footsteps of other professions so that this goal was not deviant or atypical. As this mission was pursued, however, mainstream social work largely ignored the racial and social class problems of minorities.[104]

In this quest, personal services or social casework overshadowed the social reform activities associated with the settlement houses.[105] Several major factors account for this ascendancy of social casework: Reform became unpopular as an activity, social casework appeared more "scientific" and could easily lend itself to the development of a specific knowledge base, social casework was less controversial than social reform, restrictions on immigration seemed to reduce the significance of social reform activities, the power of the social work faction supported social casework, and economic constraints led to reduced financial support for settlement house work and social reform. The "cause" base of the profession that had been concerned with facilitating change was replaced by an emphasis on "functions" of social work and the expertise underlying those functions.[106]

The external polity of the budding profession had soured on radicalism, reform, and anything that remotely touched on militancy, particularly after World War I. The "Red Scare" of the 1920s caused many groups and individuals to cower in the face of witch-hunts and mass intimidation. The climate was hostile toward agitation by or on behalf of any group, including African Americans. The public, including social workers, was silent to the raids conducted by the Attorney General that led to the deportation of thousands of Russian immigrants who were alleged to be members of Communist parties.[107] This hastened the fall of the settlement house movement and its attendant social reform. Jane Addams, yielding to the hostile polity by focusing on world brotherhood instead of Hull House activities, wrote of the effects of the raids: "Any proposed change was suspect, even those efforts that had been considered praiseworthy before the war...even social workers exhibited many symptoms of this panic and with a protective instinct *carefully avoided any phraseology of social reform*" [emphasis added].[108]

The decline of social reform was also linked to a reduction in immigration. Reform was generally seen as needed with immigrant groups, not with the ethnic/racial minorities whose social situation had changed very little. The settlement house movement modified its emphasis and approaches.

Social group work as reflected in recreation and educational activities surfaced as the primary technology, replacing social reform.[109] The settlement houses had to regain the financial support they had previously enjoyed, and to do this, they had to shed their reform image. For many settlers, *reform* was becoming a dirty word.

The noncontroversial nature of social casework became all the more important in this environment. In espousing social casework as the predominant method of social work, the profession shrouded itself with a cloak of conservatism. The primacy of individual responsibility was in step with prevailing political and social thought. It seems that, during this time, social work "success" was associated with a rejection of radicalism and militancy. Indeed, the conservative nature of social work has been discussed throughout the social work literature.[110]

Social casework stressed the social diagnosis of the individual, and Freudian approaches came to be accepted as a social diagnosis technology.[111] Social workers were developing an ideology that carried a psychological orientation to social problems.[112] Social problems started and stopped with the individual as social work defined problems in individual functioning terms. How a problem is defined also defines the solution proposed. Environmental, institutional, and/or structural bases of social problems were virtually ignored and social workers strove to change, treat, socialize, or rehabilitate the individual. Herein lies the thrust of the conservatism of social work: Society is fine and would be better if the "broken" people could be "fixed." This meant that social work virtually ignored the problems of large-scale institutional change.[113]

By narrowing their definition of social work to psychiatrically oriented casework, social workers minimized, or completely eliminated, public, social, and labor reform, as well as "less professional" techniques such as liaison and resource mobilization.[114] If the budding profession wanted public sanction and legitimacy from its external polity, the adoption of this narrow definition of social work seemed imperative. Consequently, the ideology of individual responsibility embraced during the Progressive Era was formalized in the teachings and practices of what was to become professional social work.

Grace Coyle, in 1935, offered a critique of social work and wrote, "As case work has 'gone psychiatric' it has not only concentrated upon the individual, it has further centered upon his emotional life, giving decreasing attention to environmental factors, social and economic. It has even been claimed at times that the ills that beset the unemployed could be met by proper emotional adjustment."[115] This concentration on the individual has resulted in what C. Wright Mills described as "an occupational incapacity to rise above series of 'cases.'"[116] For Mills, this trained incapacity was filled with political limitations. Because the social worker moves from case to case, he or she may be blind to a much larger picture or social context that may unify the cases. Awareness of such universal trends and commonalities may dictate an alternative professional response.

The ideology of social work differed markedly from that of ethnic/racial minorities. These groups are more likely to attribute the cause of their social condition and situation (disadvantaged status in society) to the unrelenting discrimination and racism they have historically faced.[117] Over time, many minority individuals continued to believe that White racism was the major mental health problem that needed to be addressed.[118] By adopting social casework as its dominant method, the profession of social work was ignoring the beliefs and unique histories of racial/ethnic groups in the United States—a history that is replete with discriminatory policies and practices. Social work was not just turning its back on social reform—it was turning its back on the thousands of individuals who had suffered extensively and primarily because of differential treatment they received.

Social work did, however, apply its method to work with minorities. These groups were seen as victims who were damaged by their history of oppression.[119] This led to what Henry Miller refers to as *clinicalism*—the presumption of damage and the use of psychological assistance to overcome this damage.[120] According to Miller, the history of minorities was, indeed, noted in this social work response. For African Americans, for example, this meant that slavery, exploitation, and victimization significantly damaged this group, and the results of this damage were visible in lifestyles that were viewed as maladaptive. This "clinicalism" has been applied to other groups as well. American Indians have been perceived as vulnerable for developing psychological problems because of their forced acculturation to U.S. society.[121] Social work's role, therefore, is to "correct" this damage by working with individuals because, with social casework, only individuals are "sick," not entire ethnic groups.

This individual-level orientation to ethnic/racial minorities is apparent in contemporary social work. For example, in a content analysis of 117 social work journal articles on Asian Americans, African Americans, Hispanic Americans, and American Indians published in the 1980s, McMahon and Allen-Meares found that the great majority of articles concentrated on individual intervention with these groups and concluded that "much of the surveyed social work literature is naive because it decontextualizes minority clients, intellectually removing them from the racist context in which they live."[122]

Sociologically, social work has often been considered one of the many ways in which society exerts control over its "deviant" members.[123] Ideologies and beliefs are examples of the kinds of social control that exist in U.S. society.[124] By denying the forces of discrimination in the institutions and structures of society, social work, as a profession, was validating those very institutions and structures. The endorsement of individual treatment communicated to minorities that the new profession of social work would be of little assistance in the struggle for racial equality because it perceived that efforts at social change were unnecessary. These subtle messages defined what the profession saw as the "appropriate" ways to combat social problems and attempted, either intentionally or inadvertently, to steer minorities away from social reform and social change. Social work seemed to capture America's ambivalence about the causes of social problems by trying simultaneously to enable and to control clients.[125]

Professionalization through casework practice placed the worker-client interaction and relationship at the core of social work practice. The expertise of the professional separated those who provided help from those who received help. The distance that existed during the Progressive Era between the friendly visitor and the service beneficiary was perpetuated by the distance between the expert and the client. This distance promotes practitioner objectivity and leads to assessments that may minimize client definitions of the problem. The power of the professional increases when problems are attributed to individuals because diagnostic skills become more crucial.[126] Furthermore, the power of the worker over the client became an integral part of professional social work practice.[127]

With professionalization came the "authority of expertise" predicated on the social worker's competence and the client's recognition and acceptance of that competence.[128] In addition to authority, paternalism has also been a part of casework practice. Paternalism involves acting in the best interest of the client even when his or her best interest is inconsistent with what the client wishes for himself or herself.[129] Thus, the social worker could act as a supportive father who could, when required, be authoritative.[130] Practices of the COS and settlement houses that identified for clients what they needed to do to become good Americans were institutionalized in the new profession.

To minorities, this social distance and paternalism seemed to be an extension of White superiority since very few minorities were visible in the profession. Through the professionalization of social casework, social workers could legitimately define for minority groups their problems and the course of action necessary to combat those problems. For many groups, including African Americans, this paternalism assumed that minority groups were underdeveloped and that assistance was needed to raise the values, aspirations, competence, and political sophistication of the groups.[131] This sentiment was very pervasive in U.S. society and had been so during the Progressive years. With social work, American society had a profession that actually mirrored this belief.

Had more minorities been involved in the profession during its developmental stage, perhaps the outcome would have been different. As it was, African-American and other minority social workers were extremely rare.

Figures for 1928 show that there may have been as many as 1,500 African-American social workers in the country but only about 500 were believed to have had any form of special social work training.[132] African-American social workers included 270 in private settings in 65 cities in 1932, another approximately 600 in other settings around the country, and the teaching staff at the African-American schools of social work, Atlanta University and Howard University.[133] In fact, the National Urban League was one of the largest employers of African-American social workers. These workers were needed for the numerous service sites the league operated. Training and other educational programs would not admit African Americans, and countless White agencies would not employ them. Jewish and Catholic social services were well-organized exceptions to the dominance of social work by White Protestants.[134] The need to increase the minority presence in social work has been a concern for years.[135]

Professionalization further removed social work from ethnic/minority communities. The external polity and external economy guided the path of the new profession. Legitimacy and public sanction could not be jeopardized by endorsing unpopular methods and groups. The development of any profession cannot be separated from the environment in which it forms. The internal polity of the embryonic profession charted a direction that was in consonance with the environment. The direction taken may have assured the profession of survival and public support. Any critical analysis of the profession's development must consider the internal and external forces that not only shaped but dictated particular responses. The intent here is not to rationalize or blame, but to support the contention that service delivery to minority communities must take into account the history of the alienation between the profession and those ethnic minority communities it now seeks to serve.

The Bureaucratization of the Welfare State

Funding imperatives imposed by the federal government and bureaucratization are also factors that have significantly influenced social work's response to ethnic minority communities. The growth of social practice has been spurred by major social policies that created and expanded the Welfare State. The federal government transported social services from the private to the public sector and became the predominant funder of social programs. With federal social welfare policies came social programs that required thousands of social workers and the organizations that employed them. For example, as a result of the Social Security Act of 1935 and other legislation, the number of social workers doubled during the 1930s to number about 30,000.[136] It was the passage of this act and the public funding of social programs that catapulted the United States into a Welfare State.

With the Welfare State came social work's dependency on federal sponsorship that cemented a bond between social work and the "establishment." If government is deemed an impartial provider of funding, then the social work-government relationship could be neutral. If, however, government is a vehicle for the expression of particular values, particular special-interest groups, or particular ideologies, then social work could be jeopardizing its effectiveness as a profession. For many social workers, a Welfare State potentially meant that social work could end up preserving the status quo and protecting the institutions that financed the profession.[137] Because previous social policies of the federal government had exerted an oppressive influence over ethnic/racial minorities (as discussed in Chapter 2), social work's growing relationship with the government did not raise the profession in their eyes.

With the rise of the Welfare State, the consumption of services was separated from the control of the services. As the federal government became a dominant sponsor of social services, consumption was separated from financing; this is one way that control is separated from consumption.[138] With this funding arrangement, agencies become accountable to the service sponsor and not to the service consumers. The voice of clients became heard indirectly through taxation and social policies. The separation of consumption from control reinforced the ideology of professional social work. Etzioni noted:

> The professionals are in a difficult place in this continuum. Their services, especially when organized in any administrative form, are separate from the fee charged and therefore from direct pressure by the client. Here the separation between consumption and control is supported by a strong ideology...namely, that *those who administer the service are in a better position to judge what is good for the consumer than he is for himself.* [emphasis added][139]

With the emergence of the Welfare State, ethnic and racial minorities remained outside of the mainstream as consumers rather than powerbrokers. To a certain extent, the Welfare State solidified their powerlessness, since these groups could not shape social policies—not even those policies that directly affected their lives.

Within the Welfare State, bureaucracy became the predominant organizational form.[140] According to Weber, the bureaucratic organization is characterized by its reliance on technical expertise, administrative hierarchy, specialization, formalized procedures, rationality, efficiency, and depersonalization.[141] The bureaucratic structure further distanced the client from the worker as services became administratively driven rather than client driven. The organizations also promoted a rigidity that often defied attempts at change and innovation; hence, they became less likely to adjust to changes in society. These organizations also became settings for socializing social workers into the values and norms governing bureaucratic practice.[142]

For ethnic minorities, these organizations were perceived as bastions of the status quo that seemed incapable of responding to their needs. They became entities to be manipulated, circumvented, or avoided. The impenetrable walls of bureaucratic rigidity, red tape, and coldness alienated numerous minorities as they experienced the Welfare State organizations as unresponsive.

Even some of the very programs that gave rise to the Welfare State under the Social Security Act of 1935 further alienated ethnic minorities.[143] African Americans were discriminated against in the programs of Roosevelt's New Deal as some work and housing programs practiced segregation, and other programs had requirements that could not be met by African Americans. In 1935, John Murchison of the Department of the Interior observed, "In the broad programs for economic security for the masses, moreover, the Negro in actuality still remains outside the total picture."[144]

When thousands of unemployed Hispanics applied for relief during the 1930s, they were often forced to return to Mexico. This happened to about 400,000 Hispanics from 1929 to 1934. Many, with $14.70 given them by the government, were indiscriminately railroaded to Mexico without regard for effects of deportation on families. Cornelius observed, "The door was slammed shut, and mass roundups and less obvious forms of coercion were employed to rid ourselves of the 'intolerable burden' of Mexican workers who did not leave of their own volition."[145] In addition, with the Depression, numerous Nisei (second-generation Japanese) could not find employment in engineering, manufacturing, or other areas in which they had received training. Racism toward this group contributed to the fact that almost no Nisei were employed by Whites. This racism and fear of Japanese invasion (the "yellow peril" discussed in Chapter 3) were responsible for the internment of about 120,000 Japanese Americans during World War II.

As with the COS and the settlement house movement, the Welfare State was not designed to address the issues of ethnic minority communities. For the most part, the emergence of the Welfare State and the bureaucratization of services that accompanied it deepened the wedge between social work and ethnic minority communities.

Movements to Change the Profession

The Rank-and-File Movement (RFM) of the 1930s[146] and the Human Services Movement (HSM) of the 1960s and 1970s[147] were dramatic attempts to realign goals, practices, and administration of the profession. Both movements were sparked by social policies that attempted to alleviate social suffering—policies of Roosevelt's New Deal and Johnson's Great Society's War on Poverty. With both plans, new, untrained recruits from outside the profession staffed the new social programs and brought with them a different perspective of their employment, their mission, the social work profession, and social service delivery.

The RFM social workers held talks on the worker-client relationship, sought to redefine the professional focus to emphasize client needs rather than professional status, took part in protest activities and radical movements, identified with the clients, and supported unionization. By the mid-1930s, however, the RFM workers had quieted their attack on social work and tried to develop their own method of casework that valued client-related goals. Nearing the end of the 1930s, the RFM responses to policies and practices made it a part of mainstream social work. Much of the movement's push for social reform over casework and rethinking the worker-client role had disappeared.

The agitation of the RFM did leave a mark on the profession and the profession expanded its scope to integrate some of the movement's issues. For example, because of the RFM, the profession accepted the following: public welfare as a field, even though it has never achieved a status base comparable to private agency work; groupwork and community organization as legitimate methods, even though they have continued to be overshadowed by direct practice; and a broader view of casework that fostered the "person-in-environment" perspective.

The turbulent 1960s with its civil rights movement, Chicano movement, protests, riots, and general social upheaval formed the backdrop for the Human Services Movement (HSM). The War on Poverty was a compilation of job training, community action, and youth employment programs. The community action programs mandated "maximum feasible participation of the poor" that was interpreted in varying ways at the local level. Newly developed community programs recruited paraprofessionals, minority group members, poor people, and others not typically identified with social work.

A community organization movement also developed that was at odds with the traditional theme of profession building. This movement developed outside of the profession and acknowledged the role of race and class in dividing U.S. society. Individuals, such as Saul Alinsky and Ceasar Chavez, who were not professional social workers, were instrumental in catapulting community organization to national prominence.

Client and community groups challenged the tenets of mainstream social work. National Welfare Rights Organization members, minority social workers, and other activists launched protests that disrupted professional conferences. These protests were used to force the profession to rethink poverty and racism. The HSM focused on social change, social reform, grass-roots organizing, client rights, and community development. HSM workers wanted to be agents of social change, not agents of social control, and they wanted to start with the places where clients were the most oppressed (prisons and welfare offices, for example). As with the RFM, the profession's internal polity now included a vocal faction that wanted to change the course of the profession's development.

During this period, African-American social workers grew increasingly dissatisfied with the National Association of Social Workers' (NASW) inactivity in fighting racism and advocating for African Americans. They formed the National Association of Black Social Workers in 1966 and split from NASW in 1969.[148] Because many of the Chicano social workers perceived NASW as not responding to their needs, they formed their own national social work organization, the Trabajadores de la Raza, also in 1969.[149] While the African-American social workers challenged the profession's stance on matters of race, the Chicano social workers wanted more aggressive recruitment of Chicanos for the profession as the Chicano presence in the profession was minuscule.

As with the RFM, the agitation of the HSM waned due, in part, to powerful organizational and professional norms that resisted change. Social work, for the most part, returned to business as usual. Although it was not self-sustaining, the HSM, nevertheless, left a legacy to social work: Undergraduate social work education was strengthened as the Council on Social Work Education established standards for accrediting undergraduate programs; the Bachelor of Social Work (B.S.W.) became an entry-level degree for professional practice; a human services profession emerged with its own educational program and schools; interest in community organization was renewed, even though that interest fell over time; the profession accepted the role of social advocate; and the practice of casework was critically revisited.

Wagner hypothesized more conservative changes to the profession as a result of the HSM: "While Human Service and BSW workers will seek *increasing professionalization, including dissociation from lower status work and increased association with MSW workers*, the MSW's will seek increasing work differentiation in which non-MSW's perform most direct practice, while MSW's can become supervisors, consultants, and administrators" [emphasis added].[150]

It seems likely that the dominant internal polity of the profession will continue to coopt dissidents and fractious factions while not straying too far from its conservative leanings toward professionalization. As a matter of fact, many social workers with a bachelor's degree as their highest degree are providing case management services—services that have a history based in the Charity Organization Societies.[151] According to Jansson, even the introduction of the environmental systems and ecological frameworks in the

1970s and 1980s were translated into tools for casework. He stated, "As Mary Richmond advocated decades earlier, emphasizing the environment encourages social workers to gather information about clients' living conditions. In this way, social workers need not try to change environmental conditions themselves, but can use conditions to aid clinical work."[152]

Two major movements within the profession were not powerful enough to deter the profession from its quest. As social work continues with its professionalization, it appears to be moving from serving minority communities, poor communities, and other groups that need advocacy and empowerment.[153] Those it now serves include fee-paying or third-party payment clients as the number of social workers in private practice increases.[154] The profession has devoted more of its political influence to support licensure and vendorship privileges for social work clinicians than for services to disenfranchised populations.[155]

SOCIAL WORK AND THE "MIDDLE COURSE"

In 1957, Styz described the "middle course" that some social workers took on racial issues—a middle course that, at that time, saw social workers working within the segregation framework without agreeing with it.[156] It appears that social work may be still trying to define for itself a middle course on racial issues. For today's profession, that middle course appears to be captured in support of "soft determinism" as a way of specifying the causality of social problems.[157] On one hand, there is acknowledgment of factors beyond the individual's control; on the other hand, there is acknowledgment of individual responsibility. It is the hand of individual responsibility, however, that receives the manicure.

Avoiding Controversy

As a profession, social work has had to balance the demands and expectations of its numerous and powerful constituencies that include the dominant elite both outside and inside the profession. As a profession, social work, to a large extent, has continued to be vulnerable to and dependent on its external polity and external economy. This dependency has permitted these polities to exert potent influence over the profession's position on matters of race and ethnicity. This dependency has also steered the profession along the middle, and sometimes even conservative, course.

Social work, as a nascent profession, could not afford to alienate those factions that conferred the designation of "profession." It had to equivocate on the controversial issues of race because to do otherwise would endanger its status and legitimacy to the rest of society. It needed to be in step with the rest of society and with the social and political institutions of society. Social work has been guilty of complicity with those institutions that maintained and implemented discriminatory treatment of racial and ethnic minorities. When segregation was the modus operandi of the day, social work agencies segregated despite their policy statements on nondiscrimination.[158] Racial minority clients and staff were subjected to differential treatment and differential access to services and employment. To do otherwise would have endangered the profession's credibility in the eyes of its resource holders. Social reform was held in abeyance as the profession acquiesced to the ideologies and practices of mainstream society. The middle course emerged as a reasonable response to environmental constraints. Indeed, the history of the profession appears to be a history of responding to the external environment.[159]

It took a major social movement—the civil rights movement—to shake racial attitudes and challenge race-related practices. Social workers were not in the forefront of leadership in this movement. The profession hovered around the borders of the movement with ambivalence about its role in it. Once desegregation became the law of the land, the profession was free to embrace the new mandate without fear of reprisals, for it was only acting in accordance with changing policies and changing mores. Social work schools and agencies could then actively begin to recruit minority group members.[160]

This dependency of the profession has muted its reform impulses and has given the profession a "bandwagon" quality. It seems to move with the trends and practices of society, not against them. It can join the bandwagon once the parade has begun but it cannot afford to lead the procession. This response may continue to promote the profession's survival and legitimacy, but it does little to endear the profession to ethnic and racial minorities. This response appears to make social work compliant with prevailing dominant racial attitudes, whatever they may be. For these reasons, social work's image and reputation as an establishment-oriented profession may have some credibility. As a system seeking survival and growth, this establishment-oriented image may have been in the best interest of the profession. The middle course may be the profession's attempt to manage its environmental dependencies.

Bureaucratization has also curtailed the reform impulse of the profession through rigid structures and procedures that seem immune to change and innovation. These systems seek to preserve a status quo and to continue doing business as it has always been done. Because of this, an external impetus—the civil rights movement and the resultant policy changes—was required to penetrate bureaucratic barriers to produce change. With the bureaucratization of social work, the profession became organizationally committed to the middle and conservative course.

The leadership of the elite within the profession that has knighted social casework as *the* method of social work also serves to mute the profession's reform impulse. The profession acts as an agent of social control for its members who venture outside the social work mainstream. Practitioners and scholars who challenge and critique the profession are often dubbed "radical" and their perspectives are referred to as "radical social work."[161] This so-called radical social work has challenged professional social work education, the role of social work in society, and the way the profession has related to disenfranchised groups. The very imposition of the "radical" label denotes that these perspectives are deviations from the mainstream of social work. This labeling may further serve to prevent these alternative views from being fully integrated into the profession. The profession's dominant elite appears to have supported and further forged the middle and conservative course of the profession.

The argument that social work is also an agent of social reform seems rather specious. While numerous social workers may truly believe in the profession's commitment to reform, the profession's liberalism may be associated with *individuals* within the profession rather than with the *profession* itself[162]—as was true with the settlement house movement. Those individuals who have been capable of achieving some type of social change or social reform may be held as examples of the profession's longstanding dedication to social work. The acts of a few reform-minded individuals are perhaps generalized to the profession as a whole. In fact, these activists may be individuals who also happen to be social workers and who were successful despite being social workers.

The Professionalization of Reform

The evolution of social reform into "macropractice" may also reflect an adherence to the middle course. According to the authors of a text on macropractice, this practice is a "professionally directed intervention to bring about planned change in organizations and communities" and involves the practitioner in the areas of organizations, communities, and policy.[163] It is a problem-solving method that defines and assesses needs in organizations and communities, leads to the development of strategies for intervention, and guides the selection of an appropriate tactic to bring about the planned change.

Macropractice, as currently defined, is a middle course because it acknowledges the role of external systems in shaping organizations and communities while at the same time working *within* the existing systems to bring about change. By working within these systems, the macropractitioner accepts them as impartial, effective, valid, and responsive. Civil disobedience, protests, activism, and other blatant, direct challenges to these systems that once characterized social action, social reform, and social change are approached with great trepidation, as reflected in the following observations in a macrotext: "When action system members [those working for change] deliberately engage in illegal activities, they must be ready to accept the consequences of their actions. The change agent [the macropractitioner] is responsible for making potential participants fully aware of these risks before the decision is made to proceed."[164] Only one paragraph in this entire macrotext raises the option of forcefully and vocally challenging social systems.

The social action or social reform element of community organization has virtually disappeared from macropractice to be replaced by administrative practice, community development, and social planning.[165] As the reincarnation of social reform, macropractice may represent the transformation of social reform when it becomes a part of mainstream social work. These emergent perspectives on system-level change seem also to tie social work to a middle course.

Ethnic and racial minorities are aware of the partiality, ineffectiveness, and nonresponsiveness of social systems. An acceptance of the status quo inadvertently supports the inequality these systems have perpetrated. It is difficult for many minority group members to place this awareness aside and see social and political systems as neutral, fair, and benign entities. Furthermore, social action or activism may not be the intent of these groups; rather, an awareness of the oppressive nature of these systems seems to be the crucial point. Methods of social work that recognize the injustices of institutions in society would convey the profession's commitment to advancing civil rights. An absence of this recognition seems to minimize or disregard the historical experiences of ethnic minority groups. The faith that social work has in the integrity of society's institutions and structures may not be shared by members of ethnic and racial groups. With mainstream definitions of macropractice and community organization, the gap between social work and these communities grows even wider.

CONCLUSIONS

The legacy of the Charity Organization Societies is visible throughout social work. The COS evolved into family services[166] and many of the preachings, practices, and personnel patterns are firmly imprinted on contemporary family casework. The influences of the COS on the development of social work as a profession are striking: continued adherence to individual responsibility, the dominant polity defining social problems and their solutions, an emphasis on cases rather than population aggregates, the social distance between helper and helpee, adherence to the doctrine of ethnic group responsibility, reliance on women for the provision of social services, and continued ties to the "establishment" that raises questions about the social control functions of social services.

From the settlement house movement, social work inherited advocacy, social action, policy practices, community/locality development, and social/community planning. Services to ethnic and racial minorities were not significantly integrated into this movement. A focus on socializing the individual was a central goal, which was typically minimized when the reform roots of social work are reviewed. As with the COS, the settlers also defined the needs of the communities in which they resided. In this case, however, they invited community residents to participate in achieving the goals and missions of the houses. In addition, individual responsibility also figured heavily in the beliefs of the settlers. The settlement houses did, however, stimulate the development of social policies and the provision of services. Intervention with social systems, although perhaps not to the extent or degree as commonly believed, dramatically divided the settlement movement from the COS.

The reform arm of social work, however, has been continuously overshadowed by the personal or direct practice thrust of the profession. Protests movements within the profession have been unable to deter the profession from its middle course. As social reform is also professionalized and integrated into the profession as macropractice, social work's allegiance to mainstream society becomes even more entrenched.

For ethnic minorities, the profession and its evolution have had little to do with them and their history. They have had to struggle to provide for the service needs of their communities. The next chapter provides evidence of the need for and capacity of ethnic minority communities to develop their own services.

ENDNOTES

1. For a discussion of the English roots of the settlement house movement and the history of the movement in the United States, see James Leiby, *A History of Social Welfare* (New York: Columbia University Press, 1978), pp.127–135.

2. Leiby, *A History of Social Welfare*, p. 127.

3. June Axinn and Herman Levin, *Social Welfare—A History of the American Response to Need*, Second Edition (New York: Harper & Row, 1982), p. 112.

4. Robert Woods and Albert Kennedy, *Handbook of Settlements* (New York: Charities Publication Committee, Russell Sage Foundation, 1911), p. vi.

5. Alvin Kogut, "The Settlements and Ethnicity: 1890–1914," *Social Work 17* (May 1972): 23; Leiby, *A History of Social Welfare and Social Work*, p. 128; Ralph Pumphrey and Muriel Pumphrey, "The Settlement Movement," in *The Heritage of American Social Work*, ed. Ralph Pumphrey and Muriel Pumphrey (New York: Columbia University Press, 1961), p. 193.

6. Woods and Kennedy, *Handbook of Settlements*, p. 228.

7. Woods and Kennedy, *Handbook of Settlements*, p. 53.

8. Noted in social work literature such as Ralph Dolgoff and Donald Feldstein, *Understanding Social Welfare*, Second Edition (New York: Longman, 1984), p. 263.

9. These similarities are discussed in greater detail in Dolgoff and Feldstein, *Understanding Social Welfare*, pp. 263–264.

10. Axinn and Levin, *Social Welfare*, pp. 111–113; Bruce Jansson, *The Reluctant Welfare State*, Second Edition (Pacific Grove, CA: Brooks/Cole, 1993), pp. 138-139; Ray Johns and David DeMarche, *Community Organization and Agency Responsibility*, (New York: Association Press, 1951), p. 86; Kogut, "The Settlements and Ethnicity," p. 23; Leiby, *A History of Social Welfare*, pp. 127–135; Pumphrey and Pumphrey, "The Settlement Movement," pp. 192–193.

11. Robert Reinders, "Toynbee Hall and the American Settlement Movement," *Social Service Review* 56 (March 1982): 39–54.

12. Kogut, "The Settlements and Ethnicity," p. 23

13. These expressions are quoted from Herman Hegner, "Scientific Value of the Social Settlements," *American Journal of Sociology* 3 (September 1897): 174–176.

14. Dolgoff and Feldstein, *Understanding Social Welfare*, p. 264; James Leiby, *A History of Social Welfare*, p. 129.

15. David Wagner, "Collective Mobility and Fragmentation: A Model of Social Work History," *Journal of Sociology and Social Welfare* 13 (September 1986): 671.

16. Axinn and Levin, *Social Welfare*, p. 113. Also mentioned in Pumphrey and Pumphrey, "The Settlement Movement," p. 192.

17. As detailed and quoted in Allen Davis, *Spearheads for Reforms—The Social Settlements and the Progressive Movement 1890–1914* (New Brunswick, NJ: Rutgers University Press, 1984), p. 87.

18. Howard Karger, "Minneapolis Settlement Houses in the 'Not So Roaring 20's': Americanization, Morality, and the Revolt Against Popular Culture," *Journal of Sociology and Social Welfare* 14 (June 1987): 93.

19. Woods and Kennedy, *Handbook of Settlements*.

20. Woods and Kennedy, *Handbook of Settlements*, p. 66.

21. Woods and Kennedy, *Handbook of Settlements*, p. 31.

22. Woods and Kennedy, *Handbook of Settlements*, p. 175.

23. Woods and Kennedy, *Handbook of Settlements*, p, 262.

24. Leiby, *A History of Social Welfare*, pp. 127–129.

25. Woods and Kennedy, *Handbook of Settlements*, p. 2.

26. Clarke Chambers, "Women in the Creation of the Profession of Social Work," *Social Service Review* 60 (March 1986): 12; Harry Kraus, *The Settlement House Movement in New York City, 1886–1914* (New York: Arno Press, 1980), p. 37.

27. Anthony Platt, "The Child-Saving Movement and the Origins of the Juvenile Justice System," in *The Sociology of Juvenile Delinquency*, ed. Ronald Berger (Chicago: Nelson-Hall, 1991), p. 13.

28. Chambers, "Women in the Creation of the Profession of Social Work," pp. 12–13; J. Ehrenreich, *The Altruistic Imagination: A History of Social Work and Social Policy in the United States* (Ithaca, NY: Cornell University Press, 1985), pp. 33–36.

29. Dolgoff and Feldstein, *Understanding Social Welfare*, p. 263.

30. James Gustafson, "Professions as 'Callings,'" *Social Service Review 56* (December 1982): 510, 511.

31. Platt, "The Child Saving Movement," p. 13.

32. These relationships and historical accounts are found in Platt, "The Child-Saving Movement," pp. 11–15.

33. Ehrenreich, *The Altruistic Imagination*, p. 31.

34. As noted in Leiby, *A History of Social Welfare*, p. 132.

35. Dolgoff and Feldstein, *Understanding Social Welfare*, pp. 263–264.

36. David Wagner, "Collective Mobility and Fragmentation," p. 672.

37. Davis, *Spearheads for Reform*, p. 85.

38. Kraus, *The Settlement House Movement*.

39. Louise Johnson and Charles Schwartz, *Social Welfare: A Response to Human Need*, Second Edition (Boston: Allyn and Bacon, 1991), p. 116.

40. Kraus, *The Settlement House Movement*, p. 34.

41. Woods and Kennedy, *Handbook of Settlements*, p. 33.

42. Woods and Kennedy, *Handbook of Settlements*, p. 71.

43. Woods and Kennedy, *Handbook of Settlements*, pp. 87, 282.

44. Woods and Kennedy, *Handbook of Settlements*, p. 152.

45. Woods and Kennedy, *Handbook of Settlements*, p. 53.

46. Dolgoff and Feldstein, *Understanding Social Welfare*, p. 263; Johnson and Schwartz, *Social Welfare*, p. 38; Alvin Kogut, "The Settlements and Ethnicity," p. 22; Krause, *The Settlement House Movement* p. 38; George Martin, *Social Policy in the Welfare State* (Englewood Cliffs, NJ: Prentice Hall, 1990), pp. 26–27; as reflected in the mission of the Women's Home Mission Society reported by Woods and Kennedy, *Handbook of Settlements*, p. 4;

47. Woods and Kennedy, *Handbook of Settlements*, p. 40.

48. Woods and Kennedy, *Handbook of Settlements*, p. 69.

49. Kogut, "The Settlements and Ethnicity," pp. 22–31.

50. Woods and Kennedy, *Handbook of Settlements*, p. 36.

51. Woods and Kennedy, *Handbook of Settlements*, p. 266.

52. Davis, *Spearheads for Reform*, p. 227,

53. Jansson, *The Reluctant Welfare State*, p. 138.

54. Karger, "Minneapolis Settlement Houses," p. 91.

55. Woods and Kennedy, *Handbook of Settlements*, p. 252.

56. Woods and Kennedy, *Handbook of Settlements*, p. 270.

57. Woods and Kennedy, *Handbook of Settlements*, p. 292.

58. Davis, *Spearheads for Reform*, p. 94; Judith Trolander, *Settlement Houses and the Great Depression* (Detroit: Wayne State University Press, 1975), p. 136.

59. Trolander, *Settlement Houses*, p. 137.

60. Woods and Kennedy, *Handbook of Settlements*, p. 73.

61. Trolander, *Settlement Houses*, pp. 137–138.

62. This history of neighborhood is reported in Ruth Crocker, *Social Work and Social Order: The Settlement Movement in Two Industrial Cities, 1889–1930* (Chicago: University of Illinois Press, 1992), p. 146.

63. Crocker, *Social Work and Social Order*, p. 35; Trolander, *Settlement Houses*, pp. 137–138; Woods and Kennedy, *Handbook of Settlements*, pp. 32, 150, 295.

64. Trolander, *Settlement Houses*, pp. 139–140.

65. Davis, *Spearheads for Reform*, p. 95; Woods and Kennedy, *Handbook of Settlements*, pp. 177, 210; Trolander, *Settlement Houses*, p. 24.

66. Davis, *Spearheads for Reform*, pp. 94–95.

67. W. E. B. DuBois, *Efforts for Social Betterment Among Negro Americans* (Atlanta: Atlanta University Press, 1909), p. 121.

68. Trolander, *Settlement Houses*, p. 145.

69. Woods and Kennedy, *Handbook of Settlements*, p. 268.

70. DuBois, *Efforts for Social Betterment*, pp. 121–126.

71. As quoted in DuBois, *Efforts for Social Betterment*, p. 122.

72. Crocker, *Social Work and Social Order*, p. 185.

73. Sara Collins Fernandis, "A Social Settlement in South Washington," *Charities and the Commons 15* (October 7, 1905): 66.

74. Sara Collins Fernandis, "Social Settlement Work Among Colored People," *Charities and the Commons 21* (November 21, 1908): 302.

75. Trolander, *Settlement Houses*, p. 145.

76. Krause, *The Settlement House Movement*, pp. 217–218.

77. M. A. Jimenez, "Historical Evolution and Future Challenges of the Human Services Professions," *Families in Society 71* (January 1990): 7.

78. Steven Diner, "Chicago Social Workers and Blacks in the Progessive Era," *Social Service Review 44* (December 1970): 401.

79. As quoted in W. E. B. DuBois, *The Negro Family*, Atlanta University Publications, No. 13 (Atlanta: Atlanta University Press, 1908), p. 152.

80. W. E. B. DuBois, "Social Effects of Emancipation," *The Survey 29* (February 1, 1913): 572.

81. As quoted in Edyth Ross, ed., *Black Heritage in Social Welfare 1860–1930* (Metuchen, NJ: The Scarecrow Press, 1978), p. 231.

82. Sidney Lindenberg and Ruth Zittel, "The Settlement Scene Changes," *Social Forces 14* (May 1935): 563, 564.

83. Axinn and Levin, *Social Welfare*, p. 152.

84. John Murchison, "Some Major Aspects of the Economic Status of the Negro," *Social Forces 14* (October 1935): 114.

85. August Meier, *Negro Thought in America 1880–1915* (Ann Arbor, MI: University of Michigan Press, 1966), p. 134.

86. Trolander, *Settlement Houses*, p. 145.

87. Sandra Sethno, "Public Responsibility for Dependent Black Children: The Advocacy of Edith Abbott and Sophonisba Breckinridge," *Social Service Review 62* (September 1988): 485–503.

88. Florette Henri, *Black Migration: Movement North, 1900–1920.* (Garden City, NY: Doubleday, 1975), p. 202.

89. Davis, *Spearheads for Reform*, p. 102.

90. William Foster, *The Negro People in American History* (New York: International Publishers, 1954), p. 424.

91. Axinn and Levin, *Social Welfare*, p. 152; Henri, *Black Migration*, p. 245; Jansson, *The Reluctant Welfare State*, p. 132.

92. Harold Bradley, *The United States from 1865* (New York: Charles Scribner's Sons, 1973), p. 145.

93. The Los Angeles Settlement Association, *The College Settlement* (Los Angeles: The Association, 1904–1905), p. 6.

94. Crocker, *Social Work and Social Order,* p. 146.

95. A discussion of the Neighborhood House and the Mexicans is provided by Crocker, *Social Work and Social Order,* pp. 146–147.

96. These settlements are described in Woods and Kennedy, *Handbook of Settlements,* pp. 186, 296–297.

97. Woods and Kennedy, *Handbook of Settlements,* pp. 23–24.

98. Jack Chen, *The Chinese of America* (San Francisco: Harper & Row, 1980), p. 184.

99. Woods and Kennedy, *Handbook of Settlements,* p. 235.

100. June Brown, "Primary Prevention: A Concept Whose Time Has Come for Improving the Cultural-Relevance of Family and Children's Services in Ethnic Minority Communities," in *Primary Prevention Approaches to Development of Mental Health Services for Ethnic Minorities,* ed. Samuel Miller, Gwenelle Styles, and Carl Scott (New York: Council on Social Work Education, 1982), p. 41.

101. Roy Lubove, *The Professional Altruist* (New York: Atheneum, 1969), p. 106.

102. Stanley Wenocur and Michael Reisch, *From Charity to Enterprise* (Chicago: University of Chicago Press, 1989), p. 259.

103. Stephen Kunitz, "Professionalism and Social Control in the Progressive Era: The Case of the Flexner Report," *Social Problems* 22 (October 1974): 26.

104. Wenocur and Reisch, *From Charity to Enterprise,* p. 259.

105. Numerous sources provide detailed accounts of the ascendancy of casework over social reform. The discussion presented here is based on the following readings: Axinn and Levin, *Social Welfare,* pp. 152–158; William Black, Jr., "Social Work in World War I: A Method Lost," *Social Service Review* 65 (September 1991): 379–402; Herman Borenzweig "Social Work and Psychoanalytic Theory: A Historical Analysis," *Social Work* 16 (January 1971): 7–16; Dolgoff and Feldstein, *Understanding Social Welfare,* pp. 265–274; Jansson, *The Reluctant Welfare State,* pp. 137–142; Leiby, *A History of Social Welfare,* pp. 181–190; Lubove, *The Professional Altruist,* pp. 53–84, Michael Reisch and Stanley Wenocur, "The Future of Community Organization in Social Work: Social Activism and the Politics of Profession Building," *Social Service Review* 60 (March 1986): 70–93.

106. The cause versus function discussion can be found in numerous writings, including Dolgoff and Feldstein, *Understanding Social Welfare,* p. 269; Roy Lubove, *The Professional Altruist,* pp. 157–158.

107. A more detailed discussion can be found in Borenzweig, "Social Work and Psychoanalytic Theory," pp. 11–12.

108. As quoted in Borenzweig, "Social Work and Psychoanalytic Theory," p. 11.

109. Axinn and Levin, *Social Welfare,* p. 157.

110. See, for example, David Gil, "Implications of Conservative Tendencies for Practice and Education in Social Welfare," *Journal of Sociology and Social Welfare* 17 (June 1990): 2–27; Herman Levin, "Conservatism of Social Work," *Social Service Review* 56 (December 1982): 605–615; F. Robert Schilling, Steven Schinke, and Richard Weatherly, "Service Trends in a Conservative Era: Social Workers Rediscover the Past," *Social Work* 33 (January/Febmary 1988): 5–9.

111. The reliance of social casework on Freudian approaches is also documented throughout the social work literature. See, for example, Borenzweig, "Social Work and Psychoanalytic Analysis," pp. 12–16; Lubove, *The Professional Altruist*, pp. 88–89; Martin, *Social Policy in the Welfare State*, p. 27.

112. Burton Gummer, "On Helping and Helplessness: The Structure of Discretion in the American Welfare System," *Social Service Review* 53 (June 1979): 218–219.

113. Harry Specht, "The Deprofessionalization of Social Work," *Social Work* 17 (March 1972): 3–15.

114. Philip Popple, "The Social Work Profession: A Reconceptualization," *Social Service Review* 59 (December 1985): 564.

115. Grace Coyle, "The Limitations of Social Work in Relation to Social Reorganization," *Social Forces* 14 (October 1935): 100.

116. C. Wright Mills, "The Professional Ideology of Social Pathologists," *American Journal of Sociology* 49 (September 1943): 171.

117. Miguel Montiel and Paul Wong, "A Theoretical Critique of the Minority Perspective," *Social Casework* 64 (February 1983): 112–117; Reisch and Wenocur, "The Future of Community Organization,"p. 73; Gerald Wind Sue, *Counseling the Culturally Different* (New York: John Wiley & Sons, 1981).

118. Charles Sanders, "Growth of the Association of Black Social Workers," *Social Casework* 51 (May 1970): 279.

119. Montiel and Wong, "A Theoretical Critique of the Minority Perspective," pp. 112–113.

120. Henry Miller, "Social Work in the Black Ghetto: The New Colonialism," in *Dynamics of Racism in Social Work*, ed. James A. Goodman (Washington, DC: National Association of Social Workers, 1973), pp. 271–287.

121. Teresa LaFromboise, "American Indian Mental Health Policy," *American Psychologist* 43 (May 1988): 388.

122. Anthony McMahon and Paula Allen-Meares, "Is Social Work Racist? A Content Analysis of Recent Literature," *Social Work* 37 (November 1992): 537.

123. Robert Taylor, "The Social Control Function in Casework," *Social Casework* 39 (January 1958): 17–21.

124. Margaret Vine, *Sociological Theory*, Second Edition (New York: David McKay Company, 1969), p. 171.

125. Robert Halpern, "Supportive Services for Families in Poverty: Dilemmas of Reform," *Social Service Review* 65 (September 1991): 343, 344.

126. David Powell, "Managing Organizational Problems in Alternative Service Organizations," *Administration in Social Work* 10 (Fall 1986): 65.

127. Yeheskel Hasenfeld, "Power in Social Work Practice," *Social Service Review* 61 (September 1987): 467–483.

128. Sally Palmer, "Authority: An Essential Part of Practice," *Social Work* 28 (March/April 1983): 123.

129. Marcia Abramson, "Autonomy vs. Paternalistic Beneficence: Practice Settings," *Social Casework* 70 (February 1989): 102; Frederic Reamer, "The Concept of Paternalism in Social Work," *Social Service Review* 57 (June 1983): 259.

130. Elizabeth Irvine, "Transference and Reality in the Casework Relationship," *British Journal of Psychiatric Social Work* 3 (December 1956): 15–24.

131. Miller, "Social Work in the Black Ghetto," p. 276.

132. Eugene Jones, "Social Work Among Negroes," *The Annals of the American Academy of Political and Social Science 140* (November 1928): 287–293.

133. Jacob Fisher, *The Response of Social Work to the Depression* (Boston: G. K. Hall & Co., 1980), p. 135, Leslie Leighninger, *Social Work Search for Identity* (New York: Greenwood Press, 1987), p. 10.

134. Fisher, *The Response of Social Work*, p. 10.

135. Ruth Berger, "Promoting Minority Access to the Profession," *Social Work 34* (July 1989): 346.

136. Martin, *Social Policy in the Welfare State*, p. 27.

137. Ehrenreich, *The Altruistic Imagination*, pp. 104–105.

138. Amitai Etzioni, *Modern Organizations* (Englewood Cliffs, NJ: Prentice Hall, 1964), pp. 94–96.

139. Etzioni, *Modern Organizations*, p. 97.

140. Patricia Martin, "Multiple Constituencies, Dominant Societal Values, and the Human Service Administrator: Implications for Service Delivery," *Administration in Social Work 4* (Summer 1980): 21–22.

141. Max Weber, "Bureaucracy," in *The Sociology of Organizations*, Second Edition, ed. Oscar Grusky and George Miller (New York: The Free Press, 1981), pp. 7–36; and as described in Lubove, *The Professional Altruist*, pp. 161–162.

142. David Bargal, "Social Values in Social Work: A Developmental Model," *Journal of Sociology and Social Welfare 8* (1981): 53.

143. This discussion is drawn from Jansson, *The Reluctant Welfare State*, pp. 185–192.

144. John Murchison, "Some Major Aspects of the Economic Status of the Negro," *Social Forces 14* (October 1935): 116.

145. Wayne Cornelius, "Mexican Migration to the United States: Causes, Consequences, and U.S. Responses," in *Crisis in American Institutions*, Fifth Edition, ed. Jerome Skolnick and Elliott Currie (Boston: Little, Brown, 1982), p. 159.

146. As discussed in Ehrenreich, *The Altruistic Imagination*, pp. 102–138; Fisher, *The Response of Social Work*, pp. 91–135; Leslie Leighninger, *Social Work*, pp. 39–44; Popple, "The Social Work Profession," pp. 564–565; Rick Spano, *The Rank and File Movement in Social Work* (Washington, DC: University Press of America, 1982); David Wagner, "Collective Mobility and Fragmentation: A Model of Social Work History," *Journal of Sociology and Social Welfare 13* (September 1986): 657–700; Wenocur and Reisch, *From Charity to Enterprise*, pp. 182–207.

147. As discussed in Ehrenreich, *The Altruistic Imagination*, pp. 187–264; Katherine Kendall, "A Sixty-Year Perspective of Social Work," *Social Casework 63* (September 1982): 427–428; Neil Gilbert and Harry Specht, "The Incomplete Profession," *Social Work 19* (November 1974): 667–668; George Lockhart and Joseph Vigilante, "Community Organization, Planning and the Social Work Curriculum," *Commununity Development Journal* (January 1974): 64–70; Reisch and Wenocur, "The Future of Community Organization," pp. 82–85; Robert Ross, "The New Left and the Human Service Professions," *Journal of Sociology and Social Welfare 4* (May 1977): 694–706; Stephen Sunderland, "Creating the New Profession—The Human Services," *Education and Urban Society 7* (February 1975): 141–171; David Wagner, "Radical Movements in the Social Services," *Social Service Review 63* (June 1989): 264–284.

148. Johnson and Schwartz, *Social Welfare,* p. 106; Charles Sanders, "Growth of the Association of Black Social Workers," *Social Casework 51* (May 1970): 277–284.

149. Alejandro Garcia, "The Chicano and Social Work," *Social Casework 52* (May 1971): 278.

150. Wagner, "Collective Mobility and Fragmentation," p. 687.

151. Diana DiNitto and C. Aaron McNeece, *Social Work Issues and Opportunities in a Challenging Profession* (Englewood Cliffs, NJ: Prentice Hall, 1990), p. 114; W. Joseph Heffernan, *Social Welfare Policy* (New York: Longman), p. 57.

152. Bruce Jansson, *Social Policy—From Theory to Policy Practice,* Second Edition (Pacific Grove, CA: Brooks/Cole, 1994), p. 20.

153. Jan Hagen, "Women, Work, and Welfare: Is There a Role for Social Work?" *Social Work 37* (January 1992): 9.

154. Wenocur and Reisch, *From Charity to Enterprise,* p. 268.

155. Mark Courtney, "Psychiatric Social Workers and the Early Days of Private Practice," *Social Service Review 66* (June 1992): 211.

156. Florence Styz, "Desegregation: One View from the Deep South," *Social Work 2* (July 1957): 4, 7.

157. As defined by Frederic Reamer, "The Free Will-Determinism Debate and Social Work," *Social Service Review 57* (December 1983): 631.

158 James Hackshaw, "Race and Welfare," *Encyclopedia of Social Welfare, Vol. II* (Washington, DC: National Association of Social Workers, 1971), p. 1066.

159. For additional discussion of social work and its environment, see Jansson, *Social Policy From Theory to Practice,* pp. 13–19.

160. Hackshaw, "Race and Welfare," p. 1065.

161. An example of writings in this area can be found in Roy Bailey and Mike Brake, *Radical Social Work* (New York, 1975); and a contemporary discussion on radical social work can be found in DiNitto and McNeece, *Social Work,* pp. 91–92.

162. DiNitto and McNeece, *Social Work,* p. 12.

163. F. Ellen Netting, Peter Kettner, and Steven McMurtry, *Social Work Macro Practice* (New York: Longman, 1993), p. 3.

164. Netting, Kettner, and McMurtry, *Social Work Macro Practice,* p. 256.

165. DiNitto and McNeece, *Social Work,* p. 74.

166. Johns and DeMarche, *Community Organization and Agency Responsibility,* pp. 38–40; Leighninger, *Social Work Search for Identity,* p. 11; Stadum, "A Critique of Family Case Workers," p. 75.

Chapter 6

Ethnic Services: Precedents, Perspectives, and Parameters

Ethnic social services—services provided by ethnic members to their own particular group—were not limited to ethnic and racial minorities. Religious groups established services for their members. For example, the Jewish Branch of the Roadside Settlement in Des Moines, Iowa, was organized in 1907 and supported by Jewish people; the Day Nursery and Neighborhood House was established in Newark, New Jersey, by the Jewish Sisterhood in 1905; the Harlem (New York) Federation for Jewish Communal Work was established in 1906 through the cooperation of all existing Jewish organizations in Harlem; the Brooklyn Italian Settlement opened its doors in 1901 with the help of the Italian Settlement Society; and numerous other homes emerged for specific immigrant groups, such as Catholic, Irish, and Slavonic immigrants.[1] Welfare activities for specific groups figured prominently in the lives of the immigrants and, in the absence of these groups, members of nationality groups looked to other agencies for assistance.[2]

Assistance for African Americans, Mexicans, Chinese, and Japanese was not so readily available. These groups had to develop ways of responding to what they defined as their needs. Because the assistance so readily available to the White ethnics was not forthcoming, these ethnic and racial communities had no recourse but to do for themselves. American Indians stand out as a distinct case because the intrusiveness of the government in their lives drastically limited their self-help capacity.

Minority communities, however, were not independent entities and could not determine for themselves the development of their communities and services. These communities were inexorably tied to the larger social systems in which they existed. What occurred internal to these racial and ethnic subsystems was shaped by the external polity and external economy of the U.S. society surrounding them. This state of affairs continues to prevail today. The social, political, and economic institutions of society shape the minority community experience and the community's reactions are often constrained by the larger system. According to Ringer and Lawless: "The larger society's conception of the they-ness of the ethnic group has serious consequences for the ethnic group. For the larger society tends to accept the 'validity' of its own definition and seeks to impose it in its relations with the ethnic group. Its conception of the they-ness of the group, for example, will govern its treatment of the ethnic group which in turn affects the life circumstances and opportunities of the ethnic group in the larger society."[3]

Cornell maintained that the development of a racial consciousness within an ethnic group is predicated on that group's relationship with the larger social system.[4] For example, African Americans and American Indians were of interest to society because of their labor and their land, respectively; therefore, Cornell stated that African Americans were able to form a group identity earlier than were American Indians. African-American's labor-based relationship with White America dissipated boundaries within the group and encouraged the formation of a group consciousness. Conversely, land-based relationships solidified boundaries within American-Indian groups and impeded the emergence of a group consciousness.

Each minority group suffered discriminatory treatment, but the nature and type of discrimination varied from group to group. Although each group may have had a minority status, each brought a unique reaction from the society surrounding them. As a result of these differences, the particular needs of each group also varied from group to group. For this reason, all groups cannot be lumped together. The larger society had one response to African Americans, another to American Indians, and still another for Mexicans, Chinese, and Japanese. The agenda the African-American community carved out for itself would be expected to be different from the American-Indian agenda, which would also be different from the Chinese agenda.

The internal polity and internal economy of each group has also varied. The setting of a service agenda and the mobilization of resources to implement that agenda reflected the dominance of factions within the groups. Problem causality and problem resolutions were perceived in numerous ways, and the ideology of the dominant elite within each ethnic and racial minority group prevailed. As the power of factions rose and fell, the predominant ideology also shifted. The rise and fall of particular ideologies were also linked to the prevailing conditions in the larger social system. For example, the civil rights movement and the Chicano movement occurred during a wave of unrest that swept the country. The "establishment" was being attacked on a number of fronts, and change is more likely to occur in times of turmoil. In this environment, these movements amassed a great deal of support from nonminority groups and individuals. The internal polities of the African-American and Mexican-American communities as well as the external polity were poised for change.

The external polity and external economy exerted influences that encouraged as well as forced minority communities to develop their self-help capacity. The unavailability of outside help is a major factor in stimulating this self-help.[5] Although some groups received some outside assistance, this assistance was not sufficient or deemed appropriate for the problems facing these groups. Lack of consensus between a minority group and the external polity about problem causes and problem solutions also led to the mobilization of mutual aid and self-help activities within the minority community.

As social work was planting its professional roots with the White ethnics (and, to a much lesser extent, African Americans), minority groups were beginning to create their own interventions. Mutual aid efforts of White ethnic communities preserved group culture and augmented the services of the Charity Organization Societies (COS) and settlement houses. However, mutual aid efforts of minority communities filled the void of no services or inadequate services. According to Miller: "To survive, these ethnic minority individuals and communities have had to make numerous adaptations to the institutions or create their own indigenous organizations, such as the ethnic churches and welfare institutions."[6]

This forced segregation may serve to promote the growth of a community infrastructure that reduces dependency and reliance on "outsiders" for resources.[7] Again, the community infrastructure is often shaped by the external polity and the external economy. What occurred in the minority communities was indicative of what the larger social system *permitted* or *tolerated* to occur in those communities. The capacity for self-help was constrained by the environment. These environmental constraints, in turn, influenced what these communities perceived as feasible options available to them. Consequently, ethnic communities were not totally autonomous and free to develop whatever services they desired. Needless to say, segregation may have stimulated more self-help activity than would have resulted had discrimination not been practiced.

Segregation and the emergence of community self-help also boosted the cohesiveness of ethnic minority communities. Group cohesiveness increases when members share a common external threat, when members feel that cooperation will reduce that threat, when members in low-status groups cannot elevate their status as individuals, and when stressful conditions exist.[8] For minority communities, membership in a minority group overrode the boundaries of education and social class. Because society's attack was based on the discrimination and segregation of specific groups, ethnicity became a unifying point for those affected groups. Ethnicity continues to act as a unifying theme in forming and mobilizing particular organizations.[9]

The ethnic services that evolved in minority communities were predicated on the larger society's treatment of that group, the demographics of the community, the identification of problems by the group itself, the culture of the group, and the availability of resources to mount those needed services. A brief overview of the emergence of ethnic services in specific communities is presented to illuminate the distinct issues and responses of these groups. For this reason, the overview is intended to be illustrative rather than exhaustive.

RACIAL/ETHNIC GROUPS AND ETHNIC SERVICES

African Americans and Ethnic Services

In the face of exclusionary and separatist practices, the African-American philosophy espoused historically has been one of African Americans helping African Americans. According to Meier, White discrimination and exclusionary policies were the direct cause of the establishment of segregated institutions such as African-American churches and fraternities.[10] The lack of economic advancement, compounded by growing poverty, spurred African Americans into action.[11] African-American communities began to take on the task of addressing their community needs because they felt abandoned by the federal government and neglected by service programs.

The African-American community self-help history and the primacy of the African-American church in that history have been richly documented.[12] From this history, several themes emerge: belief in the unity of the race, belief in self-help as the primary means of addressing problems and social conditions, and a commitment to improving the race.[13] African Americans fervently believed that their survival was intricately linked to self-reliance since the social, economic, and political forces surrounding them appeared to undermine that survival.

African Americans across the country accepted the doctrine of ethnic group responsibility and believed there was no one to help them but themselves. The self-help ethos was so strong that impoverished African Americans may have contributed a larger part of their income for charitable and religious causes than any group known in history.[14] Indeed, African Americans appeared to bear "almost the whole burden of their own internal social reform."[15] This self-help ethos encouraged African Americans to feel a responsibility to helping those who were less fortunate. Successful community members were expected to "reach down" and "give something back" to their community so that others could be elevated. Regardless of social class, education, and other signs of success, African Americans continued to be members of the African-American community and, as members, were expected or even obligated to use their success to help others.

Many of the writings on this subject fail to note the class distinctions inherent in the ethnic responsibility doctrine. Those who were in a more comfortable position were expected to help those who had less or nothing at all. In fact, as can be expected, the middle-class African Americans led the drive for race improvement. With their status and the power of the church behind them, it was difficult for these leaders not to be patronizing in their attitudes about the less fortunate. At the 1897 Second Atlanta University Conference, one of the African-American speakers admonished her peers for not conducting friendly visits with the poor of the community and said, "How much better off we would be if we could cease to draw these lines of caste and each of us as we climb the ladder reach down and assist a struggling sister!"[16] This speaker thought these "low-spirited" struggling sisters could benefit from "just a word of cheer and hope,...just a word of sympathy."

Improving the race meant that education was emphasized as a way out of poverty. African Americans established countless educational programs around the country and designated education as a type of self-improvement that could not be stripped away from its possessor. Education was frequently denied to African Americans and this may be the reason that these communities struggled to attain it. Education became synonymous with liberation and enlightenment. Education was also one means of assuring the betterment of the next generation. Consequently, numerous schools were established, usually through the efforts of church organizations, and they also provided a multiplicity of social welfare and child welfare functions.[17]

Improving the race also was interpreted to mean uplifting the morality of the race. "Immorality" was reflected in the high incidence of fatherless families in ghetto communities in the cities of the Progressive Era. This so-called immorality was defined as "sexual laxity" and "indifference to family ties," and was associated with "vagrancy and drunkenness" among African-American men.[18] During and since that time, numerous debates have ensued about the validity of statistics on African-American families and the effects of slavery on African-American family forms. During this period, however, these middle-class helpers were not only patronizing but they were moralizing as well.

Morality issues may also have been influenced by the presence of the church as a service delivery agent. The church was a central figure in African-American communities and was the largest and most visible African-American organization. Issues of immorality, drunkenness, and vice in general received immeasurable attention from the church. The inescapable presence of vice and the absence of law enforcement in African-American communities (as noted in Chapter 2) exacerbated issues of vice and morality in these communities.

For African Americans, the church emerged as one of the first leaders in the pursuit of the betterment of the African-American community. According to DuBois, it was natural "that charitable and rescue work among Negroes should first be found in the churches and reach there its greatest development."[19] The church was second only to the African-American extended family as a care-giving institution in these communities.[20] As the scope and extent of social needs exceeded the church's ability to respond and as the number of other voluntary organizations such as clubs and fraternities increased, the church lost its dominance as a service center.[21]

Pollard's study, as well as others, of African-American welfare developments of the Progressive Era reveals several trends that may still characterize ethnic services today.[22] First, as with the White welfare efforts, African-American services targeted populations that were perceived as the "most deserving." For African Americans, "most deserving" generally included the "most worthy" members of the community in need of assistance, such as children, young girls, widows, and the elderly.

Relief efforts for the general poor were not a priority for most U.S. communities. Although provisions could be made for some form of emergency relief, stable, ongoing relief assistance measures were not forthcoming. Groups and organizations rallied around those who were poor through no fault of their own. Those individuals deemed responsible for their poverty were extended little sympathy.

Orphanages, reformatories, homes for young girls, and homes for the aged were established for the vulnerable groups. Segregated or nonexistent services had resulted in large numbers of jailed African-American young women, children as young as age 7 "serving time" with adult criminals, and the elderly spending their twilight years in almshouses. Child welfare reform, as well as other service reforms, bypassed African-American communities and these populations appeared to be especially needy within these communities.

The concern of African-American communities about their pernicious treatment at the hands of law-enforcement officials and in jails and prisons spurred organizations to include juvenile justice and law-enforcement issues. In a 1908 visit to a Georgia court, a visitor observed that 578 boys and girls, mostly African Americans and under the age of 12, had been arrested and brought to court.[23] Offending African-American youths were either confined to jails, penitentiaries, stockades, or chain gangs. In Pollard's words, "No one worried about the soul of the black child but black people."[24]

Another trend in African-American services involved the tension between self-sufficiency and the acceptance of contributions from government and/or White philanthropists. For some African-American service providers, the ethos of self-help extended to self-help for the provision of services themselves. For other service providers, acceptance of donations from "outside" the community was necessary for the establishment and maintenance of services. The availability of outside funds indicated that Whites of the larger society supported and encouraged self-help in the African American as long as those self-help activities were consistent with White expectations. For example, White philanthropists provided significant funding for African-American education, but many were only willing to support industrial programs. White support for academic, professional, and artistic pursuits was almost nonexistent. Outside funding could serve to steer the community in the direction defined by the donors and thus act as a means of social control. The history of African-American self-help appears to be entangled with the history of White philanthrophy among African Americans.[25]

Women figured prominently in the African-American self-help movement, which parallels the pattern found in White communities. Service endeavors offered African-American women a voice in the community and they often led fund-raising and organizational development campaigns. Female participation for Whites was a way of escaping the confines of traditional roles. This was not necessarily the case for African-American women. Many African-American women were heads of households and had to work outside the home to support their families. African-American women were identified as industrious while some men were acquiring the labels of vagrant and drunk.[26] Many African-American women service leaders were not using this work to promote civic housekeeping or social mothering. The belief in racial unity brought African American men *and* women together in the struggle for racial improvement.

African-American services were for the community of African Americans as defined by race and not by geographical location. One type of service (or cluster of services) for African Americans would be utilized by African Americans in various parts of a city because such service was rare and White doors were closed. For example, as the only African-American settlement in Minneapolis, the Phyllis Wheatley House tried to serve all of the city's African Americans.[27] Because it had an African-American clientele, this house was called on to perform duties not associated with other settlement houses. Serving the city was one of these additional functions.

White welfare activities concentrated on working with individuals. However, African Americans saw their *race* as the focus of the uplift; racial improvement was the thrust. Service organizers had a vision of the African Americans, as a people, taking their place in mainstream society with status, equality, and respect. For this reason, those services with potential for elevating the future of the race were significant. The education and uplifting of children could reap benefits for generations to come and, if the tradition of ethnic group responsibility held, each generation could be better than the one before it.

Another dimension of African-American services warrants comment. Social reform and changes in public attitudes were not the goals for many of the services developed. Racial betterment, alleviating the harsh effects of poverty, and sustaining the community were primary goals of many early interventions.[28] Perhaps during this era, African Americans were acutely aware of their powerlessness in the U.S. political and social system. The times were not favorable to nor supportive of movements for integrating African Americans, and African Americans may have not yet found their political and social muscle. Also, the effects of outside funding on the course of self-help development may be a relevant factor here in guiding African Americans away from political activities. Thus, African-American services were analogous to services of mainstream America; however, in the African-American communities, individual-level change was replaced with group-level change for an entire race of people.

Social work, as an activity and as a profession, was accepted and integrated into the ethnic services of the African-American community. In an 1928 article, Jones recounted the history of social work among African Americans and indicated that social work activities as generally understood had been going on among African Americans throughout their lives in America.[29] He traced early "social work" activities back to 1793 when a New York City African-American woman organized the first Sunday school in the United States and also "reared and placed in suitable private homes forty-eight children," some of whom were White. She was no doubt among the first African Americans to work in what would now be called child placement or foster care. For Jones, as well as others, effective social work was a means of raising the social and economic level of the African-American community and developing the self-sufficiency of the group.

Several points on social work by African Americans are worthy of emphasis. First, in the history of social work in this ethnic community, specialized training appears to have been less of a prerequisite for providing services than in the White communities. As the profession was evolving its specialized knowledge base and specialized training programs, African Americans were continuing to do "social work" without the benefit of that training. As noted in Chapter 5, only about a third of African-American social workers in 1928 were thought to have had special training. Lack of access to White programs and the limited number of African-American programs contributed to this situation. For African Americans, the qualifications for doing social work and being a social worker appear to have involved factors other than special training.

African-American social workers also had distinct expectations placed on them, as Dexter observed in 1921.[30] They were expected to know their people's background; have intellectual training, a progressive outlook, and a pleasant personality; be in touch with the movements for improvement among African Americans; possess faith in the destiny of the African-American race; and deal with effects of race prejudice on the African American, something that White people were not believed to understand or realize.

As mainstream America developed mechanisms for responding to the social needs of its people, African-American communities were also developing their responses to the needs in their communities. Parallel service delivery systems were in the making, each with its own ideologies, missions, and practices.

American Indians and Ethnic Services

Policies of the U.S. government have inhibited the self-help capacity of American Indians and, for this reason, American Indians stand out as a distinct case. This history and the effects of these policies have been documented in several sources.[31] Confinement to reservations prevented these groups from continuing their cherished way of life. Forced acculturation or acculturation under duress was the country's mandate for them. Life on the reservation was dictated and controlled by the external polity and external economy of the reservation. Internally, the polity and economy did not have the resources to combat these external forces. U.S. goals for American Indians ranged from extermination and genocide, to expulsion, to exclusion, to forced Americanization, to ethnic responsibility.[32]

The U.S. government has defined the needs and solutions of American-Indian peoples, including their social welfare needs. What these people wanted for themselves was in opposition to what America wanted for them, and they were powerless to halt the imposition of U.S. policies. In essence, the country was demanding that American Indians denounce their lifestyles, their cultures, their languages, and their ways of survival. American Indians represent the most extreme example of Americanization. Even though they were denied the right to self-determination and the freedom to help themselves in the ways they thought necessary, several conclusions can be drawn from their history.

At the turn of the century, as detailed in Chapter 2, American Indians were enduring the Americanization efforts of missionaries and, in the eyes of the missionaries, were proving to be recalcitrant to those efforts. For this and perhaps other reasons, the adult American Indian was dismissed as lost or hopeless; thus, efforts focused on saving the American-Indian child. Hence, the boarding school movement was launched. The removal of children as young as 6 years old from their families and the placement of these children in institutional, off-reservation boarding schools represents one of the extreme ways in which assimilation policy operated.

Although the off-reservation boarding schools were discontinued during the depression years, mainstream child welfare followed in the practice of removing American-Indian children from their families and placing them in non-Indian settings. The perpetuation of rescuing children from "harmful" American-Indian influences was reflected in the child placement rate of American-Indian children. In 1976, for example, the out-of-home placement rate for American-Indian children was 12 to 18 times higher than that of non-Indian children, and 85 percent of the American-Indian children were placed in non-Indian homes.[33]

Because of the country's desire to save American-Indian children from the alleged harmful effects of the reservations, American Indians have been struggling to protect their children and to continue the transmission of cultural values to the next generation. Tension, and even hostility, have developed over time between American Indians and child welfare systems with their non-Indian service providers. The Indian Child Welfare Act of 1978 gives the jurisdiction of American-Indian child custody cases to the tribes. However, because many tribes are still developing their own programs, mainstream child welfare programs, the Bureau of Indian Affairs, or some nontribal entity is often used. In the aftermath of the passage of the Indian Child Welfare Act, numerous tribes struggled to hire staff, formulate program guidelines, and create program structures.

The Indian Child Welfare Act illuminates one of the paradoxes of the self-determination policies that have emerged since the 1960s and are exemplified in the Indian Self-Determination and Education Assistance Act of 1975. This act extended to tribes on reservations the right of self-government and the freedom to establish independent services. Many tribes did not have the resources to respond to these newly given rights. To a certain extent, government resources and leadership were still needed to make that transition. Deloria has been critical of these governmental efforts to foster American-Indian control of their reservations and asserted, "In the misguided hope that withdrawal of support services to the reservations would create a new wave of individualism among Indians, Congress terminated federal responsibility for them."[34]

With the Indian Self-Determination Act of 1975, American Indians could "control their relationships both among themselves and with non-Indian governments, organizations and persons" and acknowledge that "the prolonged Federal domination of Indian service programs has served to retard rather than enhance the progress of Indian People and their communities."[35] Herein lies another paradox: Policies developed and imposed by the government have resulted in a plethora of pernicious conditions on the reservations. The government then places the control of the communities in the hands of the residents to deal with these conditions. Government control was so extensive that American-Indians' self-determination was legislated— they did not have the right to decide for themselves when and how they could become self-determining. No doubt, they would have preferred tribal empowerment years earlier.

As American Indians develop self-help activities, efforts aimed at re-building or re-creating family support systems are priorities.[36] This focus is a direct response to policies that reduced the role of the extended family, clan systems, and natural child welfare systems within American-Indian communities.[37] The ethnic services now forming seem to be realistic pro-gram reactions to the damage inflicted by mainstream child welfare prac-tices and other practices of the Welfare State.

Mexican Americans and Ethnic Services

The history of Mexican-American self-help traces a path from identification with Mexico at the turn of the century to identification with the United States, as the priorities of first and subsequent generations of Mexican Americans shifted.[38] The early efforts of Mexicans in the Southwest to provide for the needs of their communities revolved around the family unit. These communities organized *mutualistas* (mutual aid funds) that provided insurance, funeral, and limited welfare benefits. These organizations served a social as well as an instrumental function, had constitutions, and con-ducted meetings. Since many of the members thought of themselves as Mexicans (rather than Mexican Americans) and anticipated returning to Mexico, politics of the United States did not dominant their time. Some of these *mutualistas* existed prior to the Treaty of Guadalupe Hidalgo.

For these first-generation Mexicans, it appears from Acuña's account that the *mutualistas* served to keep the memory of Mexico and Mexican tradition alive in the communities. These were organizations of Mexicans helping and supporting Mexicans and maintaining loyalty to Mexico. They observed Mexican holidays, traditions, and spoke Spanish.

For numerous Mexicans, a return to Mexico was not realized and they continued to reside in the United States and raise families. With this second generation, "Mexican American" was more an identity than it had been with their parents. These Mexican-Americans turned their eyes toward the United States and wanted to be part of its society. They wanted to promote their integration and change negative perceptions about them. The organi-zations they developed attempted to achieve these goals.

As a group, Mexican Americans have been subjected to deportation, regardless of whether they were citizens, legal residents, or undocumented workers. Indeed, in some situations, one's only infraction was simply "look-ing Mexican." Associations were often established to fight deportation in crisis times, such as economic slumps and depressions. These were the times the United States wanted to rid itself of expendable Mexican workers.

Some organizations were concerned with promoting the rights of Mexi-cans who were native born or who had achieved citizenship through natu-ralization. The citizen status reflected a permanency and commitment to the

United States, and the goal of these organizations was to assist Mexican Americans in obtaining their constitutional rights. One example of such an organization was *La Orden de Hijos de America* (The Order of Sons of America), founded in 1921 in San Antonio. It was the forerunner of the League of United Latin American Citizens (LULAC) established in Texas in 1928. During this period, it was more acceptable to be "Spanish" or "Latin" rather than "Mexican."[39] The anti-Mexican sentiment (discussed in Chapter 3) was a factor in the emergence of this organization.

LULAC had a integrationist perspective, as reflected in its taking an English rather than a Spanish name, with middle-class members. The organization had a commitment to children, and teaching them English was a priority as implemented in the LULAC established preschools. LULAC wanted "to develop within the members of our race the best, purest and most perfect type of a true and loyal citizen of the United States."[40] LULAC was a vehicle for Mexican-American Americanization that existed for Mexican Americans. As this organization grew, it expanded its scope to serve political as well as social functions.

Self-help community efforts among Mexican Americans were also directed toward uplifting the group. The group's status as "outsider" and "Mexican" led to harsh discriminatory treatment and the muting of their "Mexican-ness" was envisioned as leading to social acceptance and social justice.

Chinese Americans and Ethnic Services

The early Chinese communities were relatively closed social systems in which boundaries were crossed for economic purposes but the other group needs were met within the communities.[41] There were several types of associations: clans that united males of a common ancestry, *hui kuan* that united those who spoke the same dialect or came from the same geographical area of China, and tongs that were secret mutual aid associations not based on ancestry or language. In some communities, clan, *hui kuan*, and tong associations would come together to form one large organization.

One of the most powerful influences in the lives of the Chinese immigrant was the Chinese Consolidated Benevolent Association (CCBA), or the "Chinese Six Companies," established in the mid-1850s. Its membership included members of six *hui kuan*. According to the CCBA authorized historian, the CCBA "was empowered to speak and act for all the California Chinese in problems and affairs which affect the majority of the population."[42] The association collected various fees that were used to defray costs for services and community welfare.

In general, merchants, landlords, and factory owners led the voluntary organizations and served as gatekeepers and spokespersons between the community and the rest of society. In these positions, leaders often worked to maintain the separateness of the Chinese communities to protect their own power within these communities. This means that the merchant class controlled the voluntary organizations and, to some extent, exploited the immigrant laborers. On the other hand, workers who needed assistance because of sickness or loss of job had the organization's help. Wong and colleagues stated, "The benevolence of the traditional organizations in protecting their members from the vicissitudes of economic and other misfortunes must be weighed against their malevolence in maintaining as well as shielding the exploitative relationship between employers and workers in the enclave economy from external scrutiny."[43] Thus, the focus of much of the voluntary organizations' efforts seems to have been heavily economic since the protective associations acted as a type of "trades-union" that launched boycotts and strikes for better wages.[44]

The aims of the voluntary organizations were derived from the demographic makeup of the Chinese communities and the response of the larger society to the Chinese immigrants. Because of segregation, discrimination, and mob violence, the Chinese were clustered in ethnic enclaves, isolated from White Californians. All social life and activities took place within the ethnic enclave. As noted in Chapter 3, these communities were primarily male, so issues of family and children did not need attention. Because the immigrants came to the United States to work, their economic needs were of greater significance.

The isolation of the Chinese community from the "outside" world resulted in the Chinese community being perceived [by outsiders] as self-contained and able to take care of itself. An 1895 study of women in almshouses in San Francisco found that the Chinese "are practically unknown in the almshouse, probably owing to the fact that they *always care for their own poor*" [emphasis added].[45]

Although the doctrine of ethnic group responsibility was operative for this group, the group's internal polity and internal economy was driven by economic definitions of presenting problems. In addition, the barriers erected around this community, by those outside and inside the community, may have persisted over time.

Japanese Americans and Ethnic Services

The Japanese followed a pattern in social services similar to that of the Chinese. As with the Chinese immigrants, the Japanese immigrants were primarily males who came to the United States for economic reasons. They, too, formed voluntary associations that promoted economic survival and success.[46] Some of these associations provided burial and financial assistance. Members of the same *ken*, or Japanese state, frequently pooled resources for starting businesses or other economic ventures. The *tanomoshi* (to rely on or depend on) was another type of organization that assisted business ventures. The *tanomoshi* was akin to a small bank in which money was pooled and then extended, with credit, for business start-up costs.

Cohesion within the Japanese community was a key factor in the development of this community. In comparing the voluntary organizations of the early Chinese and Japanese communities, Wong, Applewhite, and Daley asserted that those in the Japanese community might have contributed more to fostering ethnic group solidarity and less to promoting class cleavage.[47] The ethnic group solidarity, as manifested in the activities of the voluntary organizations, contributed to the economic success of the ethnic group at the turn of the century.

As with the Chinese community, economic issues dominated the focus of the associations. Again, this is related to the group's purpose for immigrating to the United States, the composition of the group that immigrated, and the economic constraints confronting this group. At this point in the history of Japanese-American voluntary organizations, political issues were generally outside the purview of the community. The Issei (first generation) concentrated on economic and sociocultural interests.

OBSERVATIONS ON EARLY ETHNIC SERVICES

This cursory overview, combined with insights from the previous chapters, leads to several conclusions about early ethnic services in the United States:

1. Social work, as a practice and as a budding profession, was interwoven with the self-help activities of African-American communities. African Americans wanted and even demanded that these services be extended to them, and they wanted social work training so they could become social workers and work for the uplift of their race. Social work was a part of their world and it was growing around them, over them, beyond them, but not through them. As White programs and services proliferated, African Americans longed to bring these same kind of services to the poor and vulnerable in their communities.

African Americans were members of the U.S. society without being integrated into that society. They possessed American values and considered themselves "native Americans"—more native than the old-stock immigrants. They emulated, as much as they could, the mainstream happenings around them. If services, programs, friendly visitors, settlement houses, and the vast array of other services were going to help the immigrant become a better American, then African Americans wanted these same things to help their community members be better Americans. African Americans still clung to the hope that with education, employment, and related services they could become fully integrated into the world around them.

African Americans were defining their needs in "social work" terms and their books, articles, and newspapers documented their problems and their self-help work. Volumes of literature exist about the "colored" problem, the "Negro" problem, the "black" problem, and now the "African-American" problem. History is replete with African Americans analyzing, describing, and studying their community's problems and what should be done about them by African Americans themselves as well as society.

2. Although all racial minority groups were involved in the provision of "hard" services (tangible, concrete services), African Americans appear to be the only group that also identified a need for "soft" services (the talking services). This community encouraged individuals to become friendly visitors to lift the spirits of the less fortunate. Social work's relationship with the African-American community may have influenced this identification, and whatever services were being provided to the immigrants may have then been adopted by this group. On the other hand, the American community may have seen this service as necessary for its members.

3. White social workers knew more about the issues, needs, and conditions of African Americans than they did about any other ethnic/minority group. Through the COS and settlement houses, the plight of African-American communities was discussed, dissected, and debated. The size of the African-American population and the migration of African Americans in large numbers to centers of social work growth were factors fueling this interest. It may have led to social work historically viewing African Americans as the primary or major racial minority group in the country and to the profession displaying a greater interest in this group as opposed to the other racial groups.

4. Other ethnic minority groups did not share the African-American enthusiasm for the public discussion of its internal issues or for social work. It is doubtful that these other groups were even aware of the budding profession or of its practices. Of course, as these groups ventured into other parts of the United States, they were exposed to settlement houses and "social service," but a comparable integration of social work into their communities and into their cultures did not take place.

5. Society influenced the direction of self-help efforts in the African-American communities. These communities became a "cause" for philanthropists, settlement organizers, religious groups, and others as they funded, guided, and encouraged the self-help response among African Americans. Because African Americans were perceived by many as in a primitive stage of race development, the external polity, including social workers, were only too happy to provide the gentle nudge needed to stimulate ethnic responsibility.

6. American Indians are creating, defining, and implementing their own solutions to their issues. Although other groups have historically had opportunities to do this, American Indians had to have this right legislated because of the heavy-handedness of prior policies. Because social work has not been seen as a friend of the American Indian, the role of the profession in guiding and supporting these self-help developments is unclear. The distrust of the "system," particularly the child welfare system, held by numerous American Indians cannot be easily dismissed.

7. Mexican Americans were removed by geography, culture, and language from the development of social work so that their self-help efforts were, in fact, derived from the needs as perceived by members of this group. Because early self-help activities were geared to integration through English acquisition, language emerged as an area of great concern. They were also focused on reducing the threat of deportation, as the line between "legals" and "illegals" was firmly etched in their communities. Unfortunately, the public often refused to make this distinction and simply lumped all persons of Mexican origin in the same category; thus, the threat of deportation was very real.

8. Because the history of self-help organizations in the Chinese and Japanese communities centered around economic self-help, they are often perceived in terms of their economic success. In addition, they have maintained the image of the early communities: "closed," close-knit, and able to take care of themselves. Because of the perpetuation of this image, these communities may be perceived as problem free or not in need of "outside" help. The history of these two groups as related to exclusionary policies and practices would suggest that outside help might be received with distrust.

9. Issues related to children were priorities for African Americans, Native Americans, and Mexican Americans. These communities included families, whereas the early Chinese and Japanese communities did not. Issues related to children had to wait for the demographics of these groups to shift. For those groups that included a significant percentage of families and children, the uplifting of the group was anchored to the next generation and each successive generation. For these reasons, the communities sought to protect this investment in their future.

10. Law enforcement figured prominently in the self-help responses of African-American and Mexican communities. African-American children were subjected to the harshness of the criminal justice system and had few advocates. African Americans wanted reformatories and other services for juveniles. In the criminal justice system, race was the pivotal factor, not age, as African Americans, young and old, male and female, were jailed.

For Mexican Americans, the threat of deportation was driven by the enforcement of laws by those agents of the law. Police, border patrols, and anyone operating under the authority of a badge could rob a Mexican

American of his or her freedom, even if only temporarily. It is no wonder that early organizations tried to combat mass deportations because, during those times, law-enforcement agents may have indiscriminantly deported countless U.S.-born Mexicans. Law enforcement does not appear to have been a friend of the Mexican American, particularly in Texas and the Southwest.

11. Self-help activities of the African Americans, Mexican Americans, and Chinese Americans illuminate the intragroup issues of each culture. The African Americans were distinguished by class as the "haves" reached back/down to help the "have-nots." Some of the former could be patronizing and moralizing in their work with the poor and unfortunate. Skin color, mentioned in Chapter 2, may also be a factor in defining status within this group.

For Mexican Americans, social class and status as a native-born or naturalized citizen were important for some of the groups that formed. Middle-class, native-born "Spanish" or "Latin" individuals seemed to have had a higher status in the development of early organizations. This suggests that a gulf separated this group from the poor Mexican American and the immigrant Mexican. "Looking Mexican," mentioned in Chapter 3, may have also served to decrease one's social worth within this group.

In the Chinese communities, certain classes dominated community governance. These merchants, business owners, and others were able to offer employment in the ethnic enclave to immigrants, and this was the basis of their power.

Each group had an internal polity and an internal economy that helped to define the dominant elite of that group. An ethnic minority group may have been united by race or ethnicity, but it did not constitute a homogeneous group. Within each group, there were specific dimensions along which status and hierarchy may be plotted. The larger society may not have been aware of or interested in these intragroup differences, but the dynamics between members of the same ethnic/racial group were affected by these differences.

12. The history of ethnic minorities in the United States, the history of social work's development, and the history of ethnic self-help are relevant for forging contemporary links between social work and these diverse communities.

PERSPECTIVES ON THE ETHNIC AGENCY

The mutual aid and community self-help tradition is still apparent in ethnic minority communities and is found in the number of ethnic agencies that exist around the country. "Old" ethnic minority groups and "new" groups continue the tradition of developing, providing, and maintaining services to members of their groups. In Los Angeles, for example, the Korean Youth and Service Center serves the Korean-American community while the Russian Community Center focuses on the needs of the Russian immigrant community.

The ethnic minority agency, however, still stands out from the other agencies that exist. There is the perception that ethnic minority status creates a unique dilemma for communities that require special attention. The ethnic agency seems to set the needs of its community apart from the needs of other communities and to set its interventions apart from those used in other communities. White ethnics are seen as having the support of mainstream service plus their own ethnic services, yet the ethnic minority agency may still be propelled by *necessity* rather than by choice.

As the demand for more ethnic-sensitive services grows, these agencies should receive careful analysis so that what they do, why they do it, and how they do it can be better understood by those outside the ethnic agency system. These agencies may be an overlooked bridge between mainstream services and ethnic minority communities.

What Is the Ethnic Agency?

Before a definition of the ethnic agency is posited, it is first necessary to generate a context for this discussion. Although ethnic-specific agencies have existed throughout history, little is really known about them as a class of organizations or as an organizational type. Despite the growing diversity of the population and the growing interest in the way race/ethnicity influences organizations, there continues to be a dearth of research on and analysis of these issues.

Cox surveyed researchers and reviewed relevant literature to ascertain why this void exists. One factor uncovered was that research in this area was not a priority because it lacked "universal importance." The presumption made by sponsors of organizational research was that issues of race are only of interest to minority groups and not to the rest of the world. Cox also found that there was a tendency for issues related to a particular minority group to be subsumed under the larger rubric of "minority groups" so that emphasis on individual groups was minimized.[48]

Cox also observed a number of other factors: Minority *and* majority group members were discouraged from doing race/ethnic research; there is a perception that this type of research would be difficult to undertake because of methodological obstacles; and organizations may be unwilling to participate in research on race/ethnic issues. Minority researchers were advised not to put themselves in a "research ghetto" because this research was "inferior" and "no established person has expertise or interest in this area."[49] White researchers seeking to do research in this area generally have their credibility questioned and/or receive negative reactions from minority group members.

The paucity of research on ethnic organizations does not mean that the existing organizational literature should be dismissed. There are rays of light that can be extrapolated from the work that has been done.

What It Is and What It Is Not

In recent years, literature has emerged on alternative service organizations (ASOs). ASOs are "human service organizations founded by local initiative to offer alternatives to established human services which ASOs' initiators believe to be inadequate."[50] These agencies fill gaps, are innovative, and strive for social change. As a matter of fact, ASOs are "deeply *committed to social change*" and provide services to "*special populations* with special problems" that are not addressed by traditional agencies.[51] From the standpoint of the ASO, "The service mandates of existing agencies have evolved slowly over time and may not readily expand to meet the needs of newly emerging or newly visible client groups."[52] These agencies tend to be small, be resource poor, be staffed by the nonprofessional but ideologically committed, use staff who are members of the group being served, and engage in participatory governance.

Grass-roots agencies seem to fall within the definition of the ASOs; the designation "grass roots" describes the bottom-up approach to organizing.[53] Examples of ASOs are women's shelters, runaway shelters, crisis centers, and peer counseling centers. Ethnic agencies are typically omitted from the list.

The literature on ASOs has some limited utility for ethnic agencies. Although ethnic agencies fill service gaps, they may not necessarily be new, innovative, or social change agents. In addition, some ethnic agencies have been in operation for years and serve "old" client groups. Ethnic agencies today may concentrate on the improvement of the group it serves and may not be politically active. Ethnic agencies are not always small and resource poor, although many of them are. Many ethnic agencies are fairly large with professional staff and hierarchical structures.

The Korean Youth and Community Center of Los Angeles is an ethnic agency with a multimillion-dollar annual budget and programs that range from counseling, education, and employment to consumer education and tobacco use prevention. Its history dates back to 1975, and in 1983, it became the first Korean agency in Los Angeles to receive United Way funding. Today, this agency receives funds from federal, state, county, city, and private sources. An agency of this magnitude moves beyond the scope and definition of ASOs.

Ethnic agencies that serve new or recently visible minority immigrant groups seem closer to the ASO definition. These agencies engage in advocacy because their clients have not come to the service attention of mainstream agencies. To reach these nontraditional populations, ethnic agencies may have to be more innovative and creative in their service delivery approaches. Staff in these agencies may be indigenous workers from the community who are committed to this group. Many of these immigrant aid agencies are small with shoestring budgets.

As Haitians establish their communities in the southeastern part of the country, they are beginning to define their needs as separate from those of African Americans and are maintaining their identity as Haitians. Political needs may take priority over social service needs as this group works for legal and political status. As a service group, the specific issues of this community may be invisible to the traditional social agencies. Residents of the Haitian community may have to initiate steps to respond to these issues. As this community evolves with a base to create its own services, the definition of the ASO would then seem more applicable. Consequently, some ethnic agencies are ASOs and some are only marginally akin to ASOs.

The collectivist model of organizations may describe some ethnic agencies.[54] These agencies may have minimal formalization, a sense of community, staff recruitment based on ideology, an egalitarian stratification system, personalistic and moralistic means of social control, little or no hierarchy, group solidarity as primary, minimal division of labor, and the demystification of expertise. This definition may apply to small, grass-roots, community-based agencies. These agencies are founded on commitment and dedication but little money, and the belief in the cause ignites the organizers' desire to forge ahead. A belief in the group and the desire to serve the ethnic group form the agency's ideology.

A drug-treatment program in the Midwest for African-American women started as a collectivist agency with a small grant from an area foundation. Decisions were made by the group and few distinctions were made between clients and staff. The directorship, as well as all jobs, rotated among the workers so that everyone could perform every job. The "treatment" consisted primarily of small-group discussions. Rules were practically nonexistent and "clients" participated based on how they felt at the time. This program remained small, loosely structured, poorly funded, and collectivist until its demise. For this program, the collectivist model applies; for the Korean Youth and Community Center, however, it does not.

Some ethnic agencies evolve from the changing demography of the community in which it is housed. Just as immigration influenced service systems of the past, it is changing these systems today. For example, according to Rivera-Martinez: "Hispanics are creating and developing new agencies in the communities where they live. Most are social organizations that served White immigrants for many decades and that due to changes in the composition of the neighborhood population now find themselves serving Hispanic immigrants."[55]

The Neighborhood Youth Association (NYA) of Los Angeles is an example of an agency whose service population changed as a result of population shifts. NYA originated in 1906 as the Neighborhood Settlement Association as part of the settlement house movement to serve the new immigrants. The agency was incorporated in 1916 and received its first United Way/Community Chest funding in 1926. Because it is neighborhood and community based, it has adapted to the varying needs of its varying population. Currently, it has a Spanish-speaking director and staff who serve a large Spanish-speaking client population.

Ethnic agencies are also voluntary service agencies since they are nongovernmental, nonprofit organizations formed independently of state mandate.[56] These agencies are generally small in size (as compared with government agencies), governed by boards, and provide a range of services.[57] Ostrander reviewed the literature on these types of agencies and concluded that they support program specialization, contribute to the democratizing and decentralizing of the Welfare State when they rely on government funding and citizen participation on boards, support more government-supported services since they are the beneficiaries of government financing, and have the basis for "cross-class" political alliances in support of Welfare State services.[58]

Ostrander's analysis, however, was of mainstream family and children's agencies that are a major component of nongovernmental services. Bok criticized Ostrander's analysis because she "continues the apparent trend to discount the importance of nonmainline agencies."[59] Because it is not known to what extent ethnic agencies are in the "funding loop," the relevance of analysis of traditional agencies remains clouded. Although ethnic agencies are voluntary social service entities, their functions and structures as such may deviate from other voluntary agencies.

Because ethnic agencies are identified with specific geographical areas of a city, they may meet the definition of the neighborhood-based organization (NBO). Milofsky noted that NBOs provide services to and advocate for a particular constituency, are incorporated as nonprofits or are too small to be incorporated, are committed to the interests of their constituency, and have minimal hierarchy and specialization.[60] He indicated that examples of NBOs are the mutual aid and community betterment organizations that emerged in minority communities.

In a diverse society, ethnic agencies can, however, defy the definitions of the NBO. For example, the area of Los Angeles commonly referred to as "Koreatown" mirrors the control and culture of first-generation Koreans. The population of Koreatown is 22 percent Korean, 45 percent Hispanic, 11 percent White, 10 percent African American, and 12 percent other. This community is the center of Korean services, whereas services to the Hispanic population of the community is relatively nonexistent. The elementary school of Koreatown has an Asian-American population of 17 percent and a Hispanic population of 79 percent. It is the site of a Saturday school that offers a Korean language class to students for $250 a semester. The Hispanic community in Koreatown cannot afford a language program for their needs. The community has a clinic (Koryo Health Foundation), a community center (the Korean Community Center), as well as the Korean Youth and Community Center.

Koreatown is an example of a community that has ethnic-based services but not community-based services (since the majority of the constituency in this community is Hispanic). Koreatown acts as a magnet to attract Koreans from all parts of the county for services. The service needs of Korean Americans can be met in this community, whereas the majority of residents have to go outside the community for services. Because many ethnic agencies are committed to providing services to the identified ethnic group regardless of the geographical area in which they live, all ethnic agencies cannot be categorized as community or neighborhood based.

The ethnic agency bears some resemblance to self-help organizations that have garnered more attention over the last 20 years. Self-help organizations may be responding to some deficiency in mainstream service delivery and share three characteristics that highlight their uniqueness: (1) the majority of the members and board have some type of stigmatizing condition; (2) at least half the board or their relatives actually participate in the program; and (3) in the beginning stages of development, professional involvement is limited.[61] If ethnicity is defined as the "stigma," then numerous ethnic agencies may be subsumed under the self-help organization designation.

Self-help organizations tend to be deprofessionalized and debureaucratized; provide services that parallel, complement, or compete with mainstream services; have services delivered by peers; and fall halfway between a *folk* care system and a *professional* care system.[62] Many ethnic agencies capture these dimensions but it is not clear to what extent ethnicity interacts with them.

Although ethnic agencies may be expressions of mutual aid and self help, they appear to be outside of the self-help movement. The self-help movement involved the development of alternative service forms and structures but it was primarily a movement for the development of a "middle-class group-support system for unrelated individuals with similar psychomedical, psychosocial problems."[63] On the other hand, a small group of minority individuals can come together to brainstorm an issue or crisis affecting their community and, eventually, a new ethnic agency is born. Although not a part of the self-help movement itself, ethnic agencies may emerge as the product of self-help activities.

So What Is It?

To date, the most definitive work on the ethnic agency has been done by Shirley Jenkins and reported in *The Ethnic Dilemma in Social Services*.[64] She studied 54 agencies that served five ethnic/racial groups (Asian Americans, African Americans, Puerto Ricans, Chicanos, and Cherokees). These agencies were located in six states and included day-care centers, foster care and adoption agencies, residential centers, youth services, multipurpose service centers, and other programs providing services to children.

From this research, Jenkins concluded that an ethnic agency is the following: (1) it serves primarily ethnic clients; (2) it is staffed by a majority of individuals who are of the same ethnicity as the client group; (3) it has an ethnic majority on its board; (4) it has ethnic community and/or ethnic power structure support; (5) it integrates ethnic content into its program; (6) it views strengthening the family as a primary goal; and (7) it maintains an ideology that promotes ethnic identity and ethnic participation in the decision-making processes.

In a sample of 574 workers from the agencies studied, Jenkins also found that 43 percent of the workers had less than a B.A. degree, 18 percent had a B.A., 13 percent had some master's work, 17 percent had an M.S.W., and the remainder (9 percent) had done doctoral work. These figures reflect a tendency for these ethnic agencies to rely on paraprofessional staff.

Jenkins wanted to know more about the ethnic attitudes of social workers and asked whether workers are more likely to be helpful if (1) they have a social work degree or (2) they belong to the same ethnic group as the client. In comparing the responses of ethnic agency workers to those of a national sample of trained social workers in mainstream child welfare agencies, she found that 79 percent of the child welfare sample answered "degree" and 21 percent answered "ethnicity." For the ethnic agency workers, 62 percent replied "degree" and 38 percent replied "ethnicity." These differences were statistically significant (21 percent versus 38 percent) and further underscore the ethnic ideology of ethnic agency staff.

Additional survey questions delineated the attitudes of ethnic agency staff. Two-thirds of the ethnic agency workers believed that those minority groups who wanted to operate programs for their own group should be allowed to do so and be given public funds. About half of the national sample of workers felt this way. Over half of the ethnic agency workers thought that Spanish should be compulsory in schools of social work, yet less than a quarter of the national sample concurred. Since the Mexican-American and Puerto-Rican ethnic agency workers comprised 22 percent of the sample, their presence alone cannot account for the percentage of ethnic agency response on the Spanish question. Workers in ethnic agencies seem more likely to support those ideas and practices that promote ethnic/racial identity and consciousness in comparison to social workers in general.

Jenkins also found that African-American social workers in the ethnic agencies placed more value on credentials in comparison to the other ethnic groups studied and more of them had credentials. The place of social work in the history of African-American communities attests to the faith that many of this group have in the value and recognition of the social work degree. This may also suggest that, among those entering the ethnic agency work force, the African-American ethnic agencies will have a larger pool of degreed workers from which to choose.

For the ethnic agency workers, the social work degree was important but so was ethnicity, and the ethnic factor was also acknowledged in responding to the needs of clients. The ethnic agency is, in its own way, promoting the contemporary uplift of the group by providing services in addition to trying to assist in improving the basic primary unit of the ethnic group—the family.

This pioneering work by Jenkins amplifies the ethnic factor in service delivery that is frequently minimized in mainstream services. Unfortunately, social work has not embraced nor recognized the ethnic agency and this literature has not been fully utilized. This oversight may be part of a larger pattern in U.S. social work development—to generally ignore or devalue ethnic service organizations and ethnic social workers.[65]

An African-American social worker in Tennessee made the following comments when asked about the role of ethnic agencies in social work: "We could use more of them. You know, we black folks have always known that race made a difference in everything—how people look at you, how people treat you. It's the white people who want to play down differences, say we should only talk about what we have in common, and pretend to be colorblind while all the time making judgments about you because you're black."[66] The ethnic agency becomes one way of validating the significance of race as a factor in service delivery by treating that factor as a relevant and valued contribution to the agency/client interface.

The ethnic agency—which is primarily administered and staffed by persons from the specific group being served and which mediates between the functions of the cultural group and the service delivery system—is viewed as the most efficient way to deliver services that promote ethnic cohesiveness and identity.[67] The ethnic agency appears to offer its clients psychological well-being, cultural affinity, a nurturing environment, emotional support, the incorporation of their unique sociohistorical experiences in the treatment process, and interventions often based on the concept of empowerment.[68]

Although ethnic agencies have existed as long as traditional agencies, there is little conceptualization or empirical investigation of this type of agency. With the exception of Jenkins's work, much of the literature on this topic is filled with descriptive case studies of specific agencies.[69] Although these accounts provide some descriptive insight into the agency, additional analysis is needed to place the ethnic agency in a theoretical framework that is useful for extrapolation to mainstream agency practices.

Why Ethnic Agencies?

The debate over the purpose of the ethnic agency raises a number of issues about service delivery processes and mainstream services.

Deficiencies in Service Delivery Systems

One view of the reason for the existence of the ethnic agency cites problems in the way traditional service systems have responded (or not responded) to ethnic populations. These traditional systems may limit the access of ethnic minorities to needed services through system gatekeepers.[70] Differential access and nonresponsiveness to needs then would lead ethnic minority communities to establish their own services.[71]

Some ethnic agencies mirror traditional system services. This form of duplication is referred to as *separatism*.[72] With this form, new agencies are established outside the mainstream service delivery system, and these new agencies may not try to penetrate that system. These agencies serve disenfranchised groups that are also outside of the mainstream. Separatism may act as a political and social strategy for advocating for needs and obtaining resources.

In those settings in which access to services has been obtained, the mainstream social service may be so intrusive in the ethnic community that informal helping systems in these communities are damaged.[73] While this may be true for nonminorities, minorities may be even more susceptible to the effects of the system. For example, policies that encourage the placement of children with relatives often define *relative* to mean individuals related to the child by blood, marriage, or adoption.[74] These relative caregivers can become foster parents for the child and receive services and support. The placement policies, however, do not define *compadres* or *comadres* (godfathers or godmothers) or "kith" (fictive kin) as part of the relative definition. Although these individuals may serve as a support system in their individual cultures, service delivery systems have not embraced them officially.

Minority clients may also feel that they have no input into the systems that are providing them services. They may face what is defined by Gilbert, Specht, and Terrell as nondistributive participation (no real input) or normal participation (tokenism) without really being able to change or influence these systems.[75] The sense of powerlessness that results may be the impetus needed to mobilize residents to develop their own services.

The residents of a predominantly African-American public housing community in Washington, DC, took control of their community and eventually developed an array of social services in an attempt to improve the conditions of the community. Employment, counseling, parenting, and health services are provided in the community through agencies formed by the residents for the residents. According to Kimi Gray, one of the organizers of the Kenilworth-Parkside Residents Council, "We got tired of folks parachuting programs into our neighborhood. They weren't doing any good anyway. They had written us off. The police wouldn't come. The firemen wouldn't come. We didn't even have trash pickup. We just got tired of folks telling us what we couldn't do. Besides, we couldn't do any worse than what had already been done."[76] Through extensive community organization, Kenilworth-Parkside has evolved into a multimillion dollar corporation in addition to its social service arm.

There may be a tendency for the paternalism often associated with casework to work its way into the social planning process, and minority communities may be more likely to have programs parachuted into them. Frustration and anger can unite to form a community backlash. A program developed by the Los Angeles Police Department as part of a national Weed and Seed Program met with such organized community opposition that the proposal was withdrawn. The plan called for the "weeding" out of criminals from crime-ridden communities and the "seeding" of the communities with social programs. The communities targeted were South-Central (a Hispanic and African-American area), Pico-Union (a Hispanic immigrant community), and Koreatown.

In the aftermath of the 1992 urban unrest (that was sparked by an innocent verdict in the trial of four White police officers charged with physically assaulting an African-American male), these communities and their ethnic agencies became more vigilant in protecting the interests of citizens. Because they were not included in the planning process, these agencies and individuals denounced the Weed and Seed Program as an example of decisions being made for them. There was also concern about the effects of increased police activity in these communities. In this case, the external polity created a situation so unacceptable that the ethnic communities and their ethnic agencies became visible, vocal, and confrontational.

Myths and gross generalizations may also decrease mainstream services to ethnic minorities. For example, the "myth of the model minority" has followed many Asian Americans because of their apparent educational and economic successes.[77] This illusion of assimilation suggests that they do not warrant special attention. This myth may be so pervasive that it explains why more than 13 percent of poor Asian Americans in Los Angeles County are unnoticed by policy makers and program planners.[78]

The lumping of ethnic groups into global categories also decreases system responsiveness to these groups. *Asian American* is used typically to define Chinese, Japanese, and Korean Americans, but the term is also being expanded to include Filipino, Vietnamese, Cambodian, Samoan, and Guamanian Americans.[79] Tezcatlipoca argued that, "The terms *Hispanic* and *Latino* are insulting to Chicanos and Mexicanos because these words deny us [Chicanos] our great Native Mexican heritage."[80] Labels such as *Hispanic* or *Spanish-speaking* mask the differences that exist between Cuban, Puerto Rican, and Mexican Americans. These global labels also ignore the fact that, for some groups, Latino ethnic identification can be situational and political.[81] American Indians did not consider themselves as a collective group; rather, they were separate and distinct sovereign nations with cultural and language variations. The society around them categorized them as a group, thereby ignoring the self-identification of the nations. The imposition of artificial labels communicates a false homogeneity between ethnic groups. Services designed to meet the needs of Asian Americans and Hispanic Americans ignore between-group differences and tensions, and may only superficially attend to needs.

Many service delivery systems may not have been designed to deliver services to ethnic populations. According to Alberta Folk, program director for One Church, One Child (a national agency that promotes the adoption of African-American children by African Americans), "The system [adoption] was designed to service white families when white babies were readily available."[82] For this reason, mainstream adoption programs may not be receptive to the modifications necessary to bring African-American adoptive parents into the service delivery system.

Deficiencies in the larger social system have not been the only factor associated with the formation of ethnic agencies. Another set of explanatory factors lies in the ethnic community subsystem itself.

Cultural Barriers to Mainstream Services
Cultural barriers may prevent an ethnic group from seeking help outside the ethnic community. For example, Hammond found that this was the case for Native Hawaiians and concluded that Native Hawaiians were more similar to American Indians in their service needs and service responses.[83] Homma-True also found that cultural barriers impeded service delivery to Chinese Americans.[84] The subjects in this study were guarded about discussing their problems but did seem receptive to the possibility of using a family outreach service.

Distrust of the larger social systems figures prominently in attitudes toward mainstream services. Mass found that, although problems may exist in the Japanese-American community that exceed the family's ability to respond effectively, the Nissei (second generation) were not interested in any outside involvement in their problems. The unique history of the group in the United States has resulted in a perception of the government as not advancing the cause and interest of this community.

In a review of the literature on service utilization among Asian-American elderly, Salcido, Nakano, and Jue found distrust and skepticism played a role in the underutilization of services by Chinese Americans, Korean Americans, and Pilipino Americans.[85] For the Japanese Americans, differences were found in the attitudes between the generations. For individuals isolated from and distrustful of "outside" service systems, the ethnic agency functions as a point of contact as well as a provider of services. In this study, the ethnic agency provided needed services to individuals who otherwise would have been isolated, alone, and neglected.

Some ethnic agencies are a manifestation of a group cohesiveness that supports organizational development and organizational participation.[86] For example, in a study of American Indians' preference for counselors, Johnson and Lashley found that participants with strong commitment to the American-Indian culture preferred a same-race counselor.[87] For ethnic group members with strong ethnic identity, the ethnic agency becomes a tool for further solidifying group cohesiveness. Because participation in traditional ethnic organizations was related to success and life satisfaction among first-generation Japanese Americans, the ethnic agency can also potentially serve as a crucial source of support.[88]

THE ETHNIC AGENCY: SOCIAL SYSTEM PARAMETERS

The ethnic agency does not represent a monolithic entity; rather, it covers a range of agencies that provide a variety of services to a spectrum of ethnic groups. The ethnic agency is affected by cultural traditions that become manifested in both structure and operations.[89] Thus, as ethnic groups differ in history, cultural traditions, belief systems, and norms, these are reflected in the operations of an ethnic agency serving a particular group. There is no single model that defines the ethnic agency.

Since the ethnic agency emerges from the ethnic community, an understanding of the community itself is important for understanding the necessity of the ethnic agency. Several factors seem to determine whether ethnic agencies develop in ethnic communities. These factors include the city or part of the country where the group is located, the length of time the group has been in the United States, the degree of diversity or homogeneity of the group, intragroup class system,[90] and the group's relationship with the larger social system.[91]

Location is important because values, norms, and social systems vary by regions. For example, the Japanese Americans of St. Louis have had a different interaction with its larger social system and external polity as compared with the Japanese of California.[92] In St. Louis, the Japanese Americans were upwardly mobile and the city provided better pathways to employment and entrepreneurship. The polarization between Whites and African Americans in that city did not impede the progress of the Japanese Americans. This may have been related to the smaller size of this community in St. Louis, as compared to California, so that it was not perceived as a threat. The race conflict in St. Louis was a Black-White problem, not a Japanese-American one. The rapid integration of the Japanese into the larger social system may have reduced the need for this group to establish its own social service agencies.

Immigration patterns, as they relate to specific regions of the country, affect the nature and extent of ethnic community organization and ethnic agency development in numerous other cities and states. For example, in Miami, the polarization between African Americans and Whites is still apparent, while the Cuban American community, in general, has attained greater economic and political success in comparison to African Americans. As other "Black" groups immigrate to this part of the country, African Americans may have to aggressively launch campaigns to define themselves and their needs as distinct from Haitians and other Caribbean Islanders.

For those groups that are recent arrivals, the newness of the culture, the establishing of economic security, and the transition from the old home to the new may not immediately encourage the development of ethnic agencies. For Guatemalans immigrating to the United States (from Central America), divisions by political ideologies and districts of origin may stifle group cohesiveness and reduce the likelihood of Guatemalan ethnic agencies. As these former identifications give rise to a consensus in identity as Guatemalans, ethnic agencies that serve Guatemalans regardless of political ideology and district of origin may be forthcoming. Thus, the longer this group is in the United States, the more likely the probability of ethnic agencies emerging in this country. Recency and diversity are the factors operative here.

An ethnic group, as a subsystem, interfaces with other subsystems as well as with the larger system of which it is a member. Discriminatory practices may foster group cohesiveness and encourage ethnic agencies to develop to meet group needs and to provide intragroup support. Thus, the initial motivation to form an ethnic agency may arise from external conditions such as inadequate facilities, inappropriate facilities, or no facilities.[93]

In the prevailing environment of anti-immigration sentiment directed toward Hispanic immigrants, immigrants from Central America may find the climate less than hospitable and services less than forthcoming. They may be forced to provide for the needs of their community, and the creation of ethnic agencies may be one option. For the Central Americans, the development of ethnic agencies may be accelerated by a hostile environment.

The presence of a sizable lower class within an ethnic group may also promote the establishment of ethnic agencies. Poverty added to minority status may create a truly disadvantaged, disenfranchised class that warrants assistance from ethnic-specific agencies. Within ethnic communities, class becomes another force that propels ethnic agency development. Indeed, Jenkins found that the ethnic agencies she studied served primarily low-income groups.[94]

Class may also be an indication of some degree of integration into the larger society. For example, in a study of Korean Americans in Cleveland, Han found that middle-class Korean Americans had knowledge of mental health professionals and accepted the purpose they served.[95] This group seemed receptive to these service providers but it was not ascertained whether this belief was actually supported through action. Class could be interpreted as a measure of one's awareness of and integration into the larger social system. For middle-class ethnic group members, the ethnic agency may be less of a necessity.

The ethnic community is a dynamic, fluid entity that adapts and responds to its environment. Ethnic agencies rise and fall in tune with the system in which they are situated. Integration into and acceptance by the larger social system may decrease the need for ethnic agencies while polarization and differential treatment compel minorities to seek stations of solace. Because of the significance of these agencies to their communities, what these agencies do and how they do it command consideration.

Organizational Parameters

There seems to be a prevailing notion that ethnic agencies are "different." Articulating this difference can be challenging and perplexing, however. When clients of a small African-American ethnic agency were recently asked about the agency and their experiences, they reacted:

Client 1: It's hard to say. I mean they treat you like a human being. I mean my caseworker acts like she's glad to see me. Can you believe it?

Client 2: I can talk to the people there just like I'm talking to you. No big deal. The other day when I went there I was so mad at my daughter. I told the receptionist why I was mad and she knew exactly what I meant. I can talk to anybody there.

Client 3: It's okay. Sometimes somebody over there gets an attitude but I don't care. As long as I get what I want I don't mind.

What are these individuals really saying about the agency? What makes the ethnic agency stand out as unique type of agency?

Ethnicity and Ideology

The foremost distinction of the ethnic agency is its ideology of the value of ethnicity and its integration into the service delivery process. Ideologies reflect those beliefs that are held with fervor and help explain cause-and-effect relationships.[96] Ideologies shape the agency's receptivity to the clients and their presenting problems. Typically, these ideologies are manifested in the worker-client interaction, agency technology, agency structure, distribution of power, and the extent to which the client is held responsible for causing his or her situation.

Generally, the worker-client relationship is analyzed in terms of the degree of discretion the worker has in his or her interactions with the client; the removal of the worker-client interaction from the scrutiny of the organization; the value mutuality between the worker and client goals; and the centrality of trust and rapport in effective helping relationships.[97] Another aspect of the worker-client relationship also commands attention. According to Iglehart, the worker represents the interface between the agency and the client and, in this role, embodies the agency to the client.[98] She added that the client "sees" the agency through a worker who interprets the agency to the client. Through the worker, the client enters the organization's system. What occurs between the worker and client is frequently generalized to the rest of the agency. If the organization has a commitment to the client, workers will be expected to develop trust and rapport with these clients. Ethnicity may be a crucial factor in the commitment of the agency and the worker to the client.

Racial sameness between worker and client is assumed to foster close, sensitive interactions that are generalized to the agency. According to Etzioni, a close relationship between worker and client leads to sensitivity to the client, which in turn leads to client-responsive services.[99] In the ethnic agency, ethnicity becomes a factor that advances rather than impedes the service delivery process. For the agencies Jenkins studied, this ethnic content was located in food, music, art, history, and holidays. It seems, however, that these are just symbolic of a much deeper meaning of ethnicity.

Dexter's 1921 observation about the qualification for social work among one's own people can be generalized to other groups besides African Americans. That qualification was faith in the destiny of the race.[100] The worker who symbolizes the agency joins with the client in those steps necessary to improve and uplift the ethnic/racial group. In this regard, the worker and client become part of the same system, as opposed to being members of the helping system versus the client system. As a member of that ethnic group, the worker does not have to be convinced of, lectured to, or advised about the destiny of the race since he or she already has inside knowledge about this destiny.

Ethnicity facilitates service delivery by exposing clients to role models with whom they can identify. Freudenberger emphasized this point by noting that, in a youth drug-treatment program, it is easier for the Latino client to identify with a successful member of his own group than with someone from another group.[101] Freudenberger stated, "As staff members of minority programs it is incumbent on us to keep in mind that if there are Latino residents, then we need Latino staff; the same applies for Asian Americans, Native Americans, and Mexican Americans. This does not mean that there needs to be exclusivity, but the majority of the treatment staff in a dominant minority group neighborhood ought to be from the same ethnic background."[102]

Petr has urged workers to position themselves *within* the client system to allow for reciprocity and mutuality in the relationship.[103] If this occurs, Petr stated, "then the role of worker must be *non*interventionist, or somehow beyond intervention. Attention to the subjective world of values, meaning, and process would displace objective understanding of problems and their resolution."[104] Although this type of mutuality is not promoted by the professional and bureaucratic imperatives of mainstream agencies, the ethnic agency at least seems more sympathetic to this point of view.

In the ethnic agency, the worker and client are already more likely to attend to the world of values, meaning, and process. For example, an American-Indian client does not have to hide his or her use of native healers or other culturally sanctioned healers from the ethnic agency worker. For some groups, these healers may be a crucial source of help.[105] The worker would already have knowledge of the practice and may even inquire about it. The ethnic agency and the ethnic worker are less likely to frown on these practices and are more likely to support and validate the client's values. For example, the Papago Psychological Service (run and staffed by members of the Papago Indian tribe) uses, when necessary, the combination and cooperation of the medicine man and the mental health technician for client intervention.[106]

Cross described a ceremony that is used at the Anishnaabe Child and Family Services in Manitoba, Canada, that welcomes children returning home from placement away from the reservation.[107] This ceremony greets the children and gives the community an opportunity to begin reestablishing bonds with them. This type of community practice can probably be conducted only under the auspices of an ethnic-focused agency. Mainstream agencies may not have the capacity for this type of culturally based innovation. Besides, most child welfare agencies have diverse client populations and the special needs of one particular group may be overshadowed by the needs of other groups.

As members of the same system, the worker and clients may share the commonality of history, background, experiences, and world view. For the Chinese individual new to this country, the ethnic agency means that he or she can assume that the Chinese-American worker has some passing knowledge of Chinese cultural heritage, including some awareness of the significance of the teachings of Confucius, Laotze, and Buddha to many Chinese.[108] If the worker is working in an ethnic agency, there is a strong probability that he or she is grounded in Chinese culture.

The significance of ethnicity in the worker-client interaction may be so subtle as to be rendered invisible. Communication patterns and processes may be culturally based and so endemic to the organization, to the staff, and to the clients that these patterns and processes are a "given." Language patterns may connote a unity and familiarity to the client that he or she feels comfortable and open to staff feedback. For example, the African-American language patterns of verbal inventiveness and call/response may be understood and used freely in some African-American agencies and thus promote ethnic cohesiveness.[109]

Trust, rapport, and mutuality may be more likely to occur in the ethnic agency because the worker and client share similar ethnic-based goals. Jenkins found that the majority of the ethnic agencies she studied sought to strengthen the family.[110] For many ethnic groups, the family is the cornerstone of the group. These ethnic agencies saw individuals as members of a family *system* and worked to improve the functioning of that unit. The Kamehameha Schools/Bishop Estate, Hawaii, emphasizes parenting and early childhood education as a part of its commitment to Native-Hawaiian families.[111] In the Kenilworth-Parkside housing community, the family unit was also strengthened. In this community, a number of the families were headed by the mother. A program was launched to train these mothers to be CEOs (chief operating officers) of their households. Most other agencies would refer to this as parenting training, but this community program approached the topic in a rather creative manner.

Because the worker and client share the commonality of history, there does not seem to be a need to interpret that history to each other. As a Mexican American, the client does not need to explain to the Mexican-American worker what it is like to be a Mexican American in the United States. Although each person is different and has different experiences, there is still a thread that brings people together—the thread of ethnic group experience.

The ethnic factor suggests that barriers that often exist in mainstream agencies are minimized or are nonexistent. A layer of potential static in the communication process has been removed. For example, minority clients often have a dual consciousness that results from negotiating life in a White world and in his or her ethnic world.[112] Because these cultures do not merge, communication between Whites and minorities is frequently delivered and received at two levels—one based on the reality of being a minority and the other based on the history of minority-majority interactions. In these cross-race exchanges, the *perception* of what is being said may override what is *actually being* said. In same-race exchanges, some confusion in interpretations and meaning (the noise or state of the interaction) has been reduced.

This interaction already integrates the client's sociohistorical experiences in the process—an integration that is advocated by Beverly.[113] The ethnic factor in service delivery moves beyond the worker-client interaction. It also prevails in other aspects of organizational practice.

Empowerment as Technology
Client empowerment is also a major feature of the agency's ideology that is mirrored in agency technology. The ethnic agency attempts to foster client empowerment in the agency. Organizational level of empowerment connotes the *organization's* ability to empower individuals and communities.[114] Hasenfeld stated that "empowerment is a process through which clients obtain resources—personal, organizational, and community—that enable them to gain greater control over their environment and to attain their aspirations."[115] For example, El Centro de la Raza, a Seattle-based ethnic agency, works to increase the power, choices, and influence of its constituencies.[116]

Through its ideology of empowerment, the ethnic agency rejects the "victim" label that is all too freely attached to poor minorities, especially African Americans. The "clinicalism" of the effects of differential treatment that frequently guides mainstream casework interventions is replaced by a more powerful, uplifting ethos. Victimization breeds victimization, and as long as individuals continue to see themselves as victims, they will continue to be victimized.[117] Empowerment is a foundation for practice.

Empowerment may be a by-product of the agency's development. Ethnic workers and organizers successful enough to create and maintain a service agency for their community in a turbulent environment may feel empowered by the results of their work and may extend this air of confidence and empowerment to their clients. The feeling of accomplishment and contribution to the community may find its expression in practices that encourage clients to find their voice. A stronger sense of satisfaction may emanate from helping members of one's group. Thus, the helper benefits from organizing and contributing to the agency.

Ethnic agencies attempt to empower clients in a number of ways, such as providing them with the information they need to make decisions, providing them with information about community resources and services, involving clients in the agency decision-making process, hiring former clients as workers and/or using clients as volunteers, and creating opportunities for the client to learn the skills he or she desires.

Information, participation, and *skills* become three primary areas that distinguish the ethnic agency from other agencies. The client often has to negotiate numerous other systems in order to resolve problems and/or seek assistance. The ethnic agency can be one of those systems. The agency often begins by providing the client with the information he or she needs about the agency. In the ethnic agency, information seems readily available and, generally, freely given. In addition, information is also provided about those other agencies and services that may be of use to the clients. The importance of the worker acting as resource consultant and teacher/trainer for minority clients has also been highlighted in analyses of ethnic-sensitive practice.[118] Knowledge is an example of concrete power,[119] and when clients are provided information, they have become empowered.

The Neighborhood Youth Association (NYA), Los Angeles, in its neighborhood *ayudantes* (helper) program identified community residents who act as natural helpers in the community (largely a Spanish-speaking area). These are individuals in the community to whom residents naturally turn for help. NYA then provided the *ayudantes* information on the programs and services available to community residents. NYA wanted to empower the *ayudantes* by providing them with information that would facilitate their helping. In imparting this information, it was important that staff members not see their role as trainers or teachers because the *ayudantes* did not need these services. The role of NYA staff was to provide information. In this program, NYA was not the focal point at *ayudante* gatherings, which were held in the home of one of the *ayudantes* and not at the agency.

In this example, culture and ideology combined to generate a program that was culture specific and informative. The agency did not take on the role of expert nor did it attempt to modify and intrude in the natural pattern of helping that existed in the community. Furthermore, the agency was able to solidify its bond with its ethnic community by validating community practices and by becoming a support to these practices.

In the ethnic agency, client participation appears to be redistributive participation in which clients are able to exert influence in the agency decision-making process.[120] Over half of the ethnic workers studied by Jenkins felt that parents should have input in the decisions made in day care, whereas this was true for about 43 percent of the national social work sample.[121]

In the Papago service programs, consumers of services are also shapers of that service, and this involvement supports the values and culture of the Papago tribe.[122] The Neighborhood Youth Association (NYA) in Los Angeles includes youth representatives on its board and has youth input in its programs. In a collaboration with other agencies to develop a proposal for funding a project in an area with high minority gang activity, the absence of minority teenage representatives (the targeted client population) from the process was noted, and youth leaders were added to the coalition. The ideology of client/consumer participation is generally a major force in ethnic agencies.

Ethnic agencies also empower clients by using them as volunteers and/ or by hiring former clients. Because the worker and client are members of the same "system," the transition from client to worker is fairly smooth. The use of clients in these capacities further attests to the way in which the client becomes a partner in the helping process. The client can function as another role model for other clients and the empowerment process continues.

The satisfaction and sense of accomplishment felt by the worker is then shared with clients who become agency volunteers or with former clients who join the agency staff. The benefits of helping are passed along to the client. Thus, the helping role in and of itself has significant value to the helper as well as to the service recipient. While people are debating how to find ways of transforming recipients of help to dispensers of help,[123] many ethnic agencies have already resolved the debate.

Ethnic agencies seem to have a "group" focus in that they seek to empower the ethnic group as well as the individual client. Providing services that strengthen the family unit is indicative of this focus. In the Jenkins study, strengthening the family was the primary goal for over 90 percent of the agencies.[124] These agencies also wanted to provide growth and leadership for minority children.

The parenting classes of Kenilworth-Parkside provide a skill that has value beyond the classes themselves. Teaching clients to negotiate complex systems becomes an investment in the future. The emphasis of some agencies on job training is also another tangible commitment to the future. Because these agencies are committed to the destiny of the group, they create and provide opportunities for clients to learn skills that can uplift the group.

As noted by Jenkins, changing majority attitudes is not the agency goal.[125] The goal of these agencies, as was true with the early minority self-help efforts, is to improve the conditions of the group.

The Ethnic Agency and Nonprofessionalism

According to Powell, "The issue of professionalization is partly a question of who determines the nature of the merit good to be received by the organization's client."[126] Workers who identify with the community and its residents may define the "merit good" (services) as empowerment and the helping process as interactive. The professionally trained worker may be guided by a commitment to the profession and the tenets of professional practice.

Ethnic agencies have a pattern of relying on nonprofessional staff to carry out agency practices. This staffing is generally taken to mean that these organizations reject professionalism and the professional. Professionalization is seen as a wedge that distances the worker from the client. For those advocating client empowerment, this distance becomes a significant disadvantage to understanding and engaging the client. According to Musick and Hooyman, the client is the one who has to live with the problems, not the professional.[127] This "living with the problem" minimizes the expertise that an "outsider" brings to the intervention. Professionalism is also associated with a "clinical mentality" that reinforces responsibility to the individual and professional colleagues over a service orientation to the community.[128]

The controversy centers on who is the most qualified: the nondegreed paraprofessional with personal experience (group membership) or the degreed professional with specialized knowledge?[129] For ethnic agencies, the answer presented has been that ethnic group membership has primacy over professionalism.

This general perception of ethnicity over professionalism in ethnic agencies may be an oversimplification of a more complex issue. Ethnic agencies may be extremely interested in and supportive of professionalism. As a matter of fact, these agencies may be *rejecting the nonminority professional rather than professionalism itself.* With the issues confronting ethnic minority clients, agencies may have made the decision to subject the client to the untrained, same-group worker rather than subject him or her to the expertly trained, distanced worker.

The staffing patterns selected by an ethnic agency are based on trying to maintain an internal polity that supports a particular agency ideology. The agency seeks control of the practice, and if professionals are involved, the agency seeks control of the professional practice as well. Professionalism in the context of ethnic agency practice is the predominant goal. The ethnic agency seems to have more confidence that the untrained ethnic worker is more likely to value and maintain the "merit good" (services) to be received by clients. In the absence of identity with the clients and the community, the professionally trained nonminority individual may be more likely to define the "merit good" in other ways.

The untrained worker may be functioning more in the role of a supportive peer with a sympathetic ear. Mutuality and rapport, a basis for the helping relationship, are presumed to be established almost immediately through the bonds of ethnic identification, group cohesiveness, and sociohistorical commonality. Thus, the interaction becomes part of the intervention process in both direct and indirect practice.

Value of training and professionalism can be witnessed in the training activities that occur in ethnic agencies. For example, the Papago Psychology Service needed indigenous Papago members "because only they can establish rapport and only they can understand the subtleties communicated by the traditional Papago."[130] The recruited workers were trained by the agency in a tutorial manner because no trained Papago members were available. In addition, a program for Indian workers was developed by the Indian Health Service so that the newer staff "have the advantage of having both kinds [agency *and* formal] of training."[131]

In the Neighborhood Youth Association (NYA), nondegreed workers are hired, and after a year on the job these workers are encouraged to complete their degree. In addition, workers are also encouraged to pursue an M.S.W. (Master's of Social Work degree) if this is their interest. Two things seem to be operative here. First, the agency wants the workers to be socialized and grounded in its practices and ideologies *before* completing the degree; this grounding may protect perceptions of its practices from any erosion presumed to come with training. Second, the value of the training and degree completion are present in the agency. The approach this agency takes seems geared to bring practice and training together in a compatible union.

As previously mentioned, among the ethnic agency workers in the Jenkins study, the highest number of M.S.W. workers was found among the African Americans. African Americans may be ahead of the other ethnic groups in their involvement in professional social work education. It may be the *absence* of the professional ethnic worker that leads agencies to utilize the paraprofessional.

Jenkins also found that the highest overall level of ethnic commitment came from the M.S.W. ethnic agency workers in comparison to other ethnic agency workers and the national sample of social workers.[132] Professionalism, as reflected in the M.S.W., is strongly supportive of ethnic commitment.

Other ethnic groups are continuing to advocate for training as services are being developed for them. They desire more professionally trained ethnic workers and specific ethnic-sensitive training for the nonminority professional.[133] For ethnic agencies and ethnic services, a reconceptualization of "professionalism" appears to take place that redefines the worker-client relationship.

The Ethnic Agency and Debureaucratization

The climate or atmosphere of the ethnic agency may differ from that of most mainstream agencies. *Organizational climate* is a set of characteristics that distinguish the organization from other organizations, are relatively enduring over time, and influence the behavior of people in the organization.[134] In reviewing studies of organizational climate, Bunker and Wijnberg found that *structure* (perceptions of formality versus informality) and *social inclusion* (friendly sociability versus disagreement and criticism) were among the dimensions of this climate.[135] These two seem to have significant relevance for understanding the climate of ethnic agencies.

Within the ethnic agency, a relaxed and friendly climate seems to prevail, and this type of atmosphere is desired and maintained by the agencies. This is accomplished, in part, by the reduction in the bureaucratic red tape that is commonly associated with formal organizations. La Frontera, a service center in Tucson that works with Hispanic clients, did not drown its clients with complicated forms or red tape; the organizational atmosphere was "informal and friendly."[136] The Chicano Training Center in Los Angeles was also marked by its informality. La Clinica Familiar, a storefront agency in Los Angeles, wanted to maintain a hospitable atmosphere. By seeking to make the experience of clients as pleasant and comfortable as possible, these ethnic agencies wanted to be part of the solution and not part of the problem.

The less formal and less rigid nature of the agency climate also applies to the staff. For example, in a mental health program for American Indians, the interaction between staff was based on a "diffusion of power" that contrasted with the rigid, hierarchical structure associated with other organizations.[137] It appears that the interactions between staff members may also be less formal and the structure of the organization may be described as a flattened hierarchy.

The debureaucratized agency with its diffusion of power may serve as a source of empowerment for the workers. Workers can empower clients only if they themselves feel empowered. Worker participation in decision making and agency governance promotes the efficacy of the worker. The worker may be more committed to the agency, and the degree of worker commitment affects the quality of the worker-client interaction.[138] Worker empowerment may be correlated with job satisfaction and high worker morale. These factors may also contribute to the agency's climate.

The climate of the ethnic agency as experienced by clients may be captured by the concept of *personalismo*: "Personalismo refers to the inclination of Latin people, in general, to relate and trust people, rather than institutions, and their dislike for formal, impersonal structures and organizations. This characteristic makes Puerto Ricans more likely to use services in which they can easily reach and relate to individuals who will emphasize flexibility and availability and will minimize red tape."[139] The concept of "sameness" and ethnic group consciousness operate to reduce organizational distance and rigidity. To a degree, the ethnic agency attempts to embody *personalismo* in the relationship between workers and clients and between the workers themselves. The incorporation of *personalismo* in the agency is achieved with minimal bureaucracy.

Organizational Development

Tucson's La Frontera now has an multimillion-dollar annual budget. The Chicano Training Center evolved into El Centro, another multimillion-dollar agency. La Clinica Familiar del Barrio has been transformed into Alta-Med, a nonprofit health maintenance organization also with a multimillion-dollar budget. What has happened to the *personalismo*? What has happened to the climate and practices of these agencies?

As they grow and develop, organizations move through several stages, including (1) innovation and niche creation, (2) cohesion and commitment, (3) rule formation and structure stabilization, (4) structure elaboration, and (5) adaptation.[140]

According to Kramer, most voluntary organizations become more bureaucratic and professionalized over time in their quest for domain and identity.[141] Kramer further added that, over time, local voluntary organizations grow, prosper, and build professional staffs that obtain federal support.

The transformation of agencies is related to its search for and dependency on external funding. Hardina, for example, found that the acceptance of government funding limits the organization's flexibility in responding to client needs.[142] Fabricant recommended that public funding should not exceed 25 percent of an agency's budget if that agency wants to maintain its objectives.[143] Grants bring with them commitment to particular goals and the demands for greater formalization of operating procedures.[144] This means that agency administrators are likely to become more responsive to the wishes of the funding sources rather than to the wishes of the staff and clients.[145]

In addition to the influence of funding requirements, age contributes to agency size, complexity, and diversity independent of funding source.[146] As agencies survive, they also tend to expand and add on additional programs that require more staff. Increasing complexity and specialization are factors that promote the agency's bureaucratic development.

What does this mean for the ethnic agency? The ethnic agency appears to be a special case that may be outside the traditional organizational development pattern. For example, over 94 percent of the ethnic agencies Jenkins studied were receiving public funds.[147] The Chicano Training Center was started in 1969 with a grant from the National Institute of Mental Health. Numerous other ethnic agencies have their origins in and/or their maintenance on federal, state, and local support.

The funding base of many of the ethnic agencies are located in external and government sources; yet, it appears that these agencies have not evolved with the degree and extent of bureaucratization that would be expected. The ideology of *personalismo* still prevails in many of the multimillion-dollar operations. The climate associated with other nonethnic agencies of the size and complexity of El Centro, La Frontera, and Alta-Med does not prevail in these agencies.

Several explanations may be offered for why, comparatively speaking, ethnic agencies seem to retard their rate of bureaucratic growth: (1) agencies protect their core technologies, (2) agencies protect their clients, and (3) government funding is not as intrusive to these agencies.

According to Meyer: "The effort to maintain a structure that meets the criteria of externally defined rationality may make it necessary or wise to leave that structure inconsistent with the work that needs to get done. *Decoupling results, buffering the formal structure from ongoing activity*" [emphasis added].[148] Where decoupling is not feasible, agencies may operate as loosely coupled systems with subsystems maintaining autonomy and identity with marginal interactions.[149] This means that agencies are able to decouple their ideology and practices from the bureaucratic imperatives that accompany funding, or function as loosely coupled systems that can also protect technologies and ideologies. Conformity with the externally imposed requirements of bureaucracy and formalization occurs while the ideology and practices are minimally affected. As new programs emerge in the agency, the bureaucratic mandate is met while the prevailing ideology and technology are incorporated into the program. Each individual program can exude *personalismo* but all programs together may comprise a complex, bureaucratic system.

The agency may also seek to protect its clients from the effects of bureaucratization. According to a former director of a major ethnic agency, "The clients did not have to experience bureaucracy. That was the job of the director and the staff. We shielded the clients as much as possible." Clients were not bombarded with volumes of forms and mounds of rules. The staff attempted to keep the service delivery process as uncomplicated as possible for the clients. The agency served to buffer the client, thereby allowing the client to continue to feel that a certain informality prevailed in the agency. The director of the Neighborhood Youth Association commented that the administrative practice of her agency is to *reduce* rather than *induce* stress for the clients.[150]

It is also possible that the ethnic agency augments and complements mainstream services so that its practices and ideologies are assumed to meet the needs of a nontraditional population. Nontraditional populations may require nontraditional interventions so that the day-to-day operations of the ethnic agency may not be scrutinized. If the ethnic agency is regarded as an expert in service delivery to the ethnic population, funding sources may be less likely to want to modify the agency's practices.

The ethnic agency, as a voluntary agency, may reflect the democratizing and decentralizing of the Welfare State discussed by Ostrander, since many of them do rely on public funding.[151] This public support brings client-responsive services to communities that are more likely to be outside of mainstream service delivery. Community participation on the boards of these agencies may indirectly link these constituencies with the Welfare State. For these reasons, the organizational development of the ethnic agency may differ from that of mainstream organizations.

THE ETHNIC AGENCY AND ITS EXTERNAL POLITY

The community of the ethnic agency appears to be a powerful force in the life of the agency. The agency and its community share a symbiotic relationship. The community provides the legitimacy and the clients needed by the agency and the agency provides the services that the community needs. Agency reputation influences client trust; the better the reputation, the higher the client trust.[152] The *ethnic community* rather than an individual is the service recipient/consumer and this community bestows legitimacy and credibility. Consequently, this consumer has a powerful voice in the agency.

Mainstream social services may be funded by sources who are not the recipients of services. The agency is, however, accountable to the sponsors and not to the service recipients. This situation is radically different in the ethnic agency. The ethnic agency is a response to community need. In some instances, the community may have been the original service funders. La Frontera's first building was financed in part with money collected from the surrounding community by a door-to-door campaign spearheaded by community residents themselves. This effort reflects the commitment these residents had to the mission of the agency.

The ethnic agency belongs to the community and is accountable to its community constituency. For this reason, community participation on boards, in programs, and at meetings is necessary. Citizen involvement, especially through board membership, is vital to the agency/community relationship,[153] and the ethnic agency relies heavily on citizen involvement. The community advocates for the agency and can buffer the agency from public attack. The community can also interpret the agency to others in the larger social system. Funding cutbacks and other processes that threaten to harm the agency may be offset by community advocacy that literally protects the agency.

The agency's commitment to its community is found in the approaches it takes to client needs. For example, the agencies studied by Jenkins seemed to address as many client needs as possible.[154] This was referred to as the "more integrated approach" because many service areas were addressed. This occurred even if the agency had one or two specific service areas. The agency was to ease as many problems as possible and this may have been due to the perception that, if the agency did not help, no one else would. This attests to the strength of the agency/community link.

The agency/community link is often reflected in the agency director's relationship with the community. The distance between the director and a community resident is minimal in comparison to the distance between mainstream administrators and the community. Community residents and the ethnic agency director continue the pattern of *personalismo*. The director belongs to the community and may be called on to participate in community activities. Rich made this observation about African American administrators and the African-American community but this appears to be especially true for the ethnic agency administrator and the ethnic community.[155]

Consequently, the boundaries between the ethnic agency and the community it serves are fluid, as energy is exchanged between the two. In addition to its client responsiveness, the ethnic agency also must be community responsive if it is to survive.

THE ETHNIC AGENCY AND
SOCIAL CHANGE/SOCIAL REFORM

The ethnic agency's position on social reform bears additional comment. As previously mentioned, this agency seems to be committed to improving the condition of the community it serves. For example, in the Jenkins study, agencies seemed committed to helping clients "make it" in American society.[156] Efforts included bilingual-bicultural programs, career development programs, and supports for families. These agencies wanted their clients to have some part of the American dream.

The observations of Heiman, Burruel, and Chavez also highlighted the issues confronting agency staff: "It is unfortunate that, because staff are so busy helping individuals who have problems, they have little time to implement social and political programs addressed to the basic issues of poverty and discrimination. That frustrating situation is all too common among mental health workers treating the poor."[157] The business of facing the problems of daily living may be overwhelming for staff and clients and there is no time or energy left for planning or mounting other activities.

The question arises: To what extent is social change the *real* goal of ethnic agencies? These are *service* agencies and, with their communities, service provision is a major task. Furthermore, it appears that ethnic agencies and ethnic groups may be more concerned with obtaining their piece of the pie rather than changing the pie. For example, the protest efforts that led to the establishment of Seattle's El Centro de la Raza was a protest to obtain a building for a Latino service center.[158] The UCLA Chicano students and professor who encamped and fasted on the campus for 11 days in 1993 were fasting to protest the university administration's refusal to create a Department of Chicano Studies. These protests were not for reform or change—they were for respect, recognition, and resources.

Ethnic minorities may be accepting the intractability of institutions and structures in U.S. society. Perhaps they have no issue with them. The issue may be one of access, opportunity, and right—access to the riches and rewards of mainstream life, opportunity to participate in U.S. society, and the right to equality.

THE ETHNIC AGENCY: PITFALLS

No agency, no practice, and no ideology is perfect. The ethnic agency is no exception. Several pitfalls surround the ethnic agency and its approach to practice. Some of them are the following:

1. Because the ethnic agency may be serving an underserved population, it may try to do too much with too little. A shotgun approach to service delivery may erode the agency's effectiveness and undermine the community's confidence.
2. The most talented workers of a particular ethnic group may not view the ethnic agency as a wise career move or as a rung on the ladder to success.
3. The "we-ness" between clients and staff may result in role ambiguity as boundaries become blurred.
4. The "we-ness" of the atmosphere may inhibit client self-disclosure because of fear that confidentiality will be breached.
5. The "we-ness" may cloud worker objectivity.
6. Because workers and clients share cultural norms and values, workers may not wish to intrude in areas that may be deemed culturally inappropriate, even if this intrusion promotes effective service delivery.
7. Group cohesiveness may lead to stereotyping of the out-group.[159] In the ethnic agency, negative perceptions of White America may be perpetuated and reinforced as individuals trade "discrimination" stories. In the ethnic agency, the need for racial tolerance may not be addressed.
8. Homogeneity among ethnic agency members may stifle innovation and creativity. New ideas may be frowned on because that is not how things have been done.
9. Group cohesiveness may force individuals to conform to group norms.[160] Individuality may not be valued, as it may be a sign of deviancy.
10. Conflict within the agency may be personalized. Issues that are nonpersonal may be seen as personal and the reaction may be a personal

one. Because of the staff members' personal investment in and identification with the agency, conflict becomes personal.

11. The intragroup patterns of sexism, classism, and status differentials may persist in the ethnic agency.
12. Because "we're all in this together," the client may expect to have fewer demands placed on him or her.
13. The intensity and amount of work coupled with the degree of emotional investment may lead to worker burnout.
14. Community participation in a agency may mean participation by only a dominant few while some segments of the community may be excluded.[161]
15. Some ethnic agencies may become "sacred cows" that defy change or innovation. These agencies may be "institutionalized" in the community and have the community's support regardless of the effectiveness of the services.
16. While the ethnic agency seeks to promote the integration of the client into the larger society, it practices a type of separatism. This separatism may be needed to ensure that community needs receive attention, but the separatism may inadvertently work against integration. White America may react with skepticism and even hostility to special services for special groups. Racial polarization may be perpetuated by the presence of the ethnic agency.

These limitations may be overshadowed by the strengths and advantages that are associated with the ethnic agency.

SOCIAL WORK AND THE ETHNIC AGENCY

The very existence of the ethnic agency may be antithetical to the tenets of the social work profession. Because ethnic group members are providing services to members of their ethnic group, ethnicity serves as a type of credential needed for this practice. Thus, the ethnic agency appears to support the "insider" doctrine: You have to be one in order to understand one.[162] This doctrine suggests that, by virtue of group membership, individuals have a monopoly on or special access to the knowledge needed for practice with that particular group.

With the insider doctrine, the role of the profession's knowledge base in extending services in discounted. The existence of this knowledge base implies that social work training prepares individuals to practice with the various groups of society. Knowledge and skills are expected to be transferred from one setting to another and applications to specific ethnic groups are held to be extrapolated from this knowledge base. Because the ethnic agency emphasizes ethnicity over professional expertise, a gulf may exist between the ethnic agency and the mainstream social work agency.

The ethnic agency poses another significant challenge to the social work profession in its perceptions of and interface with the client. Rather than endorse the worker-client power differential as part of agency practice, the ethnic agency equalizes the power between the service provider and the service recipient, accepts the client's definition of the problem, actively involves client in the change process, teaches skills to the client, and advocates for the client.[163] Ethnicity is the common denominator that builds on a "one-ness" or a "we-ness" as the worker identifies with the client. Such views may define *subjective* practice as opposed to *objective* practice, and this subjective practice may be outside the boundaries of professional social work. Although ethnic agencies and mainstream social work share a commitment to service delivery, fundamental differences exist in their ideologies and methods of service delivery.

From this discussion, some propositions can be outlined to summarize the ethnic agency and its practices:

Proposition 1: The ethnic agency is controlled by, staffed by, and provides services to a specific ethnic group.

Proposition 2: The ethnic agency seems to be a special type of voluntary, self-help, alternative, community-based service agency.

Proposition 3: The ethnic agency may fill a void left by deficiencies in mainstream service delivery systems and/or be a response to cultural barriers that impede a group's utilization of traditional services.

Proposition 4: The ethnic agency is shaped by the larger social system in which it is located.

Proposition 5: Ethnicity is an integral part of the ideology and technology of the ethnic agency.

Proposition 6: The ethnic agency operationalizes the concept of empowerment.

Proposition 7: There is a tension between ethnicity and professionalism in the ethnic agency.

Proposition 8: The ethnic agency seeks to simplify the organization for the client.

Proposition 9: The ethnic agency tries to protect its ideology and technology from bureaucratic intrusion.

Proposition 10: The ethnic agency and its community share a symbiotic relationship.

Proposition 11: The ethnic agency may not be social reform oriented.

Proposition 12: The ethnic agency may augment, rather than compete, with mainstream services.

Proposition 13: There may be limitations surrounding ethnic agency practice.

Proposition 14: A tension seems to exist between the ethnic agency and mainstream social work practice.

Historically, with mainstream social work, ethnic/racial minorities have frequently been underserved or unserved, an adherence to ethnic group responsibility has prevailed, and service providers have defined problems and their solutions. The ethnic agency, in contrast, focuses primarily on an ethnic/racial minority group and engages in an interactive problem-defining/problem-resolving process with that group. The ethnic agency does seem to support the ethos of ethnic group responsibility.

According to Kwong, organizations reflect the institutionalized patterns of interactions among their members and captures the group's self-definition.[164] She further added that an understanding of an ethnic group's perspective can be achieved by studying the dynamics of the ethnic group through its ethnic organizations. Service delivery to ethnic minorities may be more effective if (1) the manner in which their agencies provide services is respected and, where feasible, adopted by other service delivery systems, and (2) these ethnic agencies are more fully incorporated into larger service delivery networks.

ENDNOTES

1. Edith Bremer, "Development of Private Social Work with the Foreign Born," *Annals of the American Academy of Political and Social Science 262* (March 1949): 139; Robert Woods and Albert Kennedy, *Handbook of Settlements* (New York: Russell Sage Foundation, 1911), pp. 85, 163, 183, 237.

2. Yaroslav Chyz and Read Lewis, "Agencies Organized by Nationality Groups in the United States," *Annals of the American Academy of Political and Social Science 262* (March 1949): 155.

3. Benjamin Ringer and Elinor Lawless, *Race-Ethnicity and Society* (New York: Routledge, 1989), p. 20.

4. Stephen Cornell, "Land, Labour and Group Formation: Blacks and Indians in the United States," *Ethnic and Racial Studies 13* (July 1990): 367–388.

5. George Weber, "Self-Help and Beliefs," in *Beliefs and Self-Help,* ed. George Weber and Lucy Cohen (New York: Human Sciences Press, 1982), p. 21.

6. Samuel Miller, "Themes and Models in Primary Prevention with Minority Populations," in *Primary Prevention Approaches to the Development of Mental Health Services for Ethnic Minorities,* ed. Samuel Miller, Gwenelle O'Neal, and Carl Scott (New York: Council on Social Work Education, 1982), pp. 122–123.

7. Carl Milofsky, "Neighborhood-Based Organizations: A Market Analogy," in *The Nonprofit Sector—A Research Handbook,* ed. Walter Powell (New Haven, CT: Yale University Press, 1987), p. 280.

8. Marcia Guttentag, "Group Cohesiveness, Ethnic Organization, and Poverty," *Journal of Social Issues 26,* number 2 (1970): 111.

9. Charles Stevens, "Organizing the Poor," *Journal of Sociology and Social Welfare 5* (September 1978): 744–762.

10. August Meier, *Negro Thought in America: 1880–1915,* Fourth Edition (Ann Arbor: University of Michigan Press, 1966).

11. Iris Carlton-LaNey, "Old Folks' Homes for Blacks during the Progressive Era," *Journal of Sociology and Social Welfare 16* (September 1989): 44.

12. See, for example, Andrew Billingsley and Jeanne Giovannoni, *Children of the Storm* (New York: Harcourt Brace Jovanovich, 1972), pp. 47–59; Lilian Brandt, "The Negroes of St. Louis," *Publications of the American Statistical Association 8* (March 1903): 206, 234, 241, 257–262; Carlton-LaNey, "Old Folks' Homes for Blacks during the Progressive Era," pp. 43–60; Steven Diner, "Chicago Social Workers and Blacks in the Progressive Era," *Social Service Review 44* (December 1970): 394, 405; John Dittmer, *Black Georgia in the Progressive Era, 1900–1920* (Urbana: University of Illinois Press, 1977), pp. 50, 62–65; W. E. B. DuBois, *Efforts for Social Betterment Among Negro Americans* (Atlanta: The Atlanta University Press, 1909); Maude Griffen, "The Negro Church and Its Social Work—St. Mark's," *Charities and the Commons 15* (October 7, 1905): 75–76; Florette Henri, *Black Migration* (Garden City, NY: Anchor Press/Doubleday, 1975), pp. 98–99; 126–131, 159, 186; Joanne Martin and Elmer Martin, *The Helping Tradition in the Black Family and Community* (Silver Spring, MD: National Association of Social Workers, 1984); Meier, *Negro Thought in America 1880–1915*, pp. 121–138; Tom Moore, "The African American Church: A Source of Empowerment, Mutual Help, and Social Change," *Prevention in Human Services 10*, number 1 (1991): 147–167; William Pollard, *A Study of Black Self Help* (San Francisco: R and E Associates, 1978); Edyth Ross, ed., *Black Heritage in Social Welfare 1860–1930* (Metuchen, NJ: The Scarecrow Press, 1978); Lennox Yearwood, "National Afro-American Organizations in Urban Communities," *Journal of Black Studies 8* (June 1978): 423–438.

13. As identified by Meier, *Negro Thought in American* pp. 121–138.

14. Martin and Martin, *The Helping Tradition,* p. 53.

15. W. E. B. DuBois, "Social Effects of Emancipation," *The Survey 29* (February 1913): 572.

16. As quoted in Pollard, *A Study of Black Self Help,* p. 63.

17. Billingsley and Giovannoni, *Children of the Storm,* pp. 47–49.

18. Henri, *Black Migration,* pp. 98, 99.

19. DuBois, *Efforts for Social Betterment,* p. 6.

20. Martin and Martin, *The Helping Tradition,* p. 38.

21. Yearwood, "National Afro-American Organizations," pp. 423–438.

22. Pollard, *A Study of Black Self Help.*

23. As detailed in Pollard, *A Study of Black Self Help,* p. 93.

24. Pollard, *A Study of Black Self Help,* p. 96.

25. Ruth Crocker, *Social Work and Social Order* (Urbana: University of Illinois Press, 1992), p. 7.

26. Henri, *Black Migration,* p. 99.

27. Judith Trolander, *Settlement Houses and the Great Depression* (Detroit: Wayne State University Press, 1975), p. 141.

28. This point is supported by the literature on the history of African-American self-help, especially Pollard, *A Study of Black Self Help.*

29. Eugene Jones, "Social Work Among Negroes," *The Annals of the American Academy of Political and Social Science 140* (November 1928): 287–293.

30. Robert Dexter, "The Negro in Social Work," *The Survey 46* (June 25, 1921): 439–440.

31. See, for example, Terry Cross, "Drawing on Cultural Tradition in Indian Child Welfare Practice," *Social Casework 67* (May 1986): 283–289; Diana DiNitto and Thomas Dye, *Social Welfare—Politics and Public Policy*, Second Edition (Englewood Cliffs, NJ: Prentice Hall, 1987), p. 256; Michael Dorris, "The Grass Still Grows, the River Still Flows: Contemporary Native Americans," *Daedalus 110* (Spring 1981): 43–69; E. Dan Edwards and Margie Egbert-Edwards, "Native American Community Development," in *Community Organizing in a Diverse Society*, ed. Felix Rivera and John Erlich (Boston: Allyn and Bacon, 1992), pp. 30–33; Grafton Hull, Jr., "Child Welfare Services to Native Americans," *Social Casework 63* (June 1982): 340–347; Teresa LaFromboise, "American Mental Health Policy," *American Psychologist 43* (May 1988): 388–397.

32. Edwards and Egbert-Edwards, "Native American Community Development," pp. 31–33.

33. Cross, "Drawing on Cultural Tradition," p. 287.

34. Vine Deloria, Jr., "Identity and Culture," *Daedalus 110* (Spring 1981): 16.

35. Dorris, "The Grass Still Grows," p. 55.

36. Hull, "Child Welfare Services to Native Americans," p. 345.

37. Cross, "Drawing on Cultural Tradition," p. 286.

38. This discussion is drawn from Rodolfo Acuña (who has one of the most detailed accounts of self-help among Mexicans and Mexican Americans), *Occupied America* (San Francisco: Canfield Press, 1972), pp. 188–190.

39. Carlos Arce, "A Reconsideration of Chicano Culture and Identity," *Daedalus 110* (Spring 1981): 184.

40. Acuña, *Occupied America*, p. 189.

41. A detailed account of the voluntary organizations in early Chinese communities, from which this discussion is drawn, can be found in Paul Wong, Steven Applewhite, and J. Michale Daley, "From Despotism to Pluralism: The Evolution of Voluntary Organizations in Chinese American Communities," *Ethnic Groups 8*, number 4 (1990): 215–233.

42. As quoted in Wong et al., "From Despotism to Pluralism," pp. 217–218.

43. Wong et al., "From Despotism to Pluralism," p. 221.

44. Philip Foner, *History of the Labor Movement in the United States*, Vol. III (New York: International Publishers, 1964), p. 274.

45. Mary Smith, "Almshouse Women," *Publications of the American Statistical Association 4* (September 1895): 228.

46. This discussion is drawn from Harry Kitano, *Japanese Americans* (Englewood Cliffs, NJ: Prentice-Hall, 1976), pp. 18–20; Kenji Murase, "Organizing in the Japanese-American Community," in *Community Organizing in a Diverse Society* (Boston: Allyn and Bacon, 1992), pp. 162–163.

47. Wong et al., "From Despotism to Pluralism," p. 221.

48. Taylor Cox, Jr. "Problems with Research by Organizational Scholars on Issues of Race and Ethnicity," *Journal of Applied Behavioral Science 26*, number 1 (1990): 5–23.

49. Cox, "Problems with Research by Organizational Scholars," p. 8.

50. David Powell, "Managing Organizational Problems in Alternative Service Organizations," *Administration in Social Work 10* (Fall 1986): 57.

51. Felice Perlmutter, "Administering Alternative Social Agencies: Educational Implications," *Administration in Social Work 12*, number 2 (1988): 110.

52. Powell, "Managing Organizational Problems," p. 57.

53. Lorraine Gutierrez and Edith Lewis, "A Feminist Perspective on Organizing with Women of Color," in *Community Organizing in a Diverse Society*, ed. Felix Rivera and John Erlich (Boston: Allyn and Bacon, 1992), p. 117.

54. As defined and detailed by Joyce Rothschild-Whitt, "The Collectivist Organization: An Alternative to Rational-Bureaucratic Models," *American Sociological Review 44* (August 1979): 509–527.

55. Carmen Rivera-Martinez, "Hispanics and the Social Services System," in *Hispanics in the United States*, ed. Pastora San Juan Cafferty and William McCready (New Brunswick: Transactional Books, 1985), p. 208.

56. Susan Ostrander, "Voluntary Social Service Agencies in the United States," *Social Service Review 59* (September 1985): 435.

57. Neil Gilbert, Harry Specht, and Paul Terrell, *Dimensions of Social Welfare Policy*, Third Edition (Englewood Cliffs, NJ: Prentice Hall, 1993), p. 7.

58. Ostrander, "Voluntary Social Service Agencies," pp. 449–450.

59. Marcia Bok, "Comments on 'Voluntary Social Service Agencies in the United States,'" *Social Service Review 60* (December 1986), p. 647.

60. Carl Milofsky, "Neighborhood-Based Organizations: A Market Analogy," in *The Nonprofit Sector—A Research Handbook*, ed. Walter Powell (New Haven, CT: Yale University Press, 1987), p. 279.

61. Robert Schilling, Steven Schinke, and Richard Weatherly, "Service Trends in a Conservative Era: Social Workers Rediscover the Past," *Social Work 33* (January/ February 1988): 6.

62. Marie Killea, "Mutual Help Organizations: Interpretations in the Literature," in *Support Systems and Mutual Help: Multidisciplinary Explorations*, ed. Gerald Caplan and Marie Killea (New York: Grune and Stratton, 1976), p. 47.

63. Stephen Schensul and Jean Schensul, "Self-Help Groups and Advocacy: A Contrast in Beliefs and Strategies," in *Beliefs and Self-Help*, ed. George Weber and Lucy Cohen (New York: Human Sciences Press, 1982), pp. 301–302.

64. Shirley Jenkins, *The Ethnic Dilemma in Social Services* (New York: The Free Press, 1981).

65. Tony Platt and Susan Chandler, "Constant Struggle: E. Franklin Frazier and Black Social Work in the 1920s," *Social Work 33* (July 1988): 293.

66. Comments made in personal conversation with the authors.

67. Elaine Pinderhughes, *Understanding Race, Ethnicity, and Power* (New York: The Free Press, 1989), p. 203.

68. Melvin Delgado and John Scott, "Strategic Intervention—A Mental Health Program for the Hispanic Community," in *Human Services for Cultural Minorities*, ed. Richard Dana (Baltimore: University Park Press, 1981), pp. 251–264; Lorraine Gutierrez, "Empowering Ethnic Minorities in the Twenty-First Century," in *Human Services as Complex Organizations*, ed. Yeheskel Hasenfeld (Newbury Park, CA: Sage Publications, 1992), pp. 320–338; Jenkins, *The Ethnic Dilemma in Social Services*; Marvin Kahn, Cecil Williams, Eugene Galvez, Linda Lejero, Rex Conrad, and George Goldstein,"The Papago Psychology Service," in *Human Services for Cultural Minori-*

ties, ed. Richard Dana (Batlimore: University Park Press, 1981), pp. 79–94; Pinderhughes, *Understanding Race, Ethnicity, and Power,* pp. 202–205; Barbara Solomon, *Black Empowerment* (New York: Columbia University Press, 1976).

69. See, for example, Delgado and Scott, "Strategic Intervention"; Charles Garvin and Fred Cox, "A History of Community Organizing Since the Civil War with Special Reference to Oppressed Communities," in *Strategies of Community Organization,* Fourth Edition, ed. Fred Cox, John Erlich, Jack Rothman, and John Tropman (Itasca, IL: F. E. Peacock, 1987); Gutierrez, "Empowering Ethnic Minorities in the Twenty-First Century," pp. 332–334; David Haber, "Church-Based Programs for Black Care-Givers of Non-Institutionalized Elders," *Journal of Gerontological Social Work 7* (July 1984): 43–55; Marvin Kahn et al., "The Papago Psychology Service"; Martin and Martin, *The Helping Tradition;* Pollard, *A Study of Black Self Help;* Charles Stevens, "Organizing the Poor," *Journal of Sociology and Social Welfare 5* (September 1978): 744–762.

70. See, for example, Lonnie Snowden and Freda Cheung, "Use of Inpatient Mental Health Services by Members of Ethnic Minority Groups," *American Psychologist 45* (March 1990): 347–355.

71. Carl Sewell, "The Impact of External Public Funding Policies on the Development of Black Community Organizations," *Black Scholar 9* (December 1977): 39.

72. Gilbert, Specht, and Terrell, *Dimensions of Social Welfare Policy,* pp. 140–141.

73. Bruce Thomas, "Protecting Abused Children: Helping Until It Hurts," *Children and Youth Services Review 4,* numbers 1/2 (1982): 139–154.

74. See, for example, Task Force on Permanency Planning for Foster Children, Inc., *Kinship Foster Care: The Double Edged Dilemma* (Rochester, NY: The Task Force, 1990), p. 4.

75. Gilbert, Specht, and Terrell, *Dimensions of Social Welfare Policy,* p. 134.

76. All field examples are from practitioners who shared their experiences through personal communication with the authors.

77. David Crystal, "Asian Americans and the Myth of the Model Minority," *Social Casework 70* (September 1989): 405–413.

78. K. Connie Kang, "Study Finds Neglect of Asian Poor," *Los Angeles Times,* 2 December 1993, section B.

79. Crystal, "Asian Americans," p. 405.

80. Leo Tezcatlipoca, "We're Chicanos—Not Latinos or Hispanics," editorial, *Los Angeles Times,* 22 November 1993, section B.

81. Felix Padilla, "On the Nature of Latino Ethnicity," *Social Science Quarterly 65,* number 2 (1984): 651–664.

82. *Los Angeles Times,* 4 December 1993, Religion section.

83. See, for example, Ormond Hammond, "Needs Assessment and Policy Development: Native Hawaiians as Native Americans," *American Psychologist 43* (May 1988): 383–387.

84. Reiko Homma-Tru, "Characteristics of Contrasting Chinatowns: 2. Oakland, Califomia," *Social Casework 57* (March 1976): 155–159.

85. Ramon Salcido, Carol Nakano, and Sally Jue, "The Use of Formal and Informal Health and Welfare Services of the Asian American Elderly: An Exploratory Study," *Californian Sociologist 3* (Summer 1990); 213–229.

86. Thomas Guterbock and Bruce London, "Race, Political Orientation, and Participation: A Empirical Test of Four Competing Theories," *American Sociological Review 48*, number 4 (1983): 439–453.

87. Mark Johnson and Karen Lashley, "Influence of Native Americans' Cultural Commitment on Preference for Counselor Ethnicity and Expectations About Counseling," *Journal of Multicultural Counseling and Development 17* (July 1989): 115–122.

88. Eric Woodrum and Nelson Reid, "Migration, Ethnic Community Organization, and Prosperity Among Japanese Americans," *Arete 12* (Summer 1987): 31–46.

89. Richard Hall and Weiman Xu, "Research Note: Run Silent, Run Deep—Cultural Influences on Organizations in the Far East," *Organizational Structures 11*, number 4 (1990): 569–576; James Lincoln, Mitsuyo Hanada, and Kerry McBride, "Organizational Structures in Japanese and U.S. Manufacturing," *Administrative Science Quarterly 31* (September 1986): 338–364.

90. These issues were raised by Jenkins, *The Ethnic Dilemma in Social Services*, p. 196.

91. Discussed by Gunter Baureiss, "Towards a Theory of Ethnic Organizations," *Canadian Ethnic Studies 14*, number 2 (1982): 21–42.

92. Miyako Inoue, "Japanese Americans in St. Louis: From Internees to Professionals," *City and Society 3* (December 1989): 14–152.

93. Felice Perlmutter, "A Theoretical Model of Social Agency Development," *Social Casework 50* (October 1969): 468.

94. Jenkins, *The Ethnic Dilemma in Social Services*, p. 45.

95. In Young Han, "A Study of Help-Seeking Patterns Among Korean Americans," Ph.D. dissertation, Case Western Reserve University, 1989.

96. This concept is defined in Chapter 1.

97. See, for example, Burton Gummer, "On Helping and Helplessness: The Structure of Discretion in the American Welfare System," *Social Service Review 53* (June 1979): 214–228; Yeheskel Hasenfeld, *Human Service Organizations* (Englewood Cliffs, NJ: Prentice Hall, 1983), pp. 197–200.

98. Alfreda Iglehart, "Adolescents in Foster Care: Factors Affecting the Worker Youth Relationship," *Children and Youth Services Review 14*, numbers 3/4 (1992): 308.

99. Amitai Etzioni, *Modern Organizations* (Englewood Cliffs, NJ: Prentice Hall, 1964), p. 100.

100. Robert Dexter, "The Negro in Social Work," *The Survey 46* (June 25, 1921): 439–440.

101. Herbert Freudenberger, "The Dynamics and Treatment of the Young Drug Abuser in an Hispanic Therapeutic Community," in *Human Services for Cultural Minorities*, ed. Richard Dana (Baltimore: University Park Press, 1981) p. 226.

102. Freudenberger, "The Dynamics and Treatment of the Young Drug Abuser," p. 226.

103. Christopher Petr, "The Worker-Client Relationship: A General Systems Perspective," *Social Casework 69* (December 1988): 625.

104. Petr, "The Worker-Client Relationship," p. 625.

105. Damian McShane, "Mental Health and North American Indian/Native Communities: Cultural Transactions, Education, and Regulation," *American Journal of Community Psychology 15*, number 1 (1987): 101–102; Scott Nelson, George McCoy,

Maria Stetter, and W. Craig Vanderwagen, "An Overview of Mental Health Services for American Indians and Alaska Natives in the 1990s," *Hospital and Community Psychiatry 43* (March 1992): 258.

106. Kahn et al. "The Papago Psychology Service," pp. 85.

107. Terry Cross, "Drawing of Cultural Tradition in Indian Child Welfare Practice," p. 289.

108. These teachings are discussed by Angela Ryan, "Cultural Factors in Casework with Chinese-Americans," *Social Casework 66* (June 1985): 333–340.

109. For a discussion of these patterns, see Anita Foeman and Gary Pressley, "Ethnic Culture and Corporate Culture: Using Black Styles in Organizations," *Communication Quarterly 35* (Fall 1987): 293–307.

110. Jenkins, *The Ethnic Dilemma in Social Services*, p. 49.

111. Ormond Hammond, "Needs Assessment and Policy Development: Native Hawaiians as Native Americans," *American Psychologist 43* (May 1988): 386.

112. Creigs Beverly, "Treatment Issues for Black, Alcoholic Clients," *Social Casework 70* (June 1989): 373–374.

113. Beverly, "Treatment Issues for Black Alcoholic Clients," pp. 370–374.

114. Gutierrez, "Empowering Ethnic Minorities," p. 330.

115. Yeheskel Hasenfeld, "Power in Social Work Practice," *Social Service Review 61* (September 1987): 478–479.

116. Gutierrez, "Empowering Ethnic Minorities," p. 333.

117. Robert Elias, *The Politics of Victimization* (New York: Oxford University Press, 1986).

118. See, for example, Hisashi Hirayama and Maummer Cetingok, "Empowerment: A Social Work Approach for Asian Immigrants," *Social Casework 69* (January 1988): 41–47; Richard Starrett, Charles Mindel, and Roosevelt Wright, Jr., "Influence of Support Systems on the Use of Social Services by the Hispanic Elderly," *Social Work Research and Abstracts 19* (Winter 1983): 39; Linda Stewart, "AIDS Risk Reduction: A Community Health Education Intervention for Minority High Risk Group Members," *Health Education Quarterly 13* (Winter 1986): 418.

119. P. Johnson, "Women and Power," *Journal of Social Issues 32*, number 3 (1976): 99–110.

120. Gilbert, Specht, and Terrell, *Dimensions of Social Welfare Policy*, p. 134.

121. Jenkins, *The Ethnic Dilemma in Social Services*, p 88.

122. Kahn et al. "The Papago Psychology Service," pp. 80–83.

123. Killilea, "Mutual Help Organizations," p. 69.

124. Jenkins, *The Ethnic Dilemma in Social Services*, p. 49.

125. Jenkins, *The Ethnic Dilemma in Social Services*, p. 49.

126. Powell, "Managing Organizational Problems in Alternative Service Organizations," p. 65.

127. John Musick and Nancy Hooyman, "Toward a Working Model for Community Organizing in the 1970's," *Journal of Sociology and Social Welfare 4* (September 1976): 14–18.

128. LaFromboise, "American Indian Mental Health Policy," p. 393.

129. E. W. Studt, "Professionalization of Substance Abuse Counseling," *Journal of Applied Rehabilitation Counseling 21* (Fall 1990): 11–15.

130. Kahn et al., "The Papago Psychology Service," p. 89.

131. Kahn et al. "The Papago Psychology Service," p. 86.

132. Jenkins, *The Ethnic Dilemma in Social Services*, p. 102.

133. Damian McShane, "Mental Health and North American Indian/Native Communities: Cultural Transactions, Education, and Regulation," *American Journal of Community Psychology 15* (February 1987): 95–116; Scott Nelson, George McCoy, Maria Stetter, and W. Craig Vanderwagen, "An Overview of Mental Health Services for American Indians and Alaska Natives in the 1990s," *Hospital and Community Psychiatry 43* (March 1992): 257–261.

134. Forehand and Gilmer, as quoted by Lawrence James and Allan Jones, "Organizational Climate: A Review of Theory and Research," *Psychological Bulletin 81*, number 12 (1974): 1097.

135. Douglas Bunker and Marion Wijnberg, "The Supervisor as a Mediator of Organizational Climate in Public Social Service Organizations," *Administration in Social Work 9* (Summer 1985): 61.

136. Elliott Heiman, Grace Burruel, and Nelba Chavez, "Factors Determining Effective Psychiatric Outpatient Treatment for Mexican Americans," *Hospital and Community Psychiatry 26* (August 1975): 516.

137. Galen Marburg, "Mental Health and Native Americans: Responding to the Challenge of the Biopsychosoical Model," *White Cloud Journal 3*, number 1 (1983): 44.

138. Hasenfeld, *Human Service Organizations*, p. 198.

139. Abad, Ramos, and Boyce, as quoted in Melvin Delgado, "Hispanics and Psychotherapeutic Groups," *International Journal of Group Psychotherapy 33* (October 1983): 510.

140. David Bargal, "The Early Stage in the Creation of Two Self-Help Organizations: An Exploratory Study," *Administration in Social Work 16*, number 3/4 (1992): 84.

141. Ralph Kramer, "Voluntary Agencies and the Personal Services," in *The Nonprofit Sector—A Research Handbook*, ed. William Powell (New Haven, CT: Yale University Press, 1987), p. 243.

142. Donna Hardina, "The Effect of Funding Sources on Client Access to Services," *Administration in Social Work 14*, number 3 (1990): 44.

143. Michael Fabricant, "Creating Survival Services," *Administration in Social Work 19* (Fall 1986): 80.

144. Carl Milofsky, "Structure and Process in Community Self-Help Organizations," in *Community Organization Studies in Resource Mobilization and Exchange*, ed. Carl Milofsky (New York: Oxford University Press, 1988), p. 211.

145. Patricia Martin, "Multiple Constituencies, Dominant Societal Values, and the Human Service Administrator: Implications for Service Delivery," *Administration in Social Work 4* (Summer 1980): 19.

146. Carl Milofsky and Frank Romo, "The Structure of Funding Arenas for Neighborhood Based Organizations," in *Community Organization Studies in Resource Mobilization and Exchange*, ed. Carl Milofsky (New York: Oxford University Press, 1988), p. 238.

147. Jenkins, *The Ethnic Dilemma in Social Services*, p. 45.

148. John Meyer, "Organizations as Ideological Systems," in *Leadership and Organizational Culture*, ed. Thomas Sergiovanni and John Corbally (Chicago: University of Illinois Press, 1984), p. 188.

149. Hasenfeld, *Human Service Organizations*, p. 150.

150. Comments made during a class presentation, October 1992.

151. Ostrander, "Voluntary Social Service Agencies in the United States."

152. Hasenfeld, *Human Service Organizations*, p. 198.

153. Ann Ward Tourigny and Joe Miller, "Community-Based Human Service Organizations: Theory and Practice," *Administration in Social Work 5* (Spring 1981): 81.

154. Jenkins, *The Ethnic Dilemma in Social Services*, pp. 48–49.

155. Wilbur Rich, "Special Role and Role Expectation of Black Administrators of Neighborhood Mental Health Programs," *Community Mental Health Journal 11* (Winter 1975): 399.

156. Jenkins, *The Ethnic Dilemma in Social Services*, pp. 60–66.

157. Heiman, Burruel, and Chavez, "Factors Determining Effective Psychiatric Outpatient Treatment for Mexican Americans," p. 517.

158. As reported in Gutierrez, "Empowering Ethnic Minorities," pp. 332–333.

159. Guttentag, "Group Cohesiveness," pp. 123–124.

160. Killilea, "Mutual Help Organizations," p. 70.

161. Gilbert, Specht, and Terrell, *Dimensions of Social Welfare Policy*, p. 135.

162. Robert Merton, "Insiders and Outsiders: A Chapter in the Sociology of Knowledge," *American Journal of Sociology 78* (July 1972): 15.

163. Gutierrez, "Empowering Ethnic Minorities," p. 331.

164. Julie Kwong, "Ethnic Organizations and Community Transformations: The Chinese in Winnipeg," *Ethnic and Racial Studies 7* (July 1984): 374–386.

Chapter 7

Service Delivery to Diverse Communities: Agency-Focused Obstacles and Pathways

As U.S. society becomes more diverse, service delivery systems are attempting to respond to the issues and problems that are accompanying these demographic shifts. The call for ethnic-sensitive service delivery is resonating around agencies throughout the country. In 1976, Mass wrote, "The social worker who acts on the stereotype of the model Japanese and expects clients to live up to this ideal will be doing his clients a great disservice."[1]

In 1989, Crystal was still admonishing social workers not to accept the "myth of the model minority" that haunts Asian Americans:

> Racism need not always take the form of white hoods and mob lynchings to be deadly. It can be just as fatal in the guise of a cultural blindness that equates service demand with need and under-utilization with mental health.[2]

Other directives have been forthcoming:

> The sooner we attempt to discover, familiarize ourselves with, respect, and work within the differences between individuals, the sooner will we arrive at more successful treatment methods useful for all. We need to incorporate in the treatment programs a sense of cultural identification, history, customs and personal natures for all ethnic groups.[3]

Consider the possibility not only of overdiagnosis, oversensitivity to disability, and overeagerness for [mental hospital] confinement for Blacks and Native Americans but also the possibility of the reverse of such biases in judging Asian American/Pacific Islanders and Whites.[4]

While there is some progress being made in social work education programs around the country, there is still insufficient training aimed at producing practitioners who can function biculturally.[5]

Indeed, advice, direction, recommendations, insight, and descriptions have been advanced to nudge agencies and workers into becoming more culturally sensitive. Practitioners and administrators have been encouraged to permit ethnic minorities more input into the programs that affect them,[6] train and hire indigenous paraprofessionals to assist in service delivery to ethnic populations,[7] engage in outreach efforts to ethnic minority communities,[8] and diversify agency staff.[9]

It seems that many of the same issues resurface periodically, and the impression given is that agencies and the profession have not taken the advice to heart and to practice. A review of the issues is warranted to disentangle the contradictions and ambivalence inherent in the development of ethnic-sensitive service delivery systems.

WHAT IS ETHNIC-SENSITIVE PRACTICE?

The meaning of ethnic-sensitive and multicultural practice can be extrapolated from the literature and from some of the preceding observations. Many of the discussions focus on the *outcome* of this practice and on the *process occurring between worker and client* rather than on ethnic-sensitive practice as an *organizational process*.[10] For example, in reviewing literature on the subject, Gutierrez defined ethnic-sensitive practice in terms of what it accomplished:

The goal of the ethnic sensitive or ethnic competent approach is to create or recreate programs and organizations that will be more responsive and responsible to the culture of minority groups. Training for cultural competence and the delivery of ethnic sensitive services requires understanding of one's own personal attributes and values, gaining knowledge about the culture of different groups, and developing skills for cross cultural work.[11]

Pinderhughes added:

> It [effective service delivery] sets goals to validate, preserve, and enhance the clients' chosen cultural identity in order to facilitate healthy relationships and group interactions; accords respect to the client's belief system [and] enables clients to gain some control over their environment and to establish a society for themselves that maintains self-esteem.[12]

These descriptions are useful for understanding the nuances of ethnic-sensitive practice and how it benefits clients—the *why* of ethnic sensitive practice—but do not expound on the organizational and structural aspects of how to achieve it. Examples of ethnic-sensitive practice frequently gloss over the pathways that led to this practice.

What is necessary for this practice to occur? What does an agency have to do to move to this kind of practice? What processes are involved? What has to change? What about agency structure? How much of it has to change? Can an agency do just a little bit of ethnic-sensitive practice or does the whole agency have to change? Is ethnic-sensitive practice consistent across agencies or are there variations?

If the practice of ethnic agencies is used as the far end of a continuum of ethnic-sensitive practice, a clearer picture of ethnic-sensitive practice surfaces. From ethnic agencies, a picture of ethnic-sensitive practice is evident. Ethnic-sensitive practice is a process whereby the agency:

1. Adopts an ideology of mutuality with the client through same-ethnic/race workers
2. Implements a technology of empowerment that focuses on building strengths
3. Buffers clients from agency bureaucracy
4. Promotes and utilizes input from clients and the ethnic community it serves
5. Is accountable to its ethnic community

The ethnic agency model can be viewed as the "ideal" type in the continuum of ethnic services because it may be the only type of agency that can realize the fullest meaning of ethnic-sensitive practice. Highlighting its service delivery dimensions is useful in formulating a framework for conceptualizing ethnic-sensitive practice. The first step in the formulation of a framework for mainstream agency-based ethnic-sensitive practice is the recognition of the barriers to the development of this practice and those forces that may overcome them.

BARRIERS TO ETHNIC-SENSITIVE PRACTICE

Numerous barriers inhibit change in organizations, and ethnic-sensitive practice is susceptible to these roadblocks. These obstacles are often imbedded in the agency itself and may not be indicators of staff attitudes toward minority groups.

The barriers can be categorized as ideological, technological, and structural. The ideology of the agency is controlled by the internal polity (dominant elite) of the agency. While all in the agency may not agree with the prevailing ideology, it remains functional in the agency because of the power of the dominant elite. The technological barriers are tied to the implementation of practice (what the agency *does* with clients), and the structure refers to power, complexity, and formalization of the agency.

The Power of Ideologies

Many agencies have established service ideologies that have been formalized and supported by the agency structure and climate. These ideologies are the beliefs held about why people need assistance and the form that assistance should take. For example, Antler and Antler traced the evolution of the child-protective movement in the United States and commented that *protecting* the family came to be interpreted as *controlling* the family.[13] As public responsibility for safeguarding the health and welfare of children grew, social work methods were integrated into the movement. Identification and investigation, indications of the significance of child-abuse reporting, suggest that society is still concerned with finding instances of abuse, determining the guilt or innocence of suspected abusers, and trying to prevent the abuse from happening again. The *prevention of the recurrence* of abuse differs markedly from the *prevention of cruelty and neglect.*[14]

Thus, prevailing ideologies around child abuse focus on correcting family situations that have already resulted in the abuse and/or neglect of children. A body of literature exists today about the correlates of child abuse and a "profile" of the abuser based on the compilation of the correlates. Abuse has been associated with such factors as poverty, substance abuse, stress, family isolation, poor self-control, and the gender of the abused child.[15] With this ideology, interventions are identified that correspond to the definition of the problem. In child-abuse cases, parents may be referred for counseling, parenting classes, substance-abuse treatment, and numerous other services geared to eradicate the abusive behavior. The abuse has been located in the traits and characteristics of the abusing parent and interventions aim to correct these inadequacies. This, then, defines the child-abuse ideology.

These service ideologies may be further refined or completely altered when they are applied to ethnic minority groups. For example, African-American families may be perceived by child welfare service providers as multiproblem, hard to work with, resistant, and hostile, while African-American children become "hard to place."[16] The overrepresentation of minority children in the foster-care system may be the manifestation of an ideology that says that these children are in greater need of protection from the effects of those harmful, dysfunctional family environments. It is conceivable that the foster-care placement rates for ethnic minorities are more reflective of the ideologies of these service delivery systems and not of the behavior of these families themselves.

Furthermore, these ideologies have confirming, reaffirming, and self-confirming qualities. Families with cultural lifestyles and patterns that deviate from the expected are "dysfunctional." Families who react with anger to the punitiveness of the child-welfare system are "hostile." Parents who are unfairly singled out for scrutiny are "uncooperative." Children who do not meet the adoption profile are "hard to place" and, since minimal efforts are expended to place them, they do become hard to place. These ideologies are perpetuated because they have been found to be "true."

Although these service ideologies interact with notions of ethnicity and the ways in which it affects service delivery, they may not be inherently racist or reflective of malicious intent of the people who believe them. Rather, agencies have operated in specific ways for so long that their members may not be able to imagine any other way of seeing things or even the necessity for seeing things differently. These ideologies are held with conviction and great tenacity. They are grounded in years of practice wisdom and professional judgments.

The organization of the workplace and the technology of the agency are the outgrowth of ideologies about problems and solutions. These ideologies are not limited to the way people perceive problems and client groups but become a blueprint for the agency. If a pathology resides with the family, then the child is removed from the pathological environment. If the parent is the problem, then an array of services may be identified and individual focused interventions are provided. Extensive reporting and investigating mirror the belief that detection is at the heart of child welfare services—a belief that society needs to find and wipe out the abuse.

New workers who enter the child-welfare system are expected to concur with the ideology of the system. One of the assumptions underlying the participation of individuals in formal organizations is that organizational goals take precedence over individual goals. Dissonance between individual belief systems and agency belief systems is resolved through the worker acting in accordance with the agency. The worker who has some issues with "the way things are done around here" is acquiescing to "the way things are done around here" by virtue of accepting membership in that agency, according to assumptions about organizational participation. Questions about the agency may be met with, "But you knew that before you took the job," and such responses act as a form of social control over worker behavior.

Continued participation in the organization often results in the cooptation of the work, so that the worker begins to accept the ideology of the agency as true. Indeed, the worker may be powerless in resisting this ideology. The organization of the work, the work itself, and the organizational climate support a particular set of beliefs about people and their problems.

The hospital is an example of the effects of ideology on the organization. In writing of the social worker performing discharge planning duties in hospitals, Iglehart stated, "In the day-to-day operations of a discharge planner...a particular manner of doing things often emerges that derives from the nature of hospitals, the nature of the tasks.... The hospital's goals, structure, technology, *ideology*, and adherence to a medical model may be more powerful than professional perspective in defining discharge planning service" [emphasis added].[17] Even though social workers may espouse professional views and ideologies that are different from those typically found in hospitals, these social work ideologies are constrained by what is taking place in the organization itself. In some situations, the way hospitals accomplish tasks takes priority over the way social workers accomplish tasks.

The organization, as a setting for the implementation of practice, is defined by the ideologies of the dominant elite in those settings. As was noted in Chapter 5, many of the ideologies found in social work practice are shaped by prevailing public attitudes.

The following case of a child-welfare worker in a large urban child welfare office illustrates the interaction between ideology and organizational behavior:

A new child-welfare worker (a White female) looked forward to the challenges of her job. As a recent M.S.W. graduate, she felt ready to meet the challenge. She wanted to conduct her job in such a way as to do as much as possible for her clients. To her, this meant establishing relationships, providing support, assisting with problem solving, and generally helping families through the crisis that faced them.

In the first month of her job, one of her clients, an African-American male, called her at the office to arrange an appointment. The abusing parent wanted to know if he could visit the worker at the office since he was going to be in that area anyway. The father was having difficulty finding the services that had been mandated by the court and he wanted to discuss this with his worker. The client was reaching out for assistance at his own initiative and the worker wanted to help him with referrals and other information.

The worker met the father in the lobby of the agency and escorted him to a chair by her desk in another part of the building. Her supervisor (a White female), who had been watching, immediately jumped up from her desk, ran over, and beckoned the worker. "Is that a *client?*" she whispered. When the worker nodded, the supervisor's shock was overwhelming. "You don't bring clients back here. We have rules about that. Didn't they tell you that in training? (They hadn't.) That could be too dangerous. What if he's angry with you or something? What if he got violent? We have special conference rooms up front for conferences with clients."

The supervisor took the worker and the father to another part of the building that had small, individual rooms—all without doors. The supervisor left for a few minutes and returned with the security guard from the parking lot. The guard patrolled the hallway during the worker's conference with the father. Although all of this was beyond the control of the worker and she was apologetic about the situation, her relationship with the father was irreparably damaged. After several years on the job, the memory of that experience faded as the worker began to see her African-American male clients as potentially threatening. Use of the conference room and the security guard became second nature to the worker.

The power of ideologies in organizations should not be denied, for they shape agency goals, structure, technology, and worker behavior.

The Old Ways Work Fine

In reality, it is not easy for agencies to change practices that have been established over a period of time. As systems, these organizations have developed their own homeostasis or steady state. According to Anderson and Carter, "A steady state occurs when the whole system is in balance. In such a state, the system is maintaining a viable relationship with its environment and its components, and its functions are being performed in such a fashion as to ensure its continued existence."[18] The work is predictable. The clients are predictable. The administrators are predictable. Processes have been routinized, informally and formally. Change—any change—is a threat to that equilibrium. The threat lies in the uncertainty of the change and its consequences. Workers and administrators strive to continue with "business as usual." "But this is how we've always done it" is one of the enemies of ethnic-sensitive practice.

The agency resists change in a battle to keep to the old ways. Indeed, Katz and Kahn observed that any internal or external factor that threatens to disrupt the system is countered by forces that *restore the system as closely as possible to its previous state.*[19] Efforts to bring about change may be coopted by the existing system. Innovative approaches may be altered or handled in such a way to accommodate existing practices.

Threats to the equilibrium may be absorbed by the agency so that they are no longer disruptive to the agency. Iglehart stressed this point in discussing organizational responses to turnover: "Turnover is commonly held to be disruptive to the agency...[but] in the face of turnover, even high rates of turnover, an agency will be likely to create mechanisms that will minimize the disruptive effects of this turnover on the organization.... Organizations, in fact, are dynamic systems capable of adapting to and gaining control over disruptive forces in order to return to the previous stability or to redefine a new stability."[20]

Attempts to import new workers, new clients, and new technologies may be neutralized by the agency as a way of protecting its equilibrium. The following, from a private, nonprofit family service agency, provides an example:

> As the population of the city was increasing in ethnic composition, the agency decided it was time to hire African-American treatment workers. Prior to these new hirings, African Americans had only been employed in the agency as secretaries. The new workers were warmly welcomed by the rest of the staff, invited to lunch with colleagues, attended social functions at colleagues' homes, and quickly became accepted as members of the staff. When one of the new workers would raise a question about an agency practice or policy, the typical response was, "Well, we don't see it that way and you're one of us now."

The agency staff members were encouraging the new workers' identification with the agency and this identification would reduce their questioning the agency. The desire to belong and to be part of the group, to be included in the network of a prestigious agency was, according to one of the new workers, "too seductive to refuse." The agency had succeeded in neutralizing and absorbing forces that could have been potentially disruptive to its operations.

The agency that opens its doors to grant access to previously unserved clients and/or to new minority staff and then continues to implement the same practices may be protecting its service delivery and its ideologies. Minority staff may be expected to provide the exact same service in the same manner as everyone else, so that the "ethnic" factor is lost as the worker becomes coopted. Consequently, ethnic *presence* in the agency does not always equal to ethnic-sensitive practice. In the situations of resistance, an *appearance* of change may occur without change itself.

Ideology: Equality over Responsiveness

Agencies may operate on the premise that equality in treatment and services is the same as responsiveness of services. Sue, Allen, and Conaway observed that it may be possible for all minorities to receive equal but unresponsive services.[21] Because all clients in an agency are treated the same without regard for ethnicity, staff and administrators may be lulled into believing that minority access and the absence of differential treatment are all that is needed for ethnic-sensitive services.

This is not to be confused with color blindness. The agency is very aware of ethnicity and race and may extend special efforts to recruit minority clients. The sensitivity is in working to promote access. If there is a disregard for ethnicity, it happens in other places in the agency. For some agencies, special attention to outreach efforts is seen as ethnic-sensitive practice rather than as a step in a continuing process.

The transformation of a residential treatment facility for girls from a predominantly White agency to one with some ethnic diversity highlights this point:

> The agency began receiving cases referred by a sister agency as part of a subcontractual arrangement. The "new" residents were African American and Hispanic. During the December holidays, the agency had typically encouraged residents to plan activities to celebrate their religious beliefs. Programs to celebrate the meaning of Hanukkah and Christmas had their dates set on the calendar at the first of each year and then these dates were protected all year long. Staff members were free to schedule other activities around these dates.
>
> As the holiday season approached, a group of the African-American girls began planning, among themselves, for a Kwanzaa program (a celebration of the principles for African-American unity) and approached staff about setting a date for the program. A date could not be set because it was too late, but they could be given a date for next year. Exception to the policy could not be extended because, "If we did it for you, we'd have to do it for everyone." The girls felt discriminated against ("They did this to us 'cause we're Black") and the atmosphere of the agency was tense during this holiday season.

A debate still goes on in the agency about the wisdom of this decision.

The Social Cost of Change

For the private, nonprofit agency with a tradition of family service to major-ity groups, the move into multicultural practice may be undesirable because it could jeopardize the agency's status. Agencies often take on the status of the clients they serve, and all clients are not equal. In order to protect its status, the agency may wish to dissociate itself from "minority" issues. As the country continues to move toward greater diversity, there will probably always be some agency somewhere that will remain untouched by the mark of multiculturalism.

This means that some agencies protect themselves from becoming too African American, too Mexican American, or too Asian American in clients served and staff hired. Controls may be informally instituted to control the access of special ethnic populations. With this controlled access, there may be little need to think or plan ethnic-sensitive practice since, in these set-tings, it is not of value.

Absence of Rewards

There may not be a structure in place to reward staff and administrators for excellence in ethnic-sensitive service delivery. Those activities of worth to the agency generally have some sanction attached to them so that worker discretion in whether to implement these activities is minimized. When left to the whim of individuals in the agency, culturally sensitive practice may be lost in the shuffle. Interventions aimed at promoting culturally aware workers may be only marginally effective if the worth of those interventions is not validated by the agency. As long as the worth of those interventions lies outside of the incentive structure, then a permanent, routinized change is not going to take place.

Evaluations of administrator and staff performance do not include per-formance measures on ability to create and maintain an ethnic-sensitive agency and ethnic-sensitive practice. Some may argue that these measures would be difficult to articulate, but if they were of worth to the agency, efforts would be underway to tackle the task.

Voiceless Clients

Hasenfeld stated, "There is generally an asymmetry of power between the agency and the client.... First, most agencies are not directly dependent on their clients for procurement of resources.... Second, the demands for ser-vices often outstrip their supply.... Third, many agencies have a quasi-monopoly over their services."[22]

Those who would benefit from ethnic-sensitive services may be the least powerful in bringing this practice to fruition. The funding structure of services works against clients and highlights the disadvantaged status of clients. Since the consumers of service may not be the sponsors of service, agencies may not be motivated to hear what these consumers have to say. This situation may be exacerbated by the powerlessness of ethnic minorities. Clients, particularly ethnic minority clients, are not the dominant elite in most agencies.

Etzioni elevated the issue to the level of society: "Here separation between consumption and control is supported by a strong ideology... namely, that those who administer the service are in a better position to judge what is good for the consumer than he is for himself; hence separation of control from consumption is the best way to maximize the happiness of the greatest number."[23] This powerlessness of clients may be part of an underlying ideology about the service delivery process. If this is true, then fee-paying clients of private agencies may have only limited control over the services they receive. Although the paying of the service increases the status of the clients, the distance between helper and client may reduce the power typically associated with that status.

The voicelessness of clients is frequently found in the lack of effort to obtain client evaluations of services. Many agencies do not routinely collect information on client opinions. Exit interviews may not be part of agency procedures. The absence of procedures for collecting evaluation data serves to retard the development of ethnic-sensitive practice.

Structure: Community Input

Private, nonprofit agencies tend to rely on the board structure of governance. Through board participation, the community can have input into the agency's operations. Ethnic minorities may be underrepresented on the boards of many of the mainstream social work agencies and, hence, not be able to influence the agency. Because many of these agencies rely on public funding,[24] they may be even less likely to "hear" minority voices. In casting a net for board members, these agencies may not target minority communities, particularly if they are not a powerful agency external constituency. Minority community input, then, is not structured into the agency's organization.

Maximum feasible participation was a popular phase in the 1960s of community groups. As noted in Chapter 5, many groups were forcing the "establishment" to listen to them. That movement has passed and the cry for citizen participation may have passed with it. As public attitudes shift, the demands placed on agencies also shifts. Grass-roots organizing seems dated as society becomes more advanced and technologically sophisticated. Citizen involvement in agencies may now be predicated on who can help the agency the most. Individuals with specialized skills may be more likely to take a seat at the agency board table than the grass-roots organizers. Thus, there is no political pressure on agencies to seek participation from a broad spectrum of the community.

Technology: Sunk Costs

Agencies also resist change because of the sunk-cost factor. According to Patti: "Sunk costs refer to the investments that have been made by an organization (or its members) to develop and sustain any institutional arrangement or pattern of behavior that is currently in force. Investment are... inputs of money, time, energy, or personal commitment."[25] The internal economy of the agency indicates the distribution of resources, and those investments may not be recovered if there is a change in the practices of the agency. The agency that has spent a great deal of time and money developing foster-home recruitment and maintenance strategies may not be willing to put those strategies aside, even temporarily, to develop culturally sensitive ones for ethnic groups.

The shift in service populations, technologies, and staff is a costly one for many agencies. The training or retraining of staff or the hiring of bilingual, bicultural workers may not be cost efficient in the eyes of the agency. The cost involved in servicing new client groups may be seen as prohibitive. In times of fiscal austerity, change may receive even less support because the agency may attempt to protect resources rather than expend them.

Agencies have significant amounts of resources committed to maintaining its steady state. The technology of "how things usually get done" requires a particular configuration of services, a particular organizational structure, and relations among staff and between staff and administrators may be derivatives of the technology. Conversions, transformations, or eliminations of the existing technology may not be feasible for the agency.

Minority Staff as Technology

Some agencies assume that the ethnic presence on the staff is a sufficient indicator of ethnic-sensitive service. Ethnic-sensitive practice is expected to occur between the minority professional and the minority client. The minority professional then becomes the embodiment of ethnic-sensitive practice. In addition, the minority is expected to impart knowledge to his or her colleagues. Wright, Saleeby, Watts, and Lecca made this assumption when they commented, "Organizations committed to hiring minority personnel can expect, in some instances, that those individuals will not be only workers and administrators but *teachers* as well" [emphasis added].[26]

This assumption subscribes to the "myth of homogeneity" because within-group differences are ignored and ethnic sensitivity is presumed to reside in the individual because of his or her ethnicity. Some minority professionals who have "made it" may have little sympathy for those who are "keeping the race down." Montiel and Wong stated, "For these professionals, 'problems' may be seen as being surmountable within the boundaries of a functional society that has provided satisfaction to its participants.

This view points to the need to examine critically the disparity between minority professionals and the minority community."[27]

The minority professional is also presumed to increase minority service utilization through her/his presence on the staff.[28] The assumption of the minority worker as the embodiment of ethnic-sensitive practice places a tremendous burden on the worker. In addition to performing daily responsibilities, he or she is expected to be the resident expert on ethnic issues, teach colleagues the nuances of ethnic-sensitive practice, and act as a magnet to attract minority clients. In this approach, the agency remains unchanged and the success or failure of ethnic-sensitive practice becomes the responsibility of the minority worker(s). Thus, the problem would continue to be seen as a *minority* problem and not an *agency* problem.

The "minority as expert" assumption disregards the kinds of issues that may hamper staff collegial interactions. Staff and administrators may assume that minority members are only expert in minority issues and with minority clients. The African American may be expected to interface with the African-American community, the Hispanic with the Hispanic community, the Asian with the Asian community, and so on. These assumptions may create tensions between staff members as professional expertise is second to ethnic group membership. Many of these agency practices are informal but well known and extremely visible in the agency.

One adoptions worker (a White female) commented:

> I really don't like it. My supervisor sends out the Black worker to assess the Black homes and she thinks she's doing those families a favor. She doesn't understand that *I* would be much better for that family than that punitive Black worker who will make that family jump through every hoop imaginable. But we don't talk about this in my agency. I wouldn't dare say anything because they'll probably think I'm being racist.

The African-American worker (female), on the other hand, sees the situation differently:

> I don't think my colleagues think I'm competent. It's not that they say anything—it's just an attitude. They probably think I'm an affirmative action hire to make the agency look good. Since I've been here, I haven't done one assessment on one White home. Now what does that tell you?

Ambivalence about the role of ethnicity at the organizational level may not be the cultivating ground for ethnic-sensitive practice.

Although all of the preceding are barriers to service and maintain a status quo of mainstream agency practice, there is a dominant prevailing myth that warrants special attention.

ETHNIC-SENSITIVE PRACTICE: THE WORKER VERSUS THE AGENCY

A major issue in the quest for ethnic-sensitive practice is the use of worker training.[29] Because the worker-client interaction is a core feature of numerous service delivery systems,[30] there is a tendency to locate ethnic-sensitive practice exclusively in this interaction. Consequently, much of the attention has been on what occurs between worker and client.

The focus on the worker implies that he or she is not performing appropriately or that he or she needs to perform better. The organization—with its structure, goals, and technology—is left intact, and workers are taught how to be culturally sensitive and relate to members of other groups. Holloway and Brager stated, "There is, we believe, a too ready disposition to define organizational problems in terms of the abilities or attitudes of incumbents and thus to overemphasize people change.... It is implicitly critical of the organization's personnel rather than the organization's program and structure or its ideology and is therefore less controversial."[31]

This presumption of "guilt" often irritates or angers some workers. For example, a White female social worker in a family service agency in the midwest had this to say after attending a mandatory training on the African-American family:

> I am so tired of hearing about the Black family. The Black family this, the Black family that. You'd think they were the only ones with families. I've been doing this work for 20 years and I know I'm a good social worker, thank you. I don't need anyone telling me how to do my job.

The trainer (an African-American female) had this reaction:

> They were really hostile. At first, I thought they were upset because they *had* to be there but, you know, I'm beginning to think they really *are* racist. They didn't want to hear anything I had to say.

Although the training was supposed to foster more ethnic-sensitive practice, it did not seem to be effective at all. As a matter of fact, it may have led to increased polarization.

For those workers who have experienced the benefits of training, they may have to deal with the frustrations of being different in a service that has not changed. In actuality, the training may educate the worker about cultural differences and thus lead to *worker* empowerment rather than to *client* empowerment. Worker empowerment, however, in an agency that is *dis*empowering may be a disservice to the worker.

Emphasis on the worker-client interaction ignores the way agency parameters shape that interaction. Glitterman and Miller asserted, "The organization influences and shapes services, problem definition, assessment and intervention, and 'careers' of clients. These in turn influence our professional behavior and view of ourselves....Organizational structures...can become the mechanisms which create numerous tensions and obstacles for professionals and clients."[32]

Worker training ignores the power of the agency in the worker-client interaction. The worker, through practice, implements the ideology and the technology of the agency. After training, the worker continues to implement the same ideology and technology, only this time with heightened cultural awareness. The worker can provide only those services sanctioned by the agency, whether these services support empowerment or not. The worker cannot visit the client in his or her neighborhood if home visits are not part of the agency's technology. The worker cannot enter into a "sameness" or "oneness" with the client if the agency's service ideology calls for professional distance and the authority of expertise. The worker alone cannot and should not bear the entire responsibility for providing ethnic-sensitive practice.

The worker-client interaction should be placed in the larger context of the agency. Ethnic-sensitive practice calls for a "paradigm shift" and the acquisition of a new world view.[33] This shift to a new world view has to pervade the agency and become a mandate for administrators and staff and become a pivotal force for technological shifts as well.

THE NEW PARADIGM

"Organizations tend to reflect the culture and society in which they are lodged. Not only their form, but also their values and goals, are reflections of their broader societal and cultural contexts."[34] The history of social work, the history of ethnic minorities, and the emergence and growth of the Welfare State illuminate the ebb and flow of public sentiment. Although the myth of the melting pot is said to be dying, that death is slow and painful. In 1970, Guttentag noted, "The dominant ethos has been against the formation of sub-group identities in favor of an overall *American* one."[35] Social work accepted this world view. It was the basis for the Americanization movement. For those minorities who could not be Americanized, social work responded by accepting the acceptable—those positions that supported the popular thought of the day.

The world view has also directed social workers to focus on the similarities and not the differences. Similarities were thought to unite individuals and differences were thought to be divisive. The mission was to overlook differences and just respond to people as individuals, and all individuals were supposed to be the same. The decontextualization of the minority client noted in the social work literature by McMahon and Allen-Meares is just an indication of the application of the ethos.[36]

Practitioners and the social work profession have struggled with various "minority" problems over the years. Numerous programs and services have been used to mold problem groups into functioning Americans. Social workers have been responsible for breathing life into these problems, but they were only acting out the mandate they had been given and that they accepted. Social work was and continues to be the practice arm of the Welfare State. The ambivalence the larger social system felt about ethnic minority groups found its way into those responses the workers had to those minorities. Social work did not invent this ambivalence. Client-blaming ideologies, professionalization, and bureaucratization work against any new paradigm. In addition, the history of the profession indicates that the shift first has to take place in other parts of the social system before social work is able to act on it.

The new paradigm calls for the integration of ethnicity in the service delivery process. It means incorporating cultural tradition and cultural heritage in the *agency's* interface with the clients. Years of trying to disregard the ethnic factor in social work cannot be undone so easily, especially when ethnicity still carries with it so many contradictions in U.S. society.

The paradigm also begs for a shift in a major way of thinking. In the new paradigm, African Americans are no longer *the* minority group of the United States. Other ethnic groups share in the minority status, and delivery systems must recognize this. The traditional ideology places African Americans at the center of concern. As noted in Chapter 6, social work and the African-American community have been historically entwined as the profession has attempted to respond to African-American needs and as the African-American community has expected social work to respond to its needs. Now, African Americans will have to share social work with other groups and social workers will have to respond more effectively with these other minority groups. This transition may be a painful one as this paradigm evolves.

A Mexican-American social worker in southern California made the following comments on the topic:

> Black people will have to know they're not the only game in town. Not anymore. Our communities need help too. I can't get over these Black people around here. They think *they're* entitled to everything. Well, this is a new day and they've got a lot to learn. But that's okay. We're pretty good teachers.

On the same subject, an African-American social worker remarked:

> Those people (Hispanics) are crazy. They've only been over here a hot minute and they think they own the place. We've (African Americans) been here for hundreds of years, slaving, fighting, working for what we

get. We didn't even *want* to come over here. Now the Hispanics want everything *handed* to them. Some nerve!

These comments capture particular views in their extreme forms and are used here to convey the full extent of the tensions that occur as transitions are in progress. Most social workers probably fall somewhere between these two extremes.

Another modification in paradigm may be needed in the way culture is identified and perceived. In the old paradigm, *culture* is something that ethnic minority groups have, and *ethnic-sensitive practice* means that White workers have to learn about minority groups. An expansion of the concept of culture suggests that *everyone* has culture and, therefore, *everyone* needs cultural awareness. The need for this awareness moves from a white-focused need to an individual-focused need that includes everyone, regardless of ethnicity. Every group then learns about every other group and the responsibility for cultural awareness is distributed throughout the population. Cultural awareness becomes necessary and of value to everyone.

The new paradigm clarifies the meaning of empowerment in contemporary social work practice. Attempts are underway to incorporate empowerment in various aspects of social work. For example, Hegar and Hunzeker promoted an empowerment approach to public child welfare.[37] This approach builds on strengths and a worker-client collaboration. Empowerment has been advocated for other groups as well.[38]

Staples pointed out one of the issues with current thinking on empowerment.[39] He urged people to move away from focusing on the empowerment of individuals to the empowerment of groups. Perhaps this is one of the fundamental distinctions between ethnic agency practice and mainstream thinking of empowerment. In the ethnic agency, the individual is empowered because, as a member of the group, his or her empowerment contributed to the greater good of the group. The individual is a subsystem of the ethnic community and not a complete system unto himself or herself.

Empowerment seems at odds with mainstream service practices that define the role of the helper as well as the role of the help recipient. Professionalization has further distanced the worker from the client. Although empowerment is a primary component of the ideology of ethnic agencies, empowerment has to be redefined in a manner that is feasible for social work. The question becomes: What should empowerment look like in social work practice? This means the definitions of empowerment and the activities that support it may vary from setting to setting.

Paradigm shifts in social work will parallel ideological shifts in society, and the transition often takes years. Does this mean that agency change is not possible? Does this mean that old paradigms will continue indefinitely? Is ethnic-sensitive practice going to be more rhetoric than practice? The answer to all these questions is *no*. The history and context of agency practice dictate that change will not come about automatically or out of the altruism of the agency. History suggests that a major impetus, internal and/ or external, has to jolt agency change.

THE FORCES OF CHANGE

Organizations wedded to old paradigms need a change catalyst to alert them to the need for ethnic-sensitive service delivery. This catalyst can be located externally or internally to the agency. Examples of external catalysts are discussed first.

Changing Funding Policies

Agency change can occur as the result of modified funding regulations that stipulate the inclusion of specific populations as service beneficiaries.[40] Agencies are dependent on sources outside their boundaries for funding and are therefore sensitive to the changes in funding directives. This sensitivity is needed to ensure the survival of the agency, as funding brings with it mandates. To this extent, agency goals are driven by the imperatives of funding policies and not necessarily by client needs.

These funding regulations may identify particular client populations that are primarily minority group members. For example, as a result of the *Youakim* v. *Miller* Supreme Court Decision of 1979, relatives who care for their kin could be eligible to receive federal foster-care benefits and receive support services.[41] Prior to the implementation of this decision, caregivers who were relatives could be informally handled by agencies and fell outside of the formal foster-care system. As more and more states fall into compliance with the decision, a new group of foster parents is steadily emerging. Foster caregiver relatives tend to be older minority women who are grandmothers or aunts to the children in their care.

Now, child-welfare agencies around the country are facing a new clientele. Traditional ways of interacting with foster parents may not be appropriate for families of color. Agency policies and practices may have to be revised as the unique needs of this group are assessed. What kinds of services do these caregivers require? What is the role of the agency in interfacing with the family? How does this affect case planning?

This is also an example in which entry and access to an agency do not necessarily result in ethnic-sensitive services. Some agencies are conducting business as usual and continue to overlook the needs of this new client group. In actuality, some agencies are functioning as if these caregivers are still outside of the formal system. The only difference is in the higher payments the caregivers receive because of their inclusion in the federal foster-care system.

Other agencies are not providing the same level of services to these caregiver relatives as they do to the nonrelative caregivers. Nonrelative, licensed foster parents tend to be White, and ethnicity may be a factor. Nonrelative caregivers continue to have more worker visits, more services, and, generally, more agency attention. The reasons for this are not yet clear. For some agencies, a two-tier system is forming that places the nonrelative White foster parent in the first tier and the minority relative caregiver in the second tier.

Child-welfare workers and agencies have a developed technology for working with foster parents who are unrelated to the foster child. The agency has helped to structure the nature of the foster parent-foster child relationship and foster parents are informed about the foster care system. Caregiver relatives have a sustaining relationship with the foster child and may not require agency assistance in structuring that relationship. The agency and worker role may be fuzzy in these cases. Family ties may have spurious effects on the relationship between race and service delivery or race could be the factor determining the type of services rendered.

Funding Priorities

All agencies, public or private, are affected by funding shifts as shrinking funds in some areas and increasing funds in other areas determine agency programs. Some issues and areas may have high profile while other areas wane in importance. Because agencies are often dependent on public and private sources of money, they may have to keep pace with complexities of the funding environment. In addition, to manage this environmental dependency, some agencies attempt to create a diversified base of support.[42]

In the search for additional funding, agencies may seek out new client populations as funding for services to these groups becomes available. A senior peer-counseling program in southern California trains senior citizens to be peer counselors for seniors. This counseling network creates a support group for individuals who would otherwise be isolated. The leadership and peer counselors are predominantly White. In the aftermath of the Los Angeles civil unrest in April 1992, the program applied for federal funds to expand its services. Agency administrators perceived a greater need for program services, since many senior citizens were isolated, frightened, and in need of emotional support.

The program received the funds it requested and was informed that additional money was available if the program could be expanded to other parts of the county to reach ethnic minority senior citizens. The administrators accepted the challenge and the funds. The very nature of the program dictated a community-focused approach to recruit seniors for training. Agency staff visited targeted communities and contacted service providers in those areas. Through this extensive community contact, seniors indigenous to the ethnic communities were recruited and trained in those communities.

Although other programs had failed, this senior peer-counseling program was able to penetrate the Samoan community in southern California. In the Samoan community, the agency director found that this community was led by 12 Samoan chiefs. An intermediary from a Samoan grass-roots organization arranged a meeting between the director and one of the chiefs. With one chief's endorsement, support from the other chiefs was easily obtained. The chiefs informed the community of the need for this program and a total of 50 Samoan senior citizens were recruited and trained at various locations in the community to provide emotional support to their fellow residents. While other traditional agencies had been struggling to gain access to the Samoan community, the senior peer-counseling agency was effective because of the recognition and respect afforded the community's culture, norms, and leadership.

Out-Group Protests

Agencies may be bombarded by the demands and protests from a traditionally unserved ethnic group and these protests are so disruptive to the agency that some agency change response is required. The tumultuous 1960s created a climate that was ripe for change as numerous "out-groups" demanded "in-group" attention.

El Centro de la Raza, as described by Gutierrez, is an outgrowth of protests led by Latino activists in Seattle who demanded a building to house a center for the community.[43] From this initial protest, El Centro de la Raza has become a complex array of services and activities. A Chicano protest in San Diego during this period resulted in the pay differential now in existence for bilingual social workers. The Chicano group staged a march, confronted the county's board of supervisors (the governing body of the county), and demanded more bilingual-bicultural workers. The board established the higher pay differential for bilingual (Spanish-English) social workers to attract those with this proficiency. San Diego County then became a model that other counties followed in trying to increase their bilingual social work force. Through this higher pay differential, the county's department of social services validated and legitimized the worth of the skill and the individual possessing it.

This ethnic presence in the county agencies increased the Chicano utilization of services and this illuminates another paradox in ethnic service delivery issue. The ethnic presence in an agency may increase ethnic utilization of the agency's services so that more resources may be needed to serve this additional population. Although some counties may be able to absorb this cost, other counties and private, nonprofit agencies may feel that the funds are not available for additional populations.

The acquisition of new funds and the new clients the funds bring may not result in ethnic-sensitive practice. A private, nonprofit residential treatment facility (predominantly White) for boys with severe emotional disabilities had been funded primarily by fees, grants, and foundations. The austere financial climate forced the agency to seek funding from other sources. To this end, it entered into a contractual arrangement with the county to accept and treat boys referred from the juvenile court system. These were boys in need of a therapeutic environment.

Although the agency was "saved" with this new and rich money source, staff and new clients did not gel. The new clients were African-American boys diagnosed as having disruptive behavior disorders (acting-out behaviors). The staff threatened to walk out in protest and the agency was in turmoil for weeks. Many staff members did leave in protest but the new workers hired to replace them included some minorities as well as workers familiar with the new client population.

In this example, the old workers' worst fears about the new clients were confirmed, although these workers were expecting the worst anyway. With a particular ideology about the differences between working with White boys and working with African-American boys firmly in place, there may have been little chance that the workers would have responded any differently regardless of the behaviors of the new clients. In the absence of the funding crisis, it is doubtful that the agency would have reached out for minority clients.

New Constituencies

The realignment of voting areas can create new minority districts that elect minority representation.[44] This new minority leadership can push for needed services in these areas. For example, Los Angeles County is governed by a five-person board of supervisors that, historically, had been all White. A protracted and contentious legal battle waged to change district boundaries to establish a new Hispanic district. This district would ensure the election of a Hispanic to the board.

In 1991, Gloria Molina became the first woman and the first Hispanic elected to the Los Angeles County Board of Supervisors. She advocates for the Hispanic community and has been instrumental in bringing programs in as well. When a county interagency gang-prevention task force began meeting to develop a countywide gang-prevention plan, Molina insisted that her constituency have an opportunity for input on this plan. She recommended that a hearing be held in her district to achieve this goal.

In a letter concerning AIDS, Molina wrote:

> As an elected official, I accepted the responsibility to be a voice for my constituents and my community.... As a Latina, I feel an even

stronger responsibility to reach the Latino Community with the message of HIV prevention and awareness.... I intend to continue to ensure that funds provided for HIV/AIDS in Los Angeles County are used appropriately and that the programs and services provided are *sensitive to the cultural needs of Latinos and other ethnic groups*. [emphasis added][45]

As more ethnic minorities fill major governmental positions, emphasis on and support for ethnic-sensitive services will grow. In all these examples, the impetus for the agency change came from forces external to the agency. Change can also occur from within the agency.

New Agency Leadership

The internal polity of an agency may shift so that a new dominant elite emerges. This may be triggered by a change in directors or a major shift in staff. As new staff members join the agency with particular skills and political positions, the agency may eventually shift as the new staff members become a majority.

An eastern family service agency hired its first African-American director who had made note of the absence of minority presence among the staff and clients. Although she had not placed issues of access on the list of immediate priorities, she began receiving calls from African-American citizens congratulating her on the new position and welcoming her to the "community." Each of the callers made a comment about their expectation of change for the agency. This was expressed as, "We're glad you're here. It's about time that place had a little color."

The director received so many comments from the African-American community, she felt she *had* to do something or lose her credibility with these residents. She and her staff planned an open house to introduce her to the entire city community. In doing this, she was especially careful to make sure invitations went out to business people, religious leaders, and other professionals in the African-American community. At the open house, she raised the possibility of a citywide coalition forming to promote those issues of importance to the city, such as youth programs and day care. The agency became the meeting place for the coalition, which included African-American members. This was the first step in opening the agency to the community. Through this coalition, the agency's image began to change and, eventually, other minorities joined the staff.

The Worker as a Change Catalyst

In the bed of bureaucracy, it is easy for workers to feel powerless in bringing about change. The forces that inhibit change activities for workers are great and the social costs may be high. There is a body of literature about how to accomplish change from within, but it is conceivable that those who do cause change may have never read that literature. This may be due to the fact that change agents may often be responding as an immediate reaction to perceived social injustice or perceived inequities. In addition, not all agency change is planned and rational.

Social work comes from a history of change catalysts, as noted in Chapter 5. The change agent role of the social worker in the agency may be minimized as the role of the worker as change agent for the *client* is maximized. Change activities initiated by the workers also threaten the agency's equilibrium and forces begin to control those change activities.

In some cases, the change is smooth without causing stress to the agency. For example, a female White worker for a private, nonprofit family service agency had been bothered by the lack of Hispanic foster homes on the agency's list of foster homes. Since this agency recruited, trained, and supervised the licensing of foster homes, she had wondered if the omission was intentional or accidental. The agency had not accepted any Hispanic referrals, so the absence of Hispanic homes was not a problem to the other staff members.

The recruitment of foster homes became a cause—a crusade—for this worker. She raised the issue at staff meetings, in conversation with her colleagues, and in conferences with her supervisor. Since the worker was well liked and respected by her colleagues, she was not perceived as threatening. In addition, her personal style was warm and engaging. In talking about the new recruitment of Hispanic homes, she would say:

> This is such a wonderful place. The people here are such good social workers. We have so much to offer kids, we should have more and different ones. There are so many things we could be doing. This is such a great place and people have such good ideas.

Over time, according to the worker, she wore down everyone's resistance and the agency now has a bilingual worker recruiting Hispanic homes. The worker commented:

> I think they wanted me to move on to talk about something else. I tell my supervisor she wanted to shut me up. She laughs but she doesn't say no. I knew we needed to do more. And we are. It's only taken three years for this to happen, but the important thing is it's happening.

This worker was committed to the issue and pursued it over time. In many agencies, issues may die and be reborn and never change because no one is making sure it remains in the forefront of agency attention. For this worker, there were no social costs to her gentle agitation.

At the other end of the continuum, there are other settings in which high social costs greet the worker who tries to be a change agent. These settings are not resistant to change; they are hostile. In these settings, workers have been known to engage in subversive tactics to stimulate change. For example, in a child-protective services agency in a midsized city, an African-American female worker believed that African-American children were being poorly supervised in foster care. She thought the White workers really did not care about the African-American children. This worker had quite a number of years invested in the job, a generous pension plan upon retirement, and could not afford to lose her job. She began, instead, to "leak" information to an African-American reporter about cases that were "sensational" and newsworthy. The newspaper stories did spark an internal audit of case handling, in-service training, and new procedures. The former worker is quick to add, "Be sure to tell people that I'm *retired* now and this happened a long time ago. I don't want anybody to think this sort of thing still goes on." Because these activities are subversive, the prevalence of their use may never be known.

Routinization of Change

Special programs may be a response adopted by agencies to meet the needs of a particular group. These special programs are developed within a larger agency to provide services to a specific ethnic group or groups.[46] The special program may be decoupled from or loosely connected with the rest of the agency. This is predicated on the agency ideology of the ethnic group served and the extent to which the program is separated from the rest of the agency. If the prevailing belief is that the program is receiving special treatment that renders it exempt from procedures that apply to everyone else, then this special program may not be well received in the agency. In most agencies, the rules of fairness are expected to apply.

In the Los Angeles County Department of Children's Services, a special Southeast Asian unit exists with Asian workers who handle Southeast Asian cases. The supervisor of that unit is Vietnamese. In this unit, the workers function as a cohesive group and, because of the language skills of the unit, the rest of the workers seem to accept the need to separate this unit. In the context of a highly bureaucratized agency, a special unit exists to serve a unique ethnic population.

The impetus for this unit was the supervisor. When he was promoted to supervisor, he began requesting workers who could work with Southeast Asian families. Over a period of several years, he advocated for the needs of Southeast Asians and developed a reputation for being an expert on this subject. He also began participating in workshops and then organized workshops on the special needs of Southeast Asian families. He became the department's expert on the topic, and this recognized expertise was an asset as he continued to put together this special unit. The department was supportive of his efforts but, in an agency of this size, the creation of the special unit took place over a long period of time.

The technology of the Southeast Asian unit is presumed to be one of empowerment (educating, training, in addition to other support services). If the workers perform their duties in the same manner as all the other workers in the agency, then, of course, empowerment is not integrated into the ideology of the program. Because the workers and clients are of the same ethnicity and because the unit is a separate one, empowerment seems likely to result.

In the ethnic unit, workers may be able to protect clients from some of the effects of bureaucracy. Workers may have greater freedom in sidestepping bureaucracy or reducing the amount of bureaucracy exposed to the client. With the ethnic unit, continuity of service can be maintained and the workers may have a heightened sense of commitment to and personal investment in the work.

Over time, these programs may become routinized. According to Zey-Ferrel, "Routinization, or institutionalization, occurs over time; when it is complete, the program is no longer designated new—most of the problems have been worked out and the structure and processes accompanying the program change have become accepted parts of the organization."[47] The goal for ethnic-sensitive practice is the institutionalization of the practice into the structure of the agency so that the practice becomes permanent, even if the workers do not.

Other Agency Considerations

Because "community" figures so prominently in ethnic-sensitive practice, factors that affect the agency's relationship with ethnic communities should be mentioned. Large, bureaucratic, complex agencies may be less accessible to ethnic communities. These agencies, many of them public, place a multitude of layers between the community resident and the director. Because they seem impenetrable, various communities may not attempt to negotiate the bureaucratic maze.

Although large bureaucratic agencies may be inaccessible to ethnic communities, these agencies may still be capable of change because they may have the resources and diversity to create innovative programs, as was mentioned earlier. This is due to the "slack resources" of these agencies.[48] On the down side, these agencies may not be able to respond as quickly to the need for change as smaller, private, nonprofit agencies.

The agency's willingness and capacity to adopt a new paradigm may be significantly influenced by the *history* of that agency with particular ethnic groups. For example, the history of American Indians in the United States would suggest that tension may exist between some group members and the mainstream child-welfare agencies. Because of the historical issues around reporting and deportation, segments of the Hispanic community may be skeptical about accessing services. Ethnic service delivery cannot disregard the history of ethnic groups in America and how agencies have responded or contributed to that history.

The Young Women's Christian Association (YWCA) of Los Angeles has branch programs located in communities throughout Los Angeles. For example, a branch is located in Koreatown that has a Korean program director, is staffed by Koreans, prints all of its materials in Korean, and responds exclusively to the Korean-American community. In addition, Korean Americans are represented in the agency's central administration and on the executive board.

This presence of and responsiveness to ethnic communities seems rooted in the history of the YWCA. For example, in 1906, the association was working in African-American schools in the south and, in 1915, at its Louisville Conference, the association affirmed:

1. That we believe the time has come for the appointing of a committee composed of white and colored women from or of the South.
2. That we recognize that the best method of cooperation in city associations is through branch relationships.[49]

Although various organizational dimensions are important for understanding the development, implementation, and routinization of ethnic-sensitive practice, the "new" paradigm may not be incompatible with all service agencies. History of the agency's contact with ethnic minorities becomes another factor for consideration.

Organizational change is a complex subject that involves ideologies, technologies, structures, people, and history. Hasenfeld summed up the issues on agency change in this manner: "While many individual human service practitioners may be change oriented and ready to intervene on behalf of clients, their organizations are often likely to resist change and innovation. On balance the forces that promote stability outweigh those that push for innovation and change. Human service organizations seem to change only when under duress—that is, when external conditions have reached a point at which they cannot be ignored."[50]

A MODEL FOR
ETHNIC-SENSITIVE PRACTICE

This chapter has discussed a definition of *ethnic-sensitive practice*, the barriers to that practice, the need for a new paradigm, and the forces that promote ethnic-sensitive practice. Examples of the range of agency responses were presented. It is clear from the examples that the extent and degree of ethnic-sensitive practice are quite varied.

The model of ethnic-sensitive practice emergent from ethnic agencies may prove helpful. For any agency, the following questions can be asked:

1. *Ideology*: What is the ideology of the agency? How are clients perceived? How are ethnic clients perceived? What are the perceived causes of the client's situation? How does the worker envision his or her role? How does the worker envision the client role? What are the desired outcomes? Why are these the desired outcomes? To what extent are clients perceived as different or the same?
2. *Technology*: What do workers actually do with clients? What are the specific activities used to bring about desired outcomes? What are the steps or stages of this process? What does the agency do to move the client from where he or she is now to where the agency thinks he or she ought to be?
3. *Structure*: What are the rules governing worker-client interactions? What are you permitted to do with clients? What are the things you cannot do with clients? How many people does the client have to encounter before he or she actually sees the worker? How rigid are the agency's rules? How high is the agency's hierarchy? How is the worker-client interaction structured? How quickly and easily can the client see someone at the top? How quickly and easily can the worker see someone at the top?
4. *Input*: Are there procedures for obtaining client input about services? Are there procedures for obtaining client assessment of services?
5. *Accountability*: Is the ethnic community identified as an agency constituency? Are there procedures for obtaining ethnic community input about agency services? To what extent is the agency accountable to the ethnic community?

From this list, several points require additional emphasis. First, ethnic-sensitive practice is not a worker-client phenomenon. Ethnic sensitivity takes place in the context of an agency with agency features that actually work to protect and maintain that practice. Workers who enter the agency are then socialized into that practice, whether they believe in it or not. The agency climate, technology, and structure create a powerful force that defies individual resistance.

Second, to protect ethnic-sensitive practice, agencies should institutionalize it so that it becomes a permanent agency feature. As formal organizations, agencies develop structures, procedures, and supports for those elements it seeks to protect. The same effort should be expended for ethnic-sensitive practice if it is to occur.

Third, an agency can create the procedures and structures to maintain ethnic-sensitive practice and at the same time buffer the client from bureaucracy. The routinization of practice does not mean the creation of complex procedures and does not mean the extension of bureaucracy into this area. In some agencies, there may be a predilection for bureaucracy and the bureaucratization of the simplest task. The structure and procedures do not have to be a complicated, complex morass and they do not have to be experienced by the client as a bureaucratic intrusion. They may serve only for the benefit of the worker and the agency to ensure that certain kinds of activities take place. If client feedback is institutionalized, for example, it may take the form of someone, not necessarily the worker, asking the client a few open-ended questions about services and recording client responses. The routinization of client input does not mean subjecting the client to a 20-page questionnaire.

Two major components emerge from this analysis of ethnic-sensitive practice that can be used as a framework for assessing the extent and type of ethnic practice taking place in service delivery settings.

One major aspect of ethnic-sensitive practice deals with the extent of *agency penetration* of that practice. This is captured in the dimensions of ideology, technology, and structure. From the field examples given, penetration ranged from access (recruitment and outreach of minority staff and clients) to the development of specialized programs within the agency (the Southeast Asian unit). Agencies may have no ethnic minority clients and/or ethnic minority staff. Other agencies may have both and still not engage in any type of ethnic practice. Those agencies that have staff, structure, and technology that support ethnic-sensitive practice appear to have institutionalized the practice in the agency.

The other major dimension of ethnic-sensitive practice is the extent of *community penetration* of that practice. Community penetration ranged in the examples from none (no community input at all) to high (community input on agency's executive board). Community participation is at the core of the agency/community interface. This was illuminated in the relationship the ethnic agency has with its community.

With these two dimensions, a grid of ethnic-sensitive practice begins to appear in which the degree of ethnic-sensitive practice in agencies is assessed as the degree of agency penetration and degree of community penetration. Figure 7–1 depicts the relationship between the dimensions. In this figure, a grid is formed with four corners that represent:

Low agency penetration and low community penetration: The agency has little or no ethnic minorities staff or clients and no ethnic community input;

High agency penetration and low community penetration: The special ethnic program within an agency is an example. This *program*, not necessarily the agency as a whole, incorporates an ideology, technology, and struc-

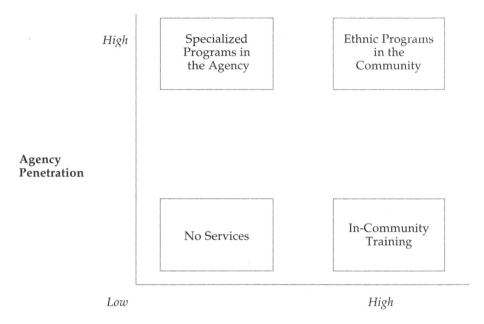

Community Penetration

FIGURE 7–1 An Overview of Ethnic-Sensitive Practice

ture that supports ethnic-sensitive practice to a specific ethnic community. The program may be decoupled from or loosely coupled with the rest of the agency to buffer the program itself. This coupling gives the program the freedom to conduct its service delivery in a manner that may differ from the rest of the agency. There may be, however, minimal or no routinized community input, so the program/community interface may be through the interactions between program staff and the ethnic community. For example, the supervisor of the Southeast Asian unit is involved in organizations in the Vietnamese community. Although the staff members may feel an added commitment to serving the ethnic community, the program is accountable to the agency and not to the community. This program/community interface is not routinized or institutionalized. With informal arrangements, a change in staff or agency organization could jeopardize informal relationships.

High community penetration and low agency penetration: The senior peer-counseling program that trained Samoan elderly to be peer counselors is an example. The agency conducts programs in the community and incorporates ethnicity and culture in its programs. There is, however, no community input in the agency and the agency/community communication is one-way—from the agency to the community.

High community penetration and high agency penetration: The YWCA Koreatown branch is an example. The branch functions as an ethnic agency with ethnic staff serving an ethnic community in the ethnic community. In addition, there is community input in the governance of the central structure of the YWCA through board participation. The communication flows both ways between the agency and the community.

This framework can then aid in determining the degree of ethnic-sensitive practice that is taking place. For example, a specialized foster-care recruitment program for Hispanic families might be moderate in agency penetration and moderate in community penetration. These programs tend to be loosely structured so that institutionalization of the program is not complete. The community penetration is moderate because community input into the program is usually through foster-parent meetings. Although feedback is provided to the agency from the community (through the foster parents), parents may not be participating in the governance structure of the agency. The "community" has limited and specific feedback to the agency.

The dimensions of ethnic-sensitive practice and the grid suggest that this type of practice does not have to continue to be a "black box" into which service providers stare and see whatever they wish to see. With a broader macroperspective on ethnic-sensitive practices, resistance can be understood as well as why its diffusion into agencies has been sluggish, at best.

Defining problem areas is only one step to resolving these areas. The next step is the development of strategies to overcome agency obstacles. Although some of these considerations may have been touched on in the previous examples, it is important to emphasize and summarize those specific steps that can lead to agency change.

BREAKING BARRIERS

Agency penetration of ethnic-sensitive practice may be difficult to achieve, but not impossible. In each of the critical areas, some movement or incremental change may be possible.

Ideology

Agency ideologies are difficult to change; however, when a new dominant elite emerges that embraces a particular perspective, a change process may occur. The emergence of this dominant elite is accelerated as new staff join the agency and old staff members resign or retire. With the passage of the old guard, the new elite in the agency may support a new world view or be open to change.

Workers may form their own factions in the agency that support a new paradigm and work within the agency to become the dominant elite. The faction may start off supporting specific issues, advocating positions, and encouraging the hiring of individuals who concur with their view.

New leadership is also a pathway that fosters change in agencies. With the new director, it is expected that some disruption will occur in the agency's equilibrium as he or she carves out an agenda and rearranges the staff. In order to accomplish change, this individual has to amass support within the agency to create a dominant elite that agrees with his or her action plan. Negotiating the organization and forming alliances are crucial to the success of new leaders with change-oriented goals. This holds true for those committed to the provision of ethnic-sensitive practice in their agencies. Knowledge of the informal power structure of the agency, participatory management (or the illusion of participatory management), availability of resources for supporting change, and the ability to mobilize a support alliance are necessary to encourage staff to adopt new approaches in working with changing client populations.

Another avenue for stimulating a paradigm shift involves advocacy in the community and in the political arena. Candidates, issues, and policies all carry with them a perspective of social problems that may reinforce old ways of thinking and responding. A significant shift in how social work and social workers deliver service requires, as history has shown, a shift in public attitudes. The support of candidates and issues that reflect a "new" way of seeing people and problems can facilitate the shift.

In some organizations, old ways persist because no one has offered alternatives. The worker committed to a new way of thinking about service delivery may have to take on the responsibility of leading change efforts. As noted in one of the previous examples, these efforts are costly in terms of time. The cost weighed against the benefits has to be determined on an individual basis.

Technology

Changing how the agency does its work requires help from a number of sources. If other organizations are changing their technology, pressure is created for similar agencies to examine their practices. If people in the agency think the world is moving ahead without them, they may grasp the opportunity to learn different skills.

If staff training is used as a means of promoting agency change, the skills developed through that training have to be (1) integrated into the work of the agency, (2) validated by rewarding excellence in the implementation of that training, (3) supported by the administration of the agency, and (4) provided to the staff by those with the skills to help them "troubleshoot" problems that may arise from using the new skills.

The training, if it is to be a step toward a new paradigm, has to be integrated into a larger plan for change. An agency analysis has to take place to determine how the training affects the usual business of the agency. If business continues as usual, then the utility of that training in changing the technology of the agency is very doubtful.

Community Participation

While the agency maintains a structure for securing community input (typically the board), other methods may be used to encourage input from the ethnic community. Agencies have established community councils, ad hoc task forces of community members, and advisory groups to meet with staff and administrators to discuss common interests, issues, and special agency needs. These are useful only if the agency responds to the issues raised by these groups. These groups are typically formed when the agency needs some type of assistance from the community in reaching special populations. For example, local community councils have been formed in African-American neighborhoods as a means of recruiting homes for African-American children.[51]

Some agencies cannot be accountable to an ethnic community because of the structure of service delivery. These agencies will continue to be accountable to the publics that sponsor them. Relationships with communities can, however, be established to create a symbiotic tie between the agency and the community in specific areas in which the tie benefits both parties. To further establish this tie, mainstream social work may have to utilize the services of ethnic agencies to reach specific communities. This is the focus of the next chapter.

ENDNOTES

1. Amy Mass, "Asians as Individuals: The Japanese Community," *Social Casework 57* (March 1976): 164.

2. David Crystal, "Asian Americans and the Myth of the Model Minority," *Social Casework 70* (September 1989): 413.

3. Herbert Freudenberger, "The Dynamics and Treatment of the Young Drug Abuser in an Hispanic Therapeutic Community," in *Human Services for Cultural Minorities*, ed. Richard Dana (Baltimore: University Park Press, 1981), p. 237.

4. Lonnie Snowden and Freda Cheung, "Use of Inpatient Mental Health Services by Members of Ethnic Minority Groups," *American Psychologist 45* (March 1990): 354.

5. Grafton Hull, "Child Welfare Services to Native Americans," *Social Casework 63* (June 1982): 347.

6. See, for example, Irving N. Berlin, "Prevention of Adolescent Suicide Among Some Native American Tribes," *Adolescent Psychiatry 12* (1985): 77–93; Terry Cross,

"Drawing on Cultural Tradition in Indian Child Welfare Practice," *Social Casework* 67 (May 1986): 283–289; Teresa LaFromboise, "American Indian Mental Health Policy," *American Psychologist 43* (May 1988): 394.

7. See, for example, Timothy Brown, Kenneth Stein, Katherine Huang, and Darrel Harris, "Mental Illness and the Role of Mental Health Facilities in Chinatown," in *Asian-Americans: Psychological Perspectives*, ed. Stanley Sue and Nathaniel Wagner (Ben Lomond, CA: Science and Behavior Books, 1973), p. 228; Hull, "Child Welfare Services to Native Americans," p. 347.

8. See, for example, Sutjit Dhooper and Thanh Van Tran, "Social Work with Asian Americans," *Journal of Independent Social Work 1* (Summer 1987): 60; T. Watkins and R. Gonzales, "Outreach to Mexican Americans," *Social Work 27* (1982): 68–73.

9. See, for example, Lee June, "Enhancing the Delivery of Mental Health and Counseling Services to Black Males: Critical Agency and Provider Responsibilities," *Journal of Multicultural Counseling and Development 14* (January 1986): 41.

10. As noted in Chapter 1; see, for example, Wynetta Devore and Elfriede Schlesinger, *Ethnic-Sensitive Social Work Practice*, Second Edition (Columbus: Merrill, 1987); John Longres, "Toward a Status Model of Ethnic Sensitive Practice," *Journal of Multicultural Practice 1*, number 1 (1991): 41–56.

11. Lorraine Gutierrez, "Empowering Ethnic Minorities in the Twenty-First Century," in *Human Services as Complex Organizations*, ed. Yeheskel Hasenfeld (Newbury Park, CA: Sage, 1992), p. 326.

12. Elaine Pinderhughes, *Understanding Race, Ethnicity, and Power* (New York: The Free Press, 1989), pp. 15–16.

13. Joyce Antler and Stephen Antler, "From Child Rescue to Family Protection," *Children and Youth Services Review 1* (Summer 1979): 177–204.

14. Antler and Antler, "From Child Rescue," p. 202.

15. Peter Pecora, James Whittaker, Anthony Maluccio, with Richard Barth and Robert Plotnick, *The Child Welfare Challenge* (New York: Aldine de Gruyter, 1992).

16. For a discussion of the history of child-welfare services and the African-American family, see Andrew Billingsley and Jeanne Giovannoni, *Children of the Storm* (New York: Harcourt Brace Jovanovich, 1972).

17. Alfreda Iglehart, "Discharge Planning: Professional Perspectives versus Organizational Effects," *Health and Social Work 15* (November 1990): 302, 306.

18. Ralph Anderson and Irl Carter, *Human Behavior in the Social Environment*, Fourth Edition (New York: Aldine de Gruter, 1990), p. 26.

19. Daniel Katz and Robert Kahn, *The Social Psychology of Organizations* (New York: Wiley, 1978), p. 27.

20. Alfreda Iglehart, "Turnover in the Social Services: Turning over to the Benefits," *Social Service Review 64* (December 1990): 649, 652–653.

21. Stanley Sue, David Allen, and Linda Conaway, "The Responsiveness and Equality of Mental Health Care to Chicanos and Native Americans," *American Journal of Community Psychology 6*, number 2 (1978): 145.

22. Yeheskel Hasenfeld, "Power in Social Work Practice," *Social Service Review 61* (September 1987): 475.

23. Amitai Etzioni, *Modern Organizations* (Englewood Cliffs, NJ: Prentice Hall, 1964), p. 97.

24. Susan Ostrander, "Voluntary Social Service Agencies in the United States," *Social Service Review 59* (September 1985): 434.

25. Rino Patti, "Organizational Resistance and Change: The View from Below," in *Social Administration*, ed. Simon Slavin (New York: Haworth Press and Council on Social Work Education, 1978), p. 551.

26. Roosevelt Wright, Dennis Saleeby, Thomas Watts, and Pedro Lecca, *Transcultural Perspectives in the Human Services* (Springfield, IL: Charles C. Thomas, 1983), p. 153.

27. Miguel Montiel and Paul Wong, "A Theoretical Critique of the Minority Perspective," *Social Casework* (February 1983): 116–117.

28. I-Hsin Wu and Charles Windle, "Ethnic Specificity in the Relative Minority Use and Staffing of Community Mental Health Centers," *Community Mental Health Journal 16* (Summer 1980): 156–168.

29. Anthony McMahon and Paula Allen-Meares, "Is Social Work Racist?: A Content Analysis of Recent Literature," *Social Work 37* (November 1992): 533–539.

30. Hasenfeld, *Human Service Organizations*, p. 10.

31. Stephen Holloway and George Brager, "Some Considerations in Planning Organizational Change," *Administration in Social Work 1* (Winter 1977): 351.

32. Alex Glitterman and Irving Miller, "The Influence of the Organization on Clinical Practice," *Clinical Social Work Journal 17* (Summer 1989): 151, 154.

33. Damian McShane, "Mental Health and North American Indian/Native Communities: Cultural Transactions, Education, and Regulation," *American Journal of Community Psychology 15* (February 1987): 112.

34. Patricia Martin, "Multiple Constituencies, Dominant Societal Values, and the Human Service Administrator: Implications for Service Delivery," *Administration in Social Work 4* (Summer 1980): 21.

35. Marcia Guttentag, "Group Cohesiveness, Ethnic Organization, and Poverty," *Journal of Social Issues 26*, number 2 (1970): 125.

36. McMahon and Allen-Meares, "Is Social Work Racist?"

37. Rebecca Hegar and Jeanne Hunzeker, "Moving toward Empowerment-Based Practice in Public Child Welfare," *Social Work 33* (November–December 1988): 501.

38. Patrick Haney, "Providing Empowerment to the Person with AIDS," *Social Work 33* (November/December 1988): 499–503.

39. Lee Staples, "Powerful Ideas About Empowerment," *Administration in Social Work 14*, number 2 (1990): 29–42.

40. Hasenfeld, *Human Service Organizations*, pp. 227–229.

41. Alfreda Iglehart, "Kinship Foster Care: Placement, Service, and Outcome Issues, " *Children and Youth Services Review 16* (1994): 108.

42. Carl Milofski and Frank Romo, "The Structure of Funding Arenas for Neighborhood Based Organizations," in *Community Organization Studies in Resource Mobilization and Exchange*, ed. Carl Milofsky (New York: Oxford University Press, 1988), p. 240.

43. Gutierrez, "Empowering Ethnic Minorities," pp. 332–333.

44. George Brager and Stephen Holloway, *Changing Human Service Organizations* (New York: The Free Press, 1978).

45. Gloria Molina, "A Message from Gloria Molina," *AIDS Link 2* (January 1994): 1, 5.

46. Gutierrez, "Empowering Ethnic Minorities," p. 329.

47. Mary Zey-Ferrell, *Dimensions of Organizations* (Santa Monica, CA: Goodyear Publishing, 1979), p. 270.

48. Mary Zey-Ferrell, *Dimensions of Organizations* (Santa Monica, CA: Goodyear Publishing, 1979), p. 287.

49. C. H. Tobias, "The Work of the Young Men's and Young Women's Christian Associations with Negro Youth," *The Annals of the American Academy of Political and Social Science 240* (November 1928): 286.

50. Hasenfeld, *Human Service Organizations*, pp. 245–246.

51. See, for example, Valora Washington, "Community Involvement in Recruiting Adoptive Homes for Black Children," *Child Welfare 66* (January/February 1987): 57–68.

Chapter 8

Service Delivery to Diverse Populations: Interorganizational Pathways

As society becomes more diverse, service demands from ethnic minority communities will increase. Mainstream social services, public and private nonprofit, will have to respond to the needs of a diverse population. It is doubtful that mainstream social services will evolve into ethnic agencies in the near future. It is also doubtful that ethnic agencies will proliferate and expand to respond to all the needs of all ethnic communities. Ethnic agencies do, however, appear to practice a type of service delivery that reaches and engages numerous communities that may be unserved or underserved, for a myriad of reasons, by mainstream services. The goals and ideology of these agencies support approaches to service delivery that appear to be responsive to ethnic communities.

Mainstream, public-supported health, welfare, and other social services, on the other hand, have a mandate to address the needs of the Welfare State. The mandate of the Welfare State includes the provision of services to its populace. The service net is cast wide enough to reach as many as possible who meet service requirements. Services and programs of the Welfare State may operate under the myth of homogeneity to develop standardized, uniform programs that may not vary, even though the communities do. Some nets may have gapping holes through which segments of the population escape services. For others, the holes are not as great and a much smaller number is excluded.

One pathway to service delivery to ethnic communities is the ethnic agency. For mainstream service providers, the ethnic agency can be a bridge to ethnic communities. These agencies have access to the community, vis-

ibility in the community, and intimate knowledge of the community's structure and processes. The ethnic agency is a subsystem of the ethnic community system. As such, it may have a significant presence in its community.

Relationships between mainstream agencies and ethnic agencies con-
nect social service systems that generally exist as parallel systems. The
purpose of this chapter is not to determine what could, should, or ought to
occur between mainstream agencies and ethnic agencies. Rather, these relationships are examined to determine those factors that affect their development, dynamics, and outcomes. The purpose is also to place these relationships in the model of ethnic-sensitive practice.

Numerous ethnic agencies are currently interacting with mainstream
agencies. As a link to the ethnic community, the ethnic agency may also
become a link between the ethnic community and the Welfare State. What is
the implication of this linkage for mainstream agencies and for ethnic agencies?

PROPOSITIONS FOR
ORGANIZATIONAL LINKAGES

In identifying those factors that influence mainstream agency and ethnic
agency linkages, it is important to develop a framework for the analysis.
There is not, however, a wealth of information on the nature of
interorganizational relations in general, and even less on those involving
ethnic agencies. Provan, Beyer, and Kruytbosch summarized three themes
that run through organizational literature relevant for analyzing
interorganizational relations.[1] The resource-dependence approach indicates
that organizations will become powerful if they can control the resources
needed by other organizations and if they can reduce their own external
dependency. A second approach looks at organization sets or organization
networks—organizations that interact and exchange resources on a frequent
and continuing basis—and the activities within them. The third approach,
the political-economy perspective, looks at the external linkages an organization has to the larger social system. Two basic types of resources are at the
core of the political-economy of interorganizational networks: money and
authority.[2]

All of these approaches incorporate the focal organization's environment and the exchange of energy (resource inputs) between that organization and others in the environment. These approaches are consistent with
the theoretical perspectives presented in Chapter 4. The ethnic agency is a
subsystem interacting within a larger system (one organization in a organizational set) as well as a system unto itself (seeking to maintain its functional independence and organizational identity[3]).

Power is a key factor in the relationships between organizations and can be defined in this manner: A has power over B to the extent that A can get B to do something B would not otherwise do.[4] Interorganizational power is frequently expressed in the negotiations that take place between organizations and according to Benson, "The powerful organization can force others to accept its terms in negotiations.... Power permits one organization to reach across agency boundaries and determine the policies or practices in weaker organizations. Failure or refusal of the weaker organization to accede to the demands of the stronger can have serious repercussions for the resource procurement of the weaker organization."[5]

The ethnic agency's ability to obtain resources and to survive become critical issues in analyzing the relations with mainstream agencies. In addition, the exchanges between systems are relevant. The points at which the ethnic agency service delivery system interfaces with mainstream service delivery systems are important for understanding when and how race and ethnicity shape these interfaces.

From what is already known about the nature of interorganizational relationships and what has been presented here on ethnic agencies, some propositions can be advanced. These propositions describe those factors that influence the ethnic agency's relationship with organizations external to the ethnic community.

Over 90 percent of the agencies Jenkins studied received public dollars.[6] This suggests that ethnic agencies are likely to receive public funds. For that reason, attention is directed to the relationships that are established between public agencies and ethnic agencies. Less attention is given to the relationships that develop between ethnic agencies and other kinds of agencies. Case illustrations will be used to further illustrate the ethnic agency's interface with other organizations.

Proposition 1.   Ethnic agencies are not in competition with mainstream social services for clients.

From previous discussions in Chapter 6, it was found that ethnic agencies do receive public funds to provide services to groups that would not ordinarily receive them or access them. Deficits in mainstream service systems and/or cultural barriers appear to create a need for ethnic agencies. Thus, as a service delivery system, the ethnic agency is not robbing mainstream services of clients.

Proposition 2.   In an interorganizational relationship, the ethnic agency is of importance because of its access to a particular ethnic population.

In the social service marketplace, ethnicity becomes a potential commodity that gives importance to the ethnic agency. According to Hasenfeld and English, because of political, social, and demographic changes in the social environment of agencies, new interorganizational relations may be developed to respond to these changes.[7] These authors further indicated that pressures to serve indigent populations may lead a family service agency, for example, to interact with an agency that has access to that population. Thus, the ethnic community represents a specialized service market to which the ethnic agency has access. The identification of neglected groups "at the boundaries of governmental welfare programs" has generally come from indigenous, less bureaucratized, less professionalized organizations.[8]

The ethnic agency does not receive interest because of its innovations, technologies, or ideologies. It receives attention because of its presence in the ethnic community and its access to clients. Although accessibility is related to its technology and ideology, the external polity and the external economy are attracted to the ethnic agency because of its relationship with specific targeted populations.

Thus, the ethnic agency has dominance of domain and its domain is the ethnic client and the ethnic community. The ownership of a domain allows the agency to operate in a particular sphere, to claim support for its services, and to define the appropriate practices within its sphere.[9] The dominance of the ethnic agency in service delivery to a particular group brings it to the attention of other agencies. For example:

> A county department of mental health began exploring the idea of school-based services as a way of providing comprehensive health and human services to children and their families. The one-stop shop approach would offer an array of services to families without the inconvenience of traveling around the city for these services. A significant percentage of the school's population was Filipino American. A small Filipino service center in the Filipino community was sought out to participate in the initial planning meetings that included representatives from several county and private agencies. Although many on the planning committee knew of the existence of the Filipino service center, they were not really aware of the center's activities. County organizers believed that, because of the Filipino students attending the school, some type of Filipino agency should be involved in the planning and delivering of services.

Proposition 3. The redefining of approaches to service delivery may promote interorganizational relations that include ethnic agencies.

As programs develop to test new configurations of service delivery, the ethnic agency may be called on to contribute to a network or constellation of services. Service delivery as a system or organizational process continues to be a dynamic process that is altered by technological, ideological, political, and economic factors. The mode of service delivery has varied from specialization to integrated, comprehensive services. As service fragmentation, duplication, and cost rise and fall as issues, the ethnic agency may be called on to participate in alternative approaches to service delivery.

Although the school-based services example is relevant here, another example also is illustrative of the proposition. The Adoption Assistance and Child Welfare Act of 1980 (P.L. 96-272) encourages the development of foster-care prevention services by making available funding for such programs.[10] Numerous child-welfare departments responded by developing family preservation programs. Family preservation services are typically rendered to families with a child at risk for placement and they are designed to prevent that placement. The services provided are home or neighborhood based, are comprehensive, and focus on the family as a unit.[11] Here is how one large, urban county approached family preservation:

> The county wanted to institute the African American Family Preservation Project and the Hispanic Preservation Project. To have the comprehensive services available for the families, the county wanted each project to be composed of networks or coalitions of ethnic agencies. This meant that the African American Family Preservation Project would have several networks composed of a range of agencies that addressed family needs. The same was true of the Hispanic Family Preservation Project.

The design of the projects brought a significant number of ethnic agencies into an exchange relationship with the county that many have never experienced. In addition, because of the number of agencies that could be involved, many smaller ethnic agencies participated in the projects.

Proposition 4.   As privatization increases, the ethnic agency will be called upon to extend services to its special population.

Proposition 4a.   Through the purchase of service contracts, mandated services can be tailored to reach specific ethnic communities.

New policies are emerging in response to government retrenchment and other environmental changes. Privatization of human services is becoming more widely embraced. According to Bendick, *privatization* is defined as shifting into nongovernmental hands some or all roles in providing a good or service that was once publicly provided.[12] Bendick also listed contracting out, franchises, grants, subsidies, and vouchers as examples of the types of privatization arrangements that can exist between government and nongovernment entities. For many years, purchase-of-service contracting has been the major mode of human service delivery nationally.[13] Government agencies frequently call on voluntary agencies to obtain specialized programs "to serve a clientele for whom there is a public responsibility" and by utilizing the "access of neighborhood-based, ethnic-sponsored organizations," government "can more effectively serve needy clients."[14]

Public social service agencies may not have the staff, other resources, and/or technologies to provide ethnic-sensitive service delivery to the array of communities it serves. For example:

> A Los Angeles County social services agency was mandated to provide AIDS education to residents of the county. Because of the ethnic diversity of the area, agency leadership decided that it was illogical and expensive to develop internal programs to respond to all these diverse communities. The agency contracted with ethnic agencies serving designated populations to provide AIDS education. With the contracting system, several ethnic agencies could then assist the county in implementing the AIDS education mandate.
>
> One contract was awarded to an Asian agency that had access to numerous Asian ethnic groups. This ethnic agency provided AIDS education and materials in Japanese, Mandarin, Vietnamese, Thai, Korean, Tagalog, and Cambodian. Indigenous volunteers worked in communities to reach citizens. Some volunteers distributed material in Filipino nightclubs while others attended the Lotus Festival (Chinese New Year). An AIDS prevention message and information number were placed in fortune cookies and distributed throughout the communities.

Proposition 5. Interorganizational relationships are more likely to develop between public agencies and the ethnic agency rather than between mainstream agencies in general and the ethnic agency.

Public agencies are mandated to meet the needs of its populations. These mandates are in the form of social policies and regulations that specify client groups, service eligibility requirements, and services to be provided. In addition, policies bring with them fiscal support for implementing them. Thus, the public agency may be a rich source of funding for ethnic agencies as particular ethnic groups are targeted for service delivery.

Proposition 5a.   In the contractual relationship with a public agency to deliver service to a special population, the ethnic agency becomes a *substitute* for government provision of those services.[15]

This further suggests that the ethnic agency becomes part of the Welfare State indirectly through the contracting process. The ethnic agency is assisting the government in the provision of mandated services and becomes the entity through which those services flow.

Proposition 5b.   The relationship between the ethnic agency and the public funding agency is usually asymmetrical.

Saidel defined an *asymmetrical relationship* as one in which two or more organizations are not equally dependent on each other for the resources each has access to or controls.[16] According to Cook, dependence is lessened to the extent that alternatives are available to an organization in the exchange network.[17] Public agencies typically have more options for reaching ethnic populations than ethnic agencies have for funding sources. The ethnic agency is more dependent on the public agency than that agency is dependent on it. To reach special populations, as was shown in Chapter 6, public agencies can create special programs, hire special staff, and/or launch aggressive outreach efforts. Although some of these options may be costly to the public agency, they nonetheless exist and may, on occasion, be utilized.

The ethnic agency, on the other hand, is far more limited in its funding options. Funding available for agencies varies from government grants/contracts to foundations to membership in a umbrella fund-raising organization to private donations. Agencies often find themselves commitment rich and cash poor. In many instances, contracts and grants from public agencies provide a rich source of support that cannot be matched in the private sector.

Proposition 5c. Because of the asymmetrical nature of the relationship, public agencies tend to have power over the ethnic agency.

Because ethnic agencies may be dependent on public agencies for resources, public agencies can influence and alter the services and service delivery processes of ethnic agencies. Diversification of funding sources as a means of managing environmental dependency is less of an option for the ethnic agency. Funding options are limited and the search for other, additional funding sources requires technical expertise, agency supports, and time. Many small ethnic agencies are not equipped to mount diversification efforts. Thus, these agencies may be more responsive to public agencies than public agencies are to them.

In the school-based services example and the AIDS education example, both agencies were responding to the opportunity to participate in service delivery activities that had not been identified by the agencies themselves. At the time the ethnic agencies became involved in these activities, neither had identified the presenting issues as problems for their communities. In both examples, contract granting bodies were instrumental in directing the focus of each agency. Another example:

> An African-American community service center in Texas provided day-care services, employment counseling, health services, family counseling, and a recreation program. The center was contacted by the county health department to consider developing a family planning program. The health department would provide the center with the names of unwed mothers in the community who had recently given birth. The new program staff would then be expected to visit with the mother to speak with her about birth control as a way of reducing the additional

number of children she would have. Money was available for support services and staff.

The center staff had not considered anything of a "family planning" nature. This was not an area that the center had identified as a priority. Some staff may have even felt that family planning was how "they" tried to control the African-American population. Community religious leaders participated on the center's board and there were numerous volunteers and staff with strong religious affiliations. Center staff assumed the African-American community equated "family planning" with "sex education," and *sex* was not a word usually heard at the center. The funding for the program was, however, quite lucrative, so the director and board discussed the program in great detail.

The center eventually decided to develop the program and call it "Loving Every Child." The program stressed the importance of only having as many children as you could love and defined "love" as the provision of emotional and material supports. Although it considered this a novel approach, the county health department assumed that the center knew how to reach its community and did not interfere with the approach taken by the center.[18]

Proposition 5d.   The greater the ethnic agency's access to the ethnic community, the more power the agency has in its funding relationships with public agencies.

Access to the ethnic community gives the ethnic agency visibility and status in relating to public agencies, and this access can be measured in number of clients served. Those external agencies attempting to reach ethnic communities may use an ethnic agency with access to the community as a means of *community penetrating*. Organizational dominance may emerge from the significant linkage the ethnic agency has to a particular racial or ethnic group, which is the reason the ethnic agency is important to other organizations.[19] The strength of this community penetration may boost the power of the ethnic agency.

The center that developed the "Loving Every Child" program is also an example here. This center was the largest ethnic agency in that African-American community. It had the largest number of staff and the largest number of clients. Because of its dominance in these areas, it was usually the first agency contacted when money was available for program planning and development in this community.

Proposition 5e.   The greater the bond between the ethnic agency and the dominant elite of the ethnic community, the more power the agency has in funding relationships with external agencies.

The dominant elite members of an ethnic community have access to the residents of the community and may serve as an interface between the community and the larger social system. The dominant elite can advocate for the community and emerge as visible members of that community. An ethnic agency that has the support and even participation of its community's elite further solidifies its *community penetration*.

> The minister of a very prominent African-American church was asked to serve on the city's human resources council. It was generally assumed he was chosen because of his visibility in the African-American community and because he could speak for that community. Discussions of community needs and city resources for addressing these needs dominated the meetings. The council became aware of the work being done by one of the African-American agencies and the role this agency could play in responding to community needs with the appropriate funding. Through this advocacy, the agency was able to expand its programs with city-sponsored grants. The minister was also president of the agency's board.

In another African-American agency in the same state:

> The agency was under contract with the county department of mental health to provide family counseling. Under the terms of the contract, the families had to attend a total of eight sessions to complete the treatment process. Agency data indicated that families attended an average of only five sessions of counseling. The board, composed of religious and business leaders from the community, contacted the county about the problems in implementing the contract and worked to have those terms modified. The county project monitor was willing to listen to the board because it represented the community. The agency, had it attempted to renegotiate the contract, would have been perceived as acting in its own interest.

Proposition 5f. The greater the ethnic agency's monopoly of services in that community, the more likely the agency is to be involved in funding relationships with external agencies.

Those ethnic agencies with a dominant presence in the community as seen in range and number of services offered may act as a magnet to attract the interest of those agencies that seek to reach that ethnic community. A prevailing public sentiment may be that if any services are to be provided in that particular community, it must go through a certain agency in order for that service to be sanctioned by the community.

The proposition may reflect "the more, the more" principle in that the more services, resources, and community penetration an agency has, the more likely it is to acquire more of these. Expansion and diversification may be indicative of the extent and degree of an agency's monopoly over the community.

Proposition 5g.   The more physically established the ethnic agency, the more likely the agency is to be involved in a funding relationship with external agencies.

Physically established here means that the ethnic agency actually has an office, space, equipment, and other support facilities. Thus, in entering into a fiscal arrangement with an external agency, the funds received by the ethnic agency are not used to literally create the physical presence of the agency.

According to a participant in the establishing of the ethnic-identified Family Preservation Projects:

> We got agencies coming out of the woodwork. Agencies no one had ever heard of. Some of them were just two rooms and a phone. They needed the money to *create* the agency. We couldn't give money to anybody like that. We needed agencies that were already up and running not those just now learning to crawl.

Proposition 5h.   The ethnic agency may not be a skilled player in the "contract game."

Bernstein discussed at length the nuances of the contract game and the informal, formal, and subtle communication that takes place.[20] This is a process that one apparently learns from repeated contract experiences. Many ethnic agencies may not have a history strong enough in this area to prepare them for the process. The rules, requirements, compliance, unofficial operations, and conflict that arise in the contracted relationship seem to call for a special expertise themselves.

> A small Asian agency wanted to respond to a request for proposals from the county to create a senior service program in the Asian community. The small staff struggled with the proposal and barely made the deadline. When they called to check on the status of the proposal, they were told that their community was geographically located in a catchment area being served by another, larger center. The staff of the agency was unaware of the county's approach to services and did not know that, as they were preparing their proposal, they could have called the county office for information. They also learned that the Asian elderly population was not a priority funding area. Although this proposal was not funded, the experience was invaluable and was the first step in promot-

ing the needs of this group and in gaining mastery of the proposal process in that county.

Proposition 5i.   A competitive funding process may work to the detriment of the ethnic agency.

According to Milofsky, an agency's ability to attract funders and funding is related to the agency's history of grant/proposal writing, the agency's history with funding agencies, and the number of people the agency has available to write proposals.[21] In a study of the contracting experiences of 57 municipal agencies, Terrell and Kramer found that most of the municipalities assigned scores based on ratings of areas such as applicant's past contract performance, staffing and training arrangements, coordination with related agencies, and financial history.[22] Many smaller ethnic agencies may not have the history and staff to develop competitive proposals. For example, Beauvais and Boueff observed that this may be particularly true for some American-Indian programs.[23]

During a televised city council meeting in a midsized city, an African-American program manager at an African-American agency made the following observations during the public comments portion of the meeting

> You tell us you want us to submit proposals. Your staff encourages us and then you turn right around and reject our proposal. That's unfair. The whole system is unfair. We can't compete with these big outfits that can put together people who don't do anything but write grants. We have a program to run. We are too busy putting out fires every day to spend all our time writing proposals. We need the money. You *know* we need the money. But then you stack the deck against us. This whole system stinks.

The competitiveness may also work against the relationships between ethnic agencies within the same community. For example, the Hispanic Family Preservation Project, mentioned earlier, caused some upheaval in the community as agencies tried to develop their networks or coalitions that would be responsible for providing a constellation of services to the community. There was not enough funding available to sponsor all the coalitions/networks that applied. Agencies looked each other over carefully to determine the best or strongest potential coalition members. The environment was created by the funding requirements of the county and the agencies were more than interested because, as one disinterested observer noted, "They had never seen that much money."

Proposition 5j.   Formal evaluation processes that accompany contracts and grants may not acknowledge those activities that reflect the strength of the ethnic agency's work.

Sewell argued that an emphasis on end products may not adequately reflect the effectiveness of an ethnic agency.[24] Thomas and Morgan suggested that formative evaluations should be the primary evaluation effort rather than summative evaluations.[25] Formative evaluation creates a feedback loop that feeds information back into the program *during* its development, whereas summative evaluation is done *after* the program has been completed.[26] One focuses on process and the other focuses on outcome.

Some ethnic agencies expend a great deal of time and resources in developing programs. Special approaches may have to be developed to tailor programs to their specific populations. The success of the program, however, is generally not measured in terms of creating the technology of service delivery but rather in the outcome of that service delivery.

> An Hispanic agency in a metropolitan city was funded to develop a teen peer-counseling program. The staff designed the program to provide teens with drug education so they could be informal counselors or advisors to their peers. The agency expended an inordinate amount of time in recruitment for the program because of the difficulty in recruiting on the high school campus that had not been foreseen. Recruitment became the priority of the agency, so that at least one class of 30 students could be assembled. The agency visited places where the students "hung out." They used posters and everything else that came to mind. The agency trained 19 students as peer counselors and the grant was not renewed. The granting agency perceived the program as not very effective. The agency believed it was successful in reaching a hard-to-reach population—adolescents—so that the 19 students who participated were signs of success.

Those who do master the proposal submission process may emerge as model agencies to implement experimental programs and receive recognition for its success. According to the director of a growing ethnic agency:

> We are on very good terms with our funders. Lots of calls back and forth. We feel like we're on the tourist route. Visitors in and out. We're being shown off to people from other cities, other states. We do just about everything that's requested of us and then some. We demonstrated a long time ago that we knew how to comply with regulations. We turned in everything on time. We have an outstanding reputation. Of course, it means we always have to worker harder. Being in the spotlight puts a lot of pressure on us.

Proposition 6. Changing federal funding requirements are developing partnerships between mainstream agencies and ethnic agencies.

Major funding sources are stipulating that the grantee must address the needs of women and minorities when developing program and service proposals. For example, the 57 municipalities studied by Terrell and Kramer were likely to use "compatibility with ethnic and foreign groups" as one of the factors on which funding proposals were rated.[27] Many mainstream agencies may not have the history, staff, or compatibility for service delivery to an ethnic community. For these agencies, the ethnic agency then becomes the vehicle for complying with this stipulation.

> A southern family service agency began developing a proposal for National Institute of Mental Health funding to become a demonstration project in the area of adolescent suicide prevention. To indicate its inclusion of ethnic considerations, an ethnic agency was asked to co-write the grant with the family service agency. This project brought these two agencies together for the first time.

Proposition 7. The ethnic agency's interface with mainstream agencies is predicated on the availability of funding to support that interface.

Because the degree of cooperation occurring between organizations in the same network is contingent on the amount of resources available to that network, a decrease in funds will affect the cooperation and/or conflict between organizations.[28] The interorganizational linkages likely to occur between mainstream agencies and ethnic agencies derive from a funding environment that supports and encourages these linkages. Increased attention to the development of partnerships in service delivery, efforts to reduce service duplication, and reaching special populations have promoted interorganizational relations and the funding mandates reflect this. A change in policy direction and/or funding directions could easily remove the ethnic presence from service delivery areas. What occurs between ethnic agencies and mainstream agencies appears to be environmentally induced.

> A county mental health department had applied for federal funds to implement a new substance-abuse education program. Word leaked out that the program was going to be contracted out to agencies in the various communities. A large family service agency took the lead in bringing agencies together to form a strong network that would cover a large segment of the city. Several ethnic agencies were part of this effort and the funds were going to be a boost for them. The county did not receive the grant and the group disbanded rather than try to secure

funding from other sources. The impetus for the coalition had been removed.

Proposition 8.   In the ebb and flow of the fiscal environment, ethnic agencies are particularly vulnerable.

Because many ethnic agencies do not have a diversified funding base, they may grow dependent on contracts and grants with publicly sponsored agencies. Smith noted that, in times of financial austerity, funds for contracts are likely to be cut first if this can be accomplished legally and politically.[29] Ethnic agencies may have to continuously scramble for funds as contracts are terminated and priority areas change.

> An African-American agency had started out several years ago as an antiviolence agency with school visits and teen education programs. Funds to support these activities were difficult to secure. The prevailing funding interest at that time was drug abuse. The agency broadened its focus to include drug-related issues ("After all, drugs do lead to violence"). Since that time, the agency has broadened its focus to include issues affecting African-American youth and has been involved in teen parenting programs, dropout programs, truancy programs, and a variety of other programs focusing on African-American youth. The agency is considering broadening its domain to include younger children so it can go after gang-prevention funds that target intervention with "wanabees" (those youngsters aspiring to be gang members).

Proposition 9.   Ideological conflicts can occur between the ethnic agency and the mainstream agencies.

While resource dependence, power, and organizational exchanges are being determined, ethnicity is an additional variable affecting the interorganizational relationship. Rose suggested that the empowerment orientation may clash with the individual defect framework associated with mainstream agencies.[30] Thus, ethnic agencies may attempt to use their technology of information, education, and participation in planning and implementing programs while program sponsors may have a different approach in mind.

> A coalition of citywide agencies in a midwestern city began meeting to formulate gang-prevention strategies and programs. Two ethnic agencies participated in the coalition. One mainstream agency defined the problem as a law-enforcement issue. "We need stronger penalties. If those gangbangers knew they'd land in jail for a spell, they wouldn't be so quick to break the law." The African-American representatives, on the other hand, saw the problem as one of scarce resources. "If they had

something else to do with their time, they wouldn't be in gangs. Our communities needs more after-school programs, more recreational programs, more well-equipped parks. We need to give them something to replace the gang activity." The city's new budget called for a reduction in parks and recreation programs and the creation of a special gang unit within the police department.

Proposition 10.   The problems of race relations that exist in the larger society permeate the dynamics of the relationship between ethnic agencies and mainstream agencies.

In the relations between ethnic agencies and mainstream agencies, the expertise of staff and administrators who are predominantly White may be interpreted by ethnic agency staff as yet another indicator of race superiority. Power, in this case, is derived from individual perceptions that are located in historical experiences and not in the interaction that is taking place. The authority of expertise, as determined by specialized skills and knowledge, may become race superiority in the eyes of ethnic agency members. Whites may be perceived as viewing the ethnic agency staff in need of teaching and leadership. Interactions are then filtered by the "color" lens and tensions develop because different individuals are responding differently to the same stimulus.

A county child-welfare agency contracted with an ethnic agency to provide parenting classes to parents referred by the court. The ethnic agency had not offered these classes before, did not have staff who had taught parenting classes, and did not have a curriculum on the subject. The county agency sought out experts in parent education to instruct the ethnic agency in curriculum development and staff training.

The expert was White. Reactions of the ethnic agency staff: "What can he tell us about teaching classes to *our* families? Did he use any of our families when he put his plan together? How many of our families live where he does?"

Reactions of the county agency staff: "We tried to be helpful. We were willing to bring in the best *person* available on this topic. But they refused our help because the consultant was White and they thought he would not be sensitive to their issues."

The propositions define the basis of power for the ethnic agency and for the other agencies in its organizational network. Exchanges often provide the source of power for an organization, particularly if it has resources in demand by other organizations. The reciprocity of the exchange is important for determining who has the most bargaining chips. The ethnic agency increases its ability to bargain by having access to special populations and access to the dominant elite of the ethnic community. In exchange for this access, the ethnic agency receives revenues and whatever legitimacy the funding may bring.

Schmidt and Kochan concluded that interorganizational relationships should be conceptualized as "mixed motive" because each organization is motivated by self-interests as well as other interests.[31] The ethnic agency seeks services for its clients while at the same time it is trying to create a secure funding niche. This is true for other agencies as well. With the ethnic agency, ethnicity becomes a fundamental part of the exchange process.

ISSUES IN CONTRACTING SERVICES

The ethnic agency does, indeed, appear to be a mediator between the ethnic community and the Welfare State when it provides services on behalf of a government agency. What are the implications of these relationships for both parties involved? What are the implications for ethnic-sensitive service delivery? By contracting with ethnic agencies to reach ethnic communities, is the public agency abdicating its responsibility? Is this a continuation of the doctrine of ethnic responsibility? Several factors have to be considered in order to answer these questions.

History

All public agencies have some type of image and reputation in the ethnic community. No public agency is neutral in the responses it elicits from residents. This history is a factor in whether public agencies can be effective in reaching ethnic communities.

> A child-welfare department in a particular county had not endeared itself to the African-American community. Historically, the agency had no African-American workers and appeared to be extremely punitive in its treatment of African-American parents suspected of abusing or neglecting their children. The workers were known by the appointment books they carried that were issued by the county. Whenever a worker was in the African-American neighborhood, people knew that someone was in trouble. When one worker passed an elderly African-American woman on the street, the older woman said, "Oh, lord. Whose child are you taking today?"
>
> The passage of time has changed this agency and its practices but the memories live on and so do the stories. African-American workers at the agency are routinely asked, "Why'd you go to work *there*?

With this type of history in the community, the agency would be predictably unsuccessful in trying to launch any type of program in this community. The images require the passage of several more years before they can be erased. For this reason, the history of a public agency in the ethnic community cannot be discounted.

Service Domain

The type of service offered affects the public agency's ability to provide it to specialized populations. The AIDS example with the Asian community is one example and the family planning program in the African-American community is another. Services that seem intrusive to the target population and/or relate to interpersonal dynamics among individuals may be more effective it they are administered by those close to or in the community. The fear of social control may lead some residents to reject those services as well as the agency offering them. The further the public agency is from the community in location, ethnicity, and ideology, the more likely the community is to resist these services. This suggests that, to a certain extent, ethnic communities function as relatively closed communities in some service areas.

Resources

The amount of resources available is another factor that determines public agency responses to the provision of ethnic-sensitive service delivery. Programs are developed within budget parameters, which may be the primary factor determining how services are provided and by whom. With increased diversity, more and more groups have to be served and the economic viability of one agency providing programs to all communities may be limited. Instead, agencies may "hire" the ethnic agency to deliver the service. In this exchange—the community penetration of the ethnic agency with location, visibility, and access in the target community—the public agency may be maximizing its reach to those communities.

As the focal organization of an organizational network, the public agency may also be able to coordinate services more effectively and to deploy resources more effectively. *Coordination* can be defined as the degree to which organizations take into consideration the activities of other organizations as they plan their own.[32] The focal agency serves as the coordinator in the organizational set. In addition, other agencies in the organizational set may be building strong relationships as they coalesce around an issue area. With one focal organization coordinating activities of the other agencies, fragmentation and duplication of services may be minimized.

Agency Penetration

In the contractual arrangement, the public agency is not penetrated by the ethnic-sensitive work of the ethnic agency. The goals, ideology, and technology of the public agency itself remains the same. It could be argued that the contracting system alters the technology of the agency itself, but this is a change and not an innovation. Change reflects some alteration in the agency's distribution of resources, distribution of power, or internal structure, whereas innovation refers to a new service, technology, or product being brought into the agency.[33]

With the "contracting out" process, public agencies continue with "business as usual" while achieving community penetration through the ethnic agency. In these cases, the image, status, and reputation of the public agency remains unchanged in the community's eyes and the agency is not receiving any direct benefits itself in these areas. The ethnic agency, however, enjoys the fruits of the contract and may have its status enhanced in the eyes of the community.

OTHER INTERORGANIZATIONAL RELATIONS

The contractual relationship is one form of interorganizational relationships. Although it may be growing in use and has particular relevance for ethnic agencies, there are other relationships that can be developed with mainstream organizations.

Ethnic agencies may be involved in *collaborative exchanges*. Collaboration takes place when an agency sees its goals as being met through assistance from and resources of other agencies.[34] Mutuality is a precondition for effective collaboration.[35] All parties feel they have something to gain from the collaboration. Some examples presented may have touched on a collaborative relationship, but another is provided for clarity:

> Several agencies, including several ethnic agencies, came together to develop a proposal for a gang-prevention program in an area of town in which they all had some interest. The agencies were not providing the same services, so there was no domain overlap and no competition between them. The meeting site was rotated so that no one agency location dominated. The agency with the most sophisticated support services took responsibility for generating the final proposal, although everyone contributed to its contents. While this was a collaborative effort, each agency was planning to provide its services at its own site.

The collaboration was in generating the proposal, not in implementing a consolidated program.

For the collaboration to be effective, all members contribute as peers and power is equalized among the members. In some cases, however, process takes priority over outcome as the goals of coordination and cooperation override original goals. Some ethnic agency staff feel, however, that they are called on solely to provide the minority presence to "legitimize" the effort and are not perceived as equal members of the team. One staff member (a male Hispanic gang-prevention worker) had this to say about his collaborative experience:

We'd meet and meet and meet about the kinds of things the program should include. We'd already figured out that we'd go for the schools and plan something. The principal was part of the team, so it was no problem getting into it. They wanted me to be there. I didn't have to say anything or do anything. When I'd make a comment or have an idea, they'd all look at me, then go back to what they were saying. It was clear from the start, I was supposed to rubber stamp the proposal.

Another Hispanic worker had this experience:

The (White) agency called us up and wanted us to work with them on this teen pregnancy proposal. I thought that was a great idea. We'd never worked with them before. Their agency director came over to talk with us about it. She came with a copy of the proposal! It was already done! She just wanted us to sign it. That took the wind right out of our sails.

Some agencies collaborate with other agencies in a subcontractual relationship, as in the following example taken from a Hispanic female in a Hispanic agency:

We work well with the (White) agency. They needed to include us because of the Hispanic population in the city and we thought this was a contact that would help us. Of course, we don't do our end of it like they do theirs, but that seems to be agreeable with them. At the beginning, we met and ironed out all the details and that first meeting went so well that we knew it was a go immediately. We listened to each other and shared ideas. It was a positive exchange of ideas. We don't see ourselves working *for* them. We work *with* them.

Another way in which the ethnic agency interfaces with mainstream agencies is through the mainstream agency's use of the ethnic agency as a site for service delivery or recruitment. Some child-welfare departments, for example, may plan adoption parties or adoption open houses at an ethnic agency to recruit potential adoptive parents. This has been done in African-American communities and serves to legitimize the adoption agency. The association with a respected agency in the community lends validity to the effort and provides access to the community. A White female adoptions worker stated:

> In the past, I would go to the Black churches and make an announcement about the need for Black parents to adopt children. That was our big outreach program. Go, say a few words, and leave. I think we may have put an ad in the paper and run an announcement on the Black radio station. We didn't get much and we really didn't expect much.
>
> One of our Black mothers who adopted through us was so happy about her little boy, she thought everybody ought to adopt. She really got us going about what we could do and she worked with us on our first adoption party. We held it at (an African-American agency) in their reception area. The place was really small but it made for a cozy feeling. It was great. The kids liked it and the adults there liked it too. There's something really special about kids that can bring people together.

Some mainstream agencies may even rent or borrow space for a "branch" office at the ethnic agency. This satellite office provides access to the community and visibility for the agency. Although this avenue of community penetration may not be widely used, it does seem to afford the mainstream a degree of visibility that other interactions may lack. Consider the following example from a White female family service worker:

> I'm at (an African-American agency) two days a week and I have my own room with telephone and desk. I do employment assistance and counseling. Mostly, I talk to people about how to look for jobs and how to do a resumé. My salary is paid out of a grant we received and we thought we'd do it this way rather than hire someone over there to do it.
>
> At first, they didn't know what to make of me.
>
> They thought I wanted to do therapy or something. The second time I went, I took posters with job-hunting tips on them and hints about how to interview well. When people stopped by my door to read the posters, I'd start a conversation with them. That worked. Once they saw I could do something and had something to offer, people started coming in. Now I have appointment sheets and I stay busy.

Other ethnic agencies may have unique needs that coincide with their unique histories. For example, Nelson and colleagues described the kinds of *technical assistance* provided by a federal agency to develop projects and secure resources.[36] For many American-Indian tribes, this area is paramount as they plan services for their reservations. Because agencies external to the reservations have dominated service delivery to reservations, the American-Indian agency's interface with mainstream services may not be a goal. Rather, the immediate goal may be the acquisition of those skills and that knowledge needed to control and direct services on the reservations.

Christian asserted that community-based agencies may also require the services of individuals from other agencies as *consultants*, educators, and other problem-solving agents.[37] June, as well as Kahn and colleagues, agreed that the services of consultants from other agencies can be useful to ethnic agencies.[38] These authors also mentioned the need for the consultant to remove himself or herself from the role of "expert" to work in partnership with the agencies. Again, the expertise of the professional consultant may be interpreted as an arrogance of race. Kahn and associates went into great detail about the role of "the non-Indian professional consultant" and advised that this individual must respect the setting and function as a student of the culture as well as a teacher. These authors emphasized the sensitivity with which the consultant should discharge the professional duties.

Although a consultant may be available and even "loaned" by the mainstream agencies, there are still some ways in which the ethnic factor presents itself. Here are two examples—the first from a White female, and the second from an African-American female:

I've been a strategic planner for years and the (Asian agency) director contacted me about doing strategic planning for her agency. My supervisor let me use agency time to work with them. I attended a staff meeting and then wanted to meet with the staff after the meeting to find out more about them and the agency. I began asking them about the agency and their work. There was not much of a discussion. I was a little uncomfortable. I was the only White person in the room. I kept thinking, "What am I doing here?" People were attentive and I think they looked to me for answers. Things have improved since then but that first meeting took me by surprise. I was surprised at my reaction.

That woman (a White female consultant) came in here and acted like she owned the place. Within fifteen minutes she thought she knew all about the place. She knew *everything*. She told us what we needed to do about that proposal. You should have seen her. "You need this. This should go here. Take that out." Listening to her made me tired.

A number of factors seem to affect the ethnic agency/mainstream agency interface and ethnicity is one of them. With the propositions and the illustrations of the ways the interface can take place, an overview of these interorganizational relationships will highlight some recurring issues.

OVERVIEW

This attention to the interorganizational relationships between ethnic agencies and mainstream agencies was needed to address the question: What is the interface between the ethnic agency and mainstream social services? The ethnic agency provides services to a particular ethnic group through staff who are of that ethnic group and these agencies are developed for this specific purpose. Mainstream social services are those provided by formal organizations that implement the policies of the Welfare State. In addition, mainstream social services are also provided by special-interest groups through formally established private nonprofit agencies.

The ethnic communities have historically developed their own services despite the existence of mainstream services. It seems as if the country has evolved two systems of service delivery. For this reason, the interface between them was addressed. There is a dearth of literature on the subject of ethnic agencies and their organizational networks. The available literature and organizational perspectives on interagency relations were briefly covered as a context within which to place the ethnic agency.

Although numerous organizational relationships exist and are developing, the goal here was not to recommend or identify one type of relationship over another. Rather, the goal was to determine predominant relationships and explore their basis. For that reason, the conclusions and interpretations advanced are cautious and conservative. The implications are informed but speculative.

Managing Dependency

The external polity and the external economy of the larger social system appear to be major factors in shaping ethnic agency programs and services. The availability of funds in some areas and not in other areas is predicated on the prevailing definitions of social problems and responses. The ethnic agency does not appear to be a powerful determinant of these attitudes and responses.

A pattern may be reflected here and Crocker's observation bears repeating.[39] She noted an interaction between African-American history and the history of White philanthropy among African Americans. Funding itself can serve as a form of social control. Programs and services may follow or "chase" dollars. Funding specifications may then determine which services emerge and which do not. Forces external to the ethnic agency and external to the ethnic community may continue a pattern in which needs are defined *for* ethnic minorities and *not* by them. This may also contribute to the notion (discussed in Chapter 6) that ethnic agencies do not appear to be reform minded.

In managing environmental dependency, ethnic agencies may either specialize or diversify. The preliminary impression is that these agencies diversify within certain parameters. As they seek funds, they may stray from their chosen path but that straying does not take it too far from the original goals. Agencies may have to decide whether to carve out a special niche and focus on that or cover many bases. Although diversification may reduce dependency, there is the risk of attempting to accomplish too much.

Some ethnic agencies have attempted to manage their dependencies by developing their own alternative federated funds. For example, Rodgers and Tartaglia reviewed efforts to organize the United Black Fund in Washington, DC, and the obstacles encountered.[40] The alternative fund movement apparently was in opposition to United Way's control over donations through the workplace and control over funding distribution.[41] Challenges to United Way dominance have been waged in courts and the success of alternative fund drives has not been determined.

External Polity

The external polity of the organizational set is creating the impetus for change by imposing mandates to ensure that social programs reach special populations. The stimulus for change continues to come from outside many agencies, and their response to the changing mandates is not optional. Organizational sets, then, behave in much the same way as individual organizations—change generally has to be thrust upon them. Organizational sets are created by social policies that promote partnerships, collaboration, and coordination. Organizations do not, of their own accord, seek relationships with other organizations unless that relationship is somehow related to the organization's survival and success. Thus, the seemingly strong interest that is emerging around the ethnic agency is indicative of the role and power of social policies in affecting change.

As has been shown throughout this book, the external polity of social service agencies wields tremendous influence over what takes place in these agencies. Since publicly funded social services are mandated by the Welfare State, then it seems that its agencies must also mirror that mandate. Prevailing ideologies, as captured in social policies, have an effect on the relationships that agencies have with each other.

As some ethnic agencies are being drawn into the service delivery network and as social policies continue to mandate services to racial/ethnic groups, an ideology supportive of diversity may be evolving. As a new ideology becomes more pervasive, additional changes may be expected in the relationships within and between agencies.

Relationships among Ethnic Agencies

This discussion has deliberately omitted the relationships that can and do develop among ethnic agencies, of the same ethnic group, or of different groups. The focus here is on the exchanges that take place between two different systems of service delivery—the ethnic agency and mainstream agencies. Because these two systems seemed to have paralleled each other, it was important to know when and how they meet. For this reason, those exchanges within the ethnic agency service delivery system were not emphasized.

Status

As policy directives recognize the need for service delivery to diverse populations, the ethnic agency is being drawn into the service delivery network. Ethnicity now brings with it a degree of status as ethnicity becomes a special commodity or segment of the market. Some agencies have higher status because of the community penetration in access to clients and access to the dominant elite of the community. Status may also be obtained from a domination of the market. As more significance is placed on service delivery to special markets, the ethnic agency will be utilized for reaching those markets.

THE DIFFUSION OF INNOVATION

Now that the overview is completed, another question remains unanswered: What is the role of the relationship between the ethnic agency and the mainstream agency? The *should* of relationships between ethnic agencies and other mainstream agencies, particularly public agencies, cannot be effectively answered until the *why* of the relationship is answered. Several responses emerge and each has an implication for ethnic-sensitive practice.

First, the relationship may be needed primarily for securing resources for ethnic agency survival and service delivery to the ethnic community. The public agency has high community penetration through the ethnic agency but does not have any penetration of its own agency. If this is the primary reason underlying the interface, then the contract system accomplishes both goals. The ethnic agency continues in its role as a mediator between the community and the Welfare State by substituting for the government. Agencies then touch boundaries and the ethnic agency is permeated by the public agency in that the ethnic agency is modifying its services and perhaps structure to comply with the terms of a contract.

By serving as a substitute for the government, the ethnic agency continues to buffer the clients from the bureaucracy of the public agencies. While the agency may, indeed, grow more bureaucratic itself, it may still protect the client from the debilitating effects of that bureaucracy The ethnic agency seems to have some degree of freedom in implementing services, and this freedom may be required to buffer clients. With this freedom, the Asian agency could develop its own approach to AIDS education and develop dissemination strategies that mirrored the cultures of the groups served.

In the contract negotiations that occur between public agencies and voluntary agencies, the burden is generally on the public agency to facilitate the exchange, and there appears to be an imbalance between the two in the equilibrium of power and influence.[42] As with other alternative organizations, relying on established organizations for financial support has a cost to it.[43] As was noted in Chapter 6, as the ethnic agency develops, it tries to protect itself from the intrusiveness of funding demands.

If the role of the interface is to *diffuse ethnic-sensitive practice throughout the mainstream agency*, then the contract system does not accomplish this. As new technologies are created, they are often disseminated or diffused throughout the organizations working in similar domains. The interorganizational relationship is one means through which this diffusion can take place and, according to Hasenfeld, interorganizational relations are important in the implementation of change.[44] For mainstream agencies, the diffusion of ethnic-sensitive practice would mean that these agencies would implement this practice. Their knowledge of this technology would be obtained through their relationship with the ethnic agency.

As was noted earlier, the ethnic agency is of value because of its access to and penetration of the ethnic community. It has not been singled out because of its technologies, although they are instrumental in securing that access. The mainstream agency may be of more interest in the outcome of that technology (number of clients reached, for example) and not the process of that technology. The technological innovations of the ethnic agency may go unrecognized.

Numerous factors exist that may explain why the ethnic agency-mainstream agency relationship does not lead to the diffusion of ethnic-sensitive practice in the mainstream agency. For example, the contract and grant process may not expose public agencies to the ethnic agency itself. Many of these reasons are similar to those raised in Chapter 7 about the resistance of mainstream agencies to change in general. The ethnic agency may not be in a strong enough position to wield power and influence.

How can the interorganizational relationship be used to diffuse innovation? Diffusion of innovation may occur when the ethnic agency and the mainstream agency relationship results in (1) the mainstream agency being penetrated by ethnic-sensitive practice and (2) the community being penetrated by the mainstream agency. Examples would include (1) joint ventures between the two systems that result in a formalized, routinized program that is part of the mainstream agency structure and is based in the ethnic community and (2) a mainstream agency locating a satellite office in the ethnic agency with staff providing ethnic-sensitive services.

The diffusion of innovation may call for programs that bypass the ethnic agency as *the* service provider. The interface would then be a pathway to ethnic-sensitive practice for the mainstream agency but the ethnic agency may be out of or less involved in the funding network. The ethnic agency may have a vested interest in protecting its turf and maintaining control over its market (the ethnic community). Once the domain (access to the community) is shared with other agencies, the bargaining power of the ethnic agency is reduced. From the ethnic agency's vantage point, the diffusion of innovation, as articulated here, may not be desirable or advantageous.

The model used in Chapter 7 (Figure 7–1) to depict the dimensions of ethnic-sensitive practice can also be applied here. Figure (8–1) shows the types of interorganizational relationships that can be associated with the agency penetration and community penetration dimensions. The four corners of the grid indicate:

Low agency penetration and high community penetration: The contract system is employed; the public agency has penetrated the community via the ethnic agency; and the public agency remains unchanged.

High agency penetration and high community penetration: The public agency establishes a branch office *in* the ethnic agency; the office is part of the public agency structure and has penetrated the community; staff members are of the same ethnic group as the clients; and the technology is ethnic-sensitive practice. The satellite office may be loosely coupled from the main office but it is part of the permanent structure of the agency. The location in the ethnic agency (on site) defines the interface between the two agencies and increases the likelihood of interagency collaboration and other relationships.

Low community penetration and low agency penetration: No collaboration takes place between the ethnic agency and the public agency.

Low community penetration and high agency penetration: Staff from the ethnic agency may be invited to assist mainstream agencies in developing services for specific populations; task forces, advisory committees, and other forms of collaborative structures may be established; programs, services, and/or staff training may result that are located *within*

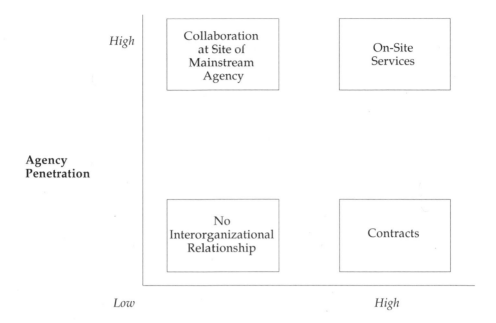

Community Penetration

FIGURE 8–1   **Model for Interorganizational Relationships**

the mainstream agency; and mainstream agency penetration of the ethnic community has not been affected by the collaboration.

From this overview, the ethnic agency seems to be continuing in its role as a mediator between the community and the agencies of the Welfare State. The three themes that have surfaced throughout this book warrant reviewing here: (1) ethnic minorities were generally ignored in the development of services, (2) the doctrine of ethnic group responsibility prevailed, and (3) the helpers defined the problems and the solutions. In the ethnic agency's interface with mainstream agencies, the needs of the ethnic communities are being addressed, the doctrine of ethnic group responsibility still prevails, and problems continue to be defined outside of the ethnic communities.

As ideologies toward diversity change, the recognition of the signficance of the ethnic agency in reaching special populations is emerging. Knowledge of its existence may be part of a process that will lead to recognition of what the agency does.

ENDNOTES

1. Keith Provan, Janice Beyer, and Carlos Kruytbosch, "Environmental Linkages and Power in Resource-Dependence Relations between Organizations," *Administrative Science Quarterly 25* (June 1980): 200–225.

2. J. Kenneth Benson, "The Interorganizational Network as a Political Economy," *Administrative Science Quarterly 20* (June 1975): 232.

3. Alvin Gouldner, "Reciprocity and Autonomy in Functional Theory," in *Symposium on Sociological Theory*, ed. Llwellyn Gross (New York: Harper and Row, 1959), pp. 241–270.

4. Mary Zey-Ferrell, *Dimensions of Organizations* (Santa Monica, CA: Goodyear Publishing, 1979), p. 142.

5. Benson, "The Interorganizational Network as Political Economy," p. 234.

6. Shirley Jenkins, *The Ethnic Dilemma in Social Services* (New York: The Free Press, 1981), p. 45.

7. Yeheskel Hasenfeld and Richard English, "Interorganizational Relations," in *Human Service Organizations*, ed. Yeheskel Hasenfeld and Richard English (Ann Arbor: University of Michigan Press, 1978), p. 543.

8. Ralph Kramer, "Voluntary Agencies and the Personal Social Services," in *The Nonprofit Sector—A Research Handbook*, ed. Walter Powell (New Haven, CT: Yale University Press, 1987), p. 249.

9. Benson, "The Interorganizational Network as a Political Economy," p. 232.

10. Jane Knitzer, "Child Welfare: The Role of Federal Policies," *Journal of Clinical Child Psychology* (Winter 1981): 3–7.

11. Anthony Maluccio, "Family Preservation: An Overview," in *Family Preservation*, ed. Alvin Sallee and June Lloyd (Riverdale, IL: National Association for Family-Based Services, 1990), pp. 17–28.

12. Marc Bendick, Jr., "Privatizing the Delivery of Social Welfare Services: An Idea to be Taken Seriously," in *Privatization and the Welfare State*, ed. Sheila Kamerman and Alfred Kahn (Princeton, NJ: Princeton University Press, 1989), p. 98.

13. Peter Kettner and Lawrence Martin, "Purchase of Service Contracting: Two Models," *Administration in Social Work 14*, number 1 (1985): 15.

14. Paul Terrell and Ralph Kramer, "Contracting with Nonprofits," *Public Welfare 42* (Winter 1984): 36.

15. For a definition of substitute services, see Kramer, "Voluntary Agencies and the Personal Social Services," p. 249.

16. Judith Saidel, "Resource Interdependence: The Relationship Between State Agencies and Nonprofit Organizations," *Public Administration Review 51* (November/December 1991): 550.

17. Karen Cook, "Exchange and Power in Networks of Interorganizational Relations," *The Sociological Quarterly 18* (Winter 1977): 66.

18. The actual name of the program used was changed to protect the identity of the center.

19. For a discussion of organizational dominance, see Benson, "The Interorganizational Network as a Political Economy," pp. 233–234.

20. Susan Bernstein, *Managing Contracted Services in the Nonprofit Agency* (Philadelphia: Temple University Press, 1991).

21. Carl Milofsky, "Neighborhood-Based Organizations: A Market Analogy," in *The Nonprofit Sector—A Research Handbook,* ed. Walter Powell (New Haven, CT: Yale University Press, 1987), pp. 277–295.

22. Paul Terrell and Ralph Kramer, "Contracting with Nonprofits," *Public Welfare 42* (Winter 1984): 34.

23. Fred Beauvais and Steve LaBoueff, "Drug and Alcohol Abuse Intervention in American Indian Communities," *The International Journal of the Addictions 20,* number 1 (1985): 157.

24. Carl Sewell, "Impact of External Public Funding Policies on the Development of Black Community Organizations," *Black Scholar 9* (December 1977): 42.

25. Stephen Thomas and Cynthia Morgan, "Evaluation of Community-Based AIDS Education and Risk Reduction Projects in Ethnic and Racial Minority Communities: A Survey of Projects Funded by the U.S. Public Health Service," *Evaluation and Program Planning 14,* number 4 (1991): 247–255.

26. Carol Weiss, *Evaluation Research* (Englewood Cliffs, NJ: Prentice Hall, 1972): 42.

27. Terrell and Kramer, "Contracting with Nonprofits," p. 34.

28. Patrick Wardell, "The Implications of Changing Interorganizational Relationships and Resource Constraints for Human Services Survival: A Case Study," *Administration in Social Work 12,* number 1 (1988): 89–105.

29. Bruce Smith, "Changing Public-Private Sector Relations: A Look at the United States," *Annals of the American Academy of Political and Social Science 466* (March 1983): 158.

30. Stephen Rose, "Community Organization: A Survival Strategy for Community-Based, Empowerment-Oriented Programs," *Journal of Sociology and Social Welfare 13* (September 1986): 491–506.

31. Stuart Schmidt and Thomas Kochan, "Interorganizational Relationship: Patterns and Motivations," *Administrative Science Quarterly 22* (June 1977): 220–234.

32. Richard Hall, John Clark, Peggy Giordano, Paul John, and Martha Van Roekel, "Patterns of Interorganizational Relationships," in *The Sociology of Organizations, Second Edition,* ed. Oscar Grusky and George Miller (New York: The Free Press, 1981), p. 479.

33. Yeheskel Hasenfeld, *Human Service Organizations* (Englewood Cliffs, NJ: Prentice Hall, 1983), p. 219.

34. Ralph Brody, *Problem Solving* (New York: Human Services Press, 1982), p. 124.

35. Rochelle Wimpfheimer, Martin Bloom, and Marge Kramer, "Inter-Agency Collaboration: Some Working Principles," *Administration in Social Work 14,* number 4 (1990): 91.

36. Scott Nelson, George McCoy, Maria Stetter, and W. Craig Vanderwagen, "An Overview of Mental Health Services for American Indians and Alaska Natives in the 1990s," *Hospital and Community Psychiatry 43* (March 1992): 260.

37. Jim Christian, "Using 'Outside Resource People' in Community-Based Organizations," *Journal of Alternative Human Services 6* (Winter 1980/81): 15–19.

38. Lee June, "Enhancing the Delivery of Mental Health and Counseling Services to Black Males: Critical Agency and Provider Responsibilities," *Journal of*

Multicultural Counseling and Development 14 (January 1986): 43; Marvin Kahn, Cecil Williams, Eugene Galvez, Linda Lejero, Rex Conrad, and George Goldstein, "The Papago Psychology Service," in *Human Services for Cultural Minorities*, ed. Richard Dana (Baltimore: University Park Press, 1981), p. 91.

39. Ruth Crocker, *Social Work and Social Order* (Chicago: University of Illinois Press, 1992), p. 7.

40. Augustus Rodgers and Leonard Tartaglia, "Constricting Resources: A Black Self-Help Initiative," *Administration in Social Work 14*, number 2 (1990): 125-137.

41. Eleanor Brilliant, "Community Planning and Community Problem Solving: Past, Present, and Future," *Social Service Review 60* (December 1986): 583.

42. Margaret Gibelman and Harold Demone, Jr., "Negotiating: A Tool for Inter-Organizational Coordination," *Administration in Social Work 14*, number 4 (1990): 37.

43. Joyce Rothschild-Whitt, "The Collectivist Organization: An Alternative to Rational-Bureaucratic Models," *American Sociological Review 44* (August 1979): 523.

44. Hasenfeld, *Human Service Organizations*, p. 242.

Chapter 9

Recurring Issues and the Next Steps

A number of issues have been raised in this analysis of mainstream social service delivery systems, the ethnic agency service delivery systems, and ethnic-sensitive practice. A synthesis of these issues seems warranted.

HISTORICAL CONTEXT

This book began with an review of the historical context in which social work, personal services, and social practice—or the "helping professions"—found roots. The nation was in the midst of transition as industrialization, urbanization, immigration, and migration cast a dark cloud over the burgeoning cities. A new poverty was invading the lives of millions of people with destitution, disease, and despair. Americans had been poor in the past and doing without at that time meant learning to sacrifice. This new poverty, however, was one of unparalleled abjection and wretchedness.

Even then, the suffering was not distributed equally throughout the tenements or throughout the country. Some people seemed to suffer poverty in its most pernicious forms, and the records of the time bear witness to this fact. The worst conditions that befell the White ethnic migrant could somehow manage to be even worse for the African-American migrants.

The "new" and unpopular White ethnic immigrants were really a temporary disruption to U.S. society. It was expected that, after a few generations, they would be indistinguishable from the native-born Americans. They could melt into the American pot and rise from the poverty and the slums they faced to join the ranks of middle America. African Americans, however, had no such prognosis. Economic success was not sufficient enough to hurdle the segregation that walled African Americans from mainstream society.

While cities swallowed the "new" White ethnics and African-American migrants, the American-Indian population suffered on the reservations. Inadequate resources resulted in an abhorrent aberration of former reservation life. The forced transition from the old ways to the new ways was an ordeal that has been referred to as *acculturation under duress*.

The American Indian had something in common with the Mexican American—their land was important but they were not. While the White ethnics and African Americans lived under the most extreme of conditions and while American Indians remained on the reservations, thousands of Mexican Americans were stripped of their land and the rights that should accompany citizenship. As immigration from Mexico increased, these immigrants were always "foreigners" who were not expected to make the United States their home. They did have *brazos fuertes* (strong arms), so they were expendable and dispensable and needed at the same time. The labor was valued but not the laborer.

While these groups were touching different locations and sentiments, the Chinese were contributing to the building of the United States, and those contributions are almost forgotten. What is left is the memory of the Chinese Exclusion Acts that banned an entire group of people from these shores. Documents of the period tell of racial hatred, violence, and fear. In the eyes of Californians and the rest of the country, the new land needed protection from the invasion of foreign countries and foreign people.

When the Japanese replaced the Chinese as immigrants, they were welcomed as another source of labor but they, too, were "foreign" and were destined to be seen that way for years to come. They reached for the American dream and their success was their downfall. Fear that they would take over and fear that they were taking land and business from "real" Americans revealed the ambivalence that the United States had about those who looked and acted "foreign."

In this time period, the sorrow of the slums could not be met in the old ways of dealing with problems. The fragmentation of efforts and the uncoordinated giving needed to be replaced with more organized approaches to poverty. The provision of alms was not enough, and the alms supply was dwindling. Throwing money at the problems could not contain the problems. The English model of poverty work was imported to the United States and the Charity Organization Societies were established with paid agents, friendly visitors, investigations, and coordination of efforts. In the Progressive Era, the beginnings of social casework or direct practice are evident.

The White ethnics needed more than friendly visiting and case investigations; they needed political advocacy, community organization, and community planning. This could be accomplished through the settlement houses, another import from England. Although the reform nature of settlement house movement is continuously emphasized, closer scrutiny of history reveals that most settlement houses were trying to Americanize the White ethnics to make them better and "real" Americans.

The Charity Organization Societies and the settlement houses gave a passing nod to African Americans and did not bother to nod at all to the American Indians, Mexicans, Chinese, and Japanese. These groups were not their target "clients"; they were not good candidates for Americanization. Although each group was different, they all had something in common— they did not conform to the image of Americans. No amount of Americanization could transform them into this image. Services extended to them were spotty, inconsistent, an afterthought, a footnote to primary services, or nonexistent.

The helping professions of today emerged from the responses of White Americans to the needs of other White Americans. Although the "new" immigrants were from unpopular parts of Europe and had religions, customs, and values that differed from those of America, these immigrants were "redeemable" and major efforts were undertaken to redeem them and protect America from erosion. Thus, the help extended had dual purposes: to assist the immigrants with adaptation to a new world and to protect White middle-class America.

Three themes dominated early helping organizations: ethnic minorities were ignored, the doctrine of ethnic group responsibility prevailed, and those extending the help defined the problems and the solutions. Ethnic minorities were assumed and expected to care for their own group members.

From the need to assist the "unfortunates" from the squalor of the slums, a new occupation eventually arose. Members who practiced its craft wanted specialized knowledge, specialized skills, and legitimacy as a profession. As these were developed, the new helping profession tended to focus on those immigrants of European stock. Casework overpowered social reform in the profession and less attention was given to the needs of the ethnic minority groups who were more concentrated in the West while the profession grew in the East.

There were those in the profession who challenged its direction and preoccupation with professionalization, but the Rank-and-File Movement of the 1930s and the Human Services Movement of the 1960s were just momentary distractions—little blips in the trajectory of the profession. These movements have been absorbed into the profession and they have expanded the profession to include new workers and new service areas. The profession, however, has had more effects on them than they have had on the profession. They were absorbed by the profession—they did not absorb it. The influence and its direction seem clear. Further, it is predicted that many people in these movements eventually aspired to be professional social workers.

While the profession was crystallizing, the ethnic minority groups were organizing their own community responses to their ills. African Americans were concerned about children, widows, the elderly, and young girls. Crime in the communities was also receiving attention. Second-generation Mexican Americans desired integration and used the acquisition of English as a tool. They were also concerned about issues of immigration and deportation because they, too, were faced with the threat just because they "looked Mexican." The Chinese and Japanese wanted to succeed in the new country and their community associations supported this desire.

The ethnic agency rose from these early community self-help efforts. These ethnic communities responded to the needs of its residents as defined by its residents. These ethnic agencies provided services to individuals who could not receive services elsewhere. In this manner, these agencies filled service gaps and substituted for government services as public agencies "hired" them to provide mandated services. The social work profession and other helping professions have not fully recognized or appreciated the ethnic agency.

THEORETICAL FRAMEWORKS

In the systems perspective, the path of social work is consistent with that of a subsystem bounded by the constraints imposed by the larger social system. The larger social system and its ideologies, structure, economy, and sociopolitical context bound the development of any helping profession. Who is helped (client eligibility), by whom (staff qualifications), why (individual versus system blame), how (technology), how much (the cost of the intervention), how long (length of intervention), and under what conditions (organizational settings) are decided by numerous factors external to the profession. A "profession" requires the sanction and legitimacy of the larger society. This is a critical input that the profession cannot extend to itself; it has to come from outside the profession. Any profession in U.S. society has to negotiate its environmental dependencies and make some adaptations.

Social work managed its environmental dependencies by becoming an established part of the larger social system. With the emergence of the Welfare State, social work joined in a partnership to become the profession that implemented and responded to the social policies of the country. Social work and those related helping professions (created in response to social work) represent the social practice of the Welfare State. This partnership guaranteed the survival of the profession, but the profession had constrained its ability to act as an agent of social change or social reform.

With the growth of the Welfare State, bureaucracy became the predominant organizational form for service delivery. As systems, these organizations also seek growth and survival, and the needs of the bureaucracy may, at times, take priority over the clients. With the Welfare State, service consumers are generally not the service sponsors; the agency's accountability is often to those who sponsor or fund the services—not to those who actually receive the services. The actual development of the Welfare State may have further separated social workers from the ethnic communities. Although more *services* may be available to ethnic minorities, the service delivery *process* may be alienating.

From the political-economy perspective, social work as a profession has been influenced by an external polity and an external economy. Although legitimacy and support are needed for the profession to survive, the internal polity and the internal economy also shape the course of the profession. The ascendancy of casework over social reform was the result of a battle that was waged within the nascent profession. The dominant elite was challenged by the two movements within the profession but the dominant elite continued to prevail. Within the profession, there is an identified place for casework practitioners and a career ladder. The profession has had difficulty defining *macropractice* and identifying a place for macropractitioners. Over time, even the definition of *macropractice* is becoming a conservative definition.

The external polity of any profession helps the profession to define the parameters of its work. This is also true for the helping professions. Social policies, as reflective of prevailing ideologies, are determined outside the profession, and often problem solutions have been articulated long before policy practice is undertaken in an agency.

As a subsystem of a community system, the ethnic agency is granted legitimacy by its external polity; that polity is the ethnic community. The agency has a symbiotic relationship with its community. The ethnic agency also seems to have need of the external economy of the larger social system because the ethnic community does not seem capable of providing for the total support of its agencies. In the search for survival, the ethnic agency may develop a resource dependency on entities located outside the community. This creates a unique situation for the ethnic agency: The identification is with the community but the resource inputs tend to be from outside the community.

Consequently, as the mainstream social system was developing, an ethnic service system was also developing. Because of the ethnic agency's emphasis on ethnicity and nonprofessionalization, the social work profession has not fully embraced it as a partner in service delivery. Although the Human Services Movement seemed to capture many of the tenets of ethnic agency practice, this movement has not been a significant force in altering mainstream service delivery to ethnic minorities.

The ethnic-sensitive practice utilized by ethnic agencies can be summarized as (1) an ideology of empowerment derived from an identification with the client and belief in the group; (2) a goal of improving the group as a whole through work with individuals of that group; (3) a technology of education, information, and participation; and (4) a structure that buffers clients from bureaucracy.

A model for ethnic-sensitive service delivery then focuses on community penetration (access to the community) and agency penetration (incorporation of ethnic-sensitive practice into the ideology, goals, technology, and structure of the agency). Hence, mainstream agencies vary in their degree of ethnic-sensitive practice. Organizational barriers serve to impede the incorporation of ethnic-sensitive practice into the agency. From the systems and political-economy perspectives, this resistance is predictable. Ideologies are difficult to change, sunk costs cannot be recovered, and change is threatening.

In its relationships with mainstream agencies, the ideologies and technologies of the ethnic agency do not appear to be permeating these other agencies. Rather, the ethnic agency seeks to protect itself from the intrusiveness of its external economy. As these agencies grow and diversify, they may attempt to buffer clients from the effects of bureaucracy by decoupling or loosely coupling its technology from its bureaucratic practices. The workers may experience the effects of bureaucracy, but the clients may not have to endure this experience.

THE ISSUES TODAY

As other immigrant groups enter the U.S. population, the past seems to be repeating itself. Jimenez stated, "The projected increase in immigration in the coming decades recalls earlier periods of American history, particularly the Progressive Era. Their [immigrants'] struggle to adjust to American society and the hardships they are likely to endure have been experienced by previous generations of American families."[1]

These groups are developing their own responses to the needs of their communities as immigration continues. Smith, Tarallo, and Kagiwada found that Chinese and Southeast Asian immigrants are developing their own social networks to survive and adjust in this new world.[2] Frey also noted the importance of mutual assistance associations in Southeast Asian communities.[3] Yu described the Filipino community organizations that emerged to meet this group's needs.[4] For example, the Filipinos in Stockton, California, had the first federally financed Filipino Center in the United States. This center was owned by a coalition of Filipino organizations called the Association of Filipino Organizations, Inc. According to Leslie and Leitch, Central Americans are coming to the United States in increasing numbers and they, too, are turning to the services in their communities.[5] Kotchek further added that Samoans are attempting to respond to the needs of the Samoan community.[6]

As was the case with ethnic minority groups of the past, these other immigrants have experienced differential treatment because of their race. Yu, for example, noted that Filipinos were not *racially* eligible for U.S. citizenship until 1946.[7] When the Philippines achieved independence, however, Filipino immigration fell under the immigration quota in the category with other countries of the Eastern Hemisphere (Japan, China, Korea) and this system was not lifted until the 1960s.

Skinner, on the other hand, has voiced concern about the status of the Vietnamese in the United States and the conflicts this group has had with members of other ethnic minority groups. He argued:

> Competition between Vietnamese and members of minority groups is to a certain extent a reflection of the fact that the Vietnamese, as well as other Indochinese, have been classified as *ethnic minorities* by some of the American institutions providing assistance.... Other recent immigrants, such as Russian Jews and Hungarians, have been considered refugees but were not subsequently classified as ethnic minorities, despite obvious ethnic distinctiveness.[8]

Ethnicity and race still figure prominently in America's response to its immigrants.

These groups will continue to provide for their own needs until these needs exceed the group's capacity to respond. When this happens, aid from the larger society is sought. Kotchek, for example, suggested that the needs of the Samoan elderly may lead to a call for *non-Samoan* assistance.[9] Hasenfeld and Law stated that "our findings indicate the voluntary sector plays a catalyst role in responding to an emerging social problem such as refugee resettlement, but its failure to respond to the increasing magnitude of the problem results in government intervention."[10] The same phenomenon seems to occur with voluntary ethnic agencies. When the magnitude of the problem surpasses the ability of the agency to respond, additional intervention is needed. As ethnic minorities reach to mainstream services for assistance, the need for ethnic-sensitive services grows.

What is being advocated for these more recent immigrants? Leslie and Leitch have urged agencies to engage in active outreach to the Central American community.[11] They also noted that there may be a fear of deportation among this group. To respond to the needs of the Vietnamese elderly, Die and Seelbach recommended that agencies serving the elderly *jointly sponsor* programs with the Vietnamese Resettlement Office because workers trained in Vietnamese are needed.[12] For work with Mexican immigrants, Peña recommended the establishment of satellite service units by public or voluntary agencies that would be staffed by individuals from the targeted community.[13]

While the incorporation of ethnic-sensitive practice into mainstream agencies is progressing, the ethnic agency will continue to serve a vital role in the ethnic community. Voluntary agencies in general have the capacity to identify community needs and to respond to those needs.[14] This role appears to be a vital one for the ethnic agency. In addition, as the government seems to approach its limits of capacity and legitimacy, the voluntary sector may be utilized more for the provision of services.[15] This means that the ethnic agencies may be increasingly called on to provide services to their communities.

The Role of History

Ethnic-sensitive practice does not start today with the here and now. Rather, it is lodged in the historical continuum that includes the unique cultural, social, political, and economic context of each group in the United States. The development and implementation of responsive service delivery systems are predicated on the awareness and acknowledgment of a group's history as *perceived by that group*. The historical experiences of African Americans, Mexican Americans, American Indians, Chinese Americans, Japanese Americans, and other ethnic minority Americans have shaped their interface with mainstream agencies. For this reason, an overview of the historical context of particular ethnic groups was presented in the earlier chapters of this book.

This history suggests that ethnic minority groups may be justified in perceiving mainstream services with suspicion and cynicism. The crumbling of many racial walls has not led these groups to warmly embrace those institutions and structures that previously delimited their opportunities for full participation in society. Services that were supposedly designed to foster upward mobility and enhance the quality of life were often guilty of reinforcing racial stereotypes, practicing racial segregation, and excluding ethnic minorities.

Some people may believe that the past is dead and should therefore be buried. Since the past cannot be changed, some may question its relevance to contemporary issues, especially if this history includes issues of racism and discrimination. The legacy of that past is often transported to the present and transformed into more subtle and insidious modes of operation. Knowledge of that past becomes crucial for protecting organizational change and innovation from the perpetuation of inequality.

What are the effects of this history today? Some groups may see their own ethnic agencies as the primary conduit for service delivery and shun mainstream agencies. Other groups may view any mainstream change as purely superficial and resist outreach efforts made to their communities. Others may wonder whether traces of past discrimination still persist today. For example, ethnic minorities, as well as other groups, were often defined in terms of how "ethnic" they looked or acted. As mentioned in Chapters 2 and 3, higher status was frequently associated with fair or light skin tones and it is not clear if skin color continues to affect the type of treatment and/or service one receives. The past thus becomes useful for identifying pitfalls to be avoided and patterns to be interrupted. Community responses may also be understood and predicted in the context of group history.

History also indicates that each ethnic group defined what it saw as major social concerns and also developed its own interventions to address those concerns. Each group had a capacity for self-help and self-determination. A significant message from the past centers around the participation of the ethnic community in the defining of problems and solutions. Thus, priorities and needs may vary from group to group and interventions should be developed in partnership with each community. History further reveals that ethnic agencies have been central to ethnic communities.

Ethnic Group Responsibility

The doctrine of ethnic group responsibility continues to receive support in the larger society as well as in ethnic communities. For example, in a text on social work, one section entitled "Early Black Prototypes" describes the work of early African-American individuals who were forerunners of social workers.[16] All the individuals cited made significant contributions to the development of African-American communities. Although the contributions of these individuals are outstanding, the discussion itself illuminates adherence to ethnic group responsibility beliefs by emphasizing African Americans working with African Americans.

This belief in the responsibility of an ethnic group to provide for its own relief may account, in part, to the reluctance of the country to respond to the needs of various ethnic groups. Ethnic responsibility in and of itself is neither desirable or undesirable. The emphasis may need to be redirected from the group itself to the external constraints placed upon a group as it attempts to help itself. The doctrine of ethnic group responsibility often disregards the effects of the external polity and the external economy in constraining self-help efforts within communities.

While social and human services are developing practice methods that may be more responsive to the needs of ethnic minorities, the minorities continue to stress the responsibility of the group to help itself. This position seems to imply the deficit model of social service delivery rather than a partnership model: Mainstream efforts are deficient in their responses to the group, so the group must do for itself. The "Lifting As We Climb" motto of the National Association of Colored Women during the early 1900s is analogous to the "what we ourselves can and must do" message of the more contemporary National Urban Coalition.[17] The deficit model is reflected in Williams's observations on intervention with minority high-risk AIDS populations: "The staff lacked sufficient data on the beliefs and attitudes of the high-risk populations necessary to design relevant risk reduction activities. Recognizing our limited awareness and accessibility to the high risk groups, a strategy was to encourage members of the high risk population to assume a leadership role in the development and implementation of the community-based program."[18] Although client participation is laudable here, it arose from the ignorance of the staff.

Ethnic group responsibility as a means of overcoming deficits in the "system" is also illuminated in the observations of an advocate for Hispanic health and mental health: "We Hispanics must work together as a unified force for change across a broad spectrum of issues. We must support and strengthen our own institutions. *When others do not respond to us, we must create our own mechanisms to meet our urgent needs."*[19] Existing service delivery systems and the doctrine of ethnic group responsibility do not appear to work in partnership to bring more effective services to ethnic minorities. There is a tension between the two, with ethnic group responsibility being evoked as a means of overcoming service delivery problems.

Defining Community Needs

Who defines the needs of a community? For ethnic minority groups, the external polity seems to have the loudest and strongest voice in determining how problems are defined and which solutions are utilized.

At the turn of the century, Mexican Americans wanted to acquire proficiency in English and wanted to be free of the threat of deportation. Hispanic immigrants continue to share these same concerns.[20] In addition, as recommendations for controlling illegal Hispanic immigration periodically push for the distribution of identification cards to legal residents as a possible solution,[21] many Mexican Americans fear that such a policy would unfairly subject them to police interrogation. Public policy responses are not always sympathetic to a minority perspective of the problem.

At the turn of the century, African Americans were concerned about the crime that preyed on their communities. They identified race prejudice and differential treatment as causes of that crime. Racial discrimination is now generally assumed to be a factor contributing to crime patterns and incarceration rates among African Americans.[22] Again, an ethnic group's definition does not necessarily lead to intervention based on that definition.

The external polity continues to define problems and solutions, and this may be seen as the larger society acting on its minority communities. The helping professions, as part of this external polity, may also be acting on ethnic communities by embracing ideologies and implementing policies that are counter to the expressed wishes of these groups.

Social service and social work may be continuing with the "middle course" by walking a fine line between the needs and desires of the larger social system and the needs and desires of ethnic subsystems. While this middle-ground position may offer some conflict resolution for the practitioners, it does not bring ethnic communities closer to social work and other helping professions.

Cultural Pluralism versus the Melting Pot

The demand for ethnic-sensitive social services is growing as the ethnic diversity of U.S. society grows. As the prevailing social environment moves toward the acknowledgment, acceptance, and appreciation of cultural differences, social institutions and systems are expected also to keep pace with the changing times. The days of the melting pot are melting away as cultural pluralism takes hold. Ethnic groups are no longer thrown into the great American pot and melted into a unique individual—the American. Rather, America the patchwork quilt and America the mosaic society rise as the new American way.

According to Kiser, "The newer concept of cultural pluralism, on the other hand, recognizes the ethnic diversity of our population.... As a philosophy, cultural pluralism denies the assumption that there is one American culture fixed once and for all by our colonial ancestors. It assumes that our culture is variegated and dynamic, and that all immigrant groups have contributed toward its enrichment."[23] Kiser made this observation in *1949* and U.S. society is still in a tug-of-war between the melting pot and cultural pluralism.

On one hand, the prevailing and dominant ethos has been against the formation and maintenance of subgroup identities in favor of an overall *American* one.[24] But, as Kiser noted, the concept of cultural pluralism differed markedly from policies and practices related to the "colored" groups. Or as Solomon said, "The proponents of the melting pot theory could be terribly cruel to ethnics who would not melt."[25]

On the other hand, ethnic and racial differences seemed too often diagnosed rather than defined, and treated rather than tolerated. Despite generations of life in the United States, some groups still bear a stigma for being "foreign." According to the director of a southern California Asian service center, "For Asian-Americans, we wear our heritage on our face and so no matter how many generations we're here, people still treat us like foreigners."[26]

Thus, American society, as well as its professions and ethnic minorities, continues to struggle with issues of race and ethnicity. Can differences be noted without penalizing those who are different? When are differences to be ignored? Can differences be ignored without jeopardizing practice effectiveness? In efforts to minimize or discount ethnic differences, ethnicity became glaring in its "invisibility." It has also become glaring in its visibility.

The period of ethnic/cultural awareness is trying to dawn while traces of the melting pot ideology persist. Social workers and other helpers are faced with the ambivalence that pervades society about the significance (or insignificance) of race and ethnicity. This ambivalence leads to questions and confusion about the meaning of ethnic-sensitive practice. This is one of the dilemmas confronting mainstream social service delivery.

Ethnicity as a Credential

Ethnic-sensitive practice may not become the new ideology of helping professions and social work until the contradictions surrounding the meaning of ethnicity in service delivery are resolved. On one hand, White practitioners are urged to become culturally sensitive, culturally aware, and culturally responsive. On the other hand, there seems to be a need for trained ethnic group members to work with members of their own group. There is a need for Hispanic-American workers, Asian-American workers, and American-Indian workers. Historically, ethnic group members have been identified with service delivery to their own communities. For example, in 1928, Jones noted:

> The first colored woman to be employed as a professional family case worker... was taken on as a case worker in the New York Charity Organization Society in 1902.... Thus it seems that [the COS secretary] was the first white social work executive to realize the value of using competent, trained Negro social workers *for work among their own people, whose problems they could understand and whose needs they could well interpret.* [emphasis added][27]

Ambivalence is reflected in discussions of the best person to work with whom. There is an implication that the *preferred* worker is the trained worker of the same ethnic group as the client. In the absence of this individual, White workers who are culturally sensitive are viewed as preferred substitutes. In reality however, the White worker who attempts to address ethnic issues or speak to ethnic concerns may be questioned because he or she is not a member of that group. Although individuals may say that ethnicity is not a credential, it still seems to be treated as if it were a credential.

With ethnicity being revered as a credential in many situations, issues are raised about the role of Whites working with minorities and the role of minorities working with Whites. The expertise of each group in working with the other is often overlooked and minimized. For ethnic-sensitive practice to take place, credentials reside with all workers who are culturally aware, regardless of their ethnicity. Culture then becomes something that everyone has and everyone learns.

Separatism versus Integration

The existence of the ethnic agency mirrors another contradiction that was noted by Jones in 1928: "The Negro attitude seems paradoxical. The whole idea of racial segregation is obnoxious to him, yet he demands that the Negro social worker specialize in the Negro's peculiar social problems, treat the problems of the Negro as special group problems."[28] The existence of special ethnic agencies that work with particular ethnic groups seems antithetical to the norms of racial integration.

Questions are then raised about the need for these agencies and about their promotion of racial separatism. This is one of the dilemmas that has to be addressed in order for ethnic-sensitive practice to find a place in mainstream social work.

Ethnic-Sensitive Practice: Whose Domain?

The ethnic agency appears to be a continuing part of the development of ethnic communities. Is ethnic practice the exclusive domain of ethnic agencies? Should ethnic practice be the exclusive practice of ethnic agencies?

A continuum of services seem to unfold in which the ethnic agency may serve as the first line of defense for filling service gaps, for responding to the needs of marginalized groups, and for helping when no other agency does. It may also substitute for public agencies in delivering uniquely packaged and specially tailored services. In the quest for ethnic-sensitive practice, it seems to be a resource that has been underutilized.

Mainstream social services and agencies will continue to vary in the degree to which they adopt ethnic-sensitive practice. This variation is due to agency history, ideologies, structure, and technologies. Mainstream agencies are responding to the needs of a mainstream America, and shifts in paradigms do take years to accomplish.

The first stage of that journey is already underway as service providers begin to acknowledge the need to do something different with different populations. That acknowledgment should now move beyond changing workers to changing systems.

ENDNOTES

1. Mary Ann Jimenez, "Historical Evolution and Future Challenges of the Human Services Professions," *Families in Society: The Journal of Contemporary Human Services 71* (January 1990): 10.

2. Michael Smith, Bernadette Tarallo, and George Kagiwada, "Colouring California: New Asian Immigrant Households, Social Networks and the Local State," *International Journal of Urban and Regional Research 15* (June 1991): 250–268.

3. Gerald Frey, "The Private Social Work Practitioner's Role in Working with Southeast Asian Organizations," *Journal of Independent Social Work 1* (Summer 1987): 41–49.

4. Elena Yu, "Filipino Migration and Community Organization in the United States," *California Sociologist 3* (Summer 1980): 76–102.

5. Leigh Leslie and M. Laurie Leitch, "A Demographic Profile of Recent Central American Immigrants: Clinical and Service Implications," *Hispanic Journal of Behavioral Sciences 11* (November 1989): 351–329.

6. Lydia Kotchek, "'Of Course, We Respect Our Old People, But..' ' Aging Among Samoan Migrants," *California Sociologist 3* (Summer 1980): 197–210.

7. Yu, "Filipino Migration," pp. 76–77.

8. Kenneth Skinner, "Vietnamese in America: Diversity in Adaptation," *California Sociologist 3* (Summer 1980): 114, 115.

9. Kotchek, "Of Course, We Respect Our Old People," p. 211.

10. Chi Kwong Law and Yesheskel Hasenfeld, "The Relationships Between the Public and the Voluntary Sectors: The Case of the Refugee Resettlement Services," *Administration in Social Work 13*, number 2 (1989): 25.

11. Leslie and Leitch, "A Demographic Profile of Recent American Immigrants," p. 327.

12. Ann Die and Wayne Seelbach, "Problems, Sources of Assistance, and Knowledge of Services Among Elderly Vietnamese Immigrants," *The Gerontologist 28* (August 1988): 451.

13. Devon Pena, "Immigration and Social Work," *Aztlan 15*, number 2 (1985): 325.

14. Susan Ostrander, "Voluntary Social Service Agencies in the United States," *Social Service Review 59* (September 1985): 449.

15. Ralph Kramer, "Voluntary Agencies and the Personal Services," in *The Nonprofit Sector—A Research Handbook*, ed. Walter Powell (New Haven, CT: Yale University Press, 1987), p. 252.

16. Diana DiNitto and C. Aaron McNeece, *Social Work* (Englewood Cliffs, NJ: Prentice Hall, 1990), pp. 10–11.

17. August Meier, *Negro Thought in American 1880-1915* (Ann Arbor: University of Michigan Press, 1966), p. 120; Wynetta Devore, "The African-American Community in 1990: The Search for Practice Method," in *Community Organizing in a Diverse Society*, ed. Felix Rivera and John Erlich (Boston: Allyn and Bacon, 1992), p. 79.

18. Linda Williams, "AIDS Risk Reduction: A Community Health Education Intervention for Minority High Risk Group Members," *Health Education Quarterly 13* (Winter 1986): 407.

19. Comments of the late Rodolfo Balli Sanchez as quoted in *NASW News,* September 1993, p. 16

20. Earl Ogletree and Vilma Ujlaki, "American Hispanics in a Pluralistic Society," *Migration Today 13,* number 3 (1985): 31–34; Devon Peña, "Immigration and Social Work," *Aztlan 15,* number 2 (1985): 309–336.

21. "Polarization Marks Debate on Immigration Policy," *Los Angeles Times,* 30 November 1993, sec. A.

22. See, for example, Louise Johnson and Charles Schwartz, *Social Welfare—A Response to Human Need,* Second Edition (Boston: Allyn and Bacon, 1991), p. 256.

23. Clyde Kiser, "Cultural Pluralism." *The Annals of the American Academy of Political and Social Science 262* (March 1949): 129.

24. Marcia Guttentag, "Group Cohesiveness, Ethnic Organization, and Poverty," *Journal of Social Issues 26,* number 2 (1970): 125.

25. Barbara Solomon, "Social Work in Multiethnic Society," in *Cross-Cultural Perspectives in Social Work Practice and Education,* ed. M. Sotomayor (New York: Council on Social Work Education, 1976), p. 2.

26. As quoted in "Asian-Americans: `We Are Still Treated Like Foreigners,'" *Los Angeles Times,* 10 November 1993, sec. B.

27. Eugene Jones, "Social Work Among Negroes," *The Annals of the American Academy of Political and Social Science 240* (November 1928): 287.

28. Jones, "Social Work Among Negroes," p. 288.

Index